W9-CEW-004

Microsoft®

Windows® 2000 and IIS 5.0

Administrator's Pocket Consultant

William R. Stanek

PUBLISHED BY
Microsoft Press
A Division of Microsoft Corporation
One Microsoft Way
Redmond, Washington 98052-6399

Library of Congress Cataloging-in-Publication Data
Stanek, William R.
    Microsoft Windows 2000 and IIS 5.0 Administrator's Pocket Consultant / William R. Stanek.
        p. cm.
    Includes index.
    ISBN 0-7356-1024-X
    1. Microsoft Windows (Computer file) 2. Web sites. 3. Computer network resources. I.
Title.

QA76.76.O63 S73448   2001
005.7'13769-dc21   2001018330

Printed and bound in the United States of America.

 2 3 4 5 6 7 8 9   MLML   6 5 4 3 2 1   *

Distributed in Canada by Penguin Books Canada Limited.

A CIP catalogue record for this book is available from the British Library.

Microsoft Press books are available through booksellers and distributors worldwide. For further information about international editions, contact your local Microsoft Corporation office or contact Microsoft Press International directly at fax (425) 936-7329. Visit our Web site at mspress.microsoft.com. Send comments to *mspinput@microsoft.com*.

Acquisitions Editor: Juliana Aldous
Project Editor: Karen Szall

Part No. X08-04128

Contents at a Glance

Part I
Microsoft Windows 2000 Web Administration Fundamentals

1   Overview of Microsoft Web Services   3

2   Core IIS Administration   17

Part II
Web Server Administration

3   Configuring Web Sites and Servers   41

4   Customizing Internet Information Services   71

5   Managing Web Server Security   111

6   Managing Microsoft Certificate Services and SSL   149

Part III
Essential Services Administration

7   Managing FTP Servers   189

8   Configuring and Maintaining SMTP   215

9   Administering the Indexing Service   251

Part IV
Performance, Optimization, and Maintenance

10   Performance Tuning and Monitoring   277

11   Tracking User Access and Logging   309

12   IIS Optimization and the Metabase   333

Table of Contents

Acknowledgments   xvii

Introduction   xix

Part I
Microsoft Windows 2000 Web Administration
Fundamentals

1   Overview of Microsoft Web Services   3

Choosing Hardware   4

Using IIS   6

Installing IIS Components and Default Sites   6

Understanding Authentication Enhancements   8

Installing Internet Services and Service-Related Accounts   8

Web Administration Tools and Techniques   9

Managing Resources with Key Administration Tools   9

Installing Administration Tools   10

Web Administration Techniques   11

2   Core IIS Administration   17

Working with IIS and URLs   17

Understanding the IIS Architecture   17

Understanding URLs   19

Internet Information Services Snap-In Essentials   22

Starting and Using the Internet Information
Services Snap-In   22

Connecting To Other Servers   24

Starting, Stopping, and Restarting All Internet Services   25

Starting, Stopping, and Pausing Individual Resources   27

Rebooting IIS Servers   28

Managing IIS Services   29

Core IIS Services   30

Starting, Stopping, and Pausing IIS Services   30

Configuring Service Startup   31

Configuring Service Recovery 32
Configuring IIS Backup and Recovery 33
Storing a Server's Configuration 33
Creating IIS Configuration Backups 35
Restoring IIS from Backup Configurations 36
Rebuilding Corrupted IIS Installations 36
Deleting Backup Configurations 37

Part II
Web Server Administration

3   **Configuring Web Sites and Servers   41**
Web Site Naming and Identification 41
Understanding IP Addresses and Name Resolution 41
Understanding Web Site Identifiers 43
Hosting Multiple Sites on a Single Server 43
Checking the Computer Name and IP Address of Servers 46
Managing Master Web Service Properties 48
Creating Web Sites 48
Managing Web Site Properties 52
Configuring a Site's Home Directory 52
Configuring Ports, IP Addresses, and Host Names
Used by Web Sites 53
Configuring Multiple Identities for a Single Web Site 55
Restricting Incoming Connections and
Setting Time-Out Values 56
Configuring HTTP Keep-Alives 57
Managing Directories 58
Understanding Physical and Virtual Directory Structures 58
Creating Physical Directories 59
Creating Virtual Directories 59
Linking IISAdmin, IISHelp, and Other System Directories 60
Modifying Directory Properties 61
Renaming Directories 61
Deleting Directories 62

Managing Web Content 62
 Opening and Browsing Files 62
 Modifying the IIS Properties of Files 62
 Renaming Files 63
 Deleting Files 63
Redirecting Browser Requests 63
 Redirecting Requests to Other Directories or Web Sites 64
 Redirecting All Requests to Another Web Site 65
 Retrieving Files from a Network Share 65
 Redirecting Requests to Applications 66
 Customizing Browser Redirection 67

4 **Customizing Internet Information Services 71**
Essentials for Working with IIS Applications 71
 Understanding ISAPI Applications 72
 Understanding ASP Applications 74
 Defining Custom Applications 75
 Using and Running Applications 77
Managing Custom IIS Applications 80
 Creating Pooled and Nonpooled Applications 80
 Configuring Application Mappings and Caching 82
 Managing Session State 85
 Controlling Application Buffering 87
 Setting Parent Paths, Default ASP Language, and
 ASP Script Time-Out 88
 Enabling and Disabling Application Debugging 89
 Configuring Application Error Messages 89
 Unloading Isolated Applications 89
 Deleting IIS Applications 90
Managing Custom ISAPI Filters 90
 Viewing and Configuring Global Filters 90
 Viewing and Configuring Local Filters 91
Customizing Web Site Content and HTTP Headers 92
 Configuring Default Documents 92

Configuring Document Footers 93

Using Content Expiration and Preventing
Browser Caching 94

Using Custom HTTP Headers 95

Using Content Ratings 96

Customizing Web Server Error Messages 98

Understanding Status Codes and Error Messages 98

Managing Custom Error Settings 100

Using MIME and Configuring Custom File Types 103

Understanding MIME 103

Viewing and Configuring MIME Types for
All Web Sites on a Server 105

Viewing and Configuring MIME Types for
Individual Sites and Directories 106

Additional Customization Tips 106

Using Update Sites to Manage Outages 107

Using Jump Pages for Advertising 108

Handling 404 Errors and Preventing Dead Ends 109

5 **Managing Web Server Security   111**

Managing Windows Security 111

Working with User and Group Accounts 112

IIS User and Group Essentials 112

Working with File and Folder Permissions 116

Working with Group Policies 121

Managing IIS Security 127

Setting Web Server Permissions 127

Configuring Distributed Authoring and Versioning 132

Setting Authentication Modes 133

Configuring IP Address and Domain Name Restrictions 137

Configuring Web Site Operators 140

More Tips for Enhancing Web Server Security 142

Using Firewalls 142

Renaming the Administrator Account 142

Disabling the Default Web Site 142

Disabling Remote Administration from the Web   143
Disabling Directory Browsing   143
Creating Legal Notices   143
Applying Service Packs, Hot Fixes, and Templates   144
Removing the IISADMPWD Virtual Directory   146
Checking for Malicious Input in Forms and
Query Strings   146
Removing Unused Application Mappings   147

6   Managing Microsoft Certificate Services and SSL   149
Understanding SSL   149
Using SSL Encryption   149
Using SSL Certificates   151
Understanding SSL Encryption Strength   153
Working with Microsoft Certificate Services   154
Understanding Certificate Services   154
Installing Certificate Services   155
Accessing Certificate Services in a Browser   158
Starting and Stopping Certificate Services   159
Backing Up and Restoring the CA   160
Approving and Declining Pending Certificate Requests   163
Generating Certificates Manually in the
Certification Authority Snap-In   163
Revoking Certificates   164
Reviewing and Renewing the Root CA Certificate   165
Creating and Installing Certificates   166
Creating Certificate Requests   167
Submitting Certificate Requests
to Third-Party Authorities   170
Submitting Certificate Requests to Certificate Services 172
Processing Pending Requests and Installing
Site Certificates   174
Deleting Pending Certificate Requests   175
Working with SSL   175

Configuring SSL Ports   175

Adding the CA Certificate to the Client Browser's
Root Store   177

Confirming that SSL Is Correctly Enabled   179

Resolving SSL Problems   179

Managing Site Certificates in the Internet
Information Services Snap-In   180

Viewing and Modifying Issued Certificates   180

Renewing, Removing, and Replacing Certificates   182

Exporting Site Certificates   183

Ignoring, Accepting, and Requiring Client Certificates   184

Requiring SSL for All Communications   185

Part III
Essential Services Administration

7   **Managing FTP Servers**   **189**

Understanding FTP   189

FTP Essentials   189

Controlling FTP Server Access   190

Working with FTP Sessions   191

FTP Site Naming and Identification   193

Managing Master FTP Service Properties   194

Creating FTP sites   194

Managing FTP Sites   196

Configuring an FTP Site's Home Directory   197

Configuring Ports and IP Addresses Used by FTP Sites   198

Restricting Incoming Connections and Setting
Time-Out Values   199

Creating Physical Directories for FTP Sites   200

Creating Virtual Directories for FTP Sites   201

Redirecting Requests to a Network Share   202

Setting the Directory Listing Style   202

Setting Welcome, Exit, and Maximum
Connection Messages   202

Managing FTP User Sessions 203
   Viewing FTP User Sessions 203
   Viewing the Total Number of Connected Users 204
   Terminating FTP User Sessions 205
Managing FTP Server Security 205
   Managing Anonymous Connections 206
   Configuring Windows Permissions on FTP Servers 208
   Configuring FTP Server Permissions 208
   Configuring IP Address and Domain Name Restrictions 210
   Configuring FTP Site Operators 213

8   Configuring and Maintaining SMTP   215

Using SMTP 215
   Understanding E-Mail Domain Usage 216
   Understanding the Mailroot 217
   Understanding Mail Processing 218
Core SMTP Administration 219
   Creating SMTP Virtual Servers 219
   Configuring Ports and IP Addresses Used by
   SMTP Servers 221
   Configuring Multiple Identities for SMTP Virtual Servers 222
   Monitoring SMTP Virtual Server Health 223
   Managing User Sessions 224
Configuring Service Domains 224
   Viewing Configured Service Domains 224
   Working with Local Domains 225
   Working with Remote Domains 227
   Configuring Smart Hosts for Remote Domains 232
   Renaming and Deleting Service Domains 233
Handling Incoming Connections 234
   Securing Access by IP Address, Subnet, or Domain 234
   Controlling Secure Communications for Incoming
   Connections 235
   Controlling Authentication for Incoming Connections 236

Restricting Incoming Connections and Setting
Time-Out Values   238
Handling Outgoing Connections   239
    Configuring Outbound Security   239
    Controlling Outgoing Connections   240
    Configuring Outgoing Message Limits for SMTP   241
    Handling Nondelivery, Bad Mail, and Unresolved
    Recipients   243
    Setting and Removing Relay Restrictions   243
Managing Message Delivery   245
    Setting Outbound Retry Intervals, Delay Notification,
    and Expiration Time-Out   245
    Setting Message Hop Count   247
    Setting Domain Name Options   247
    Configuring Reverse DNS Lookups   248
    Routing Outgoing Messages to Smart Hosts   249

9 **Administering the Indexing Service   251**
Getting Started with the Indexing Service   252
    Using the Indexing Service   252
    Indexing Service Essentials   255
    Searching Catalogs   258
Core Indexing Service Administration   260
    Setting Web Resources to Index   260
    Viewing and Creating Catalogs   261
    Viewing Indexing Status   261
    Starting, Stopping, and Pausing the Indexing Service 263
    Setting Indexing Service Properties   263
    Optimizing Indexing Service Performance   265
Managing Catalogs   268
    Viewing Catalog Properties and Directories Being
    Indexed   268
    Adding Physical Directories to a Catalog   268
    Forcing Full and Incremental Directory Rescans   270
    Starting, Stopping, and Pausing Individual Catalogs   270

Merging Catalogs 271

Specifying Web or NNTP Sites to Include in Catalogs 271

Testing Catalogs with Queries 272

Part IV
Performance, Optimization, and Maintenance

10 Performance Tuning and Monitoring   277

Monitoring IIS Performance and Activity 277

Why Monitor IIS? 277

Getting Ready to Monitor 278

Monitoring Tools and Resources 279

Detecting and Resolving IIS Errors 279

Examining the Access Logs 280

Examining the Event Logs 281

Monitoring IIS Performance 284

Choosing Counters to Monitor 284

Creating and Managing Performance Monitor Logs 289

Replaying Performance Logs 294

Configuring Alerts for Performance Counters 295

Tuning Web Server Performance 297

Monitoring and Tuning Memory Usage 298

Monitoring and Tuning Processor Usage 301

Monitoring and Tuning Disk I/O 303

Monitoring and Tuning Network Bandwidth and
Connectivity 304

11 Tracking User Access and Logging   309

Tracking Statistics: The Big Picture 309

Working with the NCSA Common Log File Format 310

Working with the Microsoft IIS Log File Format 314

Working with the W3C Extended Log File Format 316

Working with ODBC Logging 319

Understanding Logging 320

Configuring Logging for HTTP, SMTP, and FTP 322

Configuring NCSA Common Log File Format 322

Configuring Microsoft IIS Log File Format 323

Configuring W3C Extended Log File Format 325

Configuring ODBC Logging 327

Disabling Logging 331

12 IIS Optimization and the Metabase 333

Strategies for Improving IIS Performance 333

Removing Unnecessary Applications and Services 333

Optimizing Content Usage 334

Optimizing ISAPI and ASP Applications 336

Optimizing IIS Caching and Queuing 337

Configuring Automatic Restarts of IIS 338

Managing IIS Registry Settings 339

Working with the Registry 339

Controlling IIS Through the Registry 341

Controlling Indexing Service Through the Registry 342

Controlling Secure Sockets Layer Through the Registry 343

Managing IIS Metabase Settings 344

Examining and Editing the Metabase 344

Modifying Metabase Properties 345

Scripting the Metabase 348

Index 353

Tables

1 1-1. Quick Reference for Key IIS Administration Tools 10
1-2. Quick Reference for Key IIS Administration Scripts 14

2 2-1. Default Ports for IIS Resources 20
2-2. Special Characters in URLs 21
2-3. IISRESET Switches Defined 26
2-4. Core IIS Services 30

3 3-1. Redirect Variables for IIS 68

4 4-1. HTTP Request Types That Are Used with
ISAPI Extensions 73
4-2. Built-In ASP Objects 74
4-3. Pre-Built Components for ASP Applications 75
4-4. IIS Application Overhead Baselines for Sample Server 79
4-5. General Classes of Status Codes 98
4-6. Standard HTTP Error Codes and Error Messages 99
4-7. Basic MIME Types 103
4-8. Common MIME Types 104

5 5-1. File and Folder Permissions Used by Windows 2000 117
5-2. General Guidelines for Permissions Based on
Content Type 118

9 9-1. Basic Parameters for the Indexing Service 259
9-2. Quick Reference for Indexing Service Status
Conditions 262
9-3. Configurable Properties for the Indexing Service 264

10 10-1. Key Counters Used to Monitor Server Performance 285
10-2. Uncovering Memory-Related Bottlenecks 300
10-3. Uncovering Processor-Related Bottlenecks 302
10-4. Uncovering Drive-Related Bottlenecks 303

11 11-1. Basic Domain Classes 312
11-2. Status Code Classes 314
11-3. Fields for the IIS Log File Format 315
11-4. Directives Used with the Extended Log File Format 317
11-5. Prefixes Used with the Extended Log Fields 317
11-6. Field Identifiers Used with the Extended File Format 318
11-7. Process Accounting Fields Used in Extended Logs 319

11-8. Table Fields for ODBC Logging 320

11-9. Conventions for Log File Names by Log Format 321

Acknowledgments

Writing *Microsoft Windows 2000 and IIS 5.0 Administrator's Pocket Consultant* was a lot of fun—and a lot of work. It is gratifying to see techniques I've used time and again to solve problems put into a printed book so that others may benefit from them. But no man is an island, and this book couldn't have been written without help from some very special people.

As I've stated in previous *Administrator's Pocket Consultants*, the team at Microsoft Press is top-notch. Once again, I owe huge Thank Yous to the team at Microsoft Press both for recognizing the potential of my practical and useful approach to the *Pocket Consultant* series and for their willingness to run with the approach. Juliana Aldous handled acquisitions and helped make sure I had the tools I needed to write this book. Karen Szall managed the editorial process from the Microsoft Press side with Julie Miller pitching in to help part of the time. Sarah Kimnach Hains headed up the editorial process for nSight, Inc. Their professionalism, thoroughness, and attention to every detail is much appreciated!

Unfortunately for the writer (but fortunately for readers), writing is only one part of the publishing process. Next came editing and author review. I must say, Microsoft Press has the most thorough editorial and technical review process I've seen anywhere—and I've written a lot of books for many different publishers. Special thanks to Karen, Julie, and Sarah for helping me to meet review deadlines. Tony Northrup was the technical editor for the book. Thank you, Tony!

Thanks also to Studio B literary agency and my agents, David Rogelberg and Neil Salkind. David and Neil are great to work with.

Hopefully, I haven't forgotten anyone, but if I have, it was an oversight. *Honest.* ;-)

Introduction

Microsoft Windows 2000 and IIS 5.0 Administrator's Pocket Consultant is designed to be a concise and compulsively usable resource for Web administrators
using Internet Information Services and Microsoft Indexing Services. This is the
readable resource guide that you will want on your desktop at all times. The book
covers everything you need to perform core Web administration tasks for Internet
Information Services and Microsoft Indexing Services. Because the focus is on
giving you maximum value in a pocket-sized guide, you don't have to wade
through hundreds of pages of extraneous information to find what you are looking
for. Instead, you'll find exactly what you need to get the job done.

In short, the book is designed to be the one resource you turn to whenever you
have questions regarding Web administration for Internet Information Services
and Indexing Services. To this end, the book zeroes in on daily administration
procedures, frequently used tasks, documented examples, and options that are
representative while not necessarily inclusive. One of the key goals is to keep
content so concise that the book remains compact and easy to navigate, yet to
ensure that the book is packed with as much information as possible, making it
a valuable resource. Thus, rather than a hefty 1000-page tome or a lightweight
100-page quick reference, you get a valuable resource guide that can help you
quickly and easily perform common tasks, solve problems, and implement advanced IIS techniques, such as customized redirection, metabase optimization,
and automation scripts.

Who Is This Book For?

Microsoft Windows 2000 and IIS 5.0 Administrator's Pocket Consultant covers
Internet Information Services and Microsoft Indexing Services. The book is designed for:

- Current Microsoft Web administrators
- Intranet/extranet administrators
- Administrators migrating to Microsoft Web-based solutions
- Programmers, engineers, and QA personnel that manage internal or test serv-
  ers running IIS

To pack in as much information as possible, I had to assume that you have basic networking skills and a basic understanding of Web servers, and that both IIS
and Indexing Services are already successfully installed on your systems. With
this in mind, I don't devote entire chapters to understanding the Web services,
using name services, building Web sites, or installing IIS. I do, however, cover
configuration, enterprise-wide server management, performance tuning, optimization, automation, and much more.

I also assume that you are fairly familiar with the standard Windows user interface and that, if you plan to use the scripting techniques outlined in the book,

you know scripting. If you need help learning Windows or scripting, you should read *Microsoft Windows 2000 Administrator's Pocket Consultant* and *Windows 2000 Scripting Bible*. (See William R. Stanek, *Windows 2000 Scripting Bible* [IDG Books, June 2000].)

How Is This Book Organized?

Microsoft Windows 2000 and IIS 5.0 Administrator's Pocket Consultant is designed to be used in the daily administration of IIS and, as such, the book is organized according to job-related tasks rather than IIS features. If you are reading this book, you should be aware of the relationship between Pocket Consultants and Administrator's Companions. Both books are designed to be a part of an overall administrator's library. While Pocket Consultants are the "down and dirty in the trenches" books, Administrator's Companions are the comprehensive tutorials and references that cover every aspect of deploying a product or technology in the enterprise.

Speed and ease of reference is an essential part of this hands-on guide. The book has an expanded table of contents and an extensive index for finding answers to problems quickly. Many other quick-reference features have been added to the book as well. These features include quick step-by-steps, lists, tables with fast facts, and extensive cross-references. The book is broken down into both parts and chapters. The parts contain a part-opener paragraph or two about the chapters grouped in that part.

Part I, "Microsoft Windows 2000 Web Administration Fundamentals," covers the fundamental tasks you need for IIS administration. Chapter 1 provides an overview of IIS administration tools, techniques, and concepts. Chapter 2 explores core IIS administration. You'll learn about administration components, Windows services, Internet Services Manager, and server configurations.

In Part II, "Web Server Administration," you'll find the essential tasks for administering Web servers running IIS. Chapter 3 details management techniques for Web servers. You'll also learn how to create and manage virtual directories. Customizing IIS is the key focus of Chapter 4. In this chapter, you'll learn about ISAPI filters, custom HTTP headers, custom errors, and more. Chapter 5 covers Web server security. To manage server security, you'll create user logins, configure directory permissions, and assign operators. The permissions and operator privileges you assign determine the actions users can perform, as well as what areas of the Web site they can access. The final chapter in this section explores server certificates and SSL. Certificates are used to enable secure Web communications. Secure Sockets Layer (SSL) is used to protect sensitive information by encrypting the data sent between client browsers and your server.

Part III, "Essential Services Administration," focuses on administration of essential services. Essential services are those services you'll deploy time and again on your Web servers. Chapter 7 covers techniques for managing FTP servers. In Chapter 7, you'll find information about configuring FTP servers, controlling access to directories, enabling anononymous uploads and downloads, and more. Chapter 8 focuses on configuring and maintaining SMTP. You'll find detailed discussions about configuring SMTP servers, organizing messages for delivery, routing messages, message delivery options, and maintaining SMTP server security. The final chapter in this part examines Indexing Services. You'll learn all about the latest indexing techniques, creating and managing catalogs, tuning performance, and creating Indexing Service query forms.

Part IV, "Performance, Optimization, and Maintenance," covers administration tasks you'll use to enhance and maintain IIS. Chapter 10 provides the essentials for monitoring Web Server performance and solving performance problems. Chapter 11 starts by examining common tasks for tracking user access and then dives into configuring server logs. Chapter 12 explores IIS optimization. You'll learn how to update registry setting for IIS and how to work with the IIS metabase.

Conventions Used in This Book

I've used a variety of elements to help keep the text clear and easy to follow. You'll find code terms and listings in monospace type except when I tell you to actually type a command. In that case, the command appears in **bold** type. When I introduce and define a new term, I put it in *italics*.

Other conventions include:

Note To provide additional details on a particular point that needs emphasis.

Tip To offer helpful hints or additional information.

Caution To warn you when there are potential problems you should look out for.

More Info To provide more information about the subject.

Real World To provide real-world advice when discussing advanced topics.

Best Practice To explain the best technique to use when working with advanced configuration and administration concepts.

I truly hope you find that *Microsoft Windows 2000 and IIS 5.0 Administrator's Pocket Consultant* provides everything you need to perform essential administrative tasks on IIS as quickly and efficiently as possible. Your thoughts are welcome at win2000-consulting@tvpress.com. Thank you.

Support

Every effort has been made to ensure the accuracy of this book. Microsoft Press provides corrections for books through the World Wide Web at the following address:

> *http://mspress.microsoft.com/support/*

If you have comments, questions, or ideas regarding this book, please send them to Microsoft Press using either of the following methods:

Postal Mail:

> Microsoft Press
> Attn: *Microsoft Windows 2000 and IIS 5.0 Administrator's Pocket Consultant* Editor
> One Microsoft Way
> Redmond, WA 98052-6399

E-mail:

> MSPINPUT@MICROSOFT.COM

Please note that product support is not offered through the above mail addresses. For support information, visit Microsoft's Web site at *http://support.microsoft.com/directory/*.

Part I

Microsoft Windows 2000 Web Administration Fundamentals

Part I examines the fundamental tasks you need for Web administration. Chapter 1 provides an overview of Web administration tools, techniques, and concepts. Chapter 2 explores core Web administration using Microsoft Internet Information Services (IIS). You'll learn about administration components, Internet Services Manager, and server configurations.

Chapter 1

Overview of Microsoft Web Services

Microsoft Internet Information Services (IIS) is designed to provide secure, scalable solutions for creating and managing World Wide Web sites and servers. IIS can be used to publish information on intranets, extranets, and the Internet. Because today's Web sites use related services, like File Transfer Protocol (FTP), Simple Mail Transfer Protocol (SMTP), and Network News Transfer Protocol (NNTP), IIS bundles these services as part of a comprehensive offering. A separate but related service is the Indexing Service, which is used to build catalogs of documents that can be searched. When you add this capability to a Web site, it allows users to search for topics of interest using a standard Hypertext Markup Language (HTML) form.

IIS has many features. Key features that you'll want to learn about include:

- **HTTP 1.1 and HTTP Compression**   IIS fully supports the Hypertext Transfer Protocol (HTTP) 1.1 protocol and the compression enhancements it defines. Using HTTP Compression, you can compress both static and dynamic results of HTTP queries for transmission to HTTP 1.1-compliant clients.

- **Host Headers**   Host Headers allow you to host multiple Web sites on a single computer with only one Internet Protocol (IP) address. Here, IIS uses the host name passed in the HTTP header to determine the site that a client is requesting.

- **FTP Restart**   FTP Restart allows clients to resume FTP downloads without having to download the entire file again if an interruption occurs during transfer. When a connection is broken during a download, compliant clients (such as Internet Explorer 5) can re-establish their file transfer using the REST command, and the file transfer will resume where it left off.

- **Active Server Pages**   IIS supports Active Server Pages (ASP), a server-side scripting environment for creating Web server applications. Using ASP, developers can combine HTML, scripts, and Component Object Model (COM) components to create dynamic, interactive, Web-based applications.

- **Application Protection**   Application Protection settings allow ASP applications to run in separate memory space. Low protection allows applications to run in process and share resources with IIS. Medium protection allows applications to run pooled processes, meaning all applications with this priority share the same IIS process instance but do not run in process with normal IIS resources. High protection allows applications to run completely out of process, meaning the application doesn't share processes with other applications, and its failure will not affect other applications.

- **Process Accounting and Throttling** Process Accounting provides information about how individual Web sites use central processing unit (CPU) resources. Process Throttling allows you to limit CPU usage for out-of-process applications and thereby potentially reduce performance problems on the server as a whole.

- **WebDAV** Web Distributed Authoring and Versioning (WebDAV) extends the HTTP 1.1 protocol and is integrated into IIS. Using WebDAV, remote users can publish, lock, and manage resources on a Web server using an HTTP connection.

- **SSL 3.0 and TLS** Secure Sockets Layer (SSL) 3.0 and transport layer security (TLS) provide secure methods of exchanging information between clients and servers. SSL 3.0 and TLS also enable the use of client certificates that can be read by Internet Server Application Programming Interface (ISAPI) server pages. Client certificates are used to authenticate users and control access by mapping the client certificate to a Microsoft Windows user account.

- **Digest Authentication** One of many authentication mechanisms that IIS supports. During Digest Authentication, user credentials are transmitted securely between clients and servers. Digest Authentication is the most secure authentication mechanism that works correctly across proxy servers and firewalls.

Throughout this book, I'll refer to administration of IIS and Indexing Service as Microsoft Web administration or simply Web administration. As you get started with Microsoft Web administration, you should concentrate on these key areas:

- How IIS works with your hardware
- How IIS works with Windows-based operating systems
- Which administration tools are available
- Which administration techniques can be used to manage and maintain IIS

Choosing Hardware

Guidelines for choosing hardware for Internet servers are much different than those for choosing other types of servers. A Web hosting provider may host multiple sites on the same computer and may also have service level agreements that determine the level of availability and performance required. On the other hand, a busy e-commerce site may have a dedicated Web server or even multiple load-balanced servers. Given that Internet servers are used in a wide variety of circumstances and may be either shared or dedicated, here are some guidelines for choosing server hardware:

- **Memory** The amount of memory required depends on many factors, including the requirements of other services, the size of frequently accessed content files, and the random access memory (RAM) requirements of the Web applications. High-volume servers should have a minimum of 512 MB RAM. More RAM will allow more files to be cached, reducing disk requests. For detailed information on memory management and performance tuning, see Chapter 10, "Performance Tuning and Monitoring."

- **CPU** Processes the instructions received by the computer. The clock speed of the CPU and the size of the data bus determine how quickly information moves among the CPU, RAM, and system buses. Static content such as HTML and images place very little burden on the processor, and standard Windows 2000-recommended configurations should suffice. Faster clock speeds and multiple processors increase the upper capacity of a Web server, particularly for sites that rely on dynamic content.

- **SMP** IIS supports symmetric multiprocessors (SMPs) and can use additional processors to improve performance. If the system is running only IIS and does not rely on dynamic content or encryption, a single processor may suffice. Multiple processors should always be used if IIS is running alongside other services such as Microsoft SQL Server or Microsoft Exchange Server. For those sites that need greater performance, IIS 5.0 scales almost linearly to four processors.

- **Disk drives** The amount of data storage capacity you need depends entirely on the size of content files and the number of sites supported. You need enough disk space to store all your data plus workspace, system files, and virtual memory. Input/output (I/O) throughput is just as important as drive capacity. However, disk I/O is rarely a bottleneck for Web sites on the public Internet—generally, bandwidth limits throughput. High-bandwidth sites should consider hardware-based Redundant Array of Independent Disks (RAID) solutions using copper- or fiber-channel-based small computer system interfaces (SCSIs).

- **Data protection** Unless you can tolerate hours of downtime, you should add protection against unexpected drive failures by using RAID. RAID 0 (disk striping without parity) offers optimal read/write performance, but any failed drive means that IIS may not be able to continue operation until the drive is replaced. RAID 1 (disk mirroring) creates duplicate copies of data on separate drives, but recovery from drive failure may interrupt operations while you restore the failed drive from backups. RAID 5 (disk striping with parity) offers good protection against single drive failure but has poor write performance. Keep in mind that if you've configured redundant load-balanced servers, you may not need RAID. With load balancing, the additional servers offer the necessary fault tolerance.

- **UPS**   Sudden power loss and power spikes can seriously damage hardware. To prevent this, get an uninterruptible power supply (UPS). A UPS system gives you time to shut down the system properly in the event of a power outage, and it is also important in maintaining system integrity when the server uses write-back caching controllers that do not have on-board battery backups. Professional hosting providers often offer UPS systems that can maintain power indefinitely during extended power outages.

If you follow these hardware guidelines, you'll be well on your way to success with IIS.

Using IIS

The sections that follow examine the basics of working with IIS and the Indexing Service. IIS and the Indexing Service are designed to run on Windows-based operating systems. For production servers, you should install these services on Microsoft Windows 2000 Server, Microsoft Windows 2000 Advanced Server, Microsoft Windows 2000 Datacenter Server, or later versions of the operating system. For personal use, you can install these services on Microsoft Windows 2000 Professional or later versions of the operating system.

Installing IIS Components and Default Sites

You can install IIS and the Indexing Service during installation of the operating system or through the Windows Components Wizard. While the Indexing Service is installed as a single component, IIS has many subcomponents that can be added or removed at any time. These components include:

- **Common Files**   Installs common files required by IIS programs.

- **Documentation**   Installs documentation that covers server administration and publishing site content. This documentation is available using the Uniform Resource Locator (URL) *http://localhost/IISHelp/iis/misc/*.

- **File Transfer Protocol (FTP) Server**   Installs the FTP server service used to transfer files using FTP.

- **FrontPage 2000 Server Extensions**   Installs extensions that allow Web site authoring and administration using FrontPage and Microsoft Visual InterDev.

- **Internet Information Services Snap-In**   Installs the primary administration tool for IIS.

- **Internet Services Manager**   Installs a browser-based version of the IIS administration tools.

- **NNTP Service**   Installs the Network News Transfer Protocol (NNTP) service used to create and manage newsgroups.

- **SMTP Service**   Installs the SMTP service used for outgoing mail from a Web server.

- **Visual InterDev RAD Remote Deployment Support**   Allows applications to be remotely deployed to your Web servers.
- **World Wide Web Server**   Installs the Web service used to publish and manage Web sites.

When you install Internet services, default sites are created on the computer. These default sites are not active by default but can be started in the Internet Information Services snap-in. To start the snap-in, click Start, point to Programs, point to Administrative Tools, and then select Internet Services Manager. The default sites you see may include:

- **Default FTP site**   The default site for FTP services. By default, anonymous connections are allowed to FTP sites. Disable this service if you don't intend to use FTP for file transfers.
- **Default Web site**   The default site for Web services. By default, anonymous connections are allowed to Web sites. Disable anonymous connections unless your site is ready to go public.
- **Administration Web site**   The default site for browser-based administration. By default, this site is only accessible from the local system. If you wish to use this service for remote administration, change the default IP filtering.

Note   When the administration Web site is stopped, you cannot manage sites in Internet Services Manager.

- **Default SMTP Virtual Server**   The default site for SMTP services. If you don't use pages that generate e-mail messages, don't start SMTP servers. By default, only servers that authenticate themselves in the domain can relay mail on the server. This denies permission to relay e-mail through the server and protects the server from being used to deliver unsolicited e-mail messages.
- **Default NNTP Virtual Server**   The default site for NNTP services. The default configuration allows client posting and updates from news feeds and grants permission to other servers to pull articles from the server. If necessary, change these settings before starting an NNTP server.

If an IIS feature you want to use isn't available in the Internet Information Services snap-in, you can install it using the Windows Components Wizard. To access and use this wizard, follow these steps:

1. Log on to the computer using an account with administrator privileges.
2. Click Start, point to Settings, and then click Control Panel.
3. Double-click Add/Remove Programs. This displays the Add/Remove Programs dialog box.
4. Click Add/Remove Windows Components to start the Windows Components Wizard, shown in Figure 1-1.
5. Select Internet Information Services (IIS) and then click Details to add and remove individual IIS components.

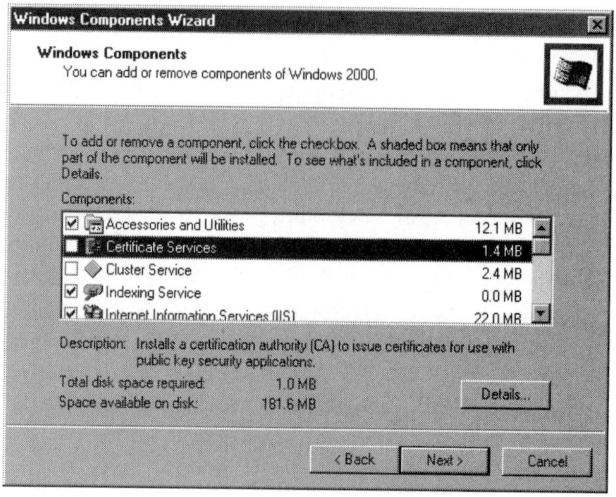

Figure 1-1. *Use the Windows Component Wizard to select components to add or remove.*

6. You can now select subcomponents to install or uninstall them.

7. When ready to continue, click Next. The selected components are then installed (or uninstalled).

Understanding Authentication Enhancements

IIS security is completely integrated with Windows domain security, allowing for authentication based on user and group memberships as well as standard Web-based authentication. These techniques make it much easier to manage logons and security. You can

- Use authentication based on Windows domain accounts only, so only users with a domain account can access the server.

- Allow anonymous access so that no username and password is required to access a resource.

- Enforce access restrictions based on IP address and domain name.

Installing Internet Services and Service-Related Accounts

When you install IIS and the Indexing Service, several services are installed on the computer. You can check for IIS-related services using the Services utility or Computer Management. Both utilities are found on the Administrative Tools menu. IIS-related services include:

- **FTP Publishing Service** Provides services for transferring files using FTP and also allows administration of an FTP server through the Internet Information Services snap-in.

- **IIS Admin Service** Allows administration of IIS through the Internet Information Services snap-in.
- **Indexing Service** Indexes the contents and properties of files, providing quick access to files through a flexible query language.
- **Simple Mail Transport Protocol (SMTP)** Provides mail transfer services and allows administration of SMTP sites through the Internet Information Services snap-in.
- **Network News Transport Protocol (NNTP)** Provides network news services and allows administration of NNTP servers through the Internet Information Services snap-in.
- **World Wide Web Publishing Service** Provides services for transferring files using HTTP and also allows administration of an HTTP server.

By default, IIS and the Indexing Service run within the local system account. This allows the services to interact with the operating system. When you install IIS, two user accounts are created as well. These accounts are:

- **IUSR_*ComputerName*** The Internet guest account used by anonymous users to access Internet sites. If this account is disabled or locked out, anonymous users cannot access Internet services.
- **IWAM_*ComputerName*** An account used by IIS to run out-of-process applications. If this account is disabled or locked out, out-of-process applications cannot start.

Tip Both accounts are members of the Guests group and have a password that never expires and cannot be changed by users. You can, however, set and manage the password for these accounts as you would for any other account.

Web Administration Tools and Techniques

Web administrators will find that there are many different ways to manage IIS and the Indexing Service. The key administration tools and techniques are covered in the sections that follow.

Managing Resources with Key Administration Tools

Many tools are available for managing Web, FTP, SMTP, NNTP, and indexing resources. Key tools you'll use are shown in Table 1-1. Most of these tools are available on the Administrative Tools menu. Click Start, point to Programs, point to Administrative Tools, and then select the tool you want to use. All of the tools shown in the table can be used to manage local and remote resources. For example, you can connect to a new computer in the Internet Information Services snap-in and then, afterward, all its sites and services can be remotely managed from your system.

Table 1-1. Quick Reference for Key IIS Administration Tools

Administration Tool	Purpose
Active Directory Users and Computers	Manages domain user, group, and computer accounts.
Computer Management	Manages services, storage, and applications. The Services And Applications node provides quick access to Indexing Service catalogs and IIS sites and servers.
Data Sources	Configures and manages Open Database Connectivity (ODBC) data sources and drivers. Data sources link Web front ends with database back ends.
DNS	Public Internet sites must have fully qualified domain names (FQDNs) to resolve properly in browsers. Use the Domain Name System (DNS) administrative snap-in to manage the DNS configuration of your Windows 2000 DNS servers.
Event Viewer	Manages events and system logs.
HTTP Monitoring Tool	Monitors HTTP activity on a server. You'll learn more about this tool in Chapter 10, "Performance Tuning and Monitoring."
IIS Administration Script Utility (ADSUTIL)	Manages the configuration of IIS from the command line. Provided as an executable and a Microsoft VBScript that can be executed using the command-line version of the Windows Script Host, CSCRIPT.EXE.
Internet Services Manager	Manages Web and FTP servers using a browser-based interface.
Performance	Tracks IIS performance, pinpoints performance problems, and configures system event logs and alerts.
Server Extensions Administrator	Manages server extensions, such as the FrontPage Server extensions for IIS.
Services	Views service information; starts and stops system services; configures service logons and automated recoveries.

Installing Administration Tools

When you add services to a server, the tools needed to manage those services are automatically installed. If you want to manage these servers remotely, you might not have these tools installed on your workstation. In this case, you need to install the administration tools on the workstation you are using.

To install the Windows 2000 administration tools, follow these steps:

1. Log on to the workstation using an account with administrator privileges.
2. Click Start, point to Settings, and then click Control Panel.
3. Double-click Add/Remove Programs.

4. To add or modify current administrative tools configuration, click Change Or Remove Programs, and then click Windows 2000 Administration Tools. This expands the entry in the right pane. Click Change.

5. To install administrative tools for the first time, click Add New Programs and then click CD Or Floppy. Click Next. Then, in the Run Installation Program dialog box, click Browse. Insert your Windows 2000 Server CD in your CD-ROM drive. In the Browse dialog box, select the CD, double-click I386, and then select ADMINPAK.MSI. Click Open, and then click Finish.

6. You should now see the Windows 2000 Administrative Tools Setup Wizard. Click Next.

7. The administrative tools are installed on your system. Click Finish to complete the process.

Web Administration Techniques

Web administrators have many options for managing IIS. The key administration tools are:

- Internet Information Services snap-in
- Internet Services Manager
- IIS Administration Objects
- Administration Scripts

The Internet Information Services snap-in provides the standard administration interface for IIS. Figure 1-2 shows the main window for the Internet Information Services snap-in. To start the Internet Information Services snap-in, click Start, point to Programs, point to Administrative Tools, and then select Internet Services Manager.

When started, the Internet Information Services snap-in automatically connects to the local IIS installation, if available. Once you connect to remote IIS installations, the Internet Information Services snap-in will automatically connect to these installations upon startup, as well. You can change this behavior by disconnecting from the remote server while in the snap-in. See Chapter 3, "Configuring Web Sites and Servers," for more information on using the Internet Information Services snap-in.

Figure 1-2. *Use the Internet Information Services snap-in to manage local and remote IIS installations.*

Internet Services Manager uses the administration Web site to access remote IIS installations. You can allow or disallow remote browser-based administration by starting or stopping this Web site. When installed, IIS randomly selects a port number from 2000 to 9999 and assigns this port number to the administration Web site. The site responds to browser requests for all permitted domains, but the administrator must specify the port name because it differs from the default HTTP port 80. For example, if the server's domain name is primary.microsoft.com and the administrative port is 9394, you can connect to the administration Web site by typing the following URL into your browser window:

http://primary.microsoft.com:9394/

Figure 1-3 shows the main window for Internet Services Manager. By default, only integrated Windows authentication is enabled. If you want to allow remote administration through the administration Web site, you must alter the IP filtering settings within the IIS security restrictions to allow outside systems access. If you are not automatically authenticated, you will be prompted for a username and password when the site is accessed. If you provide the proper logon information and are a member of the Windows Administrators group, you will be permitted to remotely administer IIS through the administration Web site.

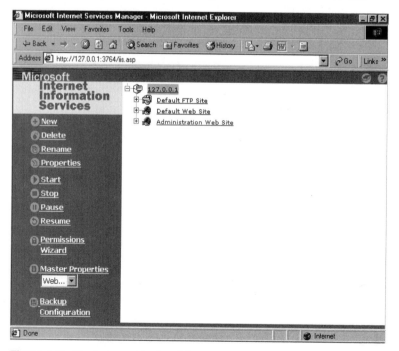

Figure 1-3. *Use Internet Services Manager to manage remote IIS installations.*

Individuals designated as Web site operators can remotely administer IIS, as well. Web site operators are a special group of users who have elevated privileges on individual Web sites. Operator privileges are limited compared to administrators', and they cannot access properties that affect IIS, the host computer, or the network. Web sites respond to browser requests from operators when the site's domain name followed by /iisadmin/ is passed to IIS. For example, if the server's domain name is primary.microsoft.com, you can connect to the operator area by typing the following URL into your browser window:

http://primary.microsoft.com/iisadmin/

As with the administrative site, only integrated Windows authentication is enabled by default. If you want to allow remote operator administration, you must alter the IP filtering settings within the IIS security restrictions to allow outside systems access. If you are not automatically authenticated, you will be prompted for a username and password when the site is accessed. If you provide the proper logon information, you will be permitted to remotely administer the Web site as an operator. See Chapter 5, "Managing Web Server Security," for more information on Web site operators.

IIS can also be managed through the Windows Scripting Host and the Active Directory services interface. Windows Scripting Host provides an architecture for building dynamic scripts that consist of a core object model, scripting hosts, and scripting engines. Active Directory service interfaces provide a set of interfaces that can be used to access the directory services built into Windows 2000 and later versions of the Windows operating system. For example, the Active Directory service interface Lightweight Directory Access Protocol (LDAP) provider offers a standard interface for LDAP-compliant services and applications, which includes Windows 2000 Active Directory and Microsoft Exchange 2000.

You will be very interested in the Active Directory service interface IIS provider. This provider defines a set of administrative objects for IIS. These objects in turn manage the IIS metabase, which contains definitions for various aspects of IIS and allows you to manage the configuration of IIS sites and servers. Thus, by manipulating IIS administrative objects, you change metabase entries and reconfigure IIS.

Two key components to working with the IIS metabase are key names and paths. A metabase key is a location in the metabase (similar to a directory in a file system). A metabase path is a sequence of keys separated by a forward slash (/) that uniquely identifies the location of a key in the metabase. You use the path of a metabase key to access the IIS administrative objects associated with the key. You'll learn more about the metabase in Chapter 12, "IIS Optimization and the Metabase."

A set of scripts is available in the \Inetpub\Adminscripts directory in the IIS installation. Table 1-2 provides an overview of each of the scripts. These scripts use the IIS administrative objects to manage core features of IIS.

Table 1-2. Quick Reference for Key IIS Administration Scripts

Administration Script	Purpose
Change Access Restrictions (CHACCESS)	Changes the type of access an IIS site or server allows. Multiple IIS resources and computers can be specified.
Continue FTP Server (CONTFTP)	Continues one or more FTP sites on one or more computers
Continue Server (CONTSRV)	Continues one or more IIS sites on one or more computers
Continue Web Server (CONTWEB)	Continues one or more Web sites on one or more computers.
Create Virtual Directory (MKWEBDIR)	Creates a virtual directory.
Create Web Site (MKW3SITE)	Creates a Web site.
Display Administrative Node (DISPNODE)	Displays configuration information for a Web site.
Display Administrative Tree (DISPTREE)	Displays the tree of administrative objects starting from the specified root node or from the top of the IIS tree.
Find Web Site (FINDWEB)	Finds the named Web site on the specified computer.
IIS Administration Script Utility (ADSUTIL)	Gets and sets IIS parameters; creates, deletes, and copies IIS sites and servers; gets IIS application status; creates, unloads, and deletes IIS applications.
Pause FTP Server (PAUSEFTP)	Pauses one or more FTP sites on one or more computers.
Pause Server (PAUSESRV)	Pauses one or more IIS sites on one or more computers.
Pause Web Server (PAUSEWEB)	Pauses one or more Web sites on one or more computers
Start FTP Server (STARTFTP)	Starts one or more FTP sites on one or more computers.
Start Server (STARTSRV)	Starts one or more IIS sites on one or more computers.
Start Web Server (STARTWEB)	Starts one or more Web sites on one or more computers.
Stop FTP Server (STOPFTP)	Stops one or more FTP sites on one or more computers.
Stop Server (STOPSRV)	Stops one or more IIS sites on one or more computers.
Stop Web Server (STOPWEB)	Stops one or more Web sites on one or more computers.

The scripts are designed to work with the command-line Windows Script Host, CSCRIPT.EXE. This host must be registered as the default scripting host on the computer you are using to execute the scripts. You can ensure that CSCRIPT.EXE is registered as the default host by entering the following command in a command prompt:

```
cscript //H:cscript
```

From the \Inetpub\Adminscripts directory, you can run a script by typing the script name on the command-line, such as:

```
dispnode -a IIS://localhost/w3svc
```

Type only the script name on the command-line to display basic help information.

Chapter 2
Core IIS Administration

Core Internet Information Services (IIS) administration tasks concern connecting to servers, managing services, and saving metabase configurations. In IIS, you connect to individual servers and manage their IIS components through the Internet Information Services snap-in or the Internet Services Manager. A single IIS server can be used to host multiple resources. World Wide Web and File Transfer Protocol (FTP) resources are referred to as Web sites and FTP sites, respectively. Simple Mail Transfer Protocol (SMTP) and Network News Transfer Protocol (NNTP) resources are referred to as SMTP virtual servers and NNTP virtual servers, respectively.

Sites and virtual servers are server processes that have their own configuration information, which can include IP addresses, port numbers, and authentication settings. To perform most administration tasks with sites and servers, you'll need to log on to the IIS server using an account that has administrator privileges. Nonadministrators designated as IIS operators can manage individual sites and virtual servers as well. Detailed information on security and operators can be found in Chapter 5, "Managing Web Server Security."

Working with IIS and URLs

Most administrators don't understand the actual underpinnings of IIS. Yet to really understand how IIS works, you have to understand the architecture and the basic techniques for accessing documents on the Internet. The sections that follow examine IIS architecture and document access using Uniform Resource Locators (URLs).

Understanding the IIS Architecture

You can think of IIS as a layer over the operating system in which, in most cases, you may need to perform a system-level task before you perform an IIS task. This is true in several key areas:

- **Directories** Web sites, virtual servers, and other resources use the Microsoft Windows 2000 file and directory structure. Before you create IIS resources, such as sites or virtual servers, you should ensure that any necessary directories have been created.

- **Permissions** Windows 2000 permissions determine whether users can access files and directories. Before users can access files and directories, you must ensure that the appropriate users and groups have access at the operating system level. After you set operating system (OS)-level permissions, you must set IIS-specific security permissions.

Windows services and processes are other areas in which Windows 2000 and IIS are tightly integrated. Figure 2-1 provides a conceptual overview of the service and process relationships. Each IIS service runs under an instance of SVCHOST.EXE. The service host process controls all resources of the same type running on a server. Because of this, Windows 2000 uses the service host to manage all instances of a specific resource, such as a Web or FTP site, running on a server. For example, if you start or stop the World Wide Web Publishing Service, you are controlling all Web sites running on the server through the related service host process. See the "Managing IIS Services" section of this chapter for details.

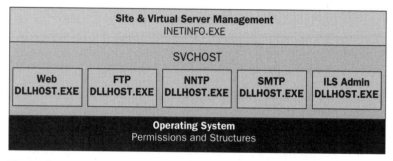

Figure 2-1. *Conceptual view of the IIS architecture.*

Because the IIS structure is layered, starting or stopping an IIS virtual server doesn't directly affect the service host. Instead, Windows 2000 uses an intermediary to control the service host for you. This intermediary is the InetInfo process. A single instance of INETINFO.EXE is used to manage the service hosts as well as Internet server application program interface (ISAPI) applications that run within the IIS process context. When you control IIS services individually, Windows 2000 controls the service host through InetInfo. InetInfo also makes it possible to manage all IIS resources running on a server. You can, for example, issue a restart command in the Internet Information Services snap-in that restarts IIS completely. See the "Starting, Stopping, and Restarting All Internet Services" section of this chapter for more details.

ISAPI applications are a key part of the IIS architecture. ISAPI applications are server-based applications that run on IIS Web sites. As Figure 2-2 shows, the dynamic-link library (DLL) host (DLLHOST.EXE) is used to manage out-of-process ISAPI applications. Any pooled ISAPI applications running on the server run within the context of a single instance of DLLHOST.EXE. In contrast, isolated ISAPI applications run within the context of separate DLL host processes.

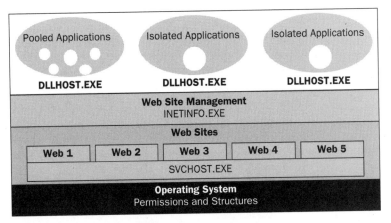

Figure 2-2. *IIS and ISAPI application architecture.*

Understanding URLs

To retrieve files from IIS servers, clients must know three things: the address of the server, where on the server the file is located, and which protocol to use to access and retrieve the file. Normally, this information is specified as a URL. URLs provide a uniform way of identifying resources that are available using Internet Protocols (IPs). The basic mechanism that makes URLs so versatile is their standard naming scheme.

URL schemes name the protocol the client will use to access and transfer the file. Clients use the name of the protocol to determine the format for the information that follows the protocol name. The protocol name is generally followed by a colon and two forward slashes. The information after the double slash marks follows a format that depends on the protocol type referenced in the URL. Here are two general formats:

protocol://hostname:port/path_to_resource

protocol://username:password@hostname:port/path_to_resource

Host name information used in URLs identifies the address to a host. Though host names can be provided in several different formats, including NetBIOS names, the most commonly used format is the fully-qualified domain name (FQDN). Common domain names for Web servers begin with www, such as *http://www.microsoft.com/*, which identifies the Microsoft Web Server in the commercial domain. Domains you can specify in your URLs include these:

- **.com**   Commercial sites
- **.edu**   Education sites
- **.gov**   Nonmilitary government sites
- **.mil**   Military sites
- **.net**   Network sites

- **.org** Organizational sites

Port information used in URLs identifies the port number to be used for the connection. Generally, you don't have to specify port numbers in your URLs unless the connection will be made to a port other than the default. As shown in Table 2-1, port 80 is the default port for Hypertext Transfer Protocol (HTTP). Let's assume you request a URL on a server using the following URL:

http://www.microsoft.com/docs/my-yoyo.htm/

Port 80 is assumed as the default port value. On the other hand, if you wanted to make a connection to port 8080, you'd need to type in the port value, such as:

http://www.microsoft.com:8080/docs/my-yoyo.htm/

Table 2-1. Default Ports for IIS Resources

Protocol	Default Port
FTP	21
SMTP	25
HTTP	80
NNTP	119
HTTPS	443

The final part of a URL is the path to the resource. This path generally follows the directory structure from the server's home directory to the resource specified in the URL.

URLs for FTP can also contain a username and password. Username and password information allow users to log on to an FTP server using a specific user account. For example, the following URL establishes a connection to the Microsoft FTP server and logs on using a named account:

ftp://sysadmin:rad$4@ftp.microsoft.com/public/download

Here, the account logon is sysadmin, the password is rad$4, the server is ftp.microsoft.com, and the requested resource is public/download.

If a connection is made to an FTP server without specifying the username and password, the FTP client (or Web browser) will assume that the user wants to establish an anonymous session. In this case, the following default values are assumed: anonymous for username and the user's e-mail address as the password.

URLs can use uppercase and lowercase letters, the numerals 0–9, and a few special characters, including these:

- Asterisk (*)
- Dollar sign ($)

- Exclamation point (!)
- Hyphen (-)
- Parentheses (left and right)
- Period (.)
- Plus sign (+)
- Single quotation mark (')
- Underscore (_)

You are limited to these characters because other characters used in URLs have specific meanings, as shown in Table 2-2.

Table 2-2. Special Characters in URLs

Character	Meaning
:	The colon is a separator. It separates the protocol from the rest of the URL scheme, the host name from the port number, and the username from the password.
//	The double slash marks indicate that the protocol uses the format defined by the Common Internet Scheme Syntax.
/	The slash is a separator and is used to separate the path from host name and port. The slash is also used to denote the directory path to the resource named in the URL.
%	The percent sign identifies an escape code. Escape codes are used to specify special characters in URLs that otherwise have a special meaning or are not allowed.
@	The at symbol is used to separate username and/or password information from the host name in the URL.
?	The question mark is used in the URL path to specify the beginning of a query string. Query strings are passed to Common Gateway Interface (CGI) scripts. All the information following the question mark is data the user submitted and is not interpreted as part of the file path.
+	The plus sign is used in query strings as a placeholder between words. Instead of using spaces to separate words the user has entered in the query, the browser substitutes the plus sign.
=	The equal sign is used in query strings to separate the key assigned by the publisher from the value entered by the user.
&	The ampersand is used in query strings to separate multiple sets of keys and values.
^	The carat is reserved for future use.
{}	Braces are reserved for future use.
[]	Brackets are reserved for future use.

To make URLs even more versatile, you can use escape codes to specify characters in URLs that are either reserved or otherwise not allowed. Escape codes have two components: a percent sign and a numeric value. The percent sign identifies the start of an escape code. The number following the percent sign identifies the character being escaped. The escape code for a space is a percent sign followed by the numeral 20 (%20). You can use this escape code in a URL as shown in the following example:

http://www.microsoft.com/docs/my%20party%20hat.htm/

Internet Information Services Snap-In Essentials

IIS is a Microsoft Management Console snap-in for managing IIS resources in Windows domains. You'll use this tool to perform routine administration tasks, such as starting Internet services, starting individual sites, and restarting services remotely.

Note Internet Services Manager provides a browser-based interface for managing Web and FTP resources. The tool has many of the same features as the Internet Information Services snap-in. For details on starting and using this tool, see the "Web Administration Techniques" section of Chapter 1, "Overview of Microsoft Web Services."

Starting and Using the Internet Information Services Snap-In

IIS is accessible in several locations. You can access the snap-in through a preconfigured console by clicking Start, pointing to Programs, pointing to Administrative Tools, and then selecting Internet Services Manager. Or you can access the snap-in through Computer Management. In Computer Management, click the plus sign (+) next to Services And Applications, and then select Internet Information Services.

Figure 2-3 shows the main window for the Internet Information Services snap-in. The snap-in automatically connects to local IIS installations (if available). You can connect to one or more remote computers as well. Each additional computer to which you connect has a separate node that you can use to manage its resources.

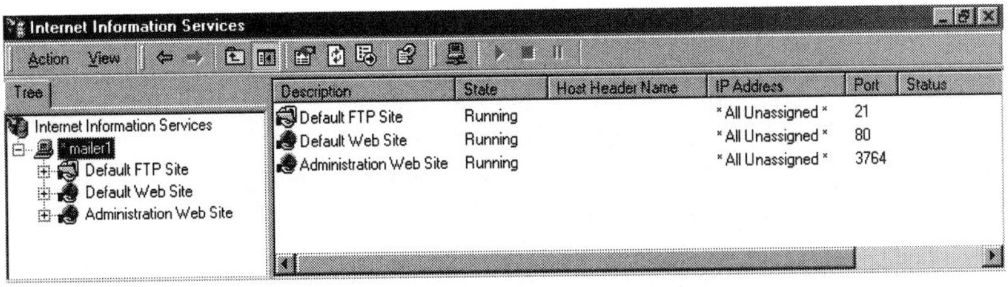

Figure 2-3. *Use the Internet Information Services snap-in to manage Web, FTP, SMTP, and NNTP resources.*

When you select the Internet Information Services node in the left pane, the right pane displays a summary of current computer connections. The connection summary provides the following information:

- **Connection Type**   Type of network connection as either Transmission Control Protocol/Internet Protocol (TCP/IP) or User Datagram Protocol (UDP).

- **Status**   Status of the computer, such as unavailable or restarting.

- **Computer**   Name of the computer to which you are connected.

- **Local**   States whether you are connected to a local or remote IIS installation. If the field value is set to Yes, you are connected to a local IIS installation. Otherwise, you are connected to a remote installation.

When you select a computer node in the left pane, the right pane displays an overview of IIS resources on the computer. The resource overview provides:

- **Description**   Basic description of site or virtual server assigned through the Properties dialog box.

- **State**   Status of the site or virtual server, such as running, stopped, paused, or unknown.

- **Host Header Name**   Host name passed in the HTTP header to clients (if applicable).

- **IP Address**   IP address of the site or virtual server. Incoming IP traffic is mapped by port and IP address to a specific site or virtual server instance. The value All Unassigned allows the HTTP, FTP, SMTP, or NNTP protocol to respond on all unassigned IP addresses that are configured on the server.

- **Port**   Port number that the site or virtual server listens on. Default ports for FTP, SMTP, HTTP, and NNTP are 21, 25, 80, and 119, respectively.

- **Status**   Additional status information for the site or virtual server.

When you access Internet Information Services through Computer Management, as shown in Figure 2-4, you'll have a slightly different display and behavior than a standard console. When first accessed, the Internet Information Services snap-in automatically connects to local IIS installations (if available). You can connect to a different computer by right-clicking the Computer Management node, selecting Connect To Another Computer, and then following the prompts.

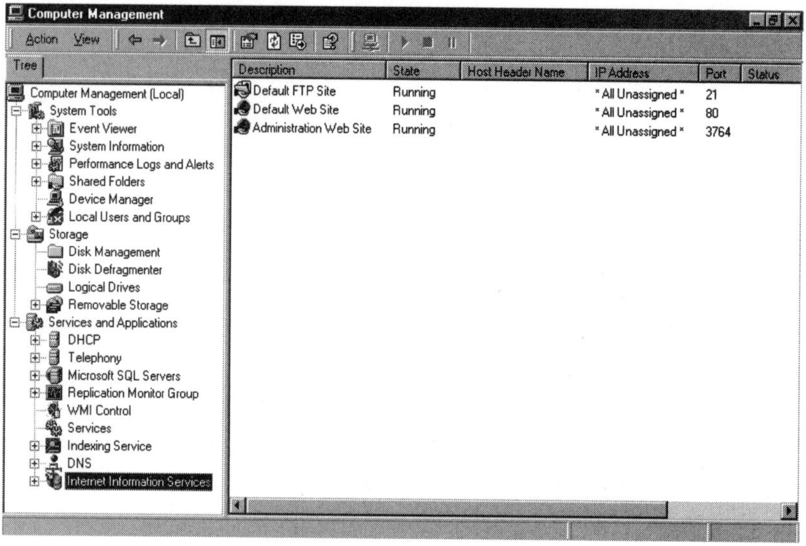

Figure 2-4. *Computer Management can be used to access Internet Information Services and Indexing Service.*

Connecting To Other Servers

Most of the time, you'll manage IIS installations from your desktop system. When you do this, you'll need to establish a remote connection to the server you want to manage. The steps for establishing remote connections are as follows:

1. Start the Internet Information Services snap-in.

2. In the left pane, right-click Internet Information Services, and then select Connect. The Connect To Computer dialog box is displayed.

3. In the Computer Name field, type the name of the computer to which you want to connect, and then click OK. You can also type the server's IP address or fully qualified domain name.

Starting, Stopping, and Restarting All Internet Services

As discussed earlier in the chapter, Windows 2000 uses the INETINFO.EXE process to manage all Internet Information Services. InetInfo is able to do this because it tracks all IIS resources running on a computer and can issue commands to these resources. As an administrator, you can control InetInfo through the Internet Information Services snap-in or the IISRESET command-line utility.

If you want to start, stop, or restart all of your Internet services from within the Internet Information Services snap-in, follow these steps:

1. In the Internet Information Services snap-in, select the icon for the computer you want to work with. If the computer isn't shown, connect to it as discussed under "Connecting To Other Servers," and then select it.

2. Click Action and then select Restart IIS. This displays the Stop/Start/Reboot dialog box, shown in Figure 2-5.

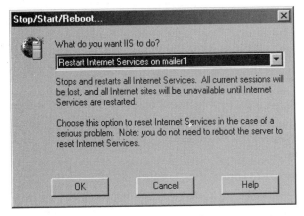

Figure 2-5. *Stop, start, and restart all Internet services.*

3. Use the selection menu to perform the following tasks:
   * **Start Internet Services** Attempts to start any IIS services that are stopped.
   * **Stop Internet Services** Attempts to stop all IIS services that are running, paused, or in an unknown state.
   * **Reboot** Attempts to restart the operating system on the server, just as if you had chosen Shutdown from that system's Start menu and selected the Restart option.
   * **Restart Internet Services** Attempts to stop and then restart IIS services. Also attempts to resolve potential problems with runaway processes or hung applications.

4. Click OK.

The sequence of tasks for the Restart Internet Services option is important to understand. The Restart Internet Services option performs the following tasks:

1. Stops all IIS services running on the computer, including World Wide Web Publishing Service, FTP Publishing Service, NNTP service, SMTP service, and IIS Admin Service.

2. Attempts to resolve potential problems with runaway processes or hung applications by stopping all Dr. Watson (DRWTSN32.EXE), Microsoft Transaction Server (MTX.EXE), and DLL Host (DLLHOST.EXE) processes.

3. Starts all IIS services and then starts DLL hosts as necessary.

You can also use the IISRESET command-line utility to start, stop, and restart Internet services. To start any IIS services that are stopped on the local computer, type the following command:

IISRESET /START

To stop all IIS services that are running, paused, or in an unknown state on the local computer, type the following command:

IISRESET /STOP

To stop and then restart IIS services on the local computer, type the following command:

IISRESET /RESTART

You can also control IIS services on remote computers. To do this, use the following syntax:

IISRESET [COMPUTERNAME] [COMMAND]

For example, type:

IISRESET ENGSVR01 /RESTART

Table 2-3 provides a listing of all switches for the IISRESET command-line utility. Rebooting computers is covered in the "Rebooting IIS Servers" section of this chapter.

Table 2-3. IISRESET Switches Defined

Switch	Definition
/DISABLE	Disables restarting of IIS services on the local system.
/ENABLE	Enables restarting of IIS services on the local system.
/NOFORCE	Does not forcefully terminate IIS services if attempting to stop them gracefully fails.
/REBOOT	Reboots the local or designated remote computer.

(continued)

Table 2-3. *(continued)*

Switch	Definition
/REBOOTONERROR	Reboots the computer if an error occurs when starting, stopping, or restarting IIS services.
/RESTART	Stops and then restarts all IIS services. Attempts to resolve potential problems with runaway processes or hung applications.
/START	Starts all IIS services that are stopped.
/STATUS	Displays the status of all IIS services.
/STOP	Stops all IIS services that are running, paused, or in an unknown state.
/TIMEOUT:*val*	Specifies the time-out value (in seconds) to wait for a successful stop of IIS services. On expiration of this time-out, the computer can be rebooted if the /REBOOTONERROR parameter is specified. With /STOP and /RESTART, an error is issued. The default value is 20 seconds for restart, 60 seconds for stop, and 0 seconds for reboot.

Starting, Stopping, and Pausing Individual Resources

You can control individual sites and virtual servers much like you do other server resources. For example, if you are changing the configuration of a site or performing other maintenance tasks, you may need to stop the site, make the changes, and then restart it. When a site is stopped, the site doesn't accept connections from users and cannot be used.

An alternative to stopping a site or virtual server is to pause it. Pausing a resource prevents new client connections but doesn't disconnect current connections. When you pause a site or virtual server, active clients can continue to retrieve documents, work with messages, and perform other tasks. No new connections are accepted, however.

To start, stop, or pause a site or virtual server, complete the following steps:

1. Start the Internet Information Services snap-in.

2. In the left pane, select the icon for the computer you want to work with. If the computer isn't shown, connect to it as discussed under "Connecting To Other Servers," and then select it.

3. Right-click the site or virtual server you want to manage. You can now do the following:

   * Select Start to start the site or virtual server.
   * Select Stop to stop the site or virtual server.

* Select Pause to pause the site or virtual server. After you pause a site or virtual server, click Pause again when you want to resume normal operations.

Note Groups of sites or virtual servers running under the same IIS service are controlled through their master process. For example, the master process for all virtual Web servers running on a computer is the World Wide Web Publishing Service. Stopping this service stops all Web sites using the process, and all connections to these sites are disconnected immediately. Starting this service restarts all Web sites that were running when the World Wide Web Publishing Service was stopped. To learn how to control IIS services, see the "Managing IIS Services" section of this chapter.

Rebooting IIS Servers

The Internet Information Services snap-in and IISRESET utility have extensions that allow you to reboot local and remote computers. To use these extensions, you must have installed IIS on the computer and you must be a member of a group that has the appropriate user rights. To reboot a local system, you must have the right to shut down the system. To reboot a remote system, you must have the right to force shutdown from a remote system. You should only reboot an IIS server if the restart IIS procedure fails.

You reboot an IIS server with the snap-in by completing the following tasks:

1. In the Internet Information Services snap-in, select the icon for the computer you want to work with. If the computer isn't shown, connect to it as discussed in the "Connecting To Other Servers" section of this chapter, and then select it.

2. Click Action and then select Restart IIS. This displays the Stop/Start/Reboot dialog box, shown previously in Figure 2-5.

3. Choose the Reboot option on the selection menu and then click OK.

4. A system shutdown message is sent to the target computer. This message explains that the computer is being shut down in 30 seconds. After completing the shutdown process, the system will reboot.

To reboot a computer using IISRESET, type the following command:

IISRESET [COMPUTERNAME] /REBOOT

For example, type:

IISRESET ENGSVR01 /REBOOT

If users are performing tasks that need to be exited gracefully, you should set a time-out value for services and processes to be stopped. By default, the time-out is 0 seconds, which forces immediate shutdown and tells Windows 2000 not to wait for services to be shut down gracefully. You could set a time-out value of 60 seconds when rebooting engsvr01 as follows:

IISRESET ENGSVR01 /REBOOT /TIMEOUT:60

Managing IIS Services

Each IIS server in the organization relies on a set of services for publishing pages, transferring files, and more. To manage IIS services, you'll use the Services node in the Computer Management console, which is started as follows:

1. Choose Start, point to Programs, point to Administrative Tools, and then select Computer Management.

2. Right-click the Computer Management entry in the console tree and, from the shortcut menu, select Connect To Another Computer. You can now choose the IIS server whose services you want to manage.

3. Expand the System Tools node by clicking the plus sign (+) next to it, and then choose Services.

Figure 2-6 shows the Services view in the Computer Management console. The key fields of this dialog box are used as follows:

- **Name** The name of the service.

- **Description** A short description of the service and its purpose.

- **Status** The status of the service as started, paused, or stopped. (Stopped is indicated by a blank entry.)

- **Startup Type** The startup setting for the service.

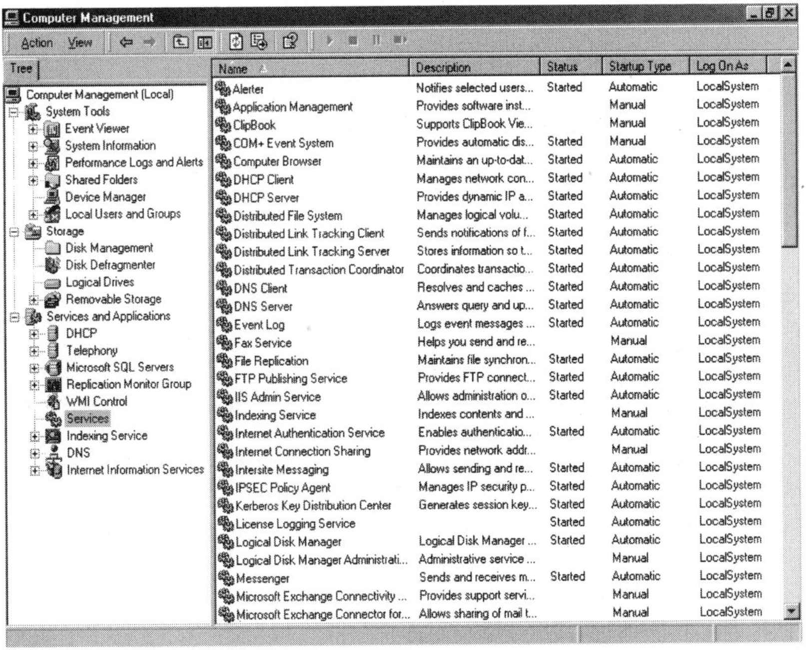

Figure 2-6. *Use the Services node to manage IIS services.*

> **Note** Automatic services are started at bootup. Manual services are started by users or other services. Disabled services are turned off and cannot be started.

- **Log On As** The account the service logs on as. The default in most cases is the local system account.

Core IIS Services

Table 2-4 provides a summary of services essential to normal IIS operations. Note that the services available on a particular IIS server depend on its configuration. Still, this is the core set of services that you'll find on most IIS servers.

Table 2-4. Core IIS Services

Name	Description
Event Log	Logs event informational, warning, and error messages issued by IIS and other applications
FTP Publishing Service	Provides services for transferring files using FTP and also allows administration of an FTP server
IIS Admin Service	Allows administration of IIS through the Internet Information Services snap-in
Indexing Service	Indexes the contents and properties of files, providing quick access to files through a flexible query language
Network News Transport Protocol (NNTP)	Provides network news services and allows administration of NNTP servers through the Internet Information Services snap-in
Simple Mail Transfer Protocol (SMTP)	Provides mail transfer services and allows administration of SMTP sites through the Internet Information Services snap-in
World Wide Web Publishing Service	Provides services for transferring files using HTTP, and also allows administration of an HTTP server

Starting, Stopping, and Pausing IIS Services

As an administrator, you'll often have to start, stop, or pause IIS services. IIS services are managed through the Computer Management console or through the Services utility. When you manage IIS services at this level, you are controlling all sites or virtual servers that use the service. For example, if a computer publishes three Web sites and you stop the World Wide Web Publishing Service, all three Web sites are stopped and are inaccessible.

To start, stop, or pause services in the Computer Management console, follow these steps:

1. Right-click the Computer Management entry in the console tree and, from the shortcut menu, select Connect To Another Computer. You can now choose the IIS server whose services you want to manage.

2. Expand the System Tools node by clicking the plus sign (+) next to it, and then choose Services.

3. Right-click the service you want to manipulate, and then select Start, Stop, or Pause as appropriate. You can also choose Restart to have Windows stop and then start the service after a brief pause. Additionally, if you paused a service, you can use the Resume option to resume normal operation.

Tip When services that are set to Start automatically fail, the status is listed as blank, and you'll usually receive notification in a pop-up dialog box. Service failures can also be logged to the system's event logs. In Windows 2000, you can configure actions to handle service failure automatically. For example, you could have Windows 2000 attempt to restart the service for you. See the "Configuring Service Recovery" section of this chapter for details.

Configuring Service Startup

Essential IIS services are configured to start automatically and normally shouldn't be configured with another startup option. That said, if you are troubleshooting a problem, you might want to start a service manually. You may also want to disable a service so that its related virtual servers don't start. For example, if you move an SMTP virtual server to a new server, you may want to disable the SMTP service on the original IIS server. In this way, the SMTP service isn't used but could be turned on if necessary (without having to re-install SMTP support).

Configure service startup as follows:

1. In the Computer Management console, connect to the IIS server whose services you want to manage.

2. Expand the Services And Applications node by clicking the plus sign (+) next to it, and then select Services.

3. Right-click the service you want to configure, and then choose Properties.

4. In the General tab, use the Startup Type selection list to choose a startup option, as shown in Figure 2-7. Select Automatic to start services at bootup. Select Manual to allow the services to be started manually. Select Disabled to turn off the service.

5. Click OK.

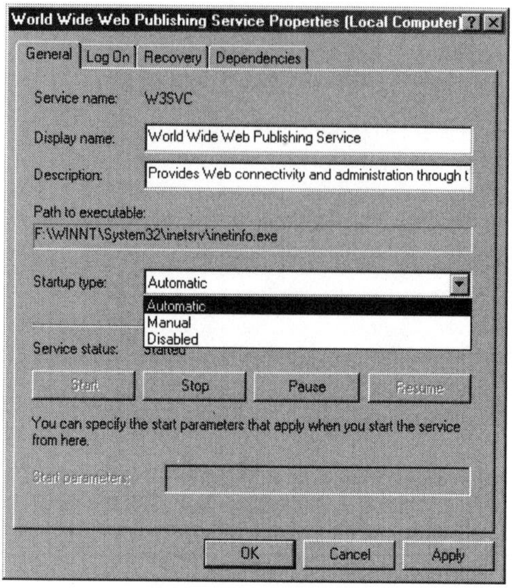

Figure 2-7. *For troubleshooting, you may want to change the service startup option.*

Configuring Service Recovery

Windows services can be configured to take specific actions when a service fails. For example, you could attempt to restart the service or reboot the server. To configure recovery options for a service, follow these steps:

1. From the Computer Management console, connect to the computer whose services you want to manage.

2. Expand the Services And Applications node by clicking the plus sign (+) next to it, and then select Services.

3. Right-click the service you want to configure, and then choose Properties.

4. Select the Recovery tab, as shown in Figure 2-8. You can now configure recovery options for the first, second, and subsequent recovery attempts. The available options are:

    * Take No Action
    * Restart The Service
    * Run A File
    * Reboot The Computer

5. Configure other options based on your previously selected recovery options. If you elected to restart the service, you'll need to specify the restart delay. After stopping the service, Windows 2000 waits for the specified delay before trying to start the service. In most cases, a delay of 1–2 minutes should be sufficient.

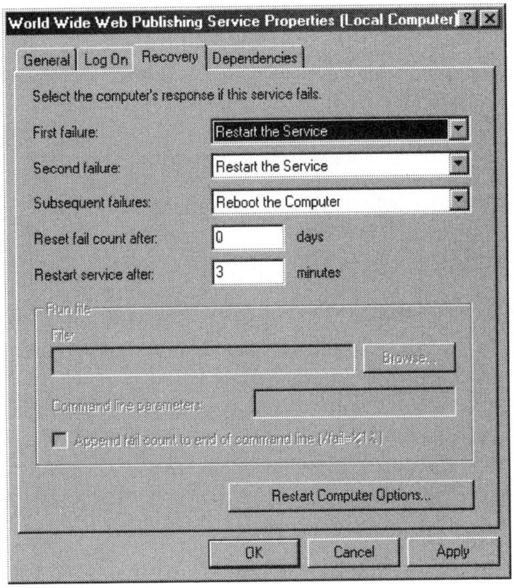

Figure 2-8. *Services can be configured to automatically recover in case of failure.*

6. Click OK.

When you configure recovery options for critical services, you may want Windows 2000 to try to restart the service on the first and second attempts and then reboot the server on the third attempt.

Configuring IIS Backup and Recovery

The sections that follow address techniques you can use to back up and recover IIS servers. These are the most important operations you'll perform as a Web administrator.

Storing a Server's Configuration

When you back up an IIS server, you need to look at the IIS configuration as well as the system configuration. This means you must:

1. Save the IIS configuration to a metadata file anytime you change the properties of the IIS installation, and maintain several configuration backups as an extra precaution.

2. Periodically back up the server using a comprehensive backup procedure, such as the one outlined in Chapter 14, "Data Backup and Recovery," of the *Windows 2000 Administrator's Pocket Consultant*.

Backing up an IIS server using this technique gives you several recovery options:

- Recover the IIS configuration settings for sites and virtual servers using the IIS configuration backup you've created.

- Recover a corrupted IIS installation by re-installing IIS and recovering the last working IIS configuration.

- Restore the server, its data files, and its IIS configuration by recovering the system from archives.

- Perform a partial server restore to retrieve missing or corrupted files from archives.

IIS configuration backups contain metadata that describes the configuration settings used by Internet sites and virtual servers. IIS uses the metadata to restore values for all resource properties, including security settings, virtual directory options, and ISAPI application configurations. IIS also uses this information to maintain the run state of sites and virtual servers. So, if you save the IIS configuration and then restore the configuration at a later date, the IIS configuration settings are restored and the IIS resources are returned to their original state (running, paused, stopped, and so on) as well.

I recommend that you create an IIS configuration backup every time you make IIS configuration changes and before you make major changes that affect the availability of resources. IIS configuration backups are saved with the .md0 file extension in the %SystemRoot%\system32\intsrv\MetaBack directory. Md0 indicates that the file contains metadata. The typical backup file is smaller than 200 KB.

IIS configuration backups can help you in many situations. You can use them to

- **Recover deleted resources**   References to all site and virtual server instances running on the server are stored with the configuration backup. If you delete a site or virtual server, you can restore the necessary resource references.

- **Restore site or server properties**   All configuration settings of sites and virtual servers are stored in the configuration backup. If you change properties, you can recover the previous IIS settings from backup.

- **Recover ISAPI application configuration**   ISAPI application settings, including App Mappings, App Options, Process Options, and App Debugging, are stored with the configuration backup. If you change the ISAPI application settings, you can recover the ISAPI application configuration.

- **Recover Web and FTP master service properties**   Master service properties and other top-level IIS settings are stored in configuration backups. This means you can recover default settings for new Web and FTP sites, bandwidth throttling settings, and Multipurpose Internet Mail Extensions (MIME)-type mappings. You cannot, however, recover master properties for server extensions.

- **Rebuild a damaged IIS installation**   If the IIS installation gets corrupted and you cannot repair it through normal means, you can rebuild the IIS installation. You do this by uninstalling IIS, re-installing IIS, and then using the configuration backup to restore the IIS settings. See the "Rebuilding Corrupted IIS Installations" section of this chapter for details.

If you were to open a backup file in a text editor, you would find that it contains metabase keys and paths that are specific to the current server installation. The significance of this is that the metabase keys and paths allow you to restore IIS settings in the Windows registry without having to manipulate the registry directly. Registry settings are machine- and instance-specific. This means you cannot restore configuration settings to other machines and you cannot restore configuration settings after re-installing the operating system.

Creating IIS Configuration Backups

Each IIS server has a configuration that must be backed up to ensure that IIS can be recovered in case of problems. To back up the IIS configuration, follow these steps:

1. In the Internet Information Services snap-in, select the icon for the computer you want to work with. If the computer isn't shown, connect to it as discussed under "Connecting To Other Servers," and then select it.

2. Click Action and then select Backup/Restore Configuration. This displays the Configuration Backup/Restore dialog box, shown in Figure 2-9.

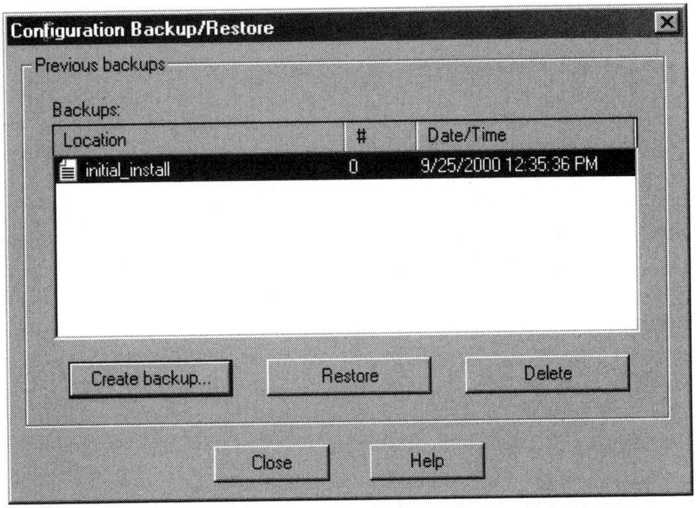

Figure 2-9. *Use Configuration Backup/Restore to create, restore, and delete IIS configuration backups.*

3. Click Create Backup, select a name for your backup file, and then click OK. IIS creates the backup file. By default, this file is stored in the %SystemRoot%\System32\Inetsrv\MetaBack directory.

4. Click Close.

Restoring IIS from Backup Configurations

You can restore IIS from backup configuration files. When you do this, the previous property settings and state are restored. Recovering the configuration won't repair a corrupted IIS installation. To repair a corrupted installation, you should follow the technique outlined in the "Rebuilding Corrupted IIS Installations" section of this chapter.

Restoring IIS from a backup configuration causes Windows 2000 to stop and then restart IIS services. Once you've notified users that IIS resources will be unavailable for several minutes, you can restore the IIS configuration by completing the following steps:

1. In the Internet Information Services snap-in, select the icon for the computer you want to work with. If the computer isn't shown, connect to it as discussed under "Connecting To Other Servers," and then select it.

2. Click Action and then select Backup/Restore Configuration. This displays the Configuration Backup/Restore dialog box shown in Figure 2-9.

3. The Backups panel shows the configuration backups that are available for the computer. Select a backup file and then click Restore. When asked whether or not you'd like to restore your configuration settings, click Yes.

Rebuilding Corrupted IIS Installations

A corrupt IIS installation can cause problems with your IIS sites and virtual servers. Resources may not run. IIS may not respond to commands. IIS may freeze intermittently. To correct these problems, you may need to rebuild the IIS installation. Rebuilding the IIS installation is a lengthy process that requires a complete outage of IIS sites and virtual servers. The outage can last from 5–15 minutes, or more.

 Caution IIS configuration backups are machine- and instance-specific. You cannot restore configuration settings to other machines and you cannot restore configuration settings after re-installing the operating system.

You rebuild a corrupt IIS installation by completing the following steps:

1. Log on locally to the computer on which you want to rebuild IIS. Make sure you use an account with Administrator privileges.

2. Click Start, point to Settings, and then click Control Panel.

3. Double-click Add/Remove Programs. This displays the Add/Remove Programs dialog box.

4. Start the Windows Components Wizard by clicking Add/Remove Windows Components.

5. In the Components list, clear the Internet Information Services check box, and then click Next. After Setup makes the configuration changes you requested, click Next again, and then click Finish.

6. In the Add/Remove Programs dialog box, click Add/Remove Components. This restarts the Windows Component Wizard.

7. Re-install IIS by selecting the Internet Information Services check box. If necessary, click Details, and then select IIS subcomponents.

8. When you are ready to continue, click Next. After Setup re-installs IIS, click Next again, and then click Finish.

9. Click Close to close the Add/Remove Programs dialog box, and then start the Internet Information Services snap-in.

10. In the Internet Information Services snap-in, right-click the local computer entry in the left pane, and then select Backup/Restore Configuration.

11. In the Configuration Backup dialog box, select the backup file that contains the correct IIS settings, and then click Restore.

12. When prompted, select Yes to confirm your decision to restore the IIS settings. After the IIS configuration has been restored, click Close to return to the Internet Information Services snap-in.

Deleting Backup Configurations

Over time, you'll gather quite a collection of IIS configuration backups. If you find that you don't need old backups anymore, you can delete them using the Configuration Backup dialog box. To do this, complete the following steps:

1. In the Internet Information Services snap-in, select the icon for the computer you want to work with. If the computer isn't shown, connect to it as discussed under "Connecting To Other Servers," and then select it.

2. Click Action and then select Backup/Restore Configuration.

The Backups panel shows the configuration backups that are available for the computer. Select the backup file or files you want to delete, and then click Delete. When asked whether or not you'd like to delete the files, click Yes.

The backup files are permanently deleted. You cannot recover the files from the Recycle Bin.

Part II

Web Server Administration

In this part, you'll find the essential tasks for administering World Wide Web servers running Internet Information Services (IIS). Chapter 3 details management techniques for Web sites and servers. You'll also learn how to create and manage virtual directories. Customizing IIS is the key focus of Chapter 4. In this chapter, you'll learn about Internet Server Application Programming Interface (ISAPI) filters, custom Hypertext Transfer Protocol (HTTP) headers, custom content, server error messages, and Multipurpose Internet Mail Extensions (MIME) types. Chapter 5 covers Web site and server security. To manage server security, you'll create user logins, configure directory permissions, and assign operators. The permissions and operator privileges you assign determine the actions users can perform as well as what areas of the Web site they can access. The final chapter in this section, Chapter 6, explores server certificates and server extensions. Certificates enable secure Web communications. Server extensions are used to for authoring and administration.

Chapter 3

Configuring
Web Sites and Servers

In this chapter, you'll learn to configure World Wide Web sites and servers. Tasks for configuring Web sites and servers are broken down into several categories. You'll find sections on Web site naming and identification, managing master Web service properties, creating Web sites, and more.

Web site properties are a key part of Web site management and configuration. Web site properties identify the site, set its configuration values, and determine where and how documents are accessed. Web site properties can be set at several levels:

- As global defaults
- As site defaults
- As directory defaults

Global defaults are set through the master Web server properties and can be inherited by all Web sites created on the server. Individual defaults are set through the Web Site Properties dialog box and apply only to the selected Web site. Directory defaults are set through the Directory Properties dialog box and apply only to the selected directory.

Web Site Naming and Identification

This section discusses Web site naming and identification techniques. Each Web site deployed in the organization has unique characteristics. Different types of Web sites can have different characteristics. Intranet Web sites typically use computer names that resolve locally and have private Internet Protocol (IP) addresses. Internet Web sites typically use fully qualified domain names and public IP addresses. Intranet and Internet Web sites can also use host header names, allowing single IP address and port assignments to serve multiple Web sites.

Understanding IP Addresses and Name Resolution

Whether you are configuring an intranet or Internet site, your Web server must be assigned a unique IP address that identifies the computer on the network. An IP address is a numeric identifier for the computer. IP addressing schemes vary depending on how your network is configured, but they're normally assigned from a range of addresses for a particular network segment. For example, if you're working with a computer on the network segment 192.55.10.0, the address range you have available for computers is usually from 192.55.10.1 to 192.55.10.254.

While numeric addresses are easy for machines to remember, they aren't easy for people to remember. Because of this, computers are assigned text names that are easy to remember. Text names have two basic forms:

- Standard computer names, which are used on private networks
- Internet names, which are used on public networks

Private networks are networks that are either indirectly connected to the Internet or completely disconnected from the Internet. Private networks use IP addresses that are reserved for private use and aren't accessible to the public Internet. Private network addresses are:

- 10.0.0.1–10.255.255.254
- 172.16.0.1–172.31.255.254
- 192.168.0.1–192.168.255.254

Private networks that use Internet technologies are called intranets. Information is delivered on intranets by mapping a computer's IP address to its text name, which is the NetBIOS name assigned to the computer. While Windows components use the NetBIOS naming convention for name resolution, Transmission Control Protocol/Internet Protocol (TCP/IP) components use the Domain Name System (DNS). Under Microsoft Windows, the DNS host name defaults to the same name as the NetBIOS computer name. For example, if you install a server with a computer name of CorpServer, this name is assigned as the NetBIOS computer name and the default DNS host name.

In contrast, public networks are networks that are connected directly to the Internet. Public networks use IP addresses that are purchased or leased for public use. Typically, you'll obtain IP address assignments for your public servers from the provider of your organization's Internet services. Internet service providers obtain blocks of IP addresses from the American Registry for Internet Numbers. Other types of organizations can purchase blocks of IP addresses as well.

On the Internet, the DNS is used to resolve text names to IP addresses. A hypothetical DNS name is www.microsoft.com. Here, *www* identifies a server name and *microsoft.com* identifies a domain name. As with public IP addresses, domain names must be leased or purchased. You purchase domain names from name registrars, such as Internet Network Information Center (InterNIC). When a client computer requests a connection to a site using a domain name, the request is transmitted to a DNS server. The DNS server returns the IP address that corresponds to the requested host name, and then the client request is routed to the appropriate site.

Don't confuse the public DNS naming system used on the Internet with the private naming system used on intranets. DNS names are configured on DNS servers and resolved to IP addresses before contacting a server. This fact makes it possible for a server to have multiple IP addresses; each with a different DNS name. For example, a server with an internal computer name of Gandolf could be configured with IP addresses of 207.46.230.210, 207.46.230.211 and 207.46.230.212. If these IP addresses are configured as www.microsoft.com, services.microsoft.com, and products.microsoft.com, respectively, in DNS server, the server can respond to requests for each of these domain names.

Understanding Web Site Identifiers

Each Web site deployed in your organization has a unique identity it uses to receive and to respond to requests. The identity includes the following:

- A computer or DNS name
- An IP address
- A port number
- An optional host header name

The way these identifiers are combined to identify a Web site depends on whether the host server is on a private or public network. On a private network, a computer called CorpIntranet could have an IP address of 10.0.0.52. If so, the Web site on the server could be accessed in the following ways:

- Using the Uniform Naming Convention (UNC) path name: \\CorpIntranet or \\10.0.0.52
- Using a Uniform Resource Locator (URL): *http://CorpIntranet/* or *http:// 10.0.0.52/*
- Using a URL and port number: *http://CorpIntranet:80/* or *http://10.0.0.52:80/*

On a public network, a computer called Dingo could be registered to use the DNS name www.microsoft.com and the IP address of 207.46.230.210. If so, the Web site on the server could be accessed:

- Using a URL: *http://www.microsoft.com/* or *http://207.46.230.210/*
- Using a URL and port number: *http://www.microsoft.com:80/* or *http:// 207.46.230.210:80/*

Hosting Multiple Sites on a Single Server

Using different combinations of IP addresses, port numbers, and host header names, one can host multiple sites on a single computer. Hosting multiple sites on a single server has definite advantages. For example, rather than installing three different Web servers, one could host www.microsoft.com, support.microsoft.com, and service.microsoft.com on the same Web server.

Note Windows 2000 Professional can host only one Web site and one FTP site. You must upgrade to Windows 2000 Server to host multiple Web or FTP sites.

One of the most efficient ways to host multiple sites on the same server is to assign multiple IP addresses to the server. An example is shown as Figure 3-1. To use this technique, you must follow these steps:

1. Configure the TCP/IP settings on the server so that there is one IP address for each site that you want to host.
2. Configure the name resolution system so that the host names and corresponding IP addresses can be resolved.
3. Configure each Web site so that it uses a specific IP address.

With this technique, users can access the sites individually by typing the unique domain name or IP address in a browser. Following the example shown in Figure 3-1, you can access the Sales intranet by typing **http://SalesIntranet/** or by typing **http://10.0.0.102/**.

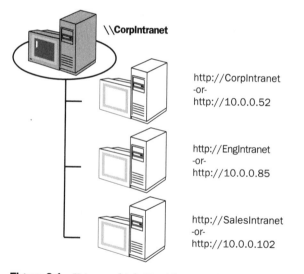

\\CorpIntranet

http://CorpIntranet
-or-
http://10.0.0.52

http://EngIntranet
-or-
http://10.0.0.85

http://SalesIntranet
-or-
http://10.0.0.102

Figure 3-1. *Using multiple IP addresses to host multiple Web sites on a single server.*

Another technique you can use to host multiple sites on a single server is to assign each site a unique port number while keeping the same IP address, as shown in Figure 3-2. Users will then be able to

1. Access the main site by typing the text name or IP address in a browser, such as *http://Intranet/* or *http://10.0.0.52/*.
2. Access other virtual servers by typing the domain name and port assignment or IP address and port assignment, such as *http://Intranet:88/* or *http://10.0.0.52:88/*.

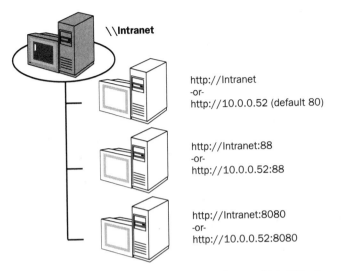

Figure 3-2. *Using multiple port numbers to host multiple Web sites on a single server.*

The final method you can use to host multiple sites on a single server is to use host header names. Host headers allow you to host multiple sites on the same IP address and port number. The key to host headers is a DNS name assignment that is configured in the name resolution system and assigned to the site in its configuration.

An example of host header assignment is shown in Figure 3-3. Here, a single server hosts the sites CorpIntranet, EngIntranet, and SalesIntranet. The three sites use the same IP address and port number assignment but have different DNS names. To use host headers, you must do the following:

1. Configure the name resolution system so that the host header names and corresponding IP addresses can be resolved.

2. Configure the primary Web site so that it responds to requests on the IP address and port number you've assigned.

3. Configure additional Web sites so that they use the same IP address and port number, and also assign a host header name.

Host headers have specific drawbacks. Earlier versions of browsers that don't support HTTP 1.1 are unable to pass host header names back to Internet Information Services (IIS). Although Microsoft Internet Explorer 3.0, Netscape Navigator 2.0, and later versions of these browsers support the use of host header names, earlier versions of these browsers do not. Visitors using earlier browsers will reach the default Web site for the IP address.

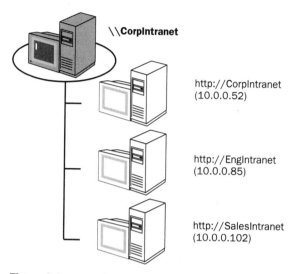

\\CorpIntranet

http://CorpIntranet
(10.0.0.52)

http://EngIntranet
(10.0.0.85)

http://SalesIntranet
(10.0.0.102)

Figure 3-3. *Using host headers to support multiple Web sites on a single server.*

Another drawback to host headers is that you cannot use host headers with Secure Sockets Layer (SSL). With SSL, Hypertext Transfer Protocol (HTTP) requests are encrypted, and the host header name within the encrypted request cannot be used to determine the correct site to which the request must be routed.

Checking the Computer Name and IP Address of Servers

Before you configure Web sites, you should check the computer name and IP address of the server. You can view the computer name by completing the following steps:

1. On the Windows Desktop, right-click My Computer, and then select Properties. This displays the System Properties dialog box.

2. Click the Network Identification tab. The tab displays the fully qualified domain name of the server and the domain membership. The fully qualified domain name is the DNS name of the computer.

3. The DNS name is the name that you normally use to access the IIS resources on the server. For example, if the DNS name of the computer is www.microsoft.com and you've configured a Web site on port 80, the URL you use to access the computer from the Internet is *http://www.microsoft.com/*.

Tip   You can change the computer and domain information by clicking Properties and entering new values. If the computer is a domain controller, you won't be able to make these changes without demoting the server. Keep in mind these settings reflect what the computer knows its name as. You must still create entries on a DNS server for proper name resolution.

You can view the IP address and other TCP/IP settings for the computer by completing the follow steps:

1. Access Network And Dial-Up Connections by clicking Start, then Settings, and then selecting Network And Dial-Up Connections.

2. Right-click Local Area Connection, and then select Properties. This opens the Local Area Connection dialog box.

3. Open the Internet Protocol (TCP/IP) Properties dialog box by double-clicking on Internet Protocol (TCP/IP). Or you could select Internet Protocol (TCP/IP) and then click Properties.

4. The IP Address and other TCP/IP settings for the computer are displayed, as shown in Figure 3-4.

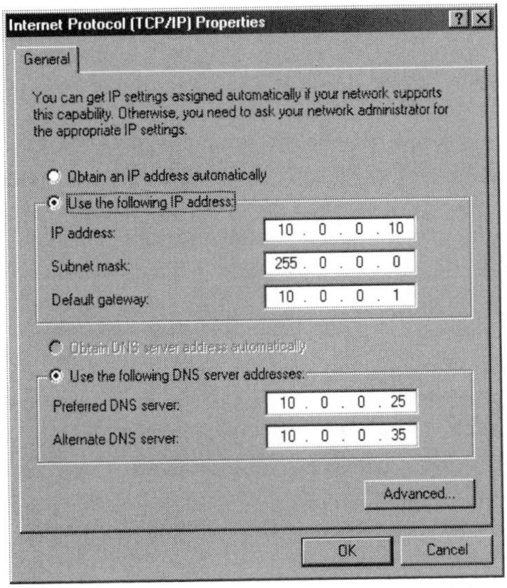

Figure 3-4. *Use the Internet Protocol (TCP/IP) Properties dialog box to view and configure TCP/IP settings.*

Real World IIS servers should use static IP addresses. If the computer is obtaining an IP address automatically, you'll need to reconfigure the TCP/IP settings. See Chapter 15, "Managing TCP/IP Networking," in *Microsoft Windows 2000 Administrator's Pocket Consultant* for details.

Managing Master Web Service Properties

The master Web service properties are used to set default property values for new Web sites created on a server. Anytime you change global properties, existing Web sites may inherit the changes as well. In some cases, you'll have the opportunity to specify which sites and directories within sites inherit changes. In other cases, the changes are applied automatically to all existing Web sites and you aren't prompted to either accept or decline.

To change the master Web service properties for a server, follow these steps:

1. In the Internet Information Services snap-in, right-click the icon for the computer you want to work with and then select Properties. If the computer isn't shown, connect to it as discussed in the "Connecting To Other Servers" section of Chapter 2, "Core IIS Administration," and then perform these tasks.

2. In the Properties dialog box, on the Master Properties panel, make sure WWW Service is selected and click Edit. This opens the WWW Service Master Properties dialog box for the computer.

3. Use the tabs and fields of the WWW Service Master Properties dialog box to configure the default property values for new Web sites. When you are finished making changes, click OK.

4. Before applying changes for permissions and authentications, IIS checks the existing settings in use for all child nodes of the selected resource (if any). If a Web site or directory within a Web site uses a different value, an Inheritance Overrides dialog box is displayed. Use this dialog box to select the site and directory nodes that should use the new setting, and then click OK.

Creating Web Sites

When you install the World Wide Web Publishing Service for IIS, a default Web site is created. In most cases, you don't need to change any network options to allow users access to the default Web site. You simply tell users the URL path that they need to type into their browser's Address field. For example, if the DNS name for the computer is www.microsoft.com and the site is configured for access on port 80, a user can access the Web site by typing *http://www.microsoft.com/* in the browser's Address field.

The default Web site is designed for beginning administrators and has many subdirectories containing documentation and helpful applications. The key directories are:

- **IISHelp** Contains online help documentation and is located in %SystemRoot%\Help\IisHelp by default. This directory is set up as a pooled Internet Server Application Programming Interface (ISAPI) application called IIS Help Application.

- **IISAdmin** Contains operator administration pages for the Web site. This directory must be configured for any Web site that you want operators to be able to control remotely. By default, the directory is located in %SystemRoot%\System32\Inetsrv\Iisadmin and is configured as a pooled ISAPI application called Administration Application.

- **IISSamples** Contains sample documents that can be helpful for administrators and developers. By default, the directory is located in the \Iissamples directory within the IIS installation and is configured as a pooled ISAPI application called Sample Application.

While the default Web site is helpful for novices, it can be the source of many problems for administrators:

- The preconfigured ISAPI applications use system resources that are better used elsewhere.

- The application files are easy targets for mischievous users who want to exploit the server.

- The \IISAdmin directory makes remote operator administration possible (when this may not be what is wanted).

For these and other reasons not stated, I recommend that you delete the default Web site and create a new Web site in its place. You can then configure any specific default directories that are needed on an individual basis. For example, if you want to make it possible to remotely administer the site, create a virtual directory called \IISAdmin that points to %SystemRoot%\System32\Inetsrv\Iisadmin as described in the "Linking IISAdmin, IISHelp, and other System Directories" section of this chapter.

You can create additional Web sites by completing the following steps:

1. If you are installing the Web site on a new server, ensure that the World Wide Web Publishing Service has been installed on the server.

2. If you want the Web site to use a new IP address, you must configure the IP address before installing the site. For details, refer to the "Assigning a Static IP Address" section of Chapter 15, "Managing TCP/IP Networking," of *Microsoft Windows 2000 Administrator's Pocket Consultant.*

3. In the Internet Information Services snap-in, right-click the icon for the computer you want to work with, point to New, and then select Web Site. If the computer isn't shown, connect to it as discussed in the "Connecting To Other

Servers" section of Chapter 2, "Core IIS Administration," and then perform this task.

4. The Web Site Creation Wizard is started. Click Next. In the Name field, type a descriptive name for the Web site, such as Corporate WWW Server. Click Next.

5. As shown in Figure 3-5, use the IP address selection list to select an available IP address. Choose (All Unassigned) to allow HTTP to respond on all unassigned IP addresses that are configured on the server. Multiple Web sites can use the same IP address provided that the sites are configured to use different port numbers or host header names.

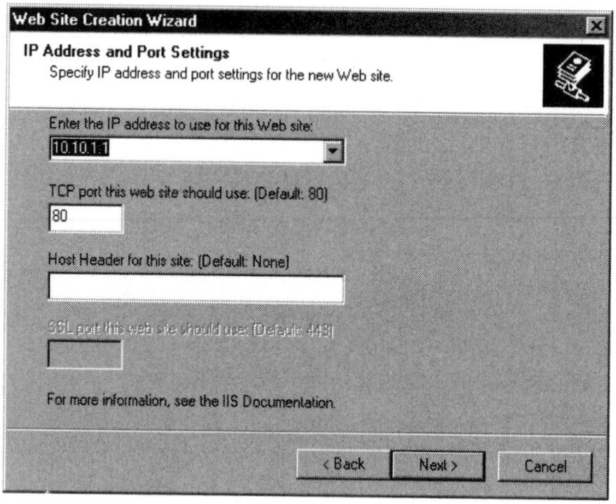

Figure 3-5. *Set the IP address and port values for the new site in the Web Site Creation Wizard.*

6. The TCP port for the Web site is assigned automatically as port 80. If necessary, type a new port number in the TCP Port field. Multiple sites can use the same port, provided that the sites are configured to use different IP addresses or host header names.

7. If you plan to use host headers for the site, type the host header name in the field provided. On a private network, the host header can be a computer name, such as EngIntranet. On a public network, the host header must be a DNS name, such as services.microsoft.com. The host header name must be unique.

8. By default, Web servers use port 443 for SSL. If you've installed an SSL certificate on the server, as discussed in Chapter 6, "Managing Microsoft Certificate Services and SSL," SSL is enabled for use and you can change the SSL port by typing a new value in the SSL Port field. Multiple sites can use the same SSL port, provided the sites are configured to use different IP addresses.

9. The next dialog box lets you set the home directory for the Web site. Click Browse to search for a folder. This folder must be created before you can select it. If necessary, use Microsoft Windows Explorer to create the directory before you browse for a folder.

Real World   I recommend that you create a top-level directory for storing the home directories and then create subdirectories for each site. The default top-level directory is C:\Inetpub. If you use this directory, you could create subdirectories called CorpWWW, CorpServices, and CorpProducts to store the files for www.microsoft.com, services.microsoft.com, and products.microsoft.com, respectively.

10. If you want to create a secure or private Web site, clear Allow Anonymous Access To This Web Site. By default, new Web sites are configured for anonymous access. This means users can access the Web site without needing to authenticate themselves.

11. Next, as shown in Figure 3-6, you can set access permissions for the Web site. Normally, you will want to set Read and Run Script permissions only. The standard permissions are:

- **Read**   Allows users to read documents, such as HTML files.

- **Run Scripts**   Allows users to run scripts, such as Activer Server Page (ASP) files or Perl scripts.

- **Execute**   Allows users to execute programs, such as ISAPI applications or executable files.

- **Write**   Allows users to upload files to the site, such as with Microsoft FrontPage.

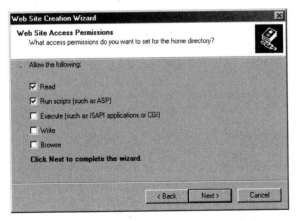

Figure 3-6. *Set access permissions for the Web site.*

- **Browse**   Allows users to view a list of files if they enter the name of a valid directory that does not have a default file.

12. Click Next and then click Finish. The Web site is created but is not started. You should finish setting the site's properties before you start the site and make it accessible to users.

Managing Web Site Properties

The sections that follow examine key tasks for managing Web site properties. Most Web site properties are configured through the Web Site Properties dialog box.

Configuring a Site's Home Directory

Each Web site on a server has a home directory. The home directory is the base directory for all documents that the site publishes. It contains a home page that links to other pages in your site. The home directory is mapped to your site's domain name or to the server name. For example, if the site's DNS name is www.microsoft.com and the home directory is C:\Inetpub\Wwwroot, then browsers use the URL *http://www.microsoft.com/* to access files in the home directory. On an intranet, the server name can be used to access documents in the home directory. For example, if the server name is CorpIntranet, then browsers use the URL *http://CorpIntranet/* to access files in the home directory.

You can view or change a site's home directory by completing the following steps:

1. Start the Internet Information Services snap-in and then, in the left pane (Console Root), click the plus sign (+) next to the computer you want to work with. If the computer isn't shown, connect to it as discussed in the "Connecting To Other Servers" section of Chapter 2, "Core IIS Administration."

2. Right-click the Web site you want to manage and then choose Properties.

3. Click the Home Directory tab, as shown in Figure 3-7.

4. If the directory you want to use is on the local computer, select A Directory Located On This Computer, and then type the directory path in the Local Path field, such as C:\Inetpub\Wwwroot. To browse for the folder, click Browse.

5. If the directory you want to use is on another computer and is accessible as a shared folder, select A Share Located On Another Computer, and then type the UNC path to the share in the Network Directory field. The path should be in the form \\ServerName\SharedFolder, such as \\Gandolf\CorpWWW. Then click Connect As and enter the username and password that should be used to connect to the shared folder.

Note If you do not specify a user name and password, the user Everyone must have access to the shared folder. Otherwise, the network connection to the folder will fail.

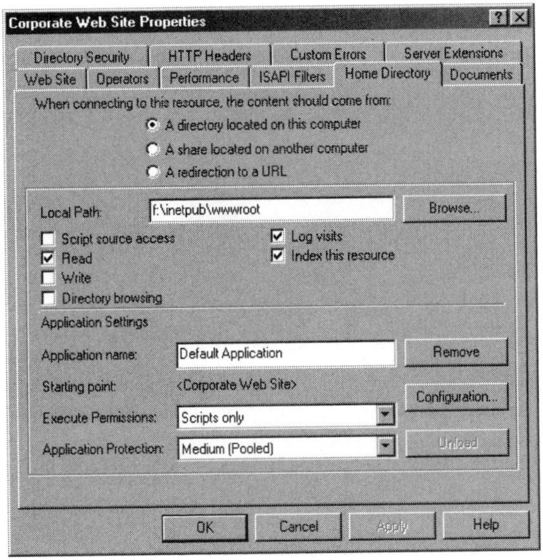

Figure 3-7. *You can change a site's home directory at any time.*

6. If you want to redirect users to another URL, select A Redirection To A URL, and then follow the techniques outlined in the "Redirecting Browser Requests" section of this chapter.

7. Click OK.

Configuring Ports, IP Addresses, and Host Names Used by Web Sites

Each Web site has a unique identity. The identity includes TCP port, SSL port, IP address, and host name settings. The default TCP port is 80. The default SSL port is 443. The default IP address setting is to use any available IP address.

To change the identity of a Web site, complete the following steps:

1. If you want the Web site to respond to a specific IP address, you must configure the IP address before updating the site. For details, refer to the "Configuring Static IP Addresses" section of Chapter 15, "Managing TCP/IP Networking," of *Microsoft Windows 2000 Administrator's Pocket Consultant.*

2. Start the Internet Information Services snap-in and then, in the left pane (Console Root), click the plus sign (+) next to the computer you want to work with. If the computer isn't shown, connect to it as discussed in the "Connecting To Other Servers" section of Chapter 2, "Core IIS Administration."

3. Right-click the Web site you want to manage and then choose Properties. The dialog box shown in Figure 3-8 is displayed.

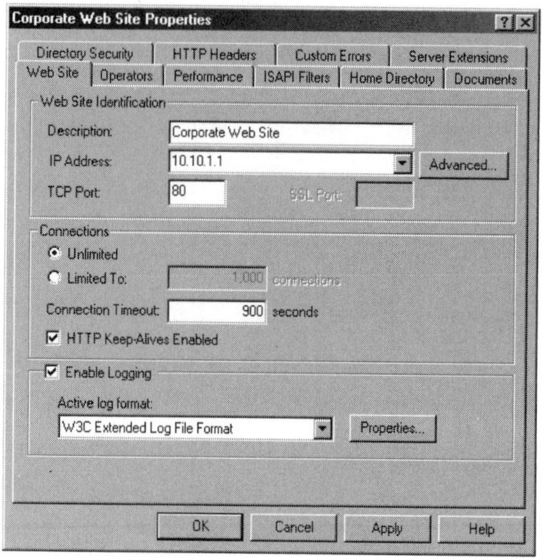

Figure 3-8. *You modify a site's identity through the Web Site tab in the Properties dialog box.*

4. The Description field shows the descriptive name for the Web site. The descriptive name is displayed in the Internet Information Services snap-in and isn't used for other purposes. You can change the current value by typing a new name in the Description field.

5. The IP address selection list shows the current IP address for the Web site. If you want to change the current setting, use the selection list to select an available IP address or choose (All Unassigned) to allow HTTP to respond on all unassigned IP addresses. Multiple Web sites can use the same IP address, provided that the sites are configured to use different port numbers or host header names.

6. The TCP port for the Web site is assigned to port 80 automatically. If necessary, type a new port number in the TCP Port field. Multiple Web sites can use the same TCP port, provided that the sites are configured to use different IP addresses or host header names.

7. If you plan to use host headers for the site, type the host header name in the field provided. On a private network, the host header can be a computer name, such as EngIntranet. On a public network, the host header must be a DNS name, such as services.microsoft.com. The host header name must be unique.

8. By default, Web servers use port 443 for SSL. If you've installed an SSL certificate on the server as discussed in Chapter 6, "Managing Microsoft Certificate Services and SSL," SSL is enabled for use, and you can change the SSL

port by typing a new value in the SSL Port field. Multiple sites can use the same SSL port, provided that the sites are configured to use different IP addresses.

9. Click OK.

Configuring Multiple Identities for a Single Web Site

Throughout this chapter, I've discussed techniques you can use to configure multiple Web sites on a single server. The focus of the discussion has been on configuring unique identities for each site. In some instances, you may want a single Web site to have multiple domain names associated with it. A Web site with multiple domain names publishes the same content for different sets of users. For example, your company may have registered domain.com, domain.org, and domain.net with InterNIC to protect your company or domain name. Rather than publishing the same content to each of these sites separately, you can publish the content to a single site that accepts requests for each of these identities.

The rules regarding unique combinations of ports, IP addresses, and host names still apply to sites with multiple identities. This means each identity for a site must be unique. You accomplish this by assigning each identity unique IP address, port, or host header name combinations.

To assign multiple identities to a Web site, complete the following steps:

1. If you want the Web site to use multiple IP addresses, you must configure the additional IP addresses before modifying the site properties. For details, refer to the "Configuring Static IP Addresses" section of Chapter 15, "Managing TCP/IP Networking," of *Microsoft Windows 2000 Administrator's Pocket Consultant*.

2. Start the Internet Information Services snap-in and then, in the left pane (Console Root), click the plus sign (+) next to the computer you want to work with. If the computer isn't shown, connect to it as discussed in the "Connecting To Other Servers" section of Chapter 2, "Core IIS Administration."

3. Right-click the Web site you want to manage and then choose Properties. The dialog box shown in Figure 3-8 is displayed.

4. On the Web Site tab, click Advanced. As Figure 3-9 shows, you can now use the Advanced Multiple Web Site Configuration dialog box to configure multiple identities for the site.

5. Use the Multiple Identities For This Web Site panel to manage the following TCP port settings:

   - **Add**   Adds a new identity. Click Add, select the IP address you want to use, and then type a TCP port and optional host header name. Click OK when you are finished.

   - **Edit**   Allows you to edit the currently selected entry in the identities list box.

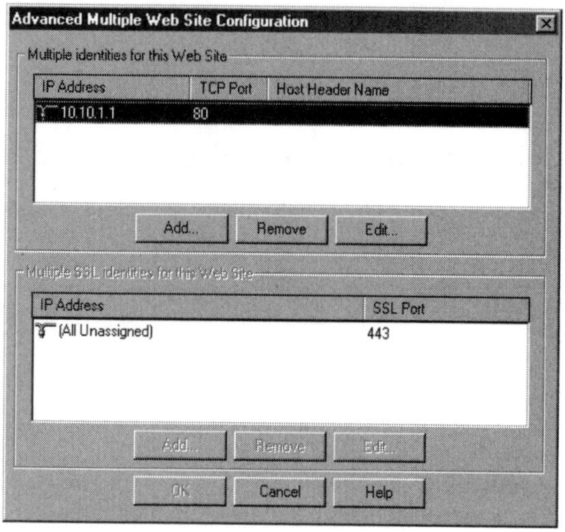

Figure 3-9. *Web sites can have multiple identities.*

* **Remove** Allows you to remove the currently selected entry from the identities list box.

6. Use the Multiple SSL Identities For This Web Site panel to manage SSL port settings. Click Add to create new entries. Use Edit or Remove to modify or delete existing entries.

7. Click OK twice to return to the Internet Information Services snap-in.

Restricting Incoming Connections and Setting Time-Out Values

You control incoming connections to a Web site in two key ways. You can set a limit on the number of simultaneous connections, and you can set a connection time-out value.

Normally, Web sites accept an unlimited number of connections and this is an optimal setting in most environments. However, a large number of connections will cause the Web site to slow down—sometimes so severely that nobody can access the site. To avoid this situation, you may want to limit the number of simultaneous connections. Once the limit is reached, no other clients are permitted to access the server. New clients must wait until the connection load on the server decreases. Currently connected users are allowed to continue browsing the site, however.

The connection time-out value determines when idle user sessions are disconnected. With the default Web site, sessions time out after they've been idle for 900 seconds (15 minutes). This prevents connections from remaining open indefinitely if browsers do not close them correctly.

You can modify connection limits and time-outs by completing the following steps:

1. Start the Internet Information Services snap-in and then, in the left pane (Console Root), click the plus sign (+) next to the computer you want to work with. If the computer isn't shown, connect to it as discussed in the "Connecting To Other Servers" section of Chapter 2, "Core IIS Administration."

2. Right-click the Web site you want to manage and then choose Properties.

3. To remove connection limits, select Unlimited on the Connections panel. To set a connection limit, select Limit To Number Of Connections, and then type a limit.

4. The Connection Timeout field controls the connection time-out. Type a new value to change the current time-out.

5. Click OK.

Configuring HTTP Keep-Alives

HTTP's original design opened a new connection for every file retrieved from a Web server. Because a connection is not maintained, no system resources are used after the transaction is completed. The drawback to this design is that when the same client requests additional data, the connection must be re-established, and this means additional traffic and delays.

Consider a standard Web page that contains a main Hypertext Markup Language (HTML) document and 10 images. With standard HTTP, a Web client requests each file through a separate connection. The client connects to the server, requests the document file, gets a response, and then disconnects. The client repeats this process for each image file in the document.

Web servers compliant with HTTP 1.1 support a feature called HTTP Keep-Alives. With this feature enabled, clients maintain an open connection with the Web server rather than re-opening a connection with each request. HTTP Keep-Alives are enabled by default for new Web sites. In most situations, clients will see greatly improved performance with HTTP Keep-Alives enabled. Keep in mind, however, that maintaining connections requires system resources. The more open connections there are, the more system resources that are used. To prevent a busy server from getting bogged down by a large number of open connections, you may want to limit the number of connections, reduce the connection time-out for client sessions, or both. For more information on managing connections, see the "Restricting Incoming Connections and Setting Time-Out Values" section of this chapter.

To enable or disable HTTP Keep-Alives, follow these steps:

1. Start the Internet Information Services snap-in and then, in the left pane (Console Root), click the plus sign (+) next to the computer you want to work

with. If the computer isn't shown, connect to it as discussed in the "Connecting To Other Servers" section of Chapter 2, "Core IIS Administration."

2. Right-click the Web site you want to manage and then choose Properties.

3. Select HTTP Keep-Alives Enabled to enable HTTP Keep-Alives. Clear this check box to disable HTTP Keep-Alives.

4. Click OK.

Managing Directories

IIS's directory structure is based primarily on the Windows 2000 file system, but it also provides additional functionality and flexibility. Understanding these complexities is critical to successfully managing IIS Web sites.

Understanding Physical and Virtual Directory Structures

Earlier in the chapter, I talked about home directories and how they were used. Beyond home directories, Microsoft Web sites also use the following:

- Physical directories
- Virtual directories

The difference between physical and virtual directories is important. A physical directory is part of the file system and must exist as a subdirectory within the home directory to be available through IIS. A virtual directory is a directory that is not necessarily contained in the home directory but is available to clients through an alias. Physical directories and virtual directories are configured and managed with the Internet Information Services snap-in, but they are displayed differently. Physical directories are indicated with a standard folder icon. Virtual directories are indicated using a folder icon with a globe in the corner.

Both physical and virtual directories have permissions and properties that can be set at the operating system level and the IIS level. You set operating system permissions and properties in Windows Explorer. You set IIS permissions and properties in the Internet Information Services snap-in.

You create physical directories by creating subdirectories within the home directory. These subdirectories are accessed by appending the directory name to the DNS name for the Web site. For example, you create a Web site with the DNS name products.microsoft.com. Users are able to access the Web site using the URL *http://www.microsoft.com/*. You then create a subdirectory within the home directory called "search." Users are able to access the subdirectory using the URL path *http://www.microsoft.com/search/*.

Even though locating your content files and directories within the home directory makes it easier to manage a Web site, you can also use virtual directories. Virtual directories act as pointers to directories that are not located in the home directory. Virtual directories are accessed by appending the directory alias to the DNS name for the site. If, for example, your home directory is D:\Inetpub\Wwwroot, and you store Microsoft Word documents in E:\Worddocs, you would need to create a virtual directory that points to the actual directory location. If the alias is *docs* for the E:\Worddocs directory, visitors to the www.microsoft.com Web site could access the directory using the URL path *http://www.microsoft.com/docs/*.

Creating Physical Directories

Within the home directory, you can create subdirectories to help organize your site's documents. You can create subdirectories within the home directory by completing the following steps:

1. Start Windows Explorer. Click Start, point to Programs, point to Accessories, and then select Windows Explorer.

2. In the Folders pane, select the home directory for the Web site.

3. In the Contents pane, right-click and then select Folder from the New menu. A new folder is added to the Contents pane. The directory name is initialized to New Folder and selected for editing.

4. Edit the name of the directory and press ENTER. The best directory names are short but descriptive, such as Images, WordDocs, or Downloads.

Tip   If possible, avoid using spaces as part of IIS directory names. Officially, spaces are illegal characters in URLs and must be replaced with an escape code. The escape code for a space is %20. While most current browsers are smart enough to replace spaces with %20 for you, earlier versions of browsers may not be and won't be able to access the page.

5. The new folder inherits the default file permissions of the home directory and the default IIS permissions of the Web site. For details on viewing or changing permissions, see Chapter 5, "Managing Web Server Security."

Tip   The Internet Information Services snap-in doesn't automatically display new folders. You may need to click the Refresh button on the toolbar to display the folder.

Creating Virtual Directories

Virtual directories are created in two stages. First, create a physical directory (which is typically not located within the home directory). Then create a virtual directory that maps to the physical directory by completing the following steps:

1. Start the Internet Information Services snap-in and then, in the left pane (Console Root), click the plus sign (+) next to the computer you want to work with. If the computer isn't shown, connect to it as discussed in the "Connecting To Other Servers" section of Chapter 2, "Core IIS Administration."

2. Right-click the Web site on which you want to create the virtual directory, point to New, and then select Virtual Directory. This starts the Virtual Directory Creation Wizard. Click Next.

3. In the Alias field, type the name you want to use to access the virtual directory. As with directory names, the best alias names are short but descriptive.

4. The next dialog box lets you set the path to the physical directory where your content is stored. Type the directory path or click Browse to search for a directory. The directory must be created before you can select it. If necessary, use Windows Explorer to create the directory before you browse for the directory.

5. Next, set access permissions for the virtual directory. Normally, you will want to set Read and Run Script permissions only. The standard permissions are these:

   - **Read**   Allows users to read documents, such as HTML files.

   - **Run Scripts**   Allows users to run scripts, such as Activer Server Page (ASP) files or Perl scripts.

   - **Execute**   Allows users to execute programs, such as ISAPI applications or executable files.

   - **Write**   Allows users to upload files to the site, such as with Microsoft FrontPage.

   - **Browse**   Allows users to view a list of files if they enter the name of a valid directory that does not have a default document.

6. Click Next and then click Finish. The virtual directory is created.

Note   By default, new virtual directories are created as pooled ISAPI applications with the application name set to the alias name. Because of this, the virtual directory is indicated with an icon that shows a document and a globe inside a box. For more information on ISAPI applications, see Chapter 4, "Customizing Internet Information Services."

Linking IISAdmin, IISHelp, and Other System Directories

IISAdmin, IISHelp, and other system directories are used to perform specific tasks. IISAdmin allows Web operators to control a site. IISHelp displays help documentation. By default, these directories are not configured for use with new sites that you create. To make these directories available, you must create a virtual directory that maps an alias to their physical location. You do this by completing the following steps:

1. Start the Internet Information Services snap-in and then, in the left pane (Console Root), click the plus sign (+) next to the computer you want to work with. If the computer isn't shown, connect to it as discussed in the "Connecting To Other Servers" section of Chapter 2, "Core IIS Administration."

2. Right-click the Web site on which you want to link the system directory, point to New, and then select Virtual Directory. This starts the Virtual Directory Creation Wizard. Click Next.

3. In the Alias field, type the name you want to use to access the system directory, such as IISAdmin.

4. The next dialog box lets you set the path to the physical directory where your content is stored. Click Browse to search for the system directory you want to use. IISHelp is located in %SystemRoot%\Help\Iishelp by default. IISAdmin is located in %SystemRoot%\System32\Inetsrv\Iisadmin by default.

5. Click Next and then set access permissions. For IISAdmin, IISHelp, and IISSamples, select Read And Run Scripts. For MSADC, select Read, Run Scripts, and Execute.

6. Click Next and then click Finish. The virtual directory is created and mapped to the system directory you referenced.

Modifying Directory Properties

You can modify the settings for a physical or virtual directory at any time. Directory permissions and general directory properties are set in Windows Explorer. IIS permissions and properties are set in the directory properties dialog box. In this Internet Information Services snap-in, right-click the directory and then select Properties.

Renaming Directories

You can rename physical and virtual directories in the Internet Information Services snap-in. When you rename a physical directory, the actual folder name of the directory is changed. When you rename a virtual directory, only the alias to the directory is changed. The name of the related physical directory is not changed.

To rename a physical or virtual directory, follow these steps:

1. In the Internet Information Services snap-in, click the plus sign (+) next to the Web site you want to work with.

2. Right-click the directory you want to rename and then select Rename. The directory name is selected for editing.

3. Edit the name of the folder and then press ENTER.

Caution Browsers store file and directory paths in bookmarks. When you change a directory name, you invalidate any URL that references the directory in its path string. Because of this, renaming a directory may cause a return visitor to experience the dreaded 404 File Not Found error. To resolve this problem, you may want to redirect browser requests to the new location using the technique discussed in the "Redirecting Browser Requests" section of this chapter.

Deleting Directories

You can delete physical and virtual directories in the Internet Information Services snap-in. When you delete a physical directory, the directory and its contents are removed and placed in the Recycle Bin. When you delete a virtual directory, only the alias to the directory is removed. The actual contents of the related physical directory are not changed.

To delete a physical or virtual directory in the Internet Information Services snap-in, follow these steps:

1. In the Internet Information Services snap-in, click the plus sign (+) next to the Web site you want to work with.

2. Right-click the directory you want to delete and then select Delete. When asked to confirm the action, click Yes.

Managing Web Content

Copying files into the home, sub, and virtual directories is in fact how you publish documents on a Web site. Documents inherit the default properties of the site and the default permissions of the Windows folder in which they are placed. These properties and permissions can be changed for each document or for all documents within a directory.

Caution As noted previously in the chapter, browsers cache file and directory paths in bookmarks. To prevent errors when renaming or deleting files, you may want to redirect browser requests to the new location using the technique discussed in the "Redirecting Browser Requests" section of this chapter.

Opening and Browsing Files

You can open files in a browser from within the Internet Information Services snap-in. To do this, right-click the file and then, from the shortcut menu, select Open. This opens the file using a directory path, such as D:\Inetpub \Wwwroot\DEFAULT.HTM.

Most types of files can be displayed in the default browser by opening them. However, if the file is an .asp document or other type of dynamic content and the Web site is running, the file will not be displayed. You must be browsing the file to view it in Internet Explorer. To browse a file, right-click the file and then, from the shortcut menu, select Browse.

Modifying the IIS Properties of Files

You can modify the settings for a Web file at any time. File permissions and general file properties are set in Windows Explorer. IIS permissions and properties are set in the file's properties dialog box. In this Internet Information Services snap-in, right-click the file, and then select Properties.

Renaming Files

You can rename Web files in the Internet Information Services snap-in. Follow these steps:

1. Start the Internet Information Services snap-in and then click the plus sign (+) next to the Web site you want to work with.

2. Right-click the file you want to rename and then select Rename. The filename is selected for editing.

3. Edit the name of the file and then press ENTER.

Deleting Files

You can delete physical and virtual directories in the Internet Information Services snap-in. When you delete a physical directory, the directory and its contents are removed and placed in the Recycle Bin. When you delete a virtual directory, only the alias to the directory is removed. The actual contents of the related physical directory are not changed.

To delete a physical or virtual directory in the Internet Information Services snap-in, follow these steps:

1. In the Internet Information Services snap-in, click the plus sign (+) next to the Web site you want to work with.

2. Right-click the directory you want to delete and then select Delete. When asked to confirm the action, click OK.

Redirecting Browser Requests

Browser redirection is a useful technique to prevent errors when you rename or delete content within a Web site. When you redirect requests, you tell a browser to take the following actions:

- Look for files in another directory.
- Look for files on a different Web site.
- Look for files on another computer.
- Look for a specific file instead of a set of files.
- Run an ISAPI application instead of accessing the requested files.

Each of these redirection techniques is examined in the sections that follow. Tips for creating customized redirection routines are examined in the "Customizing Browser Redirection" section of this chapter.

Redirecting Requests to Other Directories or Web Sites

If you rename or delete a directory, you can redirect requests for files in the directory to another directory or Web site. When a browser requests the file at the original location, the Web server instructs the browser to request the page using the new location. You redirect requests to other directories or Web sites as follows:

1. In the Internet Information Services snap-in, click the plus sign (+) next to the Web site you want to work with.

2. Right-click the directory you want to redirect and then select Properties.

3. Click the Virtual Directory or Directory tab as appropriate, and then select A Redirection To A URL, as shown in Figure 3-10.

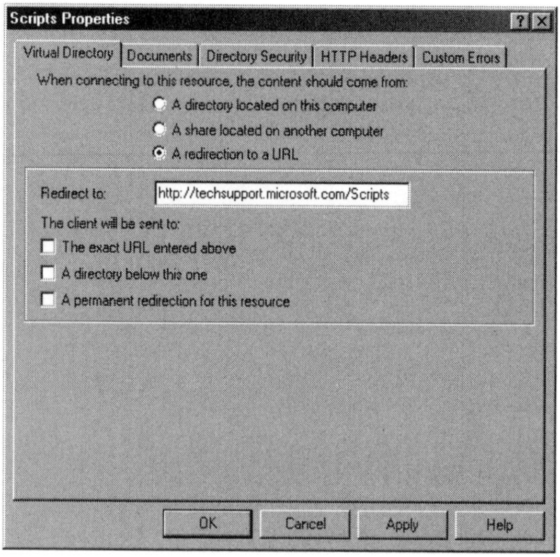

Figure 3-10. *You can redirect requests for files in one directory to another directory.*

4. In the Redirect To field, type the URL of the destination directory or Web site. For example, to redirect all requests for files in the /Docs directory to the /CorpDocs directory, type **/CorpDocs**. To redirect all requests for files located at www.microsoft.com/Docs to the techsupport.microsoft.com/CorpDocs, type **http://techsupport.microsoft.com/CorpDocs**.

5. Click OK. Now all requests for files in the old directory are mapped to files in the new directory. For example, if the browser requested *http://www.microsoft.com/Docs/adminguide.doc* and you redirected requests to *http://techsupport.microsoft.com/CorpDocs/*, the browser would request *http://techsupport.microsoft.com/CorpDocs/adminguide.doc*.

Redirecting All Requests to Another Web Site

If you stop publishing a Web site but don't want users to reach a dead end if they visit, you should redirect requests for the old Web site to a specific page at the new site. You redirect requests to a specific page at another site by completing the following steps:

1. In the Internet Information Services snap-in, right-click the Web site you want to work with, and then select Properties.

2. Click the Home Directory tab and then select A Redirection To A URL, as shown in Figure 3-11.

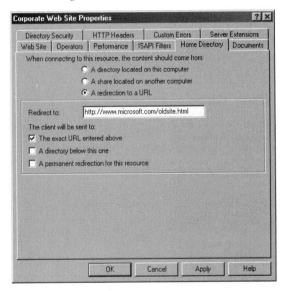

Figure 3-11. *Another redirection technique is to redirect all requests for files to a specific location at another Web site.*

3. In the Redirect To field, type the complete URL path to the page at the new site, such as *http://www.microsoft.com/oldsite.html*.

4. Select The Exact URL Entered Above and then click OK. Now all requests for files at the old site are mapped to a specific page at the new site.

Retrieving Files from a Network Share

IIS can retrieve files from a network share instead of the local hard drive. To configure this, complete the following steps:

1. In the Internet Information Services snap-in, right-click the Web site you want to work with, and then select Properties.

2. Click the Home Directory tab and then select A Share Located On Another Computer, as shown in Figure 3-12.

3. Type the UNC path to the network share in the Network Directory field. The path should be in the form \\ServerName\SharedFolder, such as \\Gandolf\CorpWWW. Afterward, click Connect As and then enter the username and password that should be used to connect to the shared folder.

4. Click OK. Now all requests for files on the Web site are mapped to files on the specified network share.

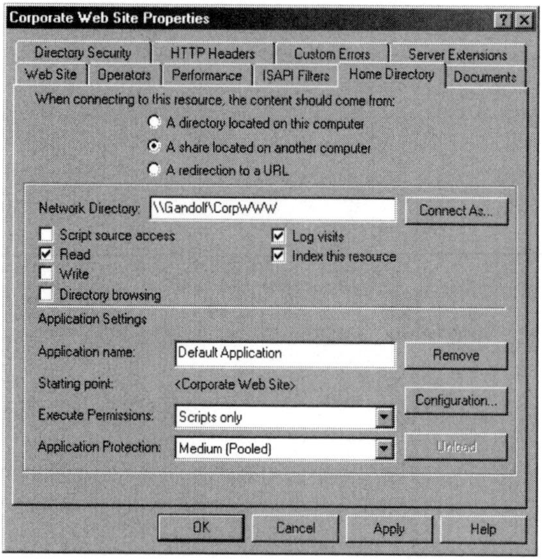

Figure 3-12. *Network shares can be used as source directories for content. To map to a share, you must use redirection.*

Redirecting Requests to Applications

If your organization's development team has created a custom application for the Web site, you can redirect all requests for files in a particular directory (or for the entire site, for that matter) to an application. Parameters passed in the URL can also be passed to the application; the technique you use to do this is as follows:

1. In the Internet Information Services snap-in, click the plus sign (+) next to the Web site you want to work with.

2. Right-click the directory you want to redirect and then select Properties. If you want to redirect all requests for the site, right-click the Web site entry and then select Properties.

3. Click the Home Directory, Virtual Directory, or Directory tab as appropriate, and then select A Redirection To A URL.

4. In the Redirection To field, type the URL of the application including any variables needed to pass parameters to the program, such as /CorpApps/ Login.exe?URL=$V+PARAMS=$P, where *$V* and *$P* are redirection variables. A complete list of redirect variables is provided in Table 3-1.

5. Select The Exact URL Entered Above and click OK. Now all requests for files in the directory or site are mapped to the application.

Customizing Browser Redirection

The previous sections looked at basic redirection techniques. Now it's time to break out the power tools and customize the redirection process. You can customize redirection anytime you select the A Redirection To A URL option.

In all of the previous discussions, when you selected A Redirection To A URL, additional options were displayed under The Client Will Be Sent To. Without selecting additional options, all requests for files in the old location were mapped automatically to files in the new location. You can change this behavior by selecting any of the following options under The Client Will Be Sent To:

- **The Exact URL Entered Above**   Redirects requests to the destination URL without adding any other portions of the original URL. You can use this option to redirect an entire site or directory to one file. For example, to redirect all requests for the /Downloads directory to the file DOWNLOAD.HTM in the home directory, select this option and then type /DOWNLOAD.HTM in the Redirect To text box.

- **A Directory Below This One**   Redirects a parent directory to a child directory. For example, to redirect your home directory (designated by /) to a subdirectory named /Current, select this option and then type **/Current** in the Redirect To text box.

- **A Permanent Redirection For This Resource**   Sends a "301—Permanent Redirect" message to the client. Without using this option, redirections are considered temporary, and the client browser receives the "302—Temporary Redirect" message. Some browsers can use the "301—Permanent Redirect" message as the signal to permanently change a URL stored in cache or in a bookmark.

You can customize redirection using redirect variables as well. As Table 3-1 shows, you can use redirect variables to pass portions of the original URL to a destination path or to prevent redirection of a specific file or subdirectory.

Table 3-1. Redirect Variables for IIS

Variable	Description	Example
$S	Passes the matched suffix of the requested URL. The server automatically performs this suffix substitution; you use the $S variable only in combination with other variables.	If /Corpapps is redirected to /Apps and the original request is for /Corpapps/LOGIN.EXE, then /LOGIN.EXE is the suffix.
$P	Passes the parameters in the original URL omitting the question mark used to specify the beginning of a query string.	If the original URL is /Scripts /COUNT.ASP?valA=1&valB=2, then the string "valA=1&valB=2" is mapped into the destination URL.
$Q	Passes the full query string to the destination.	If the original URL is /Scripts /COUNT.ASP?valA=1&valB=2, then the string "?valA=1&valB=2" is mapped into the destination URL.
$V	Passes the requested path without the server name.	If the original URL is //Gandolf /Apps/COUNT.ASP, then the string "/Apps/COUNT.ASP" is mapped into the destination URL.
$0 through $9	Passes the portion of the requested URL that matches the indicated wildcard.	
!	Use this variable to prevent redirecting a subdirectory or an individual file.	

The final way you can customize redirection is to use redirect wildcards. Use redirect wildcards to redirect particular types of files to a specific file at the destination. For example, you can use redirect wildcards to redirect all .htm files to DEFAULT.HTM and all .asp files to DEFAULT.ASP. The syntax for wildcard redirection is:

```
*;*.EXT;FILENAME.EXT[;*.EXT;FILENAME.EXT…]
```

where *.ext* is the file extension you want to redirect and *FILENAME.EXT* is the name of the file to use at the destination. As shown, begin the destination URL with an asterisk and a semicolon, and separate pairs of wildcards and destination URLs with a semicolon. Be sure to account for all document types that users may requests directly, such as .htm, .html, and .asp documents.

You can use wildcard redirection by completing the following steps:

1. In the Internet Information Services snap-in, click the plus sign (+) next to the Web site you want to work with.

2. Right-click the directory you want to redirect and then select Properties. If you want to redirect all requests for the site, right-click the Web site entry, and then select Properties.

3. Click the Home Directory, Virtual Directory, or Directory tab as appropriate, and then select A Redirection To A URL.

4. In the Redirection To field, type the wildcard redirection values. For example, if you want to redirect wildcards to redirect all .htm files to DEFAULT.HTM and all .asp files to DEFAULT.ASP, you would enter:

   `*;*.HTM;DEFAULT.HTM;*.ASP;DEFAULT.ASP`

5. Select The Exact URL Entered Above and then click OK. Now all requests for files in the directory or site are mapped using wildcards, if possible.

Chapter 4

Customizing Internet Information Services

Internet Information Services (IIS) provides a rich environment for developing custom applications. As a Web administrator, you need a strong understanding of this environment and how custom applications can be managed once they've been developed. The Internet Server Application Programmer Interface (ISAPI) provides the core functionality for custom applications.

Many other aspects of IIS can be customized as well. You can use Microsoft Active Server Pages (ASPs) to create custom applications that can be isolated from other processes. You can add custom ISAPI filters that change the behavior of IIS or that add new features, such as support for Java Servlet Pages. You can create custom headers, error messages, and Multipurpose Internet Mail Extension (MIME) types. You can design update sites, jump pages, and much more.

Essentials for Working with IIS Applications

ISAPI provides custom functions for IIS. As depicted in Figure 4.1, ISAPI acts as a layer over IIS and can be extended using ISAPI applications, Active Server Pages, and third-party extensions. The sections that follow provide an overview of ISAPI applications and ASPs. Because third-party IIS extensions behave much like ISAPI applications, they aren't examined separately.

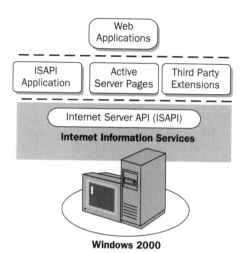

Figure 4-1. *Overview of the Web application architecture for IIS.*

Understanding ISAPI Applications

ISAPI applications fall into two categories:

- ISAPI filters
- ISAPI extensions

Both filters and extensions are used to modify the behavior of IIS. ISAPI filters are dynamic-link libraries (DLLs), or executables, that are loaded into memory when the World Wide Web Publishing Service is started and remain in memory until the IIS server is shut down. ISAPI filters are triggered when a Web server event occurs on the IIS server. For example, you could create a filter that responds to Read events by logging the client's browser type in a database.

ISAPI filters can be applied globally or locally. Global filters affect all IIS World Wide Web sites and are loaded into memory when the World Wide Web Publishing Service is started. Anytime you add new global filters or modify existing global filters you must stop and then restart the World Wide Web Publishing Service. Local filters affect a single IIS Web site and can be dynamically loaded into memory when they are added or modified, as long as the World Wide Web Publishing Service and the Web site are running.

When several filters are configured to respond to the same events, they are executed sequentially. Administrators can control the sequence by assigning priority levels to filters. Filters with higher priority are executed before filters with lower priority. Filters with the same priority are executed at the global level, as specified in the master World Wide Web properties, and then at the site level, as specified in the Web site properties. Filters with the same priority at the same level within

IIS are executed according to the order in which they were loaded into memory. If you discover a conflict, you can change the filter load order as necessary.

ISAPI extensions are similarly defined as DLLs or executables. Unlike filters, which are loaded with the World Wide Web Publishing Service, extensions are loaded on demand and are executed in response to client requests. Normally, ISAPI extensions are used to process the data received in requests for specific types of files. For example, when a client makes a request for a file using the .asp extension, IIS uses the ASP.DLL ISAPI extension to process the contents of the Active Server Pages and return the results to the client for display.

When you install IIS, many default ISAPI extensions are configured for use on the Web server. ISAPI extensions are configured to respond to specific types of Hypertext Transfer Protocol (HTTP) requests or all HTTP requests for files with a specific file extension. The key types of HTTP requests are summarized in Table 4-1.

Table 4-1. HTTP Request Types That Are Used with ISAPI Extensions

Request Type	Description
DELETE	A request to delete a resource. This request normally is not allowed unless the user has specific privileges on the Web site.
GET	A request to retrieve a resource. The standard request for retrieving files.
HEAD	A request for an HTTP header. The return request does not contain a message body.
OPTIONS	A request for information about communications options.
POST	A request to submit data as a new subordinate of a resource. Typically used for posting data from fill-out forms.
PUT	A request to store the enclosed data with the resource identifier specified. Typically used when uploading files through HTTP.
TRACE	A request to trace the client's submission (for testing or debugging).

Because ISAPI extensions are loaded on demand, you can add extensions at any time without having to restart IIS. However, if you modify an ISAPI extension that is already loaded into memory, you must stop and then restart the World Wide Web Publishing Service to apply the new configuration settings. As with ISAPI filters, ISAPI extensions have global and local context. If you set an ISAPI extension in the master World Wide Web properties, the extension is available to all Web sites on the server. On the other hand, if you set an ISAPI extension in a site's properties, the extension is only available on that site.

ISAPI extensions do not have priorities and you should not configure multiple ISAPI extensions to handle the same type of content. Additionally, ISAPI extensions always run in a single server process. This process can be the same server process as the one used by IIS, a pooled process shared by multiple applications, or an isolated process.

Understanding ASP Applications

ASP is a server-side scripting environment used to create dynamic Web applications. An ASP application is a collection of resource files and components that are grouped logically. Logically grouping files and components as an application allows IIS to share data within the application and to run the application as a shared, pooled, or isolated process. You can have multiple applications per Web site, and each application can be configured differently.

IIS resource files include ASP pages, HTML pages, GIF images, JPEG images, and other types of Web documents. An ASP page is a file that ends with the .asp extension that includes HTML, a combination of HTML and scripting, or only scripting. Scripts within ASP pages can be intended for processing by a client browser or the server itself. Scripts designed to be processed on the server are called server-side scripts and can be written using Visual Basic, Scripting Edition (VBScript), Jscript, or any other scripting language available on the server.

ASP provides an object-based scripting environment. Server-side scripts use the built-in objects to perform common tasks, such as tracking session state, managing errors, and reading HTTP requests sent by clients. A complete list of built-in objects is provided as Table 4-2.

Table 4-2. Built-In ASP Objects

Built-In Object	Description
Application	Used to share information among all users of an ASP application.
ASPError	Tracks information about error conditions that have occurred in scripts on ASP pages.
ObjectContext	Maintains information on application component instances and provides access to the built-in ASP objects. Also provides methods and events used to commit or abort transactions.
Request	Obtains the values sent in the HTTP request by the client browser.
Response	Sends the HTTP response to the client browser.
ScriptingContext	Provides access to built-in objects. Supported for backward compatibility only. Use ObjectContext instead.
Server	Used to perform server-related tasks, such as executing files and transferring state information to another ASP page, and to instantiate server components.
Session	Stores information about a specific user session (provided the user's browser supports cookies and cookies are enabled).

ASP scripts can also use IIS components. IIS components are executable programs that use the Component Object Model (COM) and Component Services to communicate with IIS. A standard IIS installation includes several pre-built components that can be used within ASP applications. These components are summarized in Table 4-3. You'll find these components in the %SystemRoot%\Inetsrv directory on the IIS server. If you remove these components from this directory, they will no longer be available to your ASP applications.

Table 4-3. Pre-Built Components for ASP Applications

Pre-Built Component	Description
Ad Rotator (ADROT.DLL)	Rotates banner ads displayed on a Web page according to a specified schedule.
Browser Capabilities (BROWSERCAP.DLL)	Determines the capabilities, type, and version of each browser that accesses your Web site.
Content Linking (NEXTLINK.DLL)	Creates tables of contents for Web pages, and provides navigational links to previous and subsequent pages.
Content Rotator (CONTROT.DLL)	Rotates Hypertext Markup Language (HTML) content on a Web page according to a specified schedule.
Counters (COUNTERS.DLL)	Creates a counter that tracks page hits for an entire Web site and access to individual pages.
Database Access (MSADO20.DLL) *(continued)*	Uses ActiveX Data Objects to access information in databases and structured data files.
File Access Component (FSCFG.DLL)	Accesses the FileSystemObject in the scripting run-time library (SCRRUN.DLL) through which the file system can be managed.
Logging Utility (LOGSCRPT.DLL)	Allows applications to read the HTTP activity log files generated by IIS.
MyInfo (MYINFO.DLL)	Tracks personal information pertaining to the site or its creator.
Page Counter (PAGECNT.DLL)	Counts and displays the number of times a Web page has been accessed.
Permission Checker (PERMCHK.DLL)	Uses IIS authentication protocols to determine whether a Web user has been granted permissions to read a file.
Status (STATUS.DLL)	Returns server status information when running Personal Web Server for Macintosh.
Tools (TOOLS.DLL)	Provides utility functions that check file existence, match site ownership, look for plug-ins (Macintosh only), process HTML form data, and generate random integers.

Defining Custom Applications

You use the Internet Information Services snap-in to configure custom applications and the Component Services snap-in to manage COM components. As part of the standard installation, Web sites have a predefined application that allows you to run custom programs without making changes to the environment. You could, for example, copy your ASP files to a site's base directory and run them without creating a separate application. Here, the ASP application you've defined runs within the context of the predefined application.

Real World The default application is often accidentally or purposefully removed by novice administrators who don't understand its purpose. If this happens, application behavior may change. For example, you suddenly might be unable to share session states between ASP pages. The reason for this is that ASP pages and other types of files that were using the default application no longer have an application context, and all associated application settings are no longer available.

To be clear, the default application allows you to run IIS applications regardless of where they may be located within the site's directory structure, as long as the directories those files are located in have the appropriate execute permissions (either Scripts Only or Scripts And Executables). If you want to delete the default application, you should create specific application contexts for each application that you want to run.

To get better control over applications, you should configure separate contexts for key applications. Application contexts are defined using basic and advanced application settings. Basic application settings include the following:

- **Application Name**   A descriptive name for the application.
- **Starting Point**   Sets the base directory for the application. All files in all subdirectories of the base directory are considered to be part of the application.
- **Execute Permissions**   Sets the level of program execution that is allowed.
- **Application Protection**   Determines how the application runs and which application resources are shared with IIS and other applications.

Advanced application settings include

- **Application Mappings**   Sets application caching and maps file extensions to DLLs for execution
- **Application Options**   Sets configuration options that control how the application runs, including time-outs, buffering, and the default scripting language
- **Application Debugging**   Enables or disables debugging and script error messages

Application settings create application contexts that your application runs within. Without an application context, your customized pages run as separate files and are unable to take advantage of key IIS features including buffering, session state, and caching. Application contexts are defined at the directory level. All files in all subdirectories of the application's based directory are considered to be part of the application. Because of this, the best way to create applications is to follow these steps:

1. In Windows Explorer, create a folder that will act as the starting point of the application, and then set appropriate access Windows permissions on the folder.

2. If necessary, use the Internet Information Services snap-in to create a virtual directory that maps to the directory.

3. Configure application settings for the directory as defined in the "Creating Pooled and Nonpooled Applications" section of this chapter.

Using and Running Applications

Each application has a starting point. The starting point sets the logical namespace for the application. That is, the starting point determines the files and folders that are included in the application. Every file and folder in the starting point is considered part of the application.

Application starting points can be defined for the following:

- An entire site
- A directory
- A virtual directory

When you define a site-wide application, all files in all subdirectories of the Web site are considered to be a part of the application. When you define an application for a standard or virtual directory, all files in all subdirectories in this directory are considered part of the application.

As stated earlier, the application starting point sets the namespace for an application. A namespace is a way of associating an area of memory with an easily recognized name that associates a group of files and components. The memory area used by an application determines its protection setting. There are three application protection settings:

- **Low**   Low protection allows applications to run in process and share resources with IIS. Low protection provides the best performance but makes it possible for a stray application to crash IIS.

- **Medium**   Medium protection allows applications to run as a pooled process, meaning all applications with this priority share the same IIS process instance but do not run in process with normal IIS resources. If a single application fails, it will affect all other applications running at medium protection—but will not affect IIS itself.

- **High**   High protection allows applications to run completely out of process, meaning the application doesn't share processes with other applications and the failure of other applications does not affect this high-priority application.

If you use medium or high protection settings, you allow IIS to isolate the application to a specific process. Process isolation protects the server's World Wide Web Publishing Service from application problems that could otherwise cause the Web server to crash or freeze. Process isolation also allows you to configure scheduled application restarts and automatic termination of application processes in case of a fatal error.

Application protection settings affect memory access. Applications that share the same process as IIS share the same memory area and are able to call each other with little overhead. Applications that share a pooled process or are isolated must use a process called *marshalling* to make requests across process boundaries. Marshalling is required whenever an application needs to interact with IIS or other applications. Because marshaled calls are slower than calls within a single process, pooled and isolated applications do not perform as well as applications sharing the IIS process.

Out-of-process applications and components, including ISAPI extensions, are not able to access metabase properties by default. This restriction is designed to prevent unauthorized changes to the metabase. If you want to allow out-of-process applications to access the metabase, you should change the identity for out-of-process applications to a specific user account and give that account access to the metabase.

 Tip You use the Component Services snap-in to manage authentication for application components. In the Component Services snap-in, expand Component Services, then Computers, then My Computer, and then COM+ Applications. Right-click IIS Out-Of-Process Pooled Applications, select Properties, and then click the Identity tab. The user context you assign the application to must have file permissions to access the metabase. To check file permissions, right-click the metabase file (Inetsrv\METABASE.BIN) in Windows Explorer, and then click the Security tab.

Application mappings are used to specify the ISAPI extensions and Common Gateway Interface (CGI) programs that are available to applications. Application mappings for Web sites are inherited from the WWW Service master properties at the time the site is created. Application mappings for individual directories are inherited from the site properties at the time the directory is created and made available to IIS. Each application mapping has three components:

- **Extension** The file extension that is associated with the ISAPI extension or CGI program. File extensions don't have to have file type associations at the operating system level and can be more than three characters.

- **Executable Path** The file path to the ISAPI extension or CGI program. IIS uses the executable path to determine which ISAPI extension or CGI program should be loaded. The associated DLL or executable must be in a directory that is accessible to IIS. Typically, this means placing the DLL or executable in the %SystemRoot% or %SystemRoot%\Inetsrv directory.

- **Verbs** The HTTP request types that are used with the ISAPI extension or CGI program. For a detailed list of HTTP request types, refer to Table 4-1.

ISAPI extensions and CGI programs with mappings are loaded dynamically into memory when IIS receives a request for a file with the designated extension, and they are unloaded when IIS is finished processing the request. You can change this behavior by enabling application caching. With caching enabled, IIS doesn't unload the associated DLL or executable and instead maintains it in memory.

Application protection and caching settings change the way memory is used on your IIS server. The operating system incurs additional overhead every time a new application is started and every time new programs are loaded into memory. The amount of overhead depends on the application configuration settings. To obtain a basic understanding of the overhead for applications, consider the following scenario.

An IIS server is configured with three Web sites: a corporate Web site, a service Web site, and an administration Web site. The server is also running an SMTP server. In the baseline configuration, the server runs the following IIS processes:

- **INETINFO.EXE** This process is used to manage the service hosts and ISAPI applications that run within the IIS process context.

- **SVCHOST.EXE** These three processes control Web resources, Simple Mail Transfer Protocol (SMTP) resources, and the baseline installation.

- **DLLHOST.EXE** This process is used to manage IIS processes (and any in-process applications that may be defined). No pooled or out-of-process applications are defined initially.

As Table 4-4 shows, these baseline processes use 27,848 KB memory on the server. To determine how application processing affects the server, I defined additional applications:

- **Pooled Application 1** An application running with medium application protection

- **Pooled Application 2** An application running with medium application protection

- **Isolated Application 1** An application running with high application protection

- **Isolated Application 2** An application running with high application protection

Table 4-4. IIS Application Overhead Baselines for Sample Server

Process	Base-line IIS	Use Pooled Application 1	Use Pooled Application 2	Use Isolated Application 1	Use Isolated Application 2
INETINFO.EXE	7568	8360	8388	8440	8472
DLLHOST.EXE	4968	4968	4968	4960	4960
DLLHOST.EXE	-	5436	5492	5080	5080
DLLHOST.EXE	-	-	-	5460	5460
DLLHOST.EXE	-	-	-	-	5248
SVCHOST.EXE	3060	3080	3080	3084	3100
SVCHOST.EXE	9908	9920	9920	9920	9920
SVCHOST.EXE	2344	2344	2344	2344	2344
Memory Usage (KB)	27,848	34,109	34,194	39,289	44,586

While the process of defining applications doesn't really affect the baseline configuration, running the applications does affect memory usage. When I use Pooled Application 1, a new DLLHOST.EXE process is started and the base memory usage changes to 34,109 KB. Because the additional DLLHOST.EXE process is used to manage all pooled applications, starting the second pooled application (Pooled Application 2) doesn't spawn any new processes, and the additional memory usage is minimal. On the other hand, each time I start a new isolated application, a new DLLHOST.EXE process is started, and an incremental amount of memory is used. Running Isolated Application 1 causes a third DLLHOST.EXE process to start, and the baseline memory usage goes to 39,289 KB. Running Isolated Application 2 causes a fourth DLLHOST.EXE process to start, and the baseline memory usage goes to 44,586 KB.

As you can see from the example, each new DLLHOST.EXE host process used about 5000 KB of additional memory, and, in the end, IIS used about 45,000 KB of memory on the server. Although this isn't a lot of memory, a server with more complex applications could use considerably more memory, especially as additional ISAPI extensions and CGI programs are loaded into memory. Servers also cache Web documents, and a portion of memory is always reserved for this file cache.

Managing Custom IIS Applications

Custom IIS applications are configured and managed through the Web Site Properties dialog box. As part of the standard installation, all Web sites created in IIS have a default application that is set as a site-wide application, meaning its starting point is the base directory for the Web site. The default application allows you to run custom applications that use the preconfigured application settings. You do not need to make any changes to the environment. You can, however, achieve better control by defining applications with smaller scope, and the sections that follow tell you how to do this.

Creating Pooled and Nonpooled Applications

IIS applications are collections of resource files and components that are grouped together to take advantage of key IIS features such as file buffering, session state, and component caching. You can create a pooled or nonpooled application by completing the following steps:

1. In the Internet Information Services snap-in, right-click the directory that you want to use as the starting point for the application, and then select Properties. Click the Home Directory, Directory, or Virtual Directory tab as appropriate. This displays the dialog box shown in Figure 4-2.

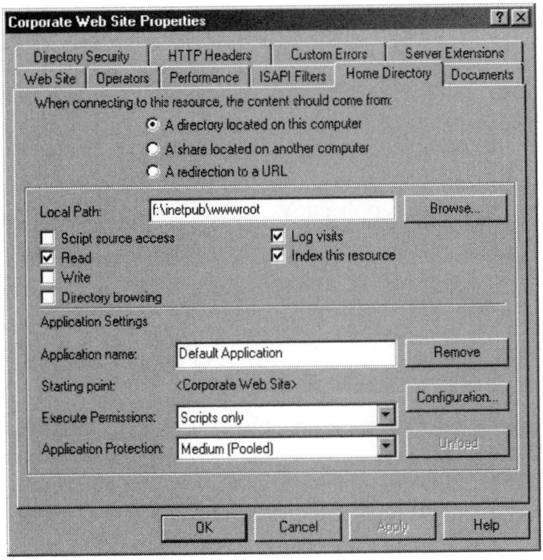

Figure 4-2. *Use the Properties dialog box to configure custom applications.*

2. Fields on the Application Settings panel are used to configure the application. If the Application Name and Application Protection fields appear dimmed, it means the directory is already within the context of another application. This is all right; you can still create your application. However, keep in mind that by doing so, you remove the directory and all its subdirectories from the current application context.

3. Click Create to start the application definition process. If an application was created by default, you may need to click Remove first.

4. The Application Name field sets a descriptive name for the application. By default, this field is set to the directory name. You can change this value by typing a new name.

5. Use the Execute Permissions selection list to set the level of program execution that is allowed for an application. Three execute permissions levels are defined:

- **None** Only static files, such as HTML or GIF files, can be accessed.
- **Scripts Only** Only scripts, such as ASP scripts, can be run.
- **Scripts And Executables** All file types can be accessed and executed.

6. Use the Application Protection selection list to specify the memory area used by the application as one of the following:

* **Low (IIS Process)** Low protection allows applications to run in process and share resources with IIS. All applications with this priority share the IIS process instance.

* **Medium (Pooled)** Medium protection allows applications to run as a pooled process. All applications with this priority share the same IIS process instance but do not run in process with normal IIS resources.

* **High (Isolated)** High protection allows applications to run completely out of process. Isolated applications don't share processes with other applications, and the failure of other applications does not affect this high-priority application.

7. Create the application by clicking Apply. You then have the option to click Configuration to configure advanced settings. Advanced settings are discussed in the sections that follow.

Configuring Application Mappings and Caching

Application mappings and caching settings control what components are available to IIS applications and how those components are managed in memory. You control application mappings and caching through the Application Mappings property sheet shown in Figure 4-3. To access this property sheet, follow these steps:

1. In the Internet Information Services snap-in, right-click the directory that is used as the starting point for the application, and then select Properties.

2. Click the Home Directory, Directory, or Virtual Directory tab as appropriate, and then click Configuration.

3. Enable application caching by selecting Cache ISAPI Applications. Clear this check box to disable caching.

Note In most instances, you'll want IIS to use application caching. The exception is when you are doing debugging or troubleshooting and want to force IIS to reload components each time they are used.

4. The Application Mappings area shows the current mappings for ISAPI extensions and CGI programs. As shown in Figure 4-3, each application mapping has an associated file extension, executable path, and verb list.

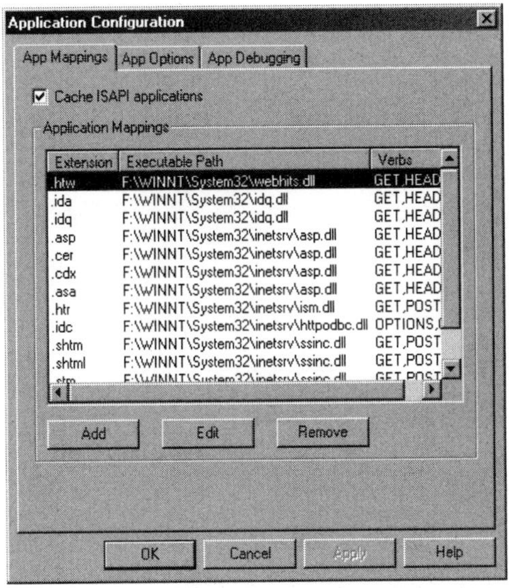

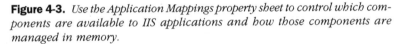

Figure 4-3. *Use the Application Mappings property sheet to control which components are available to IIS applications and how those components are managed in memory.*

Once the App Mappings property sheet is displayed, you can manage existing component mappings or create new component mappings. Techniques are examined in the sections that follow.

Adding Application Mappings

To add application mappings, follow these steps:

1. Access the App Mappings property sheet for the application and then click Add. This displays the Add/Edit Application Extension Mapping dialog box, as shown in Figure 4-4.

2. In the Executable text box, type the file path to the ISAPI extension or CGI program that you want to use. The file path should end in .EXE or .DLL, such as C:\Windows\System32\Inetsrv\ASP.DLL. If you don't know the file path, click Browse to display the Open dialog box, which you can use to find the executable.

Note   The DLL or executable must be located on a local hard disk. In most cases, DLL or executables should be placed in the %SystemRoot% or %SystemRoot%\Inetsrv directory.

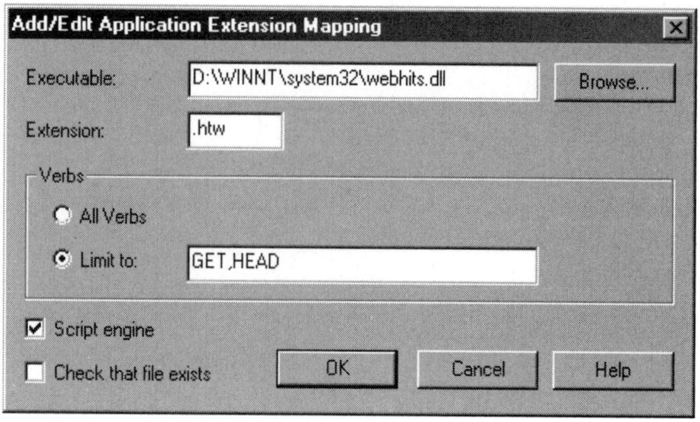

Figure 4-4. *Add new application mappings using the Add/Edit Application Extension Mapping dialog box.*

3. In the Extension field, type the file name extension that should be associated with the ISAPI extension or CGI program. Be sure to include the period (.) with the extension designator, such as .HTML.

Tip If you want the ISAPI extension or CGI program to handle requests for all file types, place an asterisk (*) in the Extension field. From then on, requests for files within the application scope are sent to the component you've specified regardless of the file extension. Keep in mind that file requests also must match the parameters set for the verb list.

4. Use the options on the Verbs panel to set the verb list for the application mapping. Select All Verbs to pass all requests with the defined extension to the application, or click Limit To and then enter request types in a comma-separated list.

Note The verb list controls the types of requests that are passed to an application. For example, you could configure one mapping to handle GET, HEAD, and POST requests for .HTM files and another mapping to handle PUT, TRACE, and DELETE requests for .HTM files.

5. Applications can run in directories with Scripts Only or Scripts And Executable permissions. If you want the ISAPI extension or CGI program to run in directories designated as Scripts Only, select the Script Engine check box. Otherwise, clear this check box and the component will only run in directories designated with Scripts And Executable permissions.

6. Select Check That File Exists to have IIS verify the existence of a requested file and to ensure that the user making the request has appropriate access permissions before running the associated ISAPI extension or CGI program. If the file does not exist or the user doesn't have access permissions, a warning message is returned to the browser and the component is not executed.

Note Check That File Exists is useful when you use scripts mapped to executables that do not send a CGI response if a script is inaccessible. One such example is Perl, which doesn't return a CGI response in this instance. Using this option can cause a performance hit on a busy server. The reason for this is that the file is opened twice—once by IIS and once by the associated component.

7. Click OK three times to return to the Internet Information Services snap-in.

Editing Application Mappings

You can edit existing application mappings by completing the following steps:

1. Access the App Mappings property sheet for the application and then click Edit. This displays the Add/Edit Application Extension Mapping dialog box shown in Figure 4-4.

2. Make the necessary adjustments to the mapping and then click OK twice.

3. The new settings are used the next time the associated DLL or executable is loaded into memory. If ISAPI caching is enabled, you must stop and then restart the Web site to enforce the changes.

Removing Application Mappings

To remove application mappings, follow these steps:

1. Access the App Mappings property sheet for the application and then click Remove.

2. When prompted to confirm the action, click Yes.

3. Click OK. The new settings are used the next time the associated DLL or executable is loaded into memory. If ISAPI caching is enabled, you must stop and then restart the Web site to enforce the changes.

Managing Session State

Session state plays a significant role in IIS performance and resource usage. When session state is enabled, IIS creates a session for each user who accesses an ASP application. Session information is used to track the user within the application and to pass user information from one page to another. For example, your company may want to track individual user preferences within an application, and you can use sessions to do this.

The way sessions work is fairly straightforward. The first time a user requests an ASP page with a specified application, IIS generates one of the following:

- A Session object containing all values set for the user session, including an identifier for the code page used to display the dynamic content, a location identifier, a session ID, and a time-out value.

- A Session.Contents collection, which contains all of the items that have been set in the session by the application (except objects created in the application's GLOBAL.ASA file).

- A Session.StaticObjects collection, which contains the static objects defined in the application's GLOBAL.ASA file.

The Session object and its associated properties are stored in memory on the server. The user's session ID is passed to the user's browser as a cookie. As long as the browser accepts cookies, the session ID is passed back to the server on subsequent requests. This is true even if the user requests a page in a different application. The same ID is used in order to reduce the number of cookies sent to the browser. Keep in mind that if the browser doesn't accept cookies, the session ID cannot be maintained and IIS cannot track the user session using this technique.

Sessions are enabled by default for all IIS applications. By default, sessions time out in 20 minutes. This means that if a user does not request or refresh a page within 20 minutes, the session ends, and IIS removes the related Session object from memory. You can change the default time-out value using the Session Timeout property on the Application Options property sheet.

As you might imagine, tracking sessions can use valuable system resources. You can reduce resource usage by reducing the time-out interval or disabling session tracking altogether. Reducing the time-out interval allows sessions to expire quicker than usual. Disabling session tracking tells IIS that sessions shouldn't be automatically created. Sessions can still be started manually within the application. Simply place the <%@ENABLESESSIONSTATE = True%> directive in individual ASP pages.

Each application configured on your server has its own session state settings. You manage the session state for an application by completing the following steps:

1. In the Internet Information Services snap-in, right-click the directory that is used as the starting point for the application, and then select Properties.

2. Click the Home Directory, Directory, or Virtual Directory tab as appropriate, and then click Configuration.

3. On the App Options tab, enable automatic session creation by selecting Enable Session State. Clear this check box to disable automatic session creation.

4. If sessions are enabled, type a session time-out value in the Session Timeout field. For a high-usage application in which you expect users to quickly move from page to page, you may want to set a fairly low time-out value, such as 15 minutes. On the other hand, if it is critical that the user's session is maintained to complete a transaction, you may want to set a long time-out value, such as 60 minutes.

5. Click OK twice.

Real World These days, most large-scale, commercial Web sites are
managed using multiple servers. In this situation, you typically have a
load balancer that distributes requests for the site URL to whichever
server is available. To use ASP session management on a load-balanced
site, you must ensure that all requests from a particular user are directed to the same Web server. The technique you use depends on your
load balancer.

Controlling Application Buffering

Buffering is another option that affects server performance and resource usage.
When buffering is enabled, IIS completely processes pages before sending content to the client browser. When buffering is disabled, IIS returns output to the
client browser as the page is processed. The advantage to buffering is that it allows
you to dynamically respond to events that occur while processing the page. You
can take one of the following actions:

* Abort sending a page or transfer the user to a different page
* Clear the buffer and send different content to the user
* Change HTTP header information from anywhere in your ASP script

A disadvantage of buffering is that users have to wait for the entire script to be
processed before content is delivered to their browser. If a script is long or complex, the user may have to wait for a long time before seeing the page. To counter
potential delays associated with buffering, developers often insert Flush commands at key positions within the script. If your development team does this, they
should be aware that this causes additional connection requests between the client
and server, which may also cause performance problems.

As with session tracking, buffering is enabled by default for all applications. You
manage buffering by completing the following steps:

1. In the Internet Information Services snap-in, right-click the directory that is
   used as the starting point for the application, and then select Properties.
2. Click the Home Directory, Directory, or Virtual Directory tab as appropriate,
   and then click Configuration.
3. On the App Options tab, enable buffering by selecting Enable Buffering. Clear
   this check box to disable buffering.

Tip If you disable buffering for an application, you can still turn on buffering for individual ASP pages. To do this, use the Response.Buffer =
True statement.

4. Click OK twice.

Setting Parent Paths, Default ASP Language, and ASP Script Time-Out

Additional options that you can set for applications pertain to parent paths, default ASP language, and ASP script time-out. Enable Parent Paths allows ASP pages to use relative paths to access the parent directory of the current directory. For example, a script could reference ../BUILD.HTM, where ".." is a reference to the parent directory of the current directory. Parent paths are enabled by default.

Default ASP Language sets the default scripting language for ASP pages. Two scripting engines are installed with a standard IIS installation. These scripting engines are for Microsoft Visual Basic Scripting Edition (VBScript) and Microsoft JScript. You can reference these scripting engines using the values VBScript and Jscript, respectively. The default scripting language is VBScript in a standard IIS installation, but you can change the default value at any time. Scripts can override the default language using the <%@LANGUAGE%> directive.

ASP Script Timeout sets the length of time IIS will allow a script to run within completing. If a script doesn't complete within the time-out interval, IIS stops the script and writes an error to the application event log. The default time-out value is 90 seconds, but you can set a new default value at any time. In an ASP page, you can override the default value using the Server.ScriptTimeout method.

To set these application options, follow these steps:

1. In the Internet Information Services snap-in, right-click the directory that is used as the starting point for the application, and then select Properties.

2. Click the Home Directory, Directory, or Virtual Directory tab as appropriate, and then click Configuration. Select the App Options tab.

3. Select Enable Parent Paths to allow scripts to use relative paths to reference the parent directory. Clear this check box to disable parent paths.

4. The default scripting language is VBScript. To change the default scripting language, type the scripting language name in the Default ASP Language field.

5. The default ASP script time-out is 90 seconds. To change the default time-out value, type a new time-out interval in the ASP Script Timeout field.

6. Click OK twice.

Enabling and Disabling Application Debugging

One of the best ways to troubleshoot an IIS application is to enable debugging. Debugging is handled through server-side and client-side configuration options. Server-side debugging allows IIS to throw errors while processing ASP pages and to display a prompt that allows you to start the Microsoft Script Debugger. You can then use the debugger to examine your ASP pages. Client-side debugging involves sending debugging information to the client browser. You can then use this information to help determine what is wrong with IIS and the related ASP page.

You can enable server-side and client-side debugging by completing the following steps:

1. In the Internet Information Services snap-in, right-click the directory that is used as the starting point for the application, and then select Properties.
2. Click the Home Directory, Directory, or Virtual Directory tab as appropriate, and then click Configuration. Select the App Debugging tab.
3. To turn on server-side debugging, select Enable ASP Server-Side Script Debugging. To turn off server-side debugging, clear this option.

Caution Server-side debugging of ASP applications is designed for development and staging servers and not necessarily production servers. If you enable server-side debugging on a production server, you may notice a severe decrease in performance for the affected application. The reason for this is that server-side debugging causes ASP to run in single-threaded mode.

4. To turn on client-side debugging, select Enable ASP Client-Side Script Debugging. To turn off client-side debugging, clear this option.

Configuring Application Error Messages

By default, applications are configured to send to clients detailed error messages that specify the filename, error message, and line number in which an error occurred. This information is great for troubleshooting problems in the code but not necessarily good for users to see when they encounter a problem. For this reason, you may want to create a text message to send instead. The text message can provide readers with an easy-to-understand text message that directs them to a location where they can get help.

You can configure application error messages by completing the following steps:

1. In the Internet Information Services snap-in, right-click the directory that is used as the starting point for the application, and then select Properties.
2. Click the Home Directory, Directory, or Virtual Directory tab as appropriate, and then click Configuration. Select the App Debugging tab.
3. To use detailed error messages, select Send Detailed ASP Error Messages To Client. Otherwise, select Send Text Error Message To Client and type a text message that is to be displayed if an error occurs.

Unloading Isolated Applications

Isolated applications are stored in a separate memory space and use a separate DLLHOST.EXE process. If you want to force IIS to remove the application from memory, you can do this by unloading the application. Now the next time a user accesses the application, IIS will reload the application into memory and start a new DLLHOST.EXE process.

You can unload an isolated application by completing the following steps:

1. In the Internet Information Services snap-in, right-click the directory that is used as the starting point for the application, and then select Properties.

2. Click the Home Directory, Directory, or Virtual Directory tab as appropriate.

3. Click Unload and then click OK.

Deleting IIS Applications

If you find that you no longer need an application, you should remove it to free up the resources it is using. To delete an application, follow these steps:

1. In the Internet Information Services snap-in, right-click the directory that is used as the starting point for the application, and then select Properties.

2. Click the Home Directory, Directory, or Virtual Directory tab as appropriate.

3. Delete the application by clicking Remove and then clicking OK.

Managing Custom ISAPI Filters

ISAPI filters are IIS applications that are used to filter requests for specific types of events, such as Read or Write. When a filter encounters an event for which it has been configured, it responds to the event by performing a set of tasks. ISAPI filters can be applied globally or locally. Global filters affect all Web sites. Local filters only affect the currently selected Web site.

Viewing and Configuring Global Filters

Global filters affect all IIS Web sites and are loaded into memory when the World Wide Web Publishing Service is started. Anytime you add new global filters or modify existing global filters, you must stop and then restart the World Wide Web Publishing Service.

To display and configure global filters, follow these steps:

1. In the Internet Information Services snap-in, right-click the computer node for the IIS server you want to work with, and then select Properties.

2. Click Edit on the Master Properties panel and then select the ISAPI Filters tab.

3. You should now see a list of the currently defined global filters. Global filters are active for all Web sites on the server and are executed according to priority in the order listed.

4. The summary list for filters shows the following information:

   • **Status** The load status of the filters. Filters that have been successfully loaded show a green up arrow. Filters that are not loaded show a red down arrow.

   • **Filter Name** The descriptive name for the filter. This name is set when you install the filter.

- **Priority** The priority of the filter as set in the source code. Filters with higher priority are executed before filters with lower priority.

Note You can obtain a detailed status for a filter by clicking it. The only additional information provided is the file path to the filter executable.

5. Use the following options to configure global filters:

- **Add** Adds a filter. To add a new global filter, click Add. Type a filter name and then type the file path to the executable for the filter. If you don't know the file path, click Browse, and then use the Open dialog box to find the filter.

- **Remove** Removes a global filter. To remove a filter, select it, and then click Remove.

- **Edit** Edits a global filter. The only filter property that you can edit is the executable file path. To edit a filter, select it, and then click Edit. Use the Properties dialog box provided to change the executable file path, and then click OK.

6. When several filters are configured to respond to the same events, they are executed sequentially. Filters with higher priority are executed before filters with lower priority. Filters with the same priority are executed at the global level and then at the site level. To change the execution order of a filter within a priority, use the green up and down arrows.

7. If you have added or changed a global filter, you should stop and then restart the World Wide Web Publishing Service. Doing this causes IIS to load the new filters into memory.

Viewing and Configuring Local Filters

Local filters affect a single IIS Web site and can be dynamically loaded into memory when they are added or modified, as long as the World Wide Web Publishing Service and the Web site are running. Because of this, you do not need to stop and then restart the World Wide Web Publishing Service when you make changes to local filters.

To display and configure local filters, follow these steps:

1. In the Internet Information Services snap-in, right-click the Web site you want to manage, and then choose Properties.

2. Select the ISAPI Filters tab. You should now see a list of the currently defined local filters. Local filters are active for the currently selected Web site only.

Note You will not see any global filters inherited from the Web server's master properties. You will see only the filters installed for the currently selected Web site, even though both sets of filters are run. While several global filters are configured by default, no local filters will exist unless an administrator has added them.

3. The summary list for filters shows the following information:

- **Status** The load status of the filters. Filters that have been successfully loaded show a green up arrow. Filters that are not loaded show a red down arrow.

- **Filter Name** The descriptive name for the filter. This name is set when you install the filter.

- **Priority** The priority of the filter as set in the source code. Filters with higher priority are executed before filters with lower priority.

 Note You can obtain a detailed status for a filter by clicking it. The only additional information provided is the file path to the filter executable.

4. Use the following options to configure local filters:

- **Add** Adds a filter. To add a new local filter, click Add. Type a filter name and then type the file path to the executable for the filter. If you don't know the file path, click Browse, and then use the Open dialog box to find the filter.

- **Remove** Removes a local filter. To remove a filter, select it, and then click Remove.

- **Edit** Edits a local filter. The only filter property that you can edit is the executable file path. To edit a filter, select it, and then click Edit. Use the Properties dialog box provided to change the executable file path, and then click OK.

5. When several filters are configured to respond to the same events, they are executed sequentially. Filters with higher priority are executed before filters with lower priority. Filters with the same priority are executed at the global level and then at the site level. To change the execution order of a filter within a priority, use the green up and down arrows.

Customizing Web Site Content and HTTP Headers

IIS sets default values for documents and HTTP headers. These default values can be modified at the site, directory, and file level.

Configuring Default Documents

Default document settings determine how IIS handles requests that do not specify a document name. If a user makes a request using a directory path that ends in a directory name or forward slash (/) rather than a filename, IIS uses the default document settings to determine how to handle the request. When default document handling is enabled, IIS searches for default documents in the order in which their names appear in the default document list and returns the first document it finds. If a match is not found, IIS checks to see if directory browsing is enabled and, if so, returns a directory listing. Otherwise, IIS returns a "404 — File Not Found" error.

Default document settings can be configured at the site or directory level. This means individual directories can have different default document settings than the site as a whole. Standard default document names include DEFAULT.HTM, DEFAULT.ASP, INDEX.HTM, and INDEX.HTML.

You can view current default document settings or make changes using the following steps:

1. In the Internet Information Services snap-in, right-click the Web site, virtual directory, or directory you want to work with, and then choose Properties.

2. Select the Documents tab. The Enable Default Document check box determines whether default documents are used. To turn on default document handling, select this check box. To turn off default document handling, clear this check box.

3. To add a new default document, click Add. Next, type the name of the default document, such as INDEX.HTML, and then click OK.

4. To remove a default document, select it in the list provided, and then click Remove.

5. To change the search order, select a document, and then click the up or down arrow buttons.

6. Click OK.

Configuring Document Footers

You can configure IIS to automatically insert an HTML-formatted footer document on the bottom of every document it sends. The footer can contain copyright information, logos, or other important information. As with default documents, document footers can be configured at the site or directory level. This means individual directories can have different footer settings than the site as a whole.

Enabling Automatic Footers

To configure automatic footers, follow these steps:

1. Create an HTML-formatted document and save it to a folder on a Web server's local hard drive. The footer document should not be a complete HTML page. Instead, it should only include the HTML tags necessary for content that is to be displayed in the footer.

2. In the Internet Information Services snap-in, right-click the Web site, virtual directory, or directory you want to work with, and then choose Properties.

3. Choose the Documents tab and then select Enable Document Footer.

4. In the text box provided, type the file path to the footer file or click Browse to display the Open dialog box, which you can use to find the file.

5. Click OK.

Disabling Automatic Footers

To disable automatic footers, follow these steps:

1. In the Internet Information Services snap-in, right-click the Web site, virtual directory, or directory you want to work with, and then choose Properties.

2. Choose the Documents tab and then clear the Enable Document Footer check box.

3. Click OK.

Using Content Expiration and Preventing Browser Caching

Most browsers store documents that users have viewed in cache so that the documents can be displayed later without having to retrieve the entire page from a Web server. You can control browser caching using content expiration. When content expiration is enabled, IIS includes document expiration information when sending HTTP results to a user. This enables the browser to determine if future requests for the same document need to be retrieved from the server, or whether a locally cached copy is still valid.

You can configure content expiration at the site, directory, or file level. Site level settings affect all pages in the site. Directory level settings affect all files in all subdirectories of the directory. File level settings affect the currently selected file only. Three content expiration settings are available:

- **Expire Immediately**   Forces cached pages to expire immediately, preventing the browser from displaying the file from cache. Use this setting when you need to make sure that the browser displays the most recent version of a dynamically generated page.

- **Expire After**   Sets a specific number of minutes, hours, or days during which the file can be displayed from cache. Use this setting when you want to ensure the browser will retrieve a file after a certain period.

- **Expire On Date At Time**   Sets a specific expiration date and time. The file can be displayed from cache until the expiration date. Use this setting for time-sensitive material that is no longer valid after a specific date, such as a special offer or event announcement.

 Tip   In ASP pages you can control content expiration by putting a Response.Expires entry in the HTTP header. Use the value Response.Expires = 0 to force immediate expiration. Keep in mind that HTTP headers must be sent to the browser before any page content is sent.

Enabling Content Expiration

Content expiration is set on site, directory, and file levels. Keep in mind individual file and directory settings override site settings. So if you don't get the behavior you expect, check for file or directory settings that may be causing a conflict.

You can configure content expiration for a site, directory, or file by completing the following steps:

1. In the Internet Information Services snap-in, right-click the site, directory, or file you want to work with, and then choose Properties.
2. Choose the HTTP Headers tab, and then select Enable Content Expiration.
3. To force cached pages to expire immediately, select Expire Immediately.
4. To set a specific number of minutes, hours, or days before expiration, select Expire After, and then configure the expiration information using the fields provided.
5. To set specific expiration date and time, select Expire On, and then configure the expiration information using the fields provided.
6. Click OK.

Disabling Content Expiration

Content expiration is set on site, directory, and file levels. Keep in mind that individual file and directory settings override site settings. So if you don't get the behavior you expect, check for file or directory settings that may be causing a conflict.

You can disable content expiration for a site, directory, or file by completing the following steps:

1. In the Internet Information Services snap-in, right-click the site, directory, or file you want to work with, and then choose Properties.
2. Choose the HTTP Headers tab and then clear the Enable Content Expiration check box.
3. Click OK.

Using Custom HTTP Headers

When a browser requests a document on a Web site handled by IIS, IIS normally passes the document with a response header prepended. Sometimes you may want to modify the standard header or create your own header for special situations. For example, you could take advantage of HTTP headers that are provided for by the HTTP standards, but for which IIS provides no interface. Other times, you may want to provide information to the client that you could not pass using standard HTML elements. To do this, you can use custom HTTP headers.

Custom HTTP headers contain information that you want to include in a document's response header. Entries in a custom header are entered as name value pairs. The Name portion of the entry identifies the value you are referencing. The Value portion of the entry identifies the actual content you are sending.

Custom HTTP headers typically provide instructions for handling the document or supplemental information. For example, the.Cache-Control HTTP header field is used to control how proxy servers cache pages. A field value of Public tells the proxy server that caching is allowed. A field value of Private tells the proxy server that caching is not allowed.

To view or manage custom HTTP headers for a site, directory, or file, follow these steps:

1. In the Internet Information Services snap-in, right-click the Web site, directory, or file you want to manage, and then choose Properties.

2. Select the HTTP Headers tab. The Custom HTTP Headers panel shows currently configured headers in name:value format.

3. Use the following options to manage existing headers or create new headers:

   • **Add**   Adds a custom HTTP header. To add a header, click Add. Type a header name and then type a header value. Complete the process by clicking OK.

   • **Remove**   Removes a custom HTTP header. To remove a header, select it, and then click Remove.

   • **Edit**   Edits a custom HTTP header. To edit a header, select it, and then click Edit. Use the Properties dialog box provided to change the header information, and then click OK.

4. Click OK to close the Properties dialog box for the site, directory, or file you are working with.

Using Content Ratings

IIS has a built-in content rating system based on the Platform for Internet Content Selection (PICS) system. PICS was developed by the Recreational Software Advisory Council (RSAC) and based on the work of Dr. Donald Roberts of Stanford University. Under the PICS rating system, content can be rated according to levels of violence, sex, nudity, and offensive language. Each rating has a separate threshold level that goes from level 0, in which no elements of the designated category are found, to level 4, in which explicit materials are used.

You can set content ratings for an entire site, individual directories, and individual files. Before setting content ratings, you should fill out an RSAC questionnaire to obtain the recommended content ratings for the type of content.

Getting Your Content Rated

To have content rated, follow these steps:

1. In the Internet Information Services snap-in, right-click a Web site, directory, or file, and then select Properties.
2. Click the HTTP Headers tab and then, under Content Ratings, click Edit Ratings.
3. Click Rating Questionnaire and then follow the instructions provided by RSAC.
4. When you are finished, close your browser and click OK twice.

Enabling Content Ratings

To set content ratings for a site, directory, or file, follow these steps:

1. In the Internet Information Services snap-in, right-click a Web site, directory, or file, and then select Properties.
2. Click the HTTP Headers tab and then, under Content Ratings, click Edit Ratings.
3. Select the Ratings tab and then select the Enable Ratings For This Resource check box.
4. In the Category list box, click a ratings category and then use the rating slider to set the level of potentially objectionable material for the category. Each setting displays a description of the rating level.
5. Type your e-mail address in the Email Name Of Person Rating This Content field, and then use the Expire On selection list to choose a ratings expiration date.
6. Click OK twice.

Disabling Content Ratings

To disable content ratings for a site, directory, or file, follow these steps:

1. In the Internet Information Services snap-in, right-click a Web site, directory, or file, and then select Properties.
2. Click the HTTP Headers tab and then, under Content Ratings, click Edit Ratings.
3. Select the Ratings tab and then clear the Enable Ratings For This Resource check box.
4. Click OK twice.

Customizing Web Server Error Messages

IIS generates HTTP error messages when Web server errors occur. These errors typically pertain to bad client requests, authentication problems, or internal server errors. As the administrator, you have complete control over how error messages are sent back to clients. You can configure IIS to send generic HTTP errors, default custom error files, or create your own custom error files.

Understanding Status Codes and Error Messages

Status codes and error messages go hand in hand. Every time a user requests a file on a server, the server generates a status code. The status code indicates the status of the user's request. If the request succeeds, the status code indicates this, and the requested file is returned to the browser. If the request fails, the status code indicates why, and the server generates an appropriate error message based on this error code. This error message is returned to the browser in place of the requested file.

A status code is a 3-digit number that may include a numeric suffix. The first digit of the status code indicates the class of the code. The next two digits indicate the error category, and the suffix (if used) indicates the specific error that occurred. For example, the status code 403 indicates an access problem, and within this access category, there are a number of specific errors that can occur; 403.1 indicates that execute access is forbidden, 403.2 indicates that read access is forbidden, and 403.3 indicates that write access is forbidden.

If you examine the Web server logs or receive an error code while trying to troubleshoot a problem, you'll see status codes. Table 4-5 shows the general classes for status codes. As you can see from the table, the first digit of the status code provides the key indicator as to what has actually happened. Status codes beginning with 1, 2, or 3 are common and generally do not indicate a problem. Status codes beginning with 4 or 5 indicate an error and a potential problem that you need to resolve.

Table 4-5. General Classes of Status Codes

Code Class	Description
1XX	Continue/protocol change
2XX	Success
3XX	Redirection
4XX	Client error/failure
5XX	Server error

Knowing the general problem is helpful when you are searching through log files or compiling statistics. When you are troubleshooting or debugging, you need to know the exact error that occurred. Look up that error code in Table 4-6, which provides a listing of the standard HTTP error messages that IIS supports, including an error code and error text. The standard HTTP error messages comply with the HTTP 1.1 protocol.

Table 4-6. Standard HTTP Error Codes and Error Messages

Error Code	Error Text
400	Bad request
401.1	Logon failed
401.2	Logon failed due to server configuration
401.3	Unauthorized due to access control list (ACL) on resource
401.4	Authorization failed by filter
401.5	Authorization failed by ISAPI/CGI application
403.1	Execute access forbidden
403.2	Read access forbidden
403.3	Write access forbidden
403.4	SSL required
403.5	SSL 128 required
403.6	IP address rejected
403.7	Client certificate required
403.8	Site access denied
403.9	Too many users
403.10	Invalid configuration
403.11	Password change
403.12	Mapper denied access
403.13	Client certificate revoked
403.14	Directory listing denied
403.15	Client Access Licenses exceeded
403.16	Client certificate untrusted or invalid
403.17	Client certificate has expired or is not yet valid
404	Not found
404.1	Site not found
405	Method not allowed
406	Not acceptable
407	Proxy authentication required
412	Precondition Failed
414	Request-URI too long
500	Internal server error
500.12	Application restarting
500.13	Server too busy
500.15	Requests for GLOBAL.ASA not allowed
500-100.ASP	ASP error
501	Not implemented
502	Bad gateway

Managing Custom Error Settings

For each of the standard errors, you can specify how the error is handled. Individual files can have different settings from their parent directory and sites, which means file settings override directory settings and directory settings override sitewide settings. The available error handling options are the following:

- **Default**   Sends a standard IIS error message to the client.
- **File**   Sends a customized error file to the client. Used with static content.
- **URL**   Sends a message that redirects the client to a specific URL. Used with dynamic content.

Custom files supplied in the standard IIS installation handle most HTTP errors. These files are located in the %SystemRoot%\Help\Iishelp\Common directory. You can edit the default error files directly, or you can create your own files. Be sure to use the File type handler with static content, such as HTML pages, and the URL type handler with dynamic content, such as .asp pages. If you don't do this, you may get unexpected results.

The sections that follow examine how you can view and edit error settings.

Real World   When you use an .asp file to handle custom errors, the error code and the original URL are passed to the ASP page as query parameters. The ASP page must be configured to read the parameters from the URL and set the status code appropriately. For example, if NOTFOUND.ASP is designed to handled 404 errors and the user accesses a page using the URL *http://www.microsoft.com/data.htm/,* then the ASP page is invoked using the following URL: *http://www.microsoft.com/NotFound.asp?404;http://www.microsoft.com/data.htm/,* and your ASP page must extract the 404 and *http://www.microsoft.com/data.htm/* parameters from the URL.

Note   In some cases, Internet Explorer may replace custom errors with its own HTTP error message. Typically, this is done when the error message is considered to be too small to be useful to the user. Internet Explorer attempts to determine message usefulness based on message size. When 403, 405, or 410 error messages are smaller than 256 bytes or when 400, 404, 406, 408, 409, 500, 500.12, 500.13, 500.15, 501, or 505 error messages are smaller than 512 bytes, the custom error message sent by IIS is replaced by a message generated by Internet Explorer.

Viewing Custom Error Settings

You can view custom error settings by following these steps:

1. In the Internet Information Services snap-in, right-click the Web site, directory, or file you want to manage, and then choose Properties.

2. Click the Custom Errors tab. As shown in Figure 4-5, you should now see a list of the standard HTTP errors and how they are handled. Entries are organized by:

   - **HTTP Error**   The HTTP status code for the error, which may include a suffix

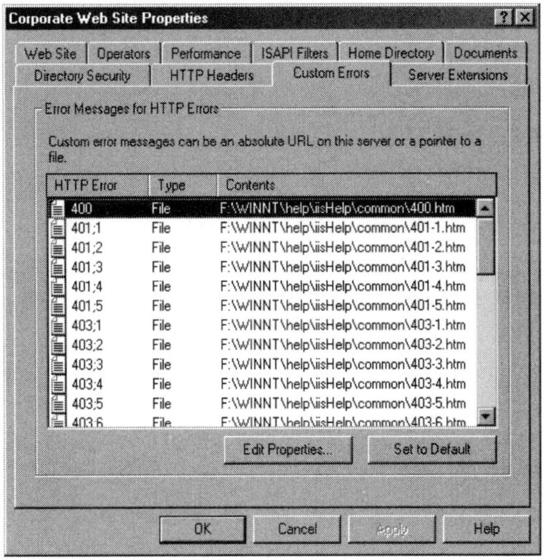

Figure 4-5. *The Custom Errors tab shows the error settings for the file, directory, or site you've selected for editing.*

   - **Type**   The method used to handle the error (default, file, or URL)
   - **Contents**   The error text, file path, or URL path associated with the error

3. Click OK when you are finished viewing the error settings.

Editing Custom Error Settings

You can edit custom error settings by completing these steps:

1. In the Internet Information Services snap-in, right-click the Web site, directory, or file you want to manage, and then choose Properties.

2. Click the Custom Errors tab. You should now see a list of the standard HTTP errors and how they are handled.

3. Click the entry for the error you want to edit, or select the entry and then click Edit Properties. The Error Mapping Properties dialog box is displayed, as shown in Figure 4-6.

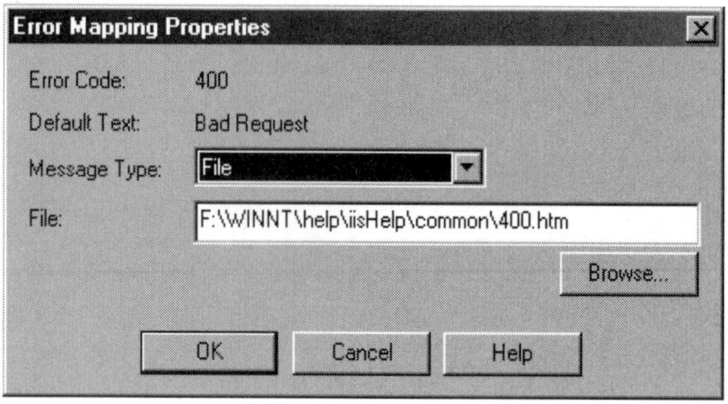

Figure 4-6. *The Error Mapping Properties dialog box provides an overview of the error and how it is handled.*

4. Use the Message Type selection list to choose the error handling technique. The options available depend on the type of error and generally include the following:

   - **Default**   Uses the default error information shown in the Error Code, Sub Error Code, and Default Text fields when returning an error message.

   - **File**   Returns the file specified when the error occurs. Type the complete file path or click Browse to search for the file.

   - **URL**   Returns the URL specified to the client. Type an absolute URL path for resources on other servers, or use a relative URL path for resources on the current server.

5. Click OK twice.

Using MIME and Configuring Custom File Types

Every file that is transferred between IIS and a client browser has a data type designator, which is expressed as a MIME type. MIME is fully supported by IIS.

Understanding MIME

To understand MIME, you need to know how servers transfer files using HTTP. HTTP is a multipurpose protocol that can be used to transfer many types of files, including full-motion video sequences, stereo sound tracks, high-resolution images, and other types of media. The transfer of media files would not be possible without the MIME standard. Web servers use MIME to identify the type of object being transferred. Object types are identified in an HTTP header field that comes before the actual data, and this allows a Web client to handle the object file appropriately.

Web servers set the MIME type using the Content_Type directive, which is part of the HTTP header sent to client browsers. MIME types are broken down into categories, with each category having a primary subtype associated with it. Basic MIME types are summarized in Table 4-7.

Table 4-7. Basic MIME Types

Type	Description
application	Binary data that can be executed or used with another application
audio	A sound file that requires an output device to preview
image	A picture that requires an output device to preview
message	An encapsulated mail message
multipart	Data consisting of multiple parts and possibly many data types
text	Textual data that can be represented in any character set or formatting language
video	A video file that requires an output device to preview
x-world	Experimental data type for world files

MIME subtypes are defined in three categories:

- **Primary** Primary type of data adopted for use as a MIME content type
- **Additional** Additional subtypes that have been officially adopted as MIME content types
- **Extended** Experimental subtypes that have not been officially adopted as MIME content types

You can easily identify extended subtypes because they begin with the letter x followed by a hyphen. Table 4-8 lists common MIME types and their descriptions.

Table 4-8. Common MIME Types

Type/Subtype	Description
application/mac-binhex40	Macintosh binary-formatted data
application/msword	Microsoft Word document
application/octet-stream	Binary data that can be executed or used with another application
application/pdf	Acrobat PDF document
application/postscript	Postscript-formatted data
application/rtf	Rich Text Format (RTF) document
application/x-compress	Data that has been compressed using UNIX compress
application/x-gzip	Data that has been compressed using UNIX gzip
application/x-tar	Data that has been archived using UNIX Tar
application/x-zip-compressed	Data that has been compressed using PKZip or WinZip
audio/basic	Audio in a nondescript format
audio/x-aiff	Audio in Apple AIFF format
audio/x-wav	Audio in Microsoft WAV format
image/gif	Image in GIF format
image/jpeg	Image in JPEG format
image/tiff	Image in TIFF format
text/html	HTML-formatted text
text/plain	Plain text with no HTML formatting included
video/mpeg	Video in the MPEG format
video/quicktime	Video in the Apple QuickTime format
video/x-msvideo	Video in the Microsoft AVI format
x-world/x-vrml	VRML world file

Hundreds of MIME types are configured using file extension to file type mappings. These mappings allow IIS to support just about any type of file that applications or utilities on the destination computer may expect. If a file doesn't end with a known extension, the file is sent as the default MIME type, which indicates the file contains application data. In most cases, use of the default MIME type means that the client is unable to handle the file or trigger other utilities that handle the file. If you expect the client to handle a new file type appropriately, you'll need to create a file extension to file type mapping.

MIME type mappings set in the master properties apply to all Web sites on the server. In the Master Properties dialog box, you can edit existing MIME types, configure additional MIME types, or delete unwanted MIME types. These changes are applied to all Web sites the next time you start IIS. You can also create additional

MIME type mappings for individual sites and directories. When you do this, the MIME type mappings are only available in the site or directory in which they are configured.

Viewing and Configuring MIME Types for All Web Sites on a Server

You can create new MIME types for all Web sites on a server by completing the following steps:

1. In the Internet Information Services snap-in, right-click the computer node for the IIS server you want to work with and then select Properties.

2. Click Edit on the Computer MIME Map panel. As shown in Figure 4-7, you should see a list of the computer MIME types. Computer MIME types are active for all Web sites on the server.

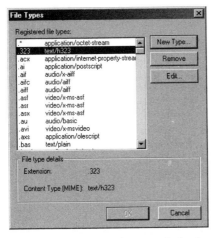

Figure 4-7. *Use the File Types dialog box to view and configure MIME types.*

3. Use the following options to configure new computer MIME types:
   - **New Type** Adds a new MIME type. Type a file extension in the Association Extension field, such as .HTML, and then type a MIME type in the Content MIME Type field, such as text/html. Complete the process by clicking OK.
   - **Remove** Removes a MIME type mapping. To remove a MIME type, select it and then click Remove.

- **Edit** Edits a MIME type mapping. To edit a MIME type, selected it and then click Edit. Use the File Type dialog box provided to change the file extension and the content MIME type.
4. Click OK twice.

Viewing and Configuring MIME Types for Individual Sites and Directories

You can limit the availability of custom MIME types by adding MIME types at the site or directory level. When you work with MIME settings at this level, the only values displayed are those you've defined.

To view or configure site or directory MIME settings, follow these steps:

1. In the Internet Information Service snap-in, right-click the Web site you want to manage, and then choose Properties.

2. On the HTTP Headers tab, click File Types. This displays the File Types dialog box.

3. Use the following options to register new MIME types:
   - **New Type** Adds a new MIME type. Type a file extension in the Association Extension field, such as .html, and then type a MIME type in the Content MIME Type field, such as text/html. Complete the process by clicking OK.
   - **Remove** Removes a MIME type mapping. To remove a MIME type, select it, and then click Remove.
   - **Edit** Edits a MIME type mapping. To edit a MIME type, select it, and then click Edit. Use the File Type dialog box provided to change the file extension and the content MIME type.
4. Click OK twice.

Note You will not see any computer MIME types inherited from the Web server's master properties. You will see only the MIME types registered for the currently selected Web site or directory, even though both sets of MIME types apply.

Additional Customization Tips

Update sites, jump pages, and error forwarding are three additional techniques you can use to customize your IIS Web sites. Each of these techniques is discussed in the sections that follow.

Using Update Sites to Manage Outages

An update site allows you to handle outages in a way that is customer-friendly. Use the update sites function to display alternate content when your primary sites are offline. So, rather than seeing an error message where the user expects to find content, the user sees a message that provides information regarding the outage as well as additional helpful information.

Each Web site you publish should have an update site. You create update sites by completing the following steps:

1. Have your Web development department create a Web page that can be displayed during outages. The page should explain that you are performing maintenance on the Web site, and that the site will be back online shortly. The page can also provide links to other sites your company publishes, so that the user has somewhere else to visit during the maintenance.

2. Use Windows Explorer to create a directory for the update site. The best location for this directory is on the Web server's local drive. Afterward, copy the content files created by the Web development team into this directory.

Tip I recommend that you create a top-level directory for storing the home directories, and then create subdirectories for each update site. For example, you can create a top-level directory D:\UpdateSites and then use subdirectories called WWWUpdate, ServicesUpdate, and ProductsUpdate to store the files for www.microsoft.com, services.microsoft.com, and products.microsoft.com, respectively.

3. Start the Internet Information Services snap-in and then, in the left pane (Console Root), click the plus sign (+) next to the computer you want to work with. If the computer isn't shown, connect to it.

4. You should now see a list of Web sites already configured on the server. Select the computer icon in the console root and note the host header, IP address, and port configuration of the primary site you want to mimic during outages.

5. Create a new site using the configuration settings you just noted. Name the site so that it clearly identifies the site as an update site. Don't start the update site.

6. Next you need to edit the site's properties. Right-click the site entry and then select Properties.

7. Use the fields on the Documents tab to perform the following tasks:
   - Enable default documents
   - Remove the existing default documents
   - Add a default document and set the document name to the name of the outage page created by your Web development department

8. Select the Custom Errors tab. Edit the properties for 400, 404, and 500 errors. These errors should have the Message Type set to File and have a file path that points to the outage page created by your Web development department.

9. Update other site properties as necessary and then close the Properties dialog box by clicking OK.

Once you create the update site, you can activate it as follows:

1. Use the Internet Information Services snap-in to stop the primary site prior to performing maintenance, and then start the related update site.

2. Confirm that the update site is running by visiting the Web site in your browser. If the site is properly configured, you should be able to append a filename to the URL and be directed to the outage page.

3. Perform the necessary maintenance on the primary site. When you are finished, stop the update site, and then start the primary site.

4. Confirm that the primary site is running by visiting the Web site in your browser.

Using Jump Pages for Advertising

A jump page is an intermediate page that redirects a user to another location. You can use jump pages to track click-throughs on banner advertisements or inbound requests from advertising done by the company.

With banner ads, jump pages ensure that users visit a page within your site before moving off to a page at an advertiser's site. This allows you to track the success of advertising on your site. Here's how it works:

1. A page in your site has a banner ad. The ad is linked to a jump page on your site.

2. A user clicks on the ad and is directed to the jump page. The Web server tracks the page access and records it in the log file.

3. The jump page is configured to redirect the user to a page on the advertiser's Web site.

With corporate advertising, jump pages ensure that you can track the source of a visit to advertising done by the company. This allows you to track the success of your company's advertising efforts. Here's how it works:

1. The marketing department develops a piece of advertising collateral. Let's say it's a product brochure. Somewhere in the brochure, there's a reference to a URL on your site. This is the URL for the jump page you've configured.

2. A user types in the URL to the jump page as it was listed in the ad. The Web server tracks the page access and records it in the log file.

3. The jump page is configured to redirect the user to a page on your Web site where the advertised product or service is covered.

Each jump page you create should be unique, or you should create a dynamic page that reads an embedded code within the URL and then redirects the user. For example, you can create a page called JUMP.ASP that reads the first parameter passed to the script as the advertising code. Then you can create a link in the banner ad that specifies the URL and the code, such as JUMP.ASP?4408.

Handling 404 Errors and Preventing Dead Ends

Users hate dead ends, and that's just what a 404 error represents. Rather than having the browser display an apparently meaningless "404 — File Not Found" error, you should throw the user a lifeline. You should consider implementing one of the following:

- Replacing the default error file with a file that provides helpful information and links
- Redirecting all 404 errors to the home page of your site

Either technique will make your Web site a better place to visit, and this could just be the one thing that separates your Web site from the pack.

Chapter 5

Managing Web Server Security

In this chapter, you learn how to manage World Wide Web server security. Web servers have different security considerations from those of standard Microsoft Windows servers. On a Web server, you have two levels of security:

- **Windows security**   At the operating system level, you create user accounts, configure access permissions for files and directories, and set policies.
- **IIS security**   At the level of Internet Information Services (IIS), you set content permissions, authentication controls, and operator privileges.

Windows security and IIS security can be completely integrated. The integrated security model allows you to use authentication based on user and group membership as well as standard Internet-based authentication. It also allows you to use a layered permission model to determine access rights and permissions for content. Before users can access files and directories, you must ensure that the appropriate users and groups have access at the operating system level. Then you must set IIS security permissions that grant permissions for content that IIS controls.

You will use the security discussion in this chapter as a stepping stone to later discussions that cover security for other IIS resources, including File Transfer Protocol (FTP), Simple Mail Transfer Protocol (SMTP), and Network News Transfer Protocol (NNTP). Later discussions focus on what's different rather than rehashing what's already been discussed in this chapter.

Managing Windows Security

Before setting IIS security permissions, you use operating system security settings to do the following tasks:

- Create and manage accounts for users and groups
- Configure access permissions for files and folders
- Set group policies for users and groups

Each of these topics is discussed in the sections that follow.

Working with User and Group Accounts

Microsoft Windows 2000 provides user accounts and group accounts. User accounts determine permissions and privileges for individuals. Group accounts determine permissions and privileges for multiple users.

IIS User and Group Essentials

User and group accounts can be set at the local computer level or the domain level. Local accounts are specific to an individual computer and are not valid on other machines or in a domain unless you specifically grant permissions. Domain accounts, on the other hand, are valid throughout a domain, which makes resources in the domain available to the account. Typically, you'll use specific accounts for specific purposes:

- Use local accounts when your IIS servers aren't part of a domain or you want to limit access to a specific computer.

- Use domain accounts when the servers are part of a Windows domain and you want users to be able to access resources throughout that domain.

User accounts that are important on IIS servers include:

- **Local System** By default, all IIS and Indexing Service users log on using the local system account. This allows the services to interact with the operating system.

- **IUSR_*ComputerName*** Internet guest account used by anonymous users to access Internet sites. If this account is disabled or locked out, anonymous users will not be able to access Internet services.

- **IWAM_*ComputerName*** Web application account used to run out-of-process applications. If this account is disabled or locked out, out-of-process applications will not be able to start.

The Internet Guest and Web application accounts are members of the Guests group and have a password that never expires and cannot be changed by users. You can make changes to these accounts if necessary. For added security, you can configure IIS to use different accounts from the standard accounts provided. You can also create additional accounts

Managing the IIS and Indexing Service Logon Accounts

IIS and Indexing Service use the local system account to log on to the server. Using the local system account allows the services to run system processes and perform system-level tasks. You really shouldn't change this configuration unless you have very specific needs or want to have strict control over the privileges and rights of the IIS logon account. If you decide not to use this account, you can reconfigure the logon account for IIS and Indexing Service by completing the following steps:

1. Start the Computer Management console. Select Start, then Programs, then Administrative Tools, and finally Computer Management.

2. In the Computer Management console, connect to the computer whose services you want to manage.

3. Expand the Services And Applications node by clicking the plus sign (+) next to it, and then select Services.

4. Right-click the service you want to configure and then choose Properties.

5. Select the Log On tab, as shown in Figure 5-1.

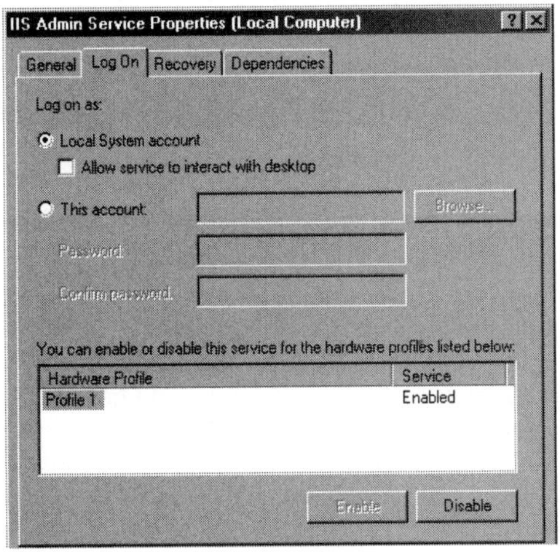

Figure 5-1. *Use the Log On tab to configure the service logon account.*

6. Select Local System Account if the service should log on using the system account (the default for most services).

7. Select This Account if the service should log on using a specific user account. Be sure to type an account name and password in the fields provided. Use the Browse button to search for a user account if necessary.

8. Click OK.

Note If you don't use the local system account, you'll need to assign privileges and logon rights to the account you use. For more information on these and other account permissions, see Chapter 3, "Monitoring Processes, Services, and Events," in the *Microsoft Windows 2000 Administrator's Pocket Consultant*.

Managing the Internet Guest Account

You manage the Internet Guest account at the IIS security level and at the Windows security level. At the IIS security level you will do the following:

• Specify the user account to use for anonymous access. Normally, anonymous access is managed at the site level, and all files and directories within the site inherit the settings you use. You can change this behavior for individual files and directories as necessary.

- Specify how the password for the anonymous user account is managed. Either you manage the password or IIS manages the password. You should only synchronize passwords for anonymous user accounts that are defined locally. If the account is defined on another computer, you should manually control the password.

To change the configuration of the anonymous user account for all Web sites and directories on a Web server, complete the following steps:

1. In the Internet Information Services snap-in, right-click the icon for the computer you want to work with, and then select Properties. This displays a Properties dialog box.

2. Select WWW Service on the Master Properties selection list, and then click Edit. This opens the WWW Service Master Properties dialog box for the computer.

3. Click the Directory Security tab or File Security tab as appropriate, and then click Edit on the Anonymous Access And Authentication Control panel.

Note When Anonymous Access is enabled, users don't have to log on using a username and password. IIS automatically logs the user on using the anonymous account information provided for the resource. If the Anonymous Access check box is not selected, the resource is configured for named account access only. You can enable anonymous access by selecting this check box. However, you should only do this if you are sure the resource does not need to be protected.

4. The Username field specifies the account used for anonymous access to the resource. If you desire, type the account name you want to use instead of the existing account, or click Browse to display the Select User dialog box.

5. Allow IIS To Control Password determines whether IIS controls the password for the anonymous access account or you do. In most cases, you'll want IIS to control the account if it is defined on the local system. If this is the case, select this check box. Otherwise, clear this check box and type in the password for the anonymous access account.

6. Click OK twice and then click OK again to save your changes.

To change the configuration of the anonymous user account at the site, directory, or file level, complete the following steps:

1. In the Internet Information Services snap-in, right-click the Web site, directory, or file you want to work with, and then choose Properties.

2. Follow steps 3 to 6 in the previous listing.

At the Windows security level you perform all other account management tasks, including:

- Enabling or disabling accounts

- Unlocking the account after it has been locked out
- Changing group membership

For details on working with user and group accounts, see Chapter 7, "Understanding User and Group Accounts," Chapter 8, "Creating User and Group Accounts," and Chapter 9, "Managing Existing User and Group Accounts," in the *Microsoft Windows 2000 Administrator's Pocket Consultant*.

Managing the Web Application Account

You manage the Web application account at the IIS security and Windows security levels only. At the IIS security level, you use the Component Services snap-in to specify the account used by out-of-process applications (both pooled and isolated). Pooled applications all use the same account. Isolated applications each can use a different account.

You access the Component Services snap-in by completing the following steps:

1. Open the Run dialog box by clicking Start and then clicking Run.
2. Type **MMC** in the Open field and then click OK. This opens the Microsoft Management Console (MMC).
3. In MMC, click Console and then click Add/Remove Snap-In. This opens the Add/Remove Snap-In dialog box.
4. On the Standalone tab, click Add.
5. In the Add Standalone Snap-In dialog box, click Component Services, and then click Add.
6. Close the Add Standalone Snap-In dialog box by clicking Close, and then click OK.

Once you've started the Component Services snap-in, you can manage the account for pooled applications by completing the following steps:

1. Expand the Component Services node by clicking the plus sign (+) next to it. You should now see the Computers node.
2. If you're connecting to a remote computer, right-click Computers, point to New, and then select Computer. Type the name of the computer you want to manage and then click OK. If you don't know the computer name, click Browse, and then use the Select Computer dialog box to select a computer.
3. Expand the node for the computer and then expand the COM+ Applications node.
4. Right-click IIS Out-Of-Process Pooled Applications, select Properties, and then click the Identity tab.
5. As shown in Figure 5-2, select This User and then, in the User field, type the account name you want to use instead of the existing account, or click Browse to display the Select User dialog box.
6. In the Password and Confirm Password fields, type the password for the account.
7. Click OK.

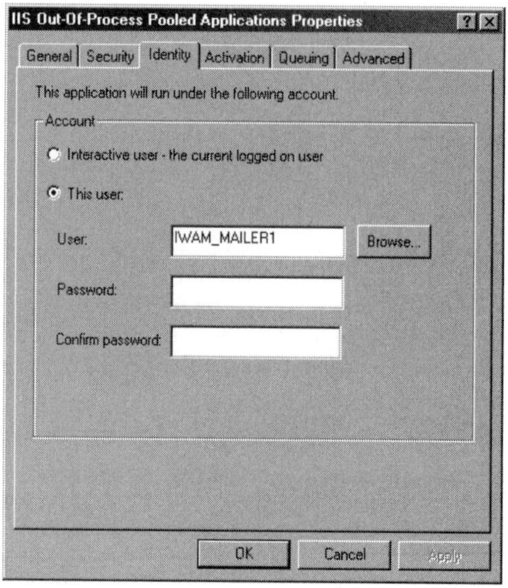

Figure 5-2. *Set the Web application account identity in the Component Services snap-in.*

You manage the account identity for isolated applications using a similar technique. The only difference is that instead of right-clicking IIS Out-Of-Process Pooled Applications, you right-click the entry for the isolated application. Each isolated application is listed by metabase path with the prefix IIS-. For example, if you created an isolated application on the Default Web Site and it was located at /Apps/Data, the associated entry would be named IIS-{Default Web Site//Root/Apps/Data}.

At the Windows security level you perform all other account management tasks for the Web application account. These tasks include the following:

- Enabling or disabling the account
- Unlocking the account after it has been locked out
- Changing group membership

For details on working with user and group accounts, see Chapter 7, "Understanding User and Group Accounts," Chapter 8, "Creating User and Group Accounts," and Chapter 9, "Managing Existing User and Group Accounts," in the *Microsoft Windows 2000 Administrator's Pocket Consultant.*

Working with File and Folder Permissions

Every folder and file used by IIS can have different access permissions. These access permissions are set at the Windows security level. The sections that follow provide an overview of permissions. You'll learn the basics, including how to view permissions and how to set permissions.

File and Folder Permission Essentials

The basic permissions you can assign to files and folders are summarized in Table 5-1. The basic permissions are created by combining special permissions, such as traverse folder and execute file, into a single easily managed permission. If you want granular control over file or folder access, you can use advanced permissions to assign special permissions individually. For more information on special permissions, see Chapter 13, "Data Sharing, Security, and Auditing," in the *Microsoft Windows 2000 Administrator's Pocket Consultant*.

Table 5-1. File and Folder Permissions Used by Windows 2000

Permission	Meaning for Folders	Meaning for Files
Read	Permits viewing and listing files and subfolders	Permits viewing or accessing the file's contents
Write	Permits adding files and subfolders	Permits writing to a file
Read & Execute	Permits viewing and listing files and subfolders as well as executing files; inherited by files and folders	Permits viewing and accessing the file's contents as well as executing the file
List Folder Contents	Permits viewing and listing files and subfolders as well as executing files; inherited by folders only	N/A
Modify	Permits reading and writing of files and subfolders; allows deletion of the folder	Permits reading and writing of the file; allows deletion of the file
Full Control	Permits reading, writing, changing, and deleting files and subfolders	Permits reading, writing, changing, and deleting the file

Anytime you work with file and folder permissions, you should keep the following in mind:

- Read is the only permission needed to run scripts. Execute permission only applies to executables.
- Read access is required to access a shortcut and its target.
- Giving a user permission to write to a file but not to delete it doesn't prevent the user from deleting the file's contents. A user can still delete the contents.
- If a user has full control over a folder, the user can delete files in the folder regardless of the permission on the files.

The following users and groups are used by IIS to configure file and folder access:

- **Administrators** This allows administrators to access IIS resources.
- **Creator Owner** This allows the account that created a resource to access the resource.
- **System** This allows the local system to access the resource.
- **Everyone** This allows interactive, dial-up, network, and authenticated users to access the content. IIS uses this group when the Web server is part of a Windows domain.
- **Users** This allows named accounts to access the resource (including the Internet Guest and Web Application accounts, which are user accounts). IIS uses this group when the Web server is part of a workgroup.

When you grant Read permission to these users and groups, anyone who has access to your Internet or intranet Web site will be able to access the files and folders. If you want to restrict access to certain files and folders, you should set specific user and group permissions and then use authenticated access rather than anonymous access. With authenticated access, IIS authenticates the user before granting access and then uses the Windows permissions to determine what files and folders the user can access.

As you evaluate the permissions you may want to use for files and folders used by IIS, you should refer to Table 5-2. This table provides general guidelines for assigning permissions based on content type.

Table 5-2. General Guidelines for Permissions Based on Content Type

File Type	File Extension	Permission
Common Gateway Interface (CGI) scripts and executables	.exe, .DLL, .cmd	Everyone (Execute) Administrators (Full Control) System (Full Control)
Dynamic content	.asp, .vbs, .js, .pl	Everyone (Read Only) Administrators (Full Control) System (Full Control)
Include files	.inc, .shtm, .shtml, .stm	Everyone (Read Only) Administrators (Full Control) System (Full Control)
Static content	.txt, .rtf, .gif, .jpg, .jpeg, .htm, .html, .doc, .ppt, .xls	Everyone (Read Only) Administrators (Full Control) System (Full Control)

Instead of setting permissions on individual files, you should organize content by type in subdirectories. For example, if your Web site used static, script, and dynamic content, you could create subdirectories called WebStatic, WebScripts, and WebDynamic. You would then store static, script, and dynamic content in these directories and assign permissions on a per-directory basis.

Viewing File and Folder Permissions

You view security permissions for files and folders by completing the following steps:

1. In Microsoft Windows Explorer, right-click the file or folder you want to work with.

2. From the pop-up menu, select Properties, and then, in the Properties dialog box, click the Security tab.

3. In the Name list box, select the user, contact, computer, or group whose permissions you want to view. If the permissions are dimmed, it means the permissions are inherited from a parent object.

Setting File and Folder Permissions

You can set permissions for files and folders by completing the following steps:

1. In Windows Explorer, right-click the file or folder you want to work with.

2. From the pop-up menu, select Properties, and then, in the Properties dialog box, click the Security tab, shown in Figure 5-3.

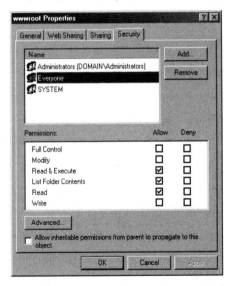

Figure 5-3. *Use the Security tab to configure basic permissions for the file or folder.*

3. Users or groups that already have access to the file or folder are listed in the Name list box. You can change permissions for these users and groups by doing the following:

   • Select the user or group you want to change.

   • Use the Permissions list box to grant or deny access permissions.

Note Inherited permissions are shaded. If you want to override an inherited permission, select the opposite permission.

4. Click Add to set access permissions for additional users, contacts, computers, or groups. This displays the Select Users, Computers, Or Groups dialog box shown in Figure 5-4.

5. Use the Select Users, Computers, Or Groups dialog box to select the users, computers, or groups for which you want to set access permissions. You can use the fields of this dialog box as follows:

- **Look In** This drop-down list box allows you to access account names from other domains. Click Look In to see a list of the current domain, trusted domains, and other resources that you can access. Select Entire Directory to view all the account names in the folder.

- **Name** This column shows the available accounts of the currently selected domain or resource.

- **Add** This button adds selected names to the selection list.

- **Check Names** This button validates the user, and group names entered in the selection list. This is useful if you type names in manually and want to make sure they're available.

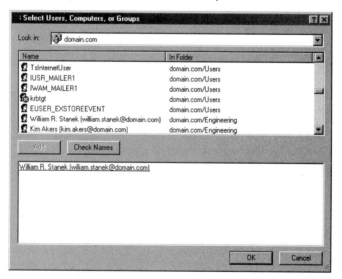

Figure 5-4. *Select users, computers, and groups that should be granted or denied access.*

6. In the Name list box, select the user, computer, or group you want to configure, and then use the fields in the Permissions area to allow or deny permissions. Repeat for other users, computers, or groups.

7. Click OK when you're finished.

Working with Group Policies

Group policies are another aspect of Windows security that you need to understand. You'll use group policies to automate key security administration tasks and to more effectively manage IIS resources.

Group Policy Essentials

Group policies provide central control over privileges, permissions, and capabilities of users and computers. You can think of a policy as a set of rules that can be applied to multiple computers and to multiple users. Because computers can be a part of larger organizational groups, multiple policies can be applied. The order in which policies are applied is extremely important in determining which rules are enforced and which rules are not.

When multiple policies are in place, the policies are applied in the following order:

1. Microsoft Windows NT 4.0 policies from NTCONFIG.POL files

2. Local group policies that affect the local computer only

3. Site group policies that affect all computers that are part of the same site, which can include multiple domains

4. Domain polices that affect all computers in a specific domain

5. Organizational unit policies that affect all computers in an organizational unit

6. Child organizational unit policies that affect all computers in a subcomponent of an organizational unit

As successive policies are applied, the rules in those policies override the rules set in the previous policy. For example, domain policy settings have precedence over the local group policy settings. Exceptions allow you to block, override, and disable policy settings; a discussion of exceptions is outside the scope of this book.

Policy settings are divided into two broad categories: those that affect computers and those that affect users. Computer policies are applied during system startup. User policies are applied during logon. You configure policies with the Group Policy snap-in. To access this snap-in to manage policies for sites, domains, and organizational units, follow these steps:

1. For sites, start the Group Policy snap-in from the Active Directory Sites And Services console. Open the Active Directory Sites And Services console.

2. For domains and organizational units, start the Group Policy snap-in from the Active Directory Users And Computers console. Open the Active Directory Users And Computers console.

3. In the console root, right-click the site, domain, or unit in which you want to create or manage a group policy. Then, from the shortcut menu, select Properties. This opens a Properties dialog box.

4. In the Properties dialog box, select the Group Policy tab. As Figure 5-5 shows, existing policies are listed in the Group Policy Object Links list.

5. To create a new policy or edit an existing policy, click New. You can now configure the policy.

6. To edit an existing policy, select the policy, and then click Edit. You can now edit the policy.

7. To change the priority of a policy, use the Up or Down buttons to change its position in the Group Policy Object Links list.

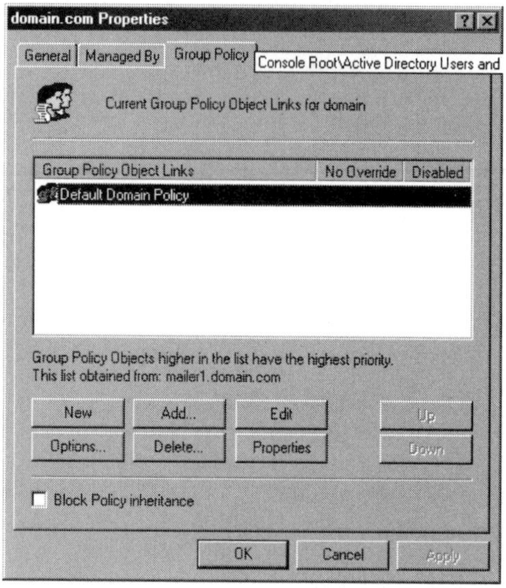

Figure 5-5. *Use the Group Policy tab to create and edit policies.*

You manage local group policies for an individual computer by completing the following steps:

1. Open the Run dialog box by clicking Start and then clicking Run.

2. Type **MMC** in the Open field and then click OK. This opens the Microsoft Management Console (MMC).

3. In MMC, click Console, and then click Add/Remove Snap-In. This opens the Add/Remove Snap-In dialog box.

4. On the Standalone tab, click Add.

5. In the Add Snap-In dialog box, click Group Policy, and then click Add. This opens the Select Group Policy Object dialog box.

6. Click Local Computer to edit the local policy on your computer or browse to find the local policy on another computer.

7. Click Finish, and then click Close.

8. Click OK. You can now manage the local policy on the selected computer.

Group policies for passwords, account lockout, and auditing are essential to the security of your Web server. Guidelines for password policies are as follows:

- Set a minimum password age for all accounts. I recommend 2-3 days.
- Set a maximum password age for all accounts. I recommend 30 days.
- Set a minimum password length. I suggest the minimum be set at 8 characters to start.
- Enable secure passwords by enforcing password complexity requirements.
- Enforce password history. Use a value of 5 or more.

Guidelines for account lockout polices include the following:

- Set an account lockout threshold. In most cases, accounts should be locked after five bad attempts.
- Set account lockout duration. In most cases, you'll want to lock out accounts indefinitely.
- Reset the lockout threshold after 30 to 60 minutes.

Guidelines for auditing include the following:

- Audit system event success and failure
- Audit logon event success and failure
- Audit failed object access attempts
- Audit successful and failed policy changes
- Audit successful and failed account management
- Audit successful and failed account logon

Techniques for managing these policies are examined in the sections that follow. For more detailed information on policy management, see Chapter 4, "Automating Administrative Tasks, Policies, and Procedures," in *Microsoft Windows 2000 Administrator's Pocket Consultant.*

Setting Account Policies for IIS Servers

You can set account policies by completing the following steps:

1. Access the group policy container you want to work with. Expand Computer Configuration, then Windows Settings, then Security Settings, and then Account Policies.

2. As shown in Figure 5-6, you can now manage account policies through the Password Policy, Account Lockout Policy, and Kerberos Policy nodes.

3. To configure a policy, double-click its entry, or right-click on it and select Security. This opens a Properties dialog box for the policy.

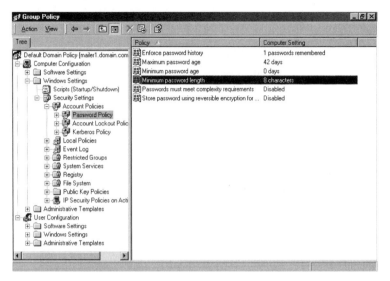

Figure 5-6. *Set policies for passwords and general account use.*

4. For a local policy, the Properties dialog box is similar to the one shown in Figure 5-7. The effective policy for the computer is displayed but you can't change it. You can change the local policy settings, however. Use the fields provided to configure the local policy. Skip the remaining steps; those steps apply to global group policies.

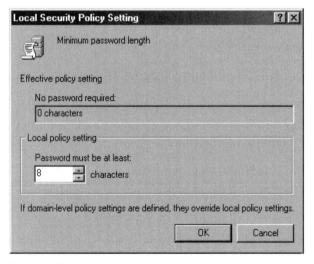

Figure 5-7. *With local policies, you'll see the effective policy as well as the local policy.*

5. For a site, domain, or organizational unit, the Properties dialog box is similar to the one shown in Figure 5-8.

6. All policies are either defined or not defined—that is, they are either configured for use or not configured for use. A policy that isn't defined in the current container could be inherited from another container.

7. Select or clear the Define This Policy Setting check box to determine whether a policy is defined.

8. Policies can have additional fields for configuring the policy. Often, these fields are option buttons labeled Enabled and Disabled.

   • Enabled turns on the policy restriction.

   • Disabled turns off the policy restriction.

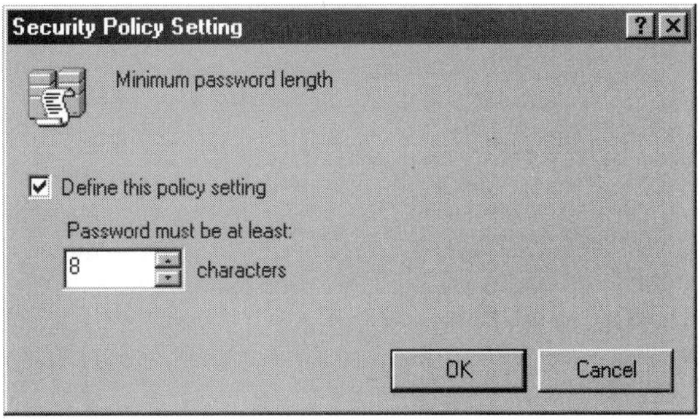

Figure 5-8. *Define and configure global group policies using the Properties dialog box.*

Setting Auditing Policies

Auditing is the best way to track what's happening on your IIS server. You can use auditing to collect information related to resource usage, such as file access, system logon, and system configuration changes. Anytime an action occurs that you've configured for auditing, the action is written to the system's security log, where it's stored for your review. The security log is accessible from Event Viewer.

You can set auditing policies by completing the following steps:

1. Access the group policy container you want to work with. Expand Computer Configuration, Windows Settings, Security Settings, and Local Policies. Then select Audit Policy, as shown in Figure 5-9.

2. You can now have access to the following auditing options:

   • **Audit Account Logon Events**   Tracks events related to user logon and logoff.

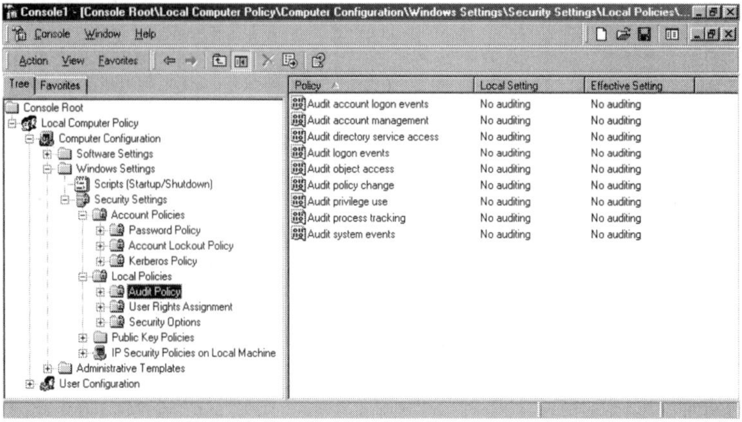

Figure 5-9. *Set auditing policies using the Audit Policy node in Group Policy.*

- **Audit Account Management** Tracks account management. Events are generated anytime user, computer, or group accounts are created, modified, or deleted.

- **Audit Directory Service Access** Tracks access to the Active Directory. Events are generated anytime users or computers access the directory.

- **Audit Logon Events** Tracks events related to user logon, logoff, and remote connections to network systems.

- **Audit Object Access** Tracks system resource usage for files, directories, shares, printers, and Active Directory objects.

- **Audit Policy Change** Tracks changes to user rights, auditing, and trust relationships.

- **Audit Privilege Use** Tracks the use of user rights and privileges, such as the right to back up files and directories, but doesn't track system logon or logoff.

- **Audit Process Tracking** Tracks system processes and the resources they use.

- **Audit System Events** Tracks system startup, shutdown, and restart, as well as actions that affect system security or the security log.

3. To configure an auditing policy, double-click its entry, or right-click and select Security. This opens a Properties dialog box for the policy.

4. Select Define These Policy Settings, and then select either the Success check box or the Failure check box, or both. Success logs successful events, such as successful logon attempts. Failure logs failed events, such as failed logon attempts.

5. Click OK when you're finished.

Managing IIS Security

After setting operating system security, use IIS security to

- Set the Web server and execute permissions for content
- Configure distributed authoring and versioning
- Configure authentication methods
- Control access by IP address or Internet domain name
- Manage Web site operator privileges

Each of these topics is discussed in the sections that follow.

Setting Web Server Permissions

Sites, directories, and files have permissions in IIS in addition to the Windows security settings. These permissions are set the same for all users. This means you cannot set different permissions for different users at the Web content level. You can, however, create secure areas of your Web site and then use Windows file and folder permissions to provide the necessary additional controls.

Understanding Web Server Permissions

The permissions you assign to Web content are applied in combination with the authentication methods and access restrictions currently being enforced for the resource. This means user requests must meet the requirements for Web content permissions, authentication, and access before they are executed. Keep in mind that all directories and files within the site inherit permissions set at the site level, and that you can override site-level permissions by setting permissions on individual directories and files.

Web server permissions also set the permissible actions for Web Distributed Authoring And Versioning (WebDAV). WebDAV publishing allows remote users to publish, lock, and manage resources on a Web server through a Hypertext Transfer Protocol (HTTP) connection. Windows 2000, Microsoft Office 2000, and Internet Explorer 5.0 or later are all WebDAV-enabled. If you have WebDAV-enabled applications, use Web server permissions to determine permitted actions for these applications and their users. You'll find more detailed information on WebDAV in the "Configuring Distributed Authoring and Versioning," section of this chapter.

You can set Web server permissions in two different ways:

- **Globally** Global permissions are configured using the WWW Server Master Properties dialog box. When you set Web server permissions in the master properties, you must also specify how these properties are inherited. When a site or directory has settings that conflict with permission changes you've made, you are given the opportunity to override the site or directory permissions with the global permissions. If you override permissions, the global permissions are applied to the site or directory and its contents. If you do not override permissions, the original settings for the site or directory are maintained.

- **Locally** Local permissions are configured at the site, directory, or file level. As with global permissions, local permissions for sites and directories can be inherited. Because of this, when you make permission changes that conflict with existing permissions on a subdirectory, you are given the opportunity to override the site or directory permissions with the local permissions. If you override permissions, the local permissions are applied to the site or directory and its contents. If you do not override permissions, the original settings for the site or directory are maintained.

IIS manages inheritance of permissions changes at the node level. Because of this, the top-level directory for a site and the individual directories within a site are seen as separate nodes. If you apply changes to a site node, the permissions are applied to the site's root folder and to files in this folder. Changes are not applied to subdirectories within the site unless you specify that they should be.

Setting Web Server Permissions Globally

To manage Web server permissions globally, complete the following steps:

1. In the Internet Information Services snap-in, right-click the icon for the computer you want to work with, and then select Properties. This displays a Properties dialog box.

2. Select WWW Service on the Master Properties selection list and then click Edit. This opens the WWW Service Master Properties dialog box for the computer.

3. As shown in Figure 5-10, click the Home Directory tab, and then use the following fields to set the Web server permissions that you want sites and directories on this computer to inherit:

   - **Directory Browsing** Allows users to view a list of files and subdirectories within the designated directory.

   - **Index This Resource** Allows the Indexing Service to index the resource. Indexing allows users to perform keyword searches for information contained in the resource.

   - **Log Visits** Used with server logging to log requests related for resource files.

   - **Read** Allows users to view the resource. For a directory, this grants the user access to the directory. For a file, this means the user can read the file and display it.

   - **Script Source Access** Allows users to access source code, including scripts in ASPs. If Read permission is also selected, users will be able to read the source file. If Write permission is also selected, users will be able to write to the source file.

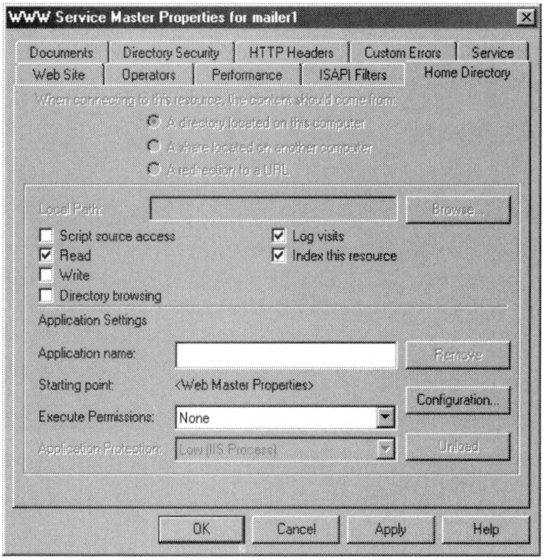

WWW Service Master Properties for mailer1					☒
Documents	Directory Security	HTTP Headers	Custom Errors	Service	
Web Site	Operators	Performance	ISAPI Filters	Home Directory	

When connecting to this resource, the content should come from:

○ A directory located on this computer
○ A share located on another computer
○ A redirection to a URL

Local Path: [   ]   [Browse...]

☐ Script source access   ☑ Log visits
☑ Read   ☑ Index this resource
☐ Write
☐ Directory browsing

Application Settings

Application name: [   ]   [Remove]

Starting point: <Web Master Properties>
                                             [Configuration...]
Execute Permissions: [None   ▼]

Application Protection: [Low (IIS Process) ▼]   [Unload]

[OK]   [Cancel]   [Apply]   [Help]

Figure 5-10. *Use the Properties dialog box to configure Web server permissions.*

Caution   Be careful when granting Script Source Access on production
servers that are on the public Internet. With this permission, anyone will
be able to read the contents of your scripts, and this may open your
servers to mischievous users. Because of this, you should only enable
this feature in a directory that requires users to authenticate themselves
before being granted access.

* **Write**   Allows users to change the resource. For a directory, this
  allows the user to create or publish files. For a file, this allows the
  user to change the content.

Caution   Write permission should be granted only to a limited number
of resources. If possible, you should create separate subdirectories that
contain only writeable files, or you should write-enable individual files
rather than entire directories. To execute application files, you must
assign Read permission to all files used by the application or to the site
or directory used to store these files. If the application posts content to
a file on the site, you must also assign Write permission (but you should
limit this to a specific file or directory).

4. If the selected resource is part of an IIS application, you may also want to set the level of program execution that is allowed for the application. To do this, use the Execute Permissions selection list to choose one of the following options:

- **None**   Only static files, such as .html or .gif files, can be accessed.
- **Scripts Only**   Only scripts, such as ASP scripts, can be run.
- **Scripts And Executables**   All file types can be accessed and executed.

5. Click Apply. Before applying permission changes, IIS checks the existing permissions in use for all Web sites and directories within Web sites. Each time a site or directory node uses a different value for a permission, an Inheritance Overrides dialog box is displayed. Use this dialog box to select the site and directory nodes, which should use the new permission value, and then click OK.

Setting Web Server Permissions Locally

To set content permissions for a site, directory, or file, complete the following steps:

1. In the Internet Information Services snap-in, right-click the site, directory, or file that you want to work with, and select Properties.

2. Click the Home Directory, Directory, or Virtual Directory tab as appropriate. This displays the dialog box shown in Figure 5-11. Then use the following fields to set the permissions for the selected resource:

- **Directory Browsing**   Allows users to view a list of files and subdirectories within the designated directory.

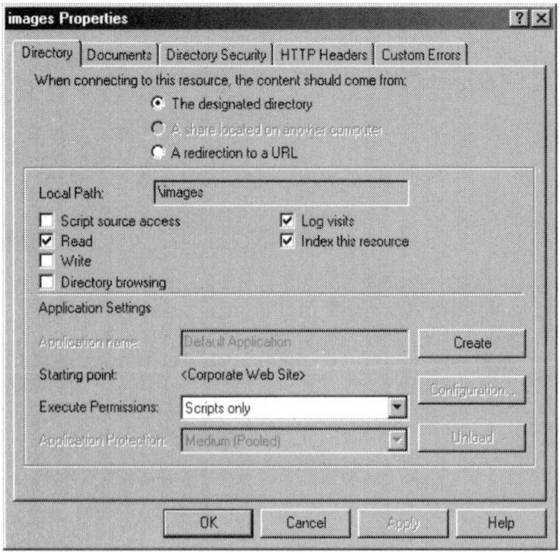

Figure 5-11. *Use the Properties dialog box to configure Web server permissions.*

- **Index This Resource**   Allows the Indexing Service to index the resource. Indexing allows users to perform keyword searches for information contained in the resource.

- **Log Visits**   Used with server logging to log requests related for resource files.

- **Read**   Allows users to view the resource. For a directory, this grants the user access to the directory. For a file, this means the user can read the file and display it.

- **Script Source Access**   Allows users to access source code, including scripts in ASP pages. If Read permission is also selected, users will be able to read the source file. If Write permission is also selected, users will be able to write to the source file.

Caution   Be careful when granting Script Source Access on production servers that are on the public Internet. With this permission, anyone will be able to read the contents of your scripts, and this may open your servers to mischievous users. Because of this, you should only enable this feature in a directory that requires users to authenticate themselves before being granted access.

- **Write**   Allows users to change the resource. For a directory, this allows the user to create or publish files. For a file, this allows the user to change the content.

Caution   Write permission should be granted to only a limited number of resources. If possible, you should create separate subdirectories that contain only writeable files, or you should write-enable individual files rather than entire directories. To execute application files, you must assign Read permission to all files used by the application or to the site or directory used to store these files. If the application posts content to a file on the site, you must also assign Write permission (but you should limit this to a specific file or directory).

3. If the selected resource is part of an IIS application, you may also want to set the level of program execution that is allowed for the application. To do this, use the Execute Permissions selection list to choose one of the following options:

   - **None**   Only static files, such as .html or .gif files, can be accessed.

   - **Scripts Only**   Only scripts, such as ASP scripts, can be run.

   - **Scripts And Executables**   All file types can be accessed and executed.

4. Click Apply. Before applying permission changes, IIS checks the existing permissions in use for all Web sites and directories within Web sites. Each time a site or directory node uses a different value for a permission, an Inheritance

Overrides dialog box is displayed. Use this dialog box to select the site and directory nodes, which should use the new permission value, and then click OK.

Configuring Distributed Authoring and Versioning

WebDAV is an extension to the HTTP 1.1 protocol that allows remote users to manage Web server resources. Using WebDAV, clients can

- Perform standard file operations, such as cut, copy, and paste
- Create and edit files and their properties at the operating system level
- Create and edit directories and their properties at the operating system level
- Lock and unlock resources to allow only one person to modify a resource while allowing multiple users to read the resource
- Search the contents and properties of files in a directory

Because WebDAV is integrated into IIS, all Web site directories on your IIS server are accessible for distributed authoring and versioning. This makes it easy to access and publish documents to your IIS server.

Permitting Distributed Authoring and Versioning

You control the permitted actions for WebDAV application using the standard Web server permissions. The Web server permissions that are directly applicable to WebDAV are

- **Directory Browsing**   Allows WebDAV clients to view the contents of directories.
- **Index This Resource**   If your Web server is running the Indexing Service, WebDAV clients can search the directory using special search utilities.
- **Read**   Allows WebDAV clients to view and run files and subdirectories within the WebDAV directory.
- **Script Source Access**   Allows WebDAV clients to download source files for scripts.
- **Write**   Allows WebDAV clients to create files or directories and to write to existing files.

To publish to a directory and see a list of files in that directory, users need Read, Write, and Browse access permissions. If users need to update script files, you must also grant Script Source Access permission. To protect your Web content, you should grant these permissions only in directories that require users to authenticate themselves. For example, you could create a directory called ForPublishing and then configure permissions on this directory so that anonymous access is not allowed, and then configure the necessary authoring and publishing permissions (Read, Write, and Browse).

When you allow script source access, you need to ensure that your source code and executables are protected. Any extension designated in the Application Mappings for the site is considered a script source file. Files with extensions that aren't mapped are treated as static .html or text files. Files with the .DLL and .exe extension are also treated as static files, unless the Scripts And Executables permission is set, which means they could be overwritten even if Script Source Access is not enabled. When the Scripts And Executables permission is set, .DLL and .exe files are not treated as static files—they are treated as executable files, and they can only be overwritten when Script Source Access is enabled.

Accessing and Publishing Documents with WebDAV

Windows 2000 and Office 2000 are both WebDAV-enabled, and you can connect to Web directories on IIS servers quite easily. In Windows 2000, you can connect to a Web directory on an IIS server by completing the following steps:

1. Double-click the My Network Places icon on your desktop, and then double-click Add Network Place. This starts the Add Network Place Wizard.

2. In the Add Network Place Wizard, type the URL of the WebDAV directory to which you want to connect, such as *http://www.microsoft.com/data/*.

3. Click Next, and then type a descriptive name for the directory.

4. When you complete the process by clicking Finish, Windows 2000 automatically accesses the directory. The next time you want to access the directory, double-click My Network Places on the desktop and then double-click the folder for the directory.

Once you've created a network place for the WebDAV directory, you can easily publish documents to it from Office 2000. Simply create a document in any Office 2000 application, then follow these steps:

1. Select Save As from the File menu and then, in the left column of the Save As dialog box, click My Network Places.

2. Select the shortcut for the WebDAV directory you want to use, or type the URL, and then click OK.

You can also connect to WebDAV directories through Internet Explorer 5.0 on the Microsoft Windows 95, Microsoft Windows 98, Windows NT 4.0, or Windows 2000 operating systems. Simply complete the following steps:

1. Start Internet Explorer 5.0 or later, and then display the Open dialog box by selecting Open from the File menu.

2. In the Open dialog box, type the URL for the WebDAV directory to which you want to connect, such as *http://www.microsoft.com/data/*.

3. Select the Open As Web Folder check box and then click OK.

Setting Authentication Modes

Authentication modes control access to IIS resources. You can use authentication to allow anonymous access to public resources, to create secure areas within a Web site, and to create controlled access Web sites. When authentication is enabled, IIS uses the account credentials supplied by a user to determine whether or not the user has access to a resource, and to determine which permissions the user has been granted.

Understanding Authentication

Four authentication modes are available. These modes are:

- **Anonymous Authentication** With anonymous authentication, IIS automatically logs users on with an anonymous or guest account. This allows users to access resources without being prompted for username and password information.

- **Basic Authentication** With basic authentication, users are prompted for logon information. When it's entered, this information is transmitted unencrypted across the network. If you've configured secure communications on the server as described in the "Working with SSL" section of Chapter 6, "Managing Microsoft Certificate Services and SSL," you can require clients to use Secure Sockets Layer (SSL). When you use SSL with basic authentication, the logon information is encrypted before transmission.

- **Integrated Windows Authentication** With integrated Windows authentication, IIS uses standard Windows security to validate the user's identity. Instead of prompting for a username and password, clients relay the logon credentials that users supply when they log on to Windows. These credentials are fully encrypted without the need for SSL, and they include the username and password needed to log on to the network. Only Internet Explorer browsers support this feature.

- **Digest Authentication** With digest authentication, user credentials are transmitted securely between clients and servers. Digest authentication is a feature of HTTP 1.1 and uses a technique that cannot be easily intercepted and decrypted. This feature is available only when the IIS server is a domain controller and the request was made by Internet Explorer 5.0 or later.

By default, both anonymous and integrated Windows authentication are enabled for IIS resources. Because of this, the default authentication process looks like this:

1. IIS attempts to access the resource using the Internet Guest account. If this has the appropriate access permissions, the user is allowed to access the resource.

2. If validation of the credentials fails or the account is disabled or locked, IIS attempts to use the user's current account credentials. If the credentials can be validated and the user has the appropriate access permissions, the user is allowed to access the resource.

3. If validation fails or the user doesn't have appropriate access permissions, the user is denied access to the resource.

As with Web server permissions, you can apply authentication on a global or local basis. Global authentication modes are configured using the master WWW properties. Local authentication modes are set using site, directory, or file properties. Anytime you make changes that conflict with existing settings IIS displays a dialog box that allows you to specify which resources inherit the new settings.

Before you start working with authentication modes, you should keep the following in mind:

- When you combine anonymous access with authenticated access, users have full access to resources that are accessible to the Internet Guest account. If this account does not have access to a resource, IIS attempts to authenticate the user using the authentication techniques you've specified. If these authentication methods fail, the user is denied access to the resource.

- When you disable anonymous access, you are telling IIS that all user requests must be authenticated using the authentication modes you've specified. Once the user is authenticated, IIS uses the user's account credentials to determine access rights.

- When you combine basic authentication with integrated or digest authentication, Internet Explorer will attempt to use integrated Windows authentication or digest authentication before using basic authentication. This means users who can be authenticated using their current account credentials won't be prompted for a username and password.

Additionally, before you can use digest authentication, you must enable reversible password encryption for each account that will connect to the server using this authentication technique. IIS and the user's Web browser use reversible encryption to manage secure transmission and unencryption of user information. To enable reversible encryption, follow these steps:

1. Start Active Directory Users And Computers. Click Start, point to Programs, point to Administrative Tools, and then select Active Directory Users And Computers.

2. Double-click the username that you want to use with Digest Authentication.

3. In Account Options, select Store Password Using Reversible Encryption.

4. Click OK. Repeat steps 1 to 4 for each account that you want to use digest authentication on.

Enabling and Disabling Authentication

You can enable or disable anonymous access to resources at the server, site, directory, or file level. If you enable anonymous access, users can access resources without having to authenticate themselves (provided the Windows permissions on the resource allow this). If you disable anonymous access, users must authenticate themselves before accessing resources. Authentication can occur automatically or manually depending on the browser used and the account credentials previously entered by the user.

You can enable or disable authentication at the server level by completing the following steps:

1. In the Internet Information Services snap-in, right-click the icon for the computer you want to work with, and then select Properties. This displays a Properties dialog box.

2. Select WWW Service on the Master Properties selection list and then click Edit. This opens the WWW Service Master Properties dialog box for the computer.

3. Select the Directory Security tab and then click Edit on the Anonymous Access And Authentication Control panel. This displays the Authentication Methods dialog box shown in Figure 5-12.

Figure 5-12. *Use the Authentication Methods dialog box to enable or disable authentication methods to meet the needs of your organization. With basic authentication, it's often helpful to set a default domain as well.*

4. To enable anonymous access, select the Anonymous Access check box. To disable anonymous access, clear this check box.

5. Select or clear Basic Authentication to enable or disable this authentication method. If you disable basic authentication, keep in mind that this may prevent some clients from accessing resources remotely. Clients can log on only when you enable an authentication method that they support.

6. A default domain isn't set automatically. If you enable basic authentication, you can choose to set a default domain that should be used when no domain information is supplied during the logon process. Setting the default domain is useful when you want to ensure that clients authenticate properly.

7. Select or clear Digest Authentication to enable or disable this authentication method. If the computer you are working with isn't a domain controller, this option will not be available.

8. Select or clear Integrated Windows Authentication to enable or disable this authentication method.

9. Click OK. Before applying changes, IIS checks the existing authentication methods in use for all Web sites and directories within Web sites. If a site or directory node uses a different value, an Inheritance Overrides dialog box is displayed. Use this dialog box to select the site and directory nodes that should use the new setting, and then click OK.

You can enable or disable authentication at the site, directory, or file level by completing these steps:

1. In the Internet Information Services snap-in, right-click the site, directory, or file that you want to work with, and then select Properties. This displays a Properties dialog box.

2. Select the Directory Security tab and then click Edit on the Anonymous Access And Authentication Control panel. This displays the Authentication Methods dialog box shown previously in Figure 5-12.

3. To enable anonymous access, select the Anonymous Access check box. To disable anonymous access, clear this check box.

4. Select or clear Basic Authentication to enable or disable this authentication method. If you disable basic authentication, keep in mind that this may prevent some clients from accessing resources remotely. Clients can log on only when you enable an authentication method that they support.

5. A default domain isn't set automatically. If you enable basic authentication, you can choose to set a default domain that should be used when no domain information is supplied during the logon process. Setting the default domain is useful when you want to ensure that clients authenticate properly.

6. Select or clear Digest Authentication to enable or disable this authentication method. If the computer you are working with isn't a domain controller, this option will not be available.

7. Select or clear Integrated Windows Authentication to enable or disable this authentication method.

8. Click OK. Before applying changes, IIS checks the existing authentication methods in use for all child nodes of the selected resource (if any). If a child node uses a different value, an Inheritance Overrides dialog box is displayed. Use this dialog box to select the site and directory nodes that should use the new setting, and then click OK.

Configuring IP Address and Domain Name Restrictions

By default, IIS resources are accessible to all IP addresses, computers, and domains, which presents a security risk that may allow your server to be misused. To control use of resources, you may want to grant or deny access by IP address, network ID, or domain. As with other Web server settings, restrictions can be applied through the Master WWW server properties or through the properties for individual sites, directories, and files.

- Granting access allows a computer to make requests for resources but doesn't necessarily allow users to work with resources. If you require authentication, users still need to authenticate themselves.

- Denying access to resources prevents a computer from accessing those resources. Therefore, users of the computer can't access the resources—even if they could have authenticated themselves with a username and password.

You can establish or remove restrictions globally through the Master WWW server properties by completing the following steps:

1. In the Internet Information Services snap-in, right-click the icon for the computer you want to work with, and then select Properties. This displays a Properties dialog box.

2. Select WWW Service on the Master Properties selection list and then click Edit. This opens the WWW Service Master Properties dialog box for the computer.

3. Select the Directory Security tab and then click Edit on the IP Address And Domain Name Restrictions panel. This displays the IP Address And Domain Name Restrictions dialog box shown in Figure 5-13.

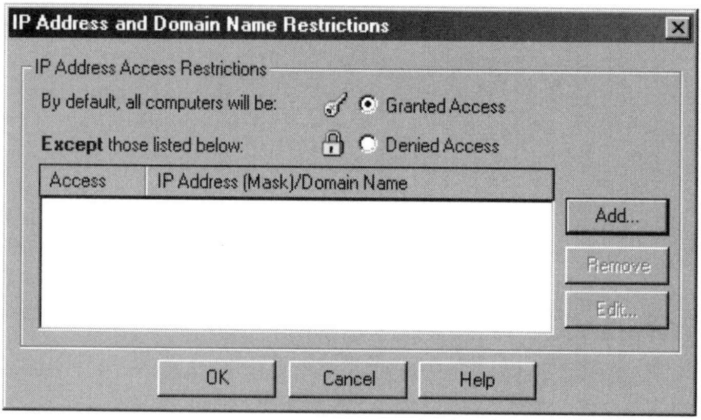

Figure 5-13. *You can grant or deny access by IP address, network ID, and domain.*

4. Select Granted Access to grant access to specific computers and deny access to all others.

5. Select Denied Access to deny access to specific computers and grant access to all others.

6. Create the grant or deny list. Click Add and then, in the Computer dialog box, specify Single Computer, Group Of Computers, or Domain.

   - For a single computer, type the IP address for the computer, such as 192.168.5.50.

   - For groups of computers, type the subnet address, such as 192.168.0.0, and the subnet mask, such as 255.255.0.0.

- For a domain name, type the fully qualified domain name, such as eng.domain.com.

Caution When you grant or deny by domain, IIS must perform a reverse Domain Name System (DNS) lookup on each connection to determine whether the connection comes from the domain. These reverse lookups can severely increase response times for the first query each user sends to your site.

7. If you want to remove an entry from the grant or deny list, select the related entry in the Computers list, and then click Remove.

8. Click Apply. Before applying changes, IIS checks the existing restrictions for all Web sites and directories within Web sites. If a site or directory node uses a different value, an Inheritance Overrides dialog box is displayed. Use this dialog box to select the site and directory nodes that should use the new setting, and then click OK.

You can establish or remove restrictions at the site, directory, or file level by completing these steps:

1. In the Internet Information Services snap-in, right-click the site, directory, or file that you want to work with, and choose Properties. This displays a Properties dialog box.

2. Select the Directory Security tab and then click Edit on the IP Address And Domain Name Restrictions panel. This displays the IP Address And Domain Name Restrictions dialog box shown previously in Figure 5-13.

3. Select Granted Access to grant access to specific computers and deny access to all others.

4. Select Denied Access to deny access to specific computers and grant access to all others.

5. Create the grant or deny list. Click Add and then, in the Computer dialog box, specify Single Computer, Group Of Computers, or Domain.

- For a single computer, type the IP address for the computer, such as 192.168.5.50.

- For groups of computers, type the subnet address, such as 192.168.0.0, and the subnet mask, such as 255.255.0.0.

- For a domain name, type the fully qualified domain name, such as eng.domain.com.

6. If you want to remove an entry from the grant or deny list, select the related entry in the Computers list, and then click Remove.

7. Click Apply. Before applying changes, IIS checks the existing restrictions for all child nodes of the selected resource (if any). If a child node uses a different value, an Inheritance Overrides dialog box is displayed. Use this dialog box to select the site and directory nodes that should use the new setting, and then click OK.

Configuring Web Site Operators

You can designate Web site operators for each Web site on your server. Operators can then manage the site remotely.

Understanding Web Site Operators

Web site operators are a special group of users who have administrative privileges. Operators can perform the following tasks:

- Manage directories on a Web site through standard create, rename, and delete procedures.

- Manage properties of directories including directory permissions, default documents, directory security, HTTP headers, and error messages.

- Manage properties of a site including site permissions, operator assignment, performance, Internet Server Application Interface (ISAPI) filters, home directory properties, default documents, directory security, HTTP headers, and error messages.

Operators cannot configure properties that affect IIS, the host computer, or the network. These limits on operators are designed to enhance security.

> **Note** Operator privileges do not extend to the Administration Web site. Users must be members of the Administrators group before they can remotely manage IIS using the Administration Web site.

Remote operator administration is made possible by the scripts, components, and applications defined in the IISAdmin directory. The IISAdmin directory must be configured for any Web site that you want operators to be able to control remotely. By default this directory is located in \%SystemRoot%\System32\Inetsrv\Iisadmin.

Operators connect to Web sites that they want to manage through a standard browser, such as Internet Explorer 5.0. The URL they type is the site's domain name followed by the name of the virtual directory used for operator administration. For example, if the server's domain name is dev.microsoft.com and the administration directory is named ops, you could connect to the operator area by typing the following URL into your browser window:

```
http://dev.microsoft.com/ops/
```

The technique used to authenticate the operator's credentials depends on the authentication methods you've enabled for the administration directory. You should never allow anonymous access to the administration directory.

You can specify accounts that have operator privileges globally or locally. Global operator assignments are automatically applied to all Web sites on the server. Local operator assignments apply only to an individual Web site.

Permitting Operator Administration of a Web Site

To permit operator administration of a Web site, you must do the following:

1. Configure a virtual directory that maps to the physical location of the IISAdmin directory.

2. Create a pooled IIS application with the designated virtual directory as the starting point. A pooled IIS application isolates the administration tasks from the main IIS processes.

3. Set Execute permissions for the administration directory to Scripts Only or Scripts And Executables.

Assigning Operators to All Web Sites on a Server

To specify operator assignments for all Web sites on a server, complete the following steps:

1. In the Internet Information Services snap-in, right-click the icon for the computer you want to work with, and then select Properties. This displays a Properties dialog box.

2. Select WWW Service on the Master Properties selection list and then click Edit. This opens the WWW Service Master Properties dialog box for the computer.

3. Select the Operators tab. The Operators list box shows the currently configured operators. The global group Administrators is the only operator configured by default.

4. To add an operator, click Add. This displays the Select Users Or Groups dialog box, which you can use to select users and groups that should be configured as operators.

5. To remove an operator, select the operator in the Operators list box, and then click Remove.

6. Click OK three times to complete the operator assignment.

Assigning Operators to an Individual Web Site

To specify operator assignments for a specific Web site, complete these steps:

1. In the Internet Information Services snap-in, right-click the site, directory, or file that you want to work with. This displays a Properties dialog box.

2. Select the Operators tab. The Operators list box shows the currently configured operators. The global group Administrators is the only operator configured by default.

3. To add an operator, click Add. This displays the Select Users Or Groups dialog box, which you can use to select users and groups that should be configured as operators.

4. To remove an operator, select the operator in the Operators list box and then click Remove.

5. Click OK twice to complete the operator assignment.

More Tips for Enhancing Web Server Security

Your Web server is only as secure as you make it. To improve the security of your server, read the additional tips provided here, and apply the ones that make sense for your server environment.

Using Firewalls

Maintaining the security of your Web server is an ongoing task that requires continual vigilance. To shield your Web servers from attacks, you need a firewall, such as the Microsoft Internet Security and Acceleration Server or the Cisco PIX 515 Firewall. When you install a firewall, close all ports that you aren't using and only open ports that are needed.

The ports you'll want to open depend on the types of IIS resources you are using. FTP uses ports 21 and 23. SMTP uses port 25 and may require port 53 for DNS resolution. HTTP uses ports 80 and 443. NNTP uses ports 119 and 563.

Renaming the Administrator Account

The Administrator account is a known account that has extensive privileges on your Web server. Malicious users often target this account in an attempt to take control of the server. You can deter malicious users by changing the name of this account. Simply select a new name for the account and then rename it using Active Directory Users and Computers. You may want to tell other administrators in your company the new name for the administrator account.

Disabling the Default Web Site

The default Web site shouldn't be used in production environments. The site has many preconfigured applications that use system resources and allow execution of the related scripts and executables. The site also automatically allows remote administration through a directory that is well known to malicious users. All of these issues can pose a security risk to your server.

To disable the default Web site, follow these steps:

1. In the Internet Information Services snap-in, right-click the default Web site, and then select Stop.
2. Exit the IIS snap-in to save this configuration state.
3. From now on, the default Web site should be stopped when you or other administrators access the Internet Information Services snap-in.

Note You can also delete the default Web site to prevent its use in the future.

Disabling Remote Administration from the Web

As you know from previous discussions, Web sites can be managed remotely through a browser. Operators connect to individual sites through the IISAdmin directory. Administrators connect to IIS through the Administration Web site. If you want to tightly control access to your server, you should disable remote administration from the Web and only allow access to the server through the IIS snap-in.

To disable remote administration from the Web, you should:

1. Stop the Administration Web site.
2. Delete the administration directory (normally named IISAdmin) or set the Execute permissions for this directory to None.

Disabling Directory Browsing

Directory browsing allows users to see the contents of directories. Most users don't need to see directory contents, so you should disable directory browsing globally. To do this, clear this Web server permission in the Master WWW Service Properties dialog box.

Creating Legal Notices

Every user who logs on to the Web server locally or through a telnet session should see a legal notice that tells the user this is a private computer system and its use is restricted to authorized personnel only. Legal notices have a caption and message text. You set the caption using the Registry key:

```
HKEY_LOCAL_MACHINE
  \Software
  \Microsoft
  \Windows
  \CurrentVersion
  \Policies
  \System
  \LegalNoticeCaption
```

You set the message text using the Registry key:

```
HKEY_LOCAL_MACHINE
  \Software
  \Microsoft
  \Windows
  \CurrentVersion
  \Policies
  \System
  \LegalNoticeText
```

Both keys can be created and modified using Registry Editor or a Windows script. If you create these keys, be sure to set the value type to REG_SZ. The REG_SZ value type is used to identify a string value type that contains a sequence of characters. When you set the key value, type a 1, followed by a comma, followed by the caption or message text, such as:

```
1,This is a private system. Use of this system is restricted to
authorized personnel only.
```

Applying Service Packs, Hot Fixes, and Templates

Microsoft regularly provides service packs and hot fixes for the Windows operating system. To maintain the security of the server, you should apply the service packs and hot fixes to production servers as soon as you've had a chance to review and test these updates on similarly configured test servers.

Microsoft also publishes security templates that can be applied to your Web servers. Security templates are available in all Windows 2000 server installations. You can preview existing templates and create your own templates using the Security Templates snap-in. You apply a template and analyze its security constraints using the Security Configuration And Analysis snap-in. These snap-ins can be accessed by completing the following steps:

1. Open the Run dialog box by clicking Start and then clicking Run.

2. Type **MMC** in the Open field and then click OK. This opens the Microsoft Management Console (MMC).

3. In MMC, click Console, and then click Add/Remove Snap-In. This opens the Add/Remove Snap-In dialog box.

4. On the Standalone tab, click Add.

5. In the Add Snap-In dialog box, click Security Templates, and then click Add.

6. Next, click Security Configuration And Analysis, and then click Add.

7. Close the Add Standalone Snap-In dialog box by clicking Close, and then click OK.

The security templates that you'll want to use are securews and hisecws. Securews is a template for Web servers that need strong security. Hisecws is a template for Web servers that need very strong security. As shown in Figure 5-14, these templates configure security for the following:

• Password, account lockout, and Kerberos policies

• Auditing, user rights assignment, and security options policies

• Event logs, system services, and file system permissions

• Registry keys for the local machine and the current user

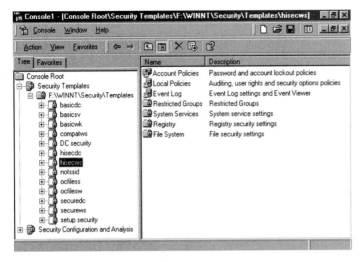

Figure 5-14. *Use the Security Templates snap-in to access existing security templates and to create new ones.*

After you select the template that you want to use, you should go through each setting that the template will apply and evaluate how the setting will affect your environment. If a setting doesn't make sense, you should modify or delete it as appropriate. When you are ready to configure and analyze the settings, complete the following steps:

1. Access the Security Configuration And Analysis snap-in in an MMC.

2. Right-click the Security Configuration And Analysis node and then select Open Database. This displays the Open Database dialog box.

3. Type a new database name in the File Name field and then click Open.

4. The Import Template dialog box is displayed next. Select the security template that you want to use and then click Open.

5. Right-click the Security Configuration And Analysis node, and then choose Analyze Computer Now. When prompted to set the error log path, click OK. The default path should be just fine.

6. Wait for the snap-in to complete the analysis of the template. Afterward, review the findings, and update the template as necessary. You can view the error log by right-clicking the Security Configuration And Analysis node and choosing View Log file.

7. When you are ready to apply the template, right-click the Security Configuration And Analysis node and choose Configure Computer Now. When prompted to set the error log path, click OK. The default path should be just fine.

8. View the configuration error log by right-clicking the Security Configuration And Analysis node and choosing View Log file. Note any problems and act as necessary.

Removing the IISADMPWD Virtual Directory

The IISADMPWD virtual directory allows you to reset Windows NT and Windows 2000 passwords. It was designed for intranets and is not installed as part of an IIS 5.0 or later installation. However, if you upgraded from IIS 4.0, this directory is not removed and it may still be available on your server. If the Web server is accessible to the Internet, you should delete this directory.

Checking for Malicious Input in Forms and Query Strings

The text that users type into forms may contain values designed to cause problems on your system. If you pass this input directly to a script or ASP page, you may allow a malicious user to gain access to the system and cause problems. To prevent this, you should check all input before passing it to a script or ASP page.

One way to ensure that input contains only text and numbers is to remove characters that aren't alphanumeric. You can do this with the following Microsoft Visual Basic Scripting Edition (VBScript) example:

```
'Start a regular expression
Set reg = New RegExp

'Check for characters that aren't 0-9a-zA-Z or '_'
reg.Pattern = "\W+"

'Remove invalid characters from input string
goodString = reg.Replace(inputString, "")
```

If you want users to be able to enter punctuation but do not want to permit possible malicious input, you should check for and remove the pipe character (|). The pipe character is used to string commands together, which could allow a user to execute a command on your server. The following command removes the pipe character and all text that follows it from an input string:

```
'Start a regular expression
Set reg = New RegExp

'Check for the pipe character
reg.Pattern = "^(.+)\|(.+)"

'Remove pipe character and any text after it
goodString = reg.Replace(inputString, "$1")
```

Many other techniques for checking user input before using it are available. Check the Microsoft TechNet at *http://www.microsoft.com/technet/* for more information.

Removing Unused Application Mappings

Application mappings are used to specify the ISAPI extensions and CGI programs that are available to applications. IIS is preconfigured to support many common ISAPI applications including ASPs, Internet Database Connector, and Index Server. If your Web site doesn't use some of these ISAPI applications, you can enhance security by removing the associated application mappings. Mappings that you may want to remove are the following:

- .htr, which is used for Web-based password reset
- .htw, .ida, and .idq, which are used by Index Server
- .idc, which is used for the Internet Database Connector
- .printer, which is used for Internet Printing
- .stm, .shtm, and .shtml, which are used for server-side includes

To remove application mappings globally for all Web sites on a server, follow these steps:

1. In the Internet Information Services snap-in, right-click the icon for the computer you want to work with, and then select Properties. This displays a Properties dialog box.

2. Select WWW Service on the Master Properties selection list and then click Edit. This opens the WWW Service Master Properties dialog box for the computer.

3. Select the Home Directory tab and then click Configuration on the Application Settings panel. This displays the Application Configuration dialog box.

4. On the App Mappings tab, select the application mappings that you want to remove, and then click Remove. When prompted to confirm the action, click Yes.

5. Click Apply. Before applying any changes, IIS checks the existing settings for all Web sites and directories within Web sites. Each time a site or directory node uses a different value, an Inheritance Overrides dialog box is displayed. Use this dialog box to select the site and directory nodes that should use the revised application mappings, and then click OK.

Chapter 6

Managing Microsoft Certificate Services and SSL

The focus of the previous chapter was on Web server security. This chapter shows how you can extend Web server security using Microsoft Certificate Services and Secure Sockets Layer (SSL). Certificate Services and SSL provide an extra layer of security that you can add to your Web server.

You use Certificate Services and SSL to protect sensitive information, such as passwords, credit card numbers, or payment information. Certificate Services and SSL protect sensitive information by encrypting the data sent between client browsers and your server. Encryption is the process of encoding information using a mathematical algorithm that makes it difficult for anyone other than the intended recipient to view the original information.

Internet Information Services (IIS) transfers encrypted data to a client browser using the SSL protocol. With SSL, servers and/or clients use certificates to provide proof of identity prior to establishing a secure connection. Once a connection is established, clients and servers use the secure SSL channel to transfer information. This information is encrypted using a technique that the clients and servers can interpret to extract the original information.

Understanding SSL

IIS supports SSL version 3.0. SSL 3.0 enables encrypted data transfers between client browsers and Web servers. The sections that follow provide an overview on how SSL works and how it is used.

Using SSL Encryption

As stated previously, encryption is the process of encoding information using a mathematical algorithm that makes it difficult for anyone other than the intended recipient to view the original information. The encryption algorithm uses a mathematical value, called a key, to scramble the data so that it can be recovered only by using the key.

Many techniques are available for encrypting information so that it can be exchanged. Some encryption techniques use a combination of public and private keys—one key can be shared and the other key can't be shared. Some encryption techniques use shared secret keys that are transferred between authenticated systems. SSL uses a technique called public key encryption, which combines private, public, and shared secret (session) keys.

In public key encryption, there are three keys:

* A public key available to any application that requests it
* A private key known only to its owner
* A session key created using public and private key data

IIS uses the public key encryption component in SSL to establish sessions between clients and servers. You should use SSL anytime you want to provide additional protection for data that is transferred between clients and servers. Some specific instances in which you may want to use Certificate Services and SSL are the following:

* When you remotely manage the Web server using the Administration Web site or operator administration pages
* When your World Wide Web site has secure areas that contain sensitive company documents
* When your Web site has pages that collect sensitive personal or financial information from visitors
* When your Web site processes orders for goods or services and you collect credit information from customers

With SSL, users connect to Web pages using a secure Uniform Resource Locator (URL) that begins with *https://*. The *https* designator tells the browser to try to establish a secure connection with IIS. SSL connections for Web pages are made on port 443 by default, but you can change the port designator as necessary. As you set out to work with SSL, keep in mind that you cannot use host headers with SSL. With SSL, Hypertext Transfer Protocol (HTTP) requests are encrypted, and the host header name within the encrypted request cannot be used to determine the correct site to which a request must be routed.

After the client browser contacts the server using a secure URL, the server sends the browser its public key and server certificate. Next the client and server negotiate the level of encryption to use for the secure communications. The server will always attempt to use the highest level of encryption it supports. Once the encryption level is established, the client browser creates a session key and uses the server's public key to encrypt this information for transmission. Anyone intercepting the message at this point would not be able to read the session key—only the server's private key can decrypt the message.

The IIS server decrypts the message sent by the client using its private key. The SSL session between the client and the server is now established. The session key can be used to encrypt and decrypt data transmitted between the client and server.

To recap, secure SSL sessions are established using the following technique:

1. The user's Web browser contacts the server using a secure URL.

2. The IIS server sends the browser its public key and server certificate.

3. The client and server negotiate the level of encryption to use for the secure communications.

4. The client browser encrypts a session key with the server's public key and sends the encrypted data back to the server.

5. The IIS Server decrypts the message sent by the client using its private key, and the session is established.

6. Both the client and the server use the session key to encrypt and decrypt transmitted data.

Using SSL Certificates

Not reflected in the previous discussion is the way in which SSL uses certificates. You can think of a certificate as an identity card that contains information needed to establish the identity of an application or user over a network. Certificates enable Web servers and users to authenticate one another before establishing a connection. Certificates also contain keys that need to establish SSL sessions between clients and servers.

In most cases, certificates used by IIS, Web browsers, and Certificate Services conform to the X.509 standard. For this reason, they are often referred to as X.509 certificates. Different versions of the X.509 standard have been issued. These versions have been extended from time to time as well. Two types of X.509 certificates are used:

- Client certificates, which contain identifying information about a client

- Server certificates, which contain identifying information about a server

Certificate authorities (CAs) issue both types of certificates. A CA is a trusted agency responsible for confirming the identity of users, organizations, and their servers and then issuing certificates that confirm these identities. Before issuing a client certificate, CAs require you to provide information that identifies you, your organization, and the client application you are using. Before issuing a server certificate, CAs require you to provide information that identifies your organization and the server you are using.

This chapter focuses on server certificates. You have several options when choosing CAs to create your server certificates. If you use Certificate Services, your organization can act as its own CA. When you act as your own CA, you enable SSL on your Web server using the following process:

1. Install Certificate Services on a server in the domain and then generate the root CA certificate.

2. Generate a certificate request file for each Web site on your server that has a unique name, and then use the certificate request files to create server certificates for your Web sites.

3. Install the certificates and then enable SSL on each applicable Web site.

4. Your root CA certificate won't be recognized and trusted by client browsers. To get browsers to trust the root CA, the user must install the certificate in the browser's authorities store.

5. Initiate SSL connections by using URLs that begin with *https://*.

You can also use third-party CAs—and there's an advantage here. The third-party authority can vouch for your identity, and dozens of vendors are already configured as trusted CAs in Web browsers. In Microsoft Internet Explorer 5.0, you can obtain a list of trusted authorities by completing the following steps:

1. From the Tools menu, select Internet Options. This displays the Internet Options dialog box.

2. Click the Content tab and then click Certificates. This displays the Certificates dialog box.

3. Click the Trusted Root Certification Authorities tab. You should now see a list of trusted root CAs.

When you use a trusted third-party authority, you enable SSL on your Web server using a different process from when you act as your own root CA. This process is as follows:

1. Generate a certificate request file for each Web site on your server that has a unique name.

2. Submit the certificate request files to a trusted third-party authority, such as Entrust, Equifax, Valicert, or Verisign. The CA will process the requests and send you back certificates.

3. Install the certificates and then enable SSL on each applicable Web site.

4. Client browsers initiate SSL sessions using a secure URL beginning with *https://*.

Regardless of whether you act as your own CA or use a trusted CA, you must still manage the server certificates, and you use Certificate Services to do this. Server certificates can expire or be revoked, if necessary. For example, if your organization is an Internet service provider (ISP) that issues its own certificates, you may want your customers' server certificates to expire on an annual basis. This forces customers to update their certificate information at least once per year to ensure it is current. You may also want to revoke a certificate when a customer cancels service.

Understanding SSL Encryption Strength

The encryption strength of an SSL session is directly proportional to the number of bits in the session key. This means that session keys with a greater number of bits are considerably more difficult to crack and, thus, are more secure.

The two most commonly used encryption levels for SSL sessions are 40-bit and 128-bit. Encryption at the 40-bit level is adequate for most needs, including e-commerce. Encryption at the 128-bit level provides added protection for sensitive personal and financial information. Versions of Microsoft Windows 2000 shipped in the United States are configured with 128-bit encryption. Export versions of Windows 2000 have 40-bit encryption. To upgrade a server from 40-bit encryption to 128-bit encryption, you must install the 128-bit upgrade patch, which is available from Microsoft.

Don't confuse the encryption level for SSL sessions (the strength of the session key expressed as bits) with the encryption level for SSL certificates (the strength of the certificate's public and private keys expressed as bits). Most encryption keys (public and private) have a bit length of 512 or 1024. Domestic U.S. and export versions of most applications and operating systems support encryption keys with a bit length of 512. However, encryption keys with a bit length of 1024 or greater are not supported in the export versions of most applications and operating systems.

When a user attempts to establish an SSL session with your Web server, the user's browser and the server use the bit length of their encryption keys to determine the strongest level of encryption possible. If the encryption keys use 512 bits, the level of encryption is set to 40 bits. If the encryption keys use 1024 bits, the level of encryption is set to 128 bits. Other key bit lengths and encryption levels are available.

Working with Microsoft Certificate Services

Microsoft Certificate Services allows you to issue and revoke digital certificates. These certificates can be used to enable SSL sessions and to authenticate the identity of your intranet, extranet, or Internet Web site.

Understanding Certificate Services

Certificate Services is a Windows service that runs on a designated certificate server. Certificate servers can be configured as one of four types of certification authorities:

- **Enterprise root CA**   An enterprise root CA is the certificate server at the root of the hierarchy for a Windows domain. It is the most trusted CA in the enterprise and must have access to Active Directory service.

- **Enterprise subordinate CA**   An enterprise subordinate CA is a certificate server that will be a member of an existing CA hierarchy. It can issue certificates but must obtain its own CA certificate from the enterprise root CA.

- **Stand-alone root CA**   A stand-alone root CA is the certificate server at the root of a nonenterprise hierarchy. It is the most trusted CA in its hierarchy and doesn't need access to Active Directory service.

- **Stand-alone subordinate CA**   A stand-alone subordinate CA is a certificate server that will be a member of an existing nonenterprise hierarchy. It can issue certificates but must obtain its own CA certificate from the stand-alone root CA in its hierarchy.

Certificate servers don't have to be dedicated to Certificate Services and can be the same servers you use for Web publishing. However, it is a good idea to designate specific servers in your domain that will act as certificate servers and to use these servers only for that purpose. Once you install Certificate Services on a computer, you are limited in what you can and cannot do with the computer. Specifically, you cannot do the following:

- You cannot rename a computer running Certificate Services.

- You cannot change the domain membership of a computer running Certificate Services.

Certificate Services is managed using a Microsoft Management Console snap-in called Certification Authority snap-in, and a Web-based Active Server Page (ASP) application that can be accessed in a standard Web browser. In the snap-in, you have full control over Certificate Services. The Web-based application, on the other hand, is primarily used to retrieve certificate revocation lists (CRLs), to request certificates, and to check on pending certificates.

Figure 6-1 shows the main window of the Certification Authority snap-in. As you can see, there are four nodes under the root authority. These nodes are used as follows:

- **Revoked Certificates**   Contains all certificates that have been issued and then revoked.

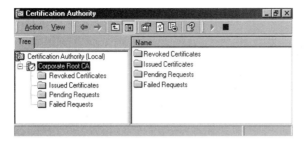

Figure 6-1. *Use the Certification Authority snap-in to manage Certificate Services.*

- **Issued Certificates** Contains all certificates that have been approved and issued by the Certificate Services administrator.

- **Pending Requests** Contains all pending certificate requests for this CA. If you are an administrator on the certificate server, you can approve requests by right-clicking them and selecting Issue.

- **Failed Requests** Contains any declined certificate requests for this CA. If you are an administrator on the certificate server, you can deny requests by right-clicking them and selecting Deny.

Note The label for the root node of the snap-in is set to the name of the CA. In the example, the CA name is Corporate Root CA.

Installing Certificate Services

Installing Certificate Services is a multipart process. First, you must create a folder that Certificate Services can use to store certificates and configuration files. The folder must be stored on the local machine where Certificate Services will be installed. The folder must also be configured with Read permission for the implicit group Everyone. This allows users to access the folder and to install certificates from it. Second, if the server isn't running IIS and you want to be able to retrieve CRLs to request certificates or to check on pending certificates via a browser, you must install IIS on the certificate server.

After you create the certificate folder and install IIS, if necessary, you need to install Certificate Services. To do this, complete the following steps:

1. Log on to the certificate server using an account with Administrator privileges, or Domain Administrator privileges if you're creating an enterprise CA.

2. Click Start, point to Settings, and then click Control Panel.

3. Double-click Add/Remove Programs. This displays the Add/Remove Programs dialog box.

4. Start the Windows Components Wizard by clicking Add/Remove Windows Components.

5. Select the Certificate Services check box. When prompted to confirm the action, click Yes, and then click Next.

6. As shown in Figure 6-2, select the CA type. The options are as follows:

   - **Enterprise Root CA** Establishes the root CA in an Active Directory domain. This option is only available if your server participates in a domain.

   - **Enterprise Subordinate CA** Establishes a subordinate CA that will be a member of an existing hierarchy. This option also requires connectivity to Active Directory service.

   - **Stand-Alone Root CA** Establishes a stand-alone root CA that doesn't require connectivity to Active Directory service.

   - **Stand-Alone Subordinate CA** Establishes a subordinate CA that will be a member of an existing hierarchy. The server doesn't require connectivity to Active Directory service.

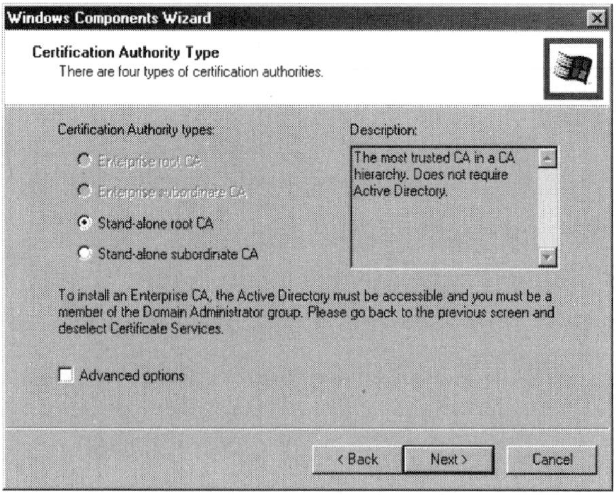

Figure 6-2. *Choose the type of CA that you want to install.*

Note Select Advanced Options if you want to choose the cryptographic service provider and hashing algorithms used to generate keys. In most cases, however, the default values are acceptable.

7. Next, as shown in Figure 6-3, enter information to identify the CA and to set the expiration date of the root CA certificate. Provide complete entries for the following fields:

   - **CA Name** Sets the name of the CA, such as Microsoft Corporation Root CA.

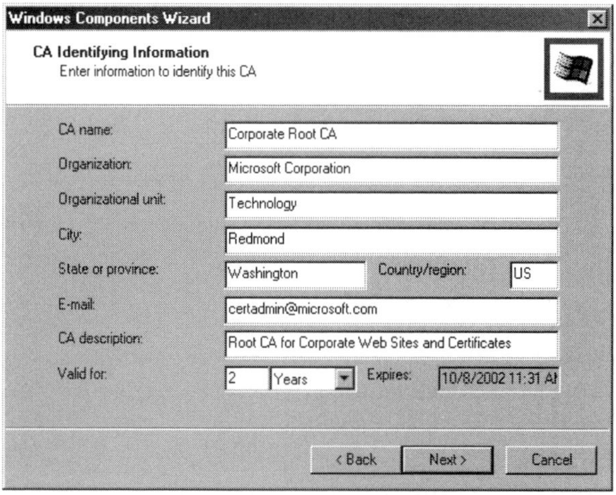

Figure 6-3. *Identify the certification authority and set an expiration date for the root CA certificate.*

- **Organization**   Sets the legal name of your company, such as Microsoft Corporation.

- **Organizational Unit**   Sets the division in your company responsible for the CA, such as Technology Department.

- **City**   Sets the city or locality in which your company is located.

- **State Or Province**   Sets the name of the state or province in which your company is located.

- **Country/Region**   Sets the country or region for your company.

- **E-Mail**   Sets the e-mail address for the certificate administrator.

- **CA Description**   Sets a description for the CA.

- **Valid For**   Sets the root CA's certificate expiration date and time. This certificate is generated when you install the CA.

8. Next, specify the storage location for the configuration data, database, and log. By default, the certificate database and log are stored in the \%SystemRoot%\System32\CertLog folder. Also, use the Shared Folder field to specify the location of the certificate folder you created earlier, or click Browse to find this folder.

9. Click Next. If IIS is running on the certificate server, Windows will need to shut down the related services before continuing. Click OK when prompted to do this. The Windows Components Wizard will begin installing and configuring Certificate Services.

10. Click Finish to complete the process. If you installed Certificate Services on a computer running IIS, you can configure these services for Web access (see the section of this chapter titled, "Accessing Certificate Services in a Browser").

Accessing Certificate Services in a Browser

When you install Certificate Services on a computer running IIS, the default (or primary) Web site is updated so that you can perform key certificate tasks via a Web browser. These tasks include

- Retrieving CRLs
- Requesting certificates
- Checking on pending certificates

The structures that make Web-based requests possible are files configured for use in three virtual directories:

- **CertSrv** Contains files necessary for Web-based access to Certificate Services and is located in \%SystemRoot%\System32\CertSrv by default. This directory is set up as an in-process Internet Server Application Programming Interface (ISAPI) application called CertSrv.

- **CertControl** Contains files necessary for controlling Certificate Services and is located in \%SystemRoot%\System32\CertSrv\CertControl by default.

- **CertEnroll** Contains files necessary for controlling Certificate Services and is located in \%SystemRoot%\System32\CertSrv\CertEnroll by default.

If these directories are not available for some reason, you can create virtual directories that map aliases to their physical locations. You do this by completing the following steps:

1. Start the Internet Information Services snap-in and then, in the left panel (Console Root), click the plus sign (+) next to the computer you want to work with. If the computer isn't shown, connect to it as discussed in the "Connecting To Other Servers" section of Chapter 2, "Core IIS Administration."

2. Right-click the Web site on which you want to link the system directory, point to New, and then select Virtual Directory. This starts the Virtual Directory Creation Wizard. Click Next.

3. In the Alias field, type the name you want to use to access the system directory, such as CertSrv.

4. The next dialog box lets you set the path to the physical directory where your content is stored. Click Browse to search for the system directory you want to use.

5. Click Next and then set access and execute permissions. For CertSrv, CertControl, and CertEnroll, select Read, and then select Scripts Only.

6. Click Next and then click Finish. The virtual directory is created and mapped to the system directory you referenced. The CertSrv directory should be configured as an ISAPI application with a starting point that points to its base directory. CertControl and CertEnroll should be a part of an application as well, but these don't need to be configured as separate applications.

Once you've configured Web-based access to Certificate Services, you can access these services by typing the following URL:

http://hostname/certsrv/

where *host name* is the DNS or NetBIOS name of the host server, such as ca.microsoft.com or CASrv. Figure 6-4 shows the main page for Certificate Services.

Figure 6-4. *Use the Web-based interface to retrieve CA certificates or revocation lists, to request certificates, or to check on pending certificates.*

Starting and Stopping Certificate Services

Microsoft Certificate Services runs as a Windows service on the certificate server. You can stop and start this service on a local system by completing the following steps:

1. Start the Certification Authority snap-in, then right-click the root node for the CA (Root CA) and point to All Tasks.

2. Select Stop Service to stop Certificate Services.

3. Select Start Service to start Certificate Services.

You can stop and start services on a remote system by completing the following steps:

1. Start the Certification Authority snap-in and then right-click the CA node.

2. To display the Certification Authority dialog box, from the shortcut menu, select Retarget Certification Authority.

3. As shown in Figure 6-5, select Another Computer, type the name of the computer to which you want to connect, and then click Finish. You can also type the server's Internet Protocol (IP) address or fully qualified domain name (FQDN).

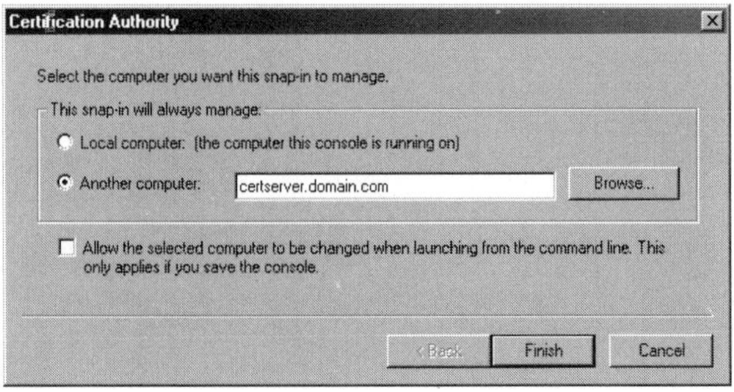

Figure 6-5. *You can connect to both local and remote certification authorities.*

4. In the Certification Authority snap-in, right-click the root node for the CA (Root CA), then point to All Tasks.

5. Select Stop Service to stop Certificate Services.

6. Select Start Service to start Certificate Services.

Backing Up and Restoring the CA

If your organization publishes its own CA, you should routinely back up the CA information. Backing up the CA information ensures that you can recover critical CA data, including

- CA private key and certificate
- CA configuration information
- CA log and pending request queue

You can perform two types of backups:

- **Standard** Creates a full copy of certificate logs and pending request queues.
- **Incremental** Creates a partial copy of certificate logs and pending request queues. This copy contains only the changes since the last standard backup.

In a very large CA implementation, you can perform incremental backups of logs and queues by selecting Perform Incremental Backups. To use incremental backups, you must do the following:

1. First perform a standard backup.

2. Perform successive incremental backups at later dates.

When you use incremental backups, you must also incrementally restore. To do this, complete the following steps:

1. Stop Certificate Services.

2. Restore the last standard backup.

3. Restore each incremental backup in order.

4. Start Certificate Services.

Creating CA Backups

To back up the CA information on your certificate server, complete the following steps:

1. Create a folder that Certificate Services can use to store the backup information. This directory must be empty and it should created on the local machine where Certificate Services is installed.

2. Start the Certification Authority snap-in, right-click the root node for the CA (Root CA), point to All Tasks, and then select Backup CA. This starts the Certification Authority Backup Wizard.

Note Certificate Services must be running when you back up the CA. If the service isn't running, you'll see a prompt asking you if you want to start the service. Click OK.

3. Click Next and then select the items you want to back up, as shown in Figure 6-6. The options are

    - Private Key And CA Certificate
    - Configuration Information
    - Issued Certificate Log And Pending Certificate Request Queue

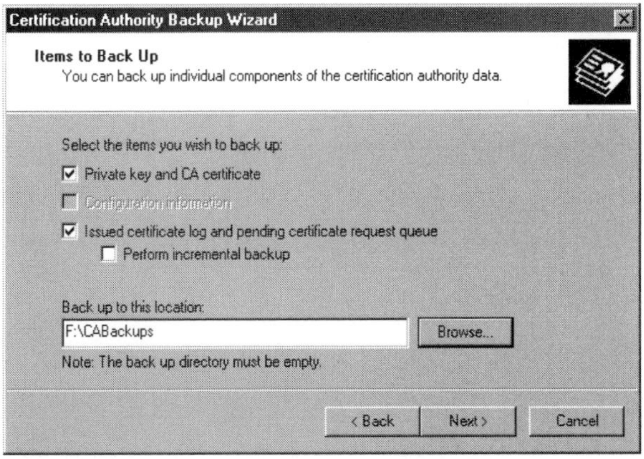

Figure 6-6. *Specify the certification items that you want to back up.*

4. If this is an incremental backup, select Perform Incremental Backup.

5. Type the file path to the backup folder in the Back Up To This Location field, or click Browse to search for this folder. If you specify a folder that does not already exist, you will be given the option of having it created.

6. Click Next. Type and then confirm a password that will be used to protect the private key and CA certificate files.

7. Click Next and then click Finish. The wizard creates a backup of the selected data.

Recovering CA Information

If you ever need to recover the CA information, you can do this by completing the following steps:

1. The Certificate Services cannot be running when you restore the CA. In the Certification Authority snap-in, right-click the root node for the CA (Root CA), point to All Tasks, and then select Stop Service.

2. Right-click the root node a second time, point to All Tasks, and then select Restore CA. This starts the Certification Authority Restore Wizard.

3. Click Next and then select the items you want to restore, as shown in Figure 6-7. The options are

   * Private Key And CA Certificate
   * Configuration Information
   * Issued Certificate Log And Pending Certificate Request Queue

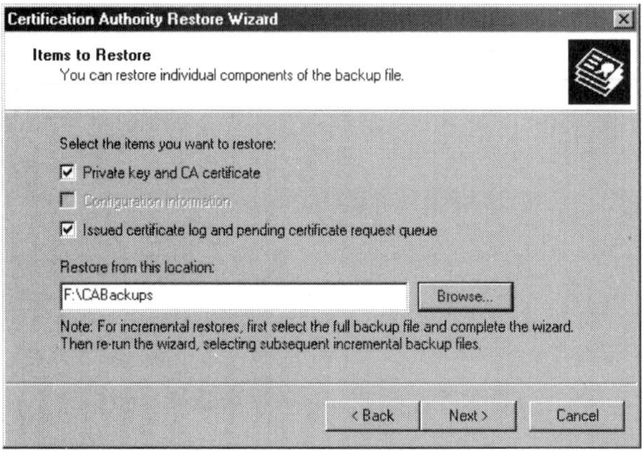

Figure 6-7. *Specify the certification items that you want to restore from a backup.*

4. Type the file path to the backup folder in the Restore From This Location field, or click Browse to search for this folder. You should always restore the last complete backup before restoring any incremental backups.

5. Click Next. Type the password used to protect the CA files and then click Next again.

6. Click Finish. The wizard restores the selected data. When the operation is complete, you have the option of starting Certificate Services. Click Yes if this is only a backup to restore. Otherwise, click No, and repeat this process to apply incremental backups as well.

Approving and Declining
Pending Certificate Requests

Pending certificate requests are displayed in the Pending Requests node of the Certification Authority snap-in.

You can approve pending requests as follows:

1. Start the Certification Authority snap-in and then select the Pending Requests node. You should see a list of pending requests.

2. Right-click the request that you want to approve, point to All Tasks, and then select Issue.

3. Certificate Services generates a certificate based on the request and places this certificate in the Issued Certificates queue.

4. Certificates are valid for one year. After this period, they must be renewed.

You can decline pending certificate requests as follows:

1. Start the Certification Authority snap-in and then select the Pending Requests node. You should see a list of pending requests.

2. Right-click the request that you want to decline, point to All Tasks, and then select Deny.

3. When prompted to confirm the action, select Yes.

4. Denied requests are moved to the Failed Requests queue and cannot be restored. The user must resubmit a new request.

Generating Certificates Manually
in the Certification Authority Snap-In

Once you've issued a certificate, you can manually create the certificate file that you need to install on the Web site. To do this, complete the following steps:

1. Start the Certification Authority snap-in and then select the Issued Certificates node. You should see a list of certificates issued by this root CA.

2. Right-click the certificate that you want to generate and select Open. This displays the Certificates dialog box.

3. Select the Details tab and then select Copy To File. This starts the Certificate Export Wizard. Click Next.

4. Select the Base-64 Encoded X.509 export file format, and then click Next.

5. Specify the name of the file you want to export. Be sure to use .cer as the file extension. Click Browse if you want to use the Save As dialog box to set the file location and name.

6. Click Next and then click Finish. Click OK after the Certificate Export Wizard confirms that the certificate was successfully exported. You can now install the certificate file on the Web site as described in the section of this chapter titled "Processing Pending Requests and Installing Site Certificates."

Revoking Certificates

Server certificates are valid for one year and can be revoked if necessary. Typically, you revoke a certificate when there is a change in the status of the site or when the customer for whom you issued the certificate cancels the service subscription. To revoke a certificate, complete the following steps:

1. Start the Certification Authority snap-in and then select the Issued Certificates node. You should see a list of issued certificates.

2. Right-click the certificate that you want to revoke, point to All Tasks, and then select Revoke Certificate. The Certificate Revocation dialog box is displayed.

3. As shown in Figure 6-8, use the Reason Code to specify a reason for the revocation, and then click Yes.

4. The CA marks the certificate as revoked and moves it to the Revoked Certificates node.

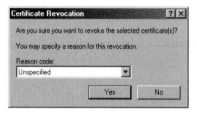

Figure 6-8. *Specify the reason you are revoking the certificate.*

By default, CAs publish CRLs weekly. You can change this setting through the Revoked Certificates Properties dialog box.

1. Start the Certification Authority snap-in and then right-click the Revoked Certificates node.

2. Select Properties and then use the Publication Interval fields to set a new interval for publishing the CRL, as shown in Figure 6-9.

3. Click OK.

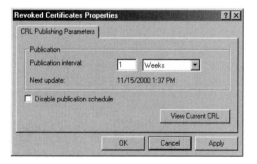

Figure 6-9. *Set the schedule for publishing the CRL. By default, the publication interval is one week.*

Reviewing and Renewing the Root CA Certificate

The root CA certificate is valid for the period specified when the certificate was created. To view the expiration date or to review the certificate properties, complete the following steps:

1. Start the Certification Authority snap-in. Right-click the root node for the CA (Root CA) and then select Properties. This displays the Root CA Properties dialog box.

2. Click View Certificate on the General tab.

3. As shown in Figure 6-10, use the Certificate dialog box to review the properties of the root CA certificate, including the valid from and to dates.

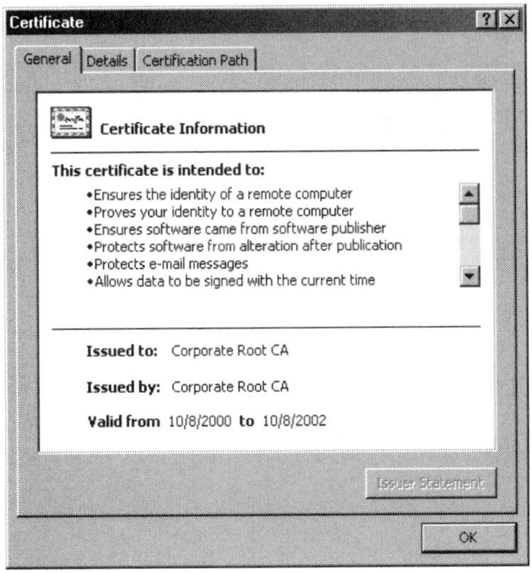

Figure 6-10. *The Certificate dialog box shows the properties of the root CA certificate, including the valid from and to dates.*

Usually, the root CA certificate is valid for two years. If you are approaching the end of the two-year period, you should renew the certificate. You should also renew the root CA certificate if one of the following situations exists:

• The signing key is compromised

• A program requires a new signing key to be used with a new certificate

• The current CRL is too big and you want to move some of the information to a new CRL

To renew the root CA certificate, complete the following steps:

1. The Certificate services cannot be running when you renew the CA. In the Certification Authority snap-in, right-click the root node for the CA (Root CA), point to All Tasks, and then select Stop Service.

2. Right-click the root node for the CA (Root CA) again, point to All Tasks, and then select Renew CA Certificate. This displays the Renew CA Certificate dialog box shown in Figure 6-11.

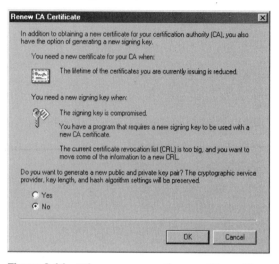

Figure 6-11. *When you renew the root CA certificate, you can generate new public and private keys. Do this if the key has been compromised or a new key is required.*

3. In the Renew CA Certificate dialog box, select Yes if you want to generate a new public and private key pair. Otherwise, click No.

4. Click OK. Certificate Services is restarted automatically and a new certificate is issued.

Creating and Installing Certificates

You have two options for creating and installing certificates. You can use your own Certificate Services to generate your certificates or you can use a trusted third-party authority. When you use Certificate Services, you manage the certificate creation, expiration, and revocation process. When you create certificates through trusted third-party authorities, you let the trusted authority manage the certificate creation, expiration, and revocation process. Either way, the basic tasks you need to perform, create, and install a certificate are as follows:

1. Create a certificate request.

2. Submit the request to the authority of your choice or to your own root authority.

3. When you receive the response from the authority, process the pending request and install the certificate.

4. Ensure that SSL is enabled and that secure communications are configured properly.

Creating Certificate Requests

Each Web site hosted on your Web server needs a separate certificate if you want SSL to work properly. The first step in the certificate creation process is to generate a certificate request. You can generate a certificate request by completing the following steps:

1. In the Internet Information Services snap-in, right-click the site for which you want to generate the certificate and select Properties.

2. From the Directory Security tab, select Server Certificate. This starts the Web Server Certificate Wizard. Click Next.

Note If you or someone else has already generated a certificate request for the site, you'll see the Pending Certificate Request dialog box, shown in Figure 6-17. You must either process the request or delete the request to continue. See the sections of this chapter titled "Processing Pending Requests and Installing Site Certificates" and "Approving and Declining Pending Certificate Requests" for more information.

3. As shown in Figure 6-12, select Create A New Certificate, and then click Next.

Figure 6-12. *To create a certificate, select Create A New Certificate.*

4. Select Prepare The Request Now to prepare a request and manually submit it to an authority, and then click Next.

5. Next, as shown in Figure 6-13, you must assign the certificate a name and select a bit length. The name should be descriptive and easy to refer to. The bit length sets the encryption strength of your public and private keys. In most cases, you should choose the highest bit length you are allowed to use.

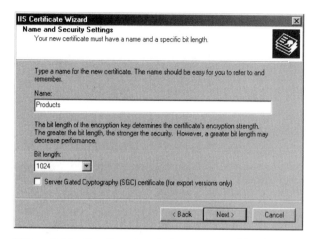

Figure 6-13. *Specify a descriptive name and bit length for the certificate.*

Tip If you are outside the United States, you might want to generate a Server Gated Cryptography certificate. If so, select the Server Gated Cryptography (SGC) Certificate check box. Selecting this option does not mean that you'll get issued an SGC certificate automatically. You'll still have to go through an SGC verification process with the trusted authority.

Caution A high level of encryption might slow down a CPU-intensive application when it is running over SSL. If you use SSL with ASP applications extensively and your Web server demonstrates high CPU utilization, you may want to experiment with different levels of encryption and determine where the acceptable levels of performance are achieved.

6. Click Next. You have now created a public and private key pair. These keys are stored locally on the Web server. The final steps are used to create a certificate-signing request (CSR). The information in the request identifies the owner of the key and is displayed on your certificate. The CSR is used only to request the certificate. Certain characters must be excluded from your CSR fields, or your certificate may not work. Do not use any of the following characters:

! @ # $ % ^ * ( ) ~ ? > < & / \

7. Enter your organization information in the fields provided:

- **Organization** Sets the legal name of your company, such as Microsoft Corporation
- **Organizational Unit** Sets the division in your company responsible for the certificate, such as Technology Department

Note Third-party authorities will use the organization name, the site's common name, and the geographical information you supply to validate your request for a certificate. If you don't enter this information correctly, you won't be issued a certificate.

8. Click Next, and enter your Web site's common name. When the certificate will be used on an intranet (or internal network), the common name may be one word, and it can also be the NetBIOS name of the server, such as CorpIntranet. When the certificate will be used on the Internet, the common name must be a valid DNS name, such as www.domain.com. Click Next.

Real World The common name is typically composed of Host + Domain Name, such as www.domain.com or products.domain.com. Certificates are specific to the common name that they have been issued to at the Host level. The common name must be the same as the Web address you will be accessing when connecting to a secure site. For example, a certificate for the domain domain.com will receive a warning if accessing a site named www.domain.com or services.domain.com, as www.domain.com and services.domain.com are different from domain.com. You would need to create a certificate for the correct common name.

9. As shown in Figure 6-14, enter the geographic information for your company in the fields provided, and then click Next:

   - **Country/Region** Type the country or region for your company.
   - **State/Province** Type the full name of the state or province in which your company is located.
   - **City/Locality** Type the city or locality in which your company is located.

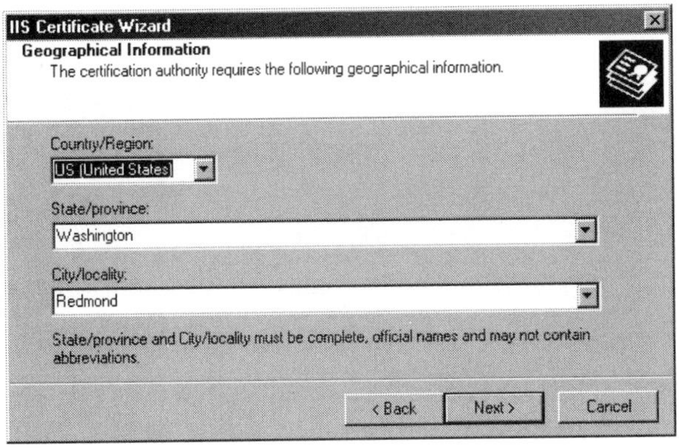

Figure 6-14. *Type complete entries for geographic information. Don't use abbreviations for state, province, city, or locality.*

Caution Do not use abbreviations. Some authorities won't accept abbreviated geographic information and you'll have to resubmit your request.

10. Next, you need to specify the filename and path for the certificate request file. By default, the filename and path are set to C:\CERTREQ.TXT. Type a new path, or click Browse to select a path and filename using the Save As dialog box.

11. Click Next twice and then click Finish to complete the request generation process.

Submitting Certificate Requests to Third-Party Authorities

After you create a CSR, you can submit it to a third-party authority, such as Entrust, Equifax, Valicert, or Verisign. The certificate-signing request is stored as ASCII text in the file you specified in Step 10 under "Creating Certificate Requests." It contains your site's public key and your identification information. When you open this file, you'll find the encrypted contents of the request, such as:

```
----BEGIN NEW CERTIFICATE REQUEST----

MIXCCDCCAnECAQAwczERMA8GA1UEAxMIZW5nc3ZyMDExEzARBgNVBAsTClRlY2hu
b2xvZ3kxEzARBgNVBAoTCkRvbWFpbi5Db20xEjAQBgNVBAcTCVZhbmNvdXZlcjET
MBEGA3UECBMKV2FzaGluZ3RvbjELMAkGA1UEBhMCVVMwgZ8wDQYJKoZIhvcNAQEB
BQADgY0AMIGJAoGBALE1brvIZNRB+gvkdcf9b7tNns24hB2Jgp5BhKi4NXc/twR7
C+GuDnyTqRs+C2AnNHgb9oQkpivqQNKh2+N18bKU3PEZUzXH0pxxjhaiT8aMFJhi
3bFvD+gTCQrw5BWoV9/Ff5Ud3EF5TRQ2WJZ+J1uQQewo/mXv5ZnbHsM+aLy3AgMB
AAGgggFTMBoGCisGAQQBgjcNAgMxDBYKNS4wLjIxOTUuMjA1BgorBgEEAYI3AgEO
MScwJTAOBgNVHQ8BAf8EBAMCBPAwEwYDVR01BAwwCgYIKwYWWQUHAwEwgf0GCisG
AQQBgjcNAgIxge4wgesCAQEeWgBNAGkAYwByAG8AcwBvAGYAdAAgAFIAUwBBACAA
UwBDAGgAYQBuAG4AZQBsACAAQwByAHkAcAB0AG8AZwByAGEAcABoAGkAYwAgAFAA
cgBvAHYAaQBkAGUAUAcgOBiQBfE24DPqBwFp1R15/xZDY8Cugoxbyymtwq/tAPZ6dz
Pr9Zy3MNnkKQbKcsbLR/4t9/tWJIMmrFhZonrx12qBfICoiKUXreSK890ILrLEto
1frm/dycoXHhStSsZdm25vszv827FKKk5bRW/vIIeBqfKnEPJHOnoiG6UScvgA8Q
fgAAAAAVVAAAMA0GCSqGSIb3DQEBBQUAA4GBAFZc6K4S04BMUnR/8Ow3J/MS3TYi
HAvFuxnjG0CefTq8Sakzvq+uazU03waBqHxZ1f32qGr7karoD+fq8dX27nmh0zpp
Rz1DXrxR35mMC/yP/fpLmLb51sxOt1379PdS4trvWUFkfY93/CkUi+nrQt/uZHY3
N0SThxf73VkfbsE3

----END NEW CERTIFICATE REQUEST----
```

Most CAs have you submit the certificate request as part of a formal site registration process. In this registration process, you'll be asked to submit the request file in an e-mail or through an online form. When using e-mail, you simply attach the request file to the e-mail and send it. When using an online form, you must copy the entire text of the request—including the BEGIN and END statements—to the clipboard and paste this into the online form. You can use Microsoft Notepad to do this.

After the CA reviews your certificate request, the CA will either approve or decline your request. If the CA approves the request, you will receive an e-mail with the signed certificate attached or a notice to visit a location where you can retrieve the signed certificate. The certificate is an ASCII text file that you can view in Notepad, and it can only be decrypted with the private key you generated previously. As before, the contents of the file are encrypted and include BEGIN and END statements like this:

```
----BEGIN CERTIFICATE----

MXXCWjCCAgQCED1pyIenknxBt43eUZ7JF9YwDQYJKoZIhvcNAQEEBQAwgakxFjAU

BgNERAoTDVZ1cm1TaWduLCBJbmMxRzBFBgNVBAsTPnd3dy52ZXJpc2lnbi5jb20v

cmVwb3NpdG9yeS9UZXN0Q0Q1BTIE1uY29ycC4gQnkgUmVmLiBMaWFiLiBMVEQuMUYw

RAYDVQQLEz1G45IgVmVyaVNpZ24gYXV0aG9yaXplZCB0ZXN0aW5nIG9ubHkuIeev

IGFzc3VyYW5jZXMgKEM345MxOTk3MB4XDTAwMTEwNzAwMDAwMFoXDTAwMTEyMTIz

NTk1OVowczELMAkGA1UEBhMCVVMxEzARBgNVBAgTC1dhc2hpbmd0b24xEjAQBgNV

BAcUCVZhbmNvdXZlcjETMBEGA1UEChQKRG9tYW1uLkNvbTETMBEGA1UECxQKVGVj

aG5vbG9neTERMA8GA1UEAxQIZW5nc3ZyQWEwgZ8wDQYJKoZIhvcNAQEBBQADgY0A

MIGJAoGBALElbrvIZNRB+gvkdcf9b7tNns24hB2Jgp5BhKi4NXc/twR7C+GuDnyT

qRs+C2AnNHgb9oQkpivqQNKh2+N18bKU3PEZUzXH0prtyhaiT8aMFJhi3bFvD+gT

CQrw5BWoV9/Ff5Ud3EF5TRQ2WJZ+J1uQQewo/mXnTZnbHsM+aLy3AgMBAAEwDQYJ

KoZIhvcNAQEEBQADQQCQIrhq5UmsPYzwzKVHIiLDDnkYunbhUpSNaBfUSYdv1AU1

Ic/37OrdN/E1ZmOut0MbCWIXKr0Jk5q8F6T1bqwe

----END CERTIFICATE----
```

Save the certificate file to a location that you can access when using the Internet Information Services snap-in. You should use .cer as the file extension. Then process and install the certificate as described in the "Processing Pending Requests and Installing Site Certificates" section of this chapter.

Submitting Certificate Requests to Certificate Services

After you create a certificate-signing request, you can submit it to Certificate Services using the Web-based interface. To do this, complete the following steps:

1. The certificate-signing request is stored as ASCII text in the file you specified in Step 10 under "Creating Certificate Requests." Open this file in Notepad and copy the entire text of the request, including the BEGIN and END statements, to the clipboard (press Ctrl+A and then press Ctrl+C).

2. You are now ready to submit the request to Certificate Services. Start your Web browser and type in the Certificate Services URL, such as *http://ca.microsoft.com/certsrv/*. You should see the main page for Certificate Services, as shown in Figure 6-15.

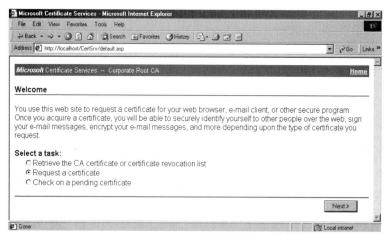

Figure 6-15. *When you access the Certificate Services URL, you should see the main page for the Web-based interface. If you don't, you may not have configured Web access correctly.*

3. Select Request A Certificate and then click Next.

4. On the Choose Request Type page, select Advanced Request, and then click Next.

5. As shown in Figure 6-16, select the second option on the Advanced Certificate Requests page and then click Next. This option tells Certificate Services that you are going to submit a request that is base64-encoded.

6. Paste the request into the Saved Request text box and then click Submit.

7. If you've completed this process correctly, the final page shows you that your request has been received and is pending approval by the CA. If there is a problem with the request, you'll see an error page telling you to contact your administrator for further assistance. On the error page, you can click Details

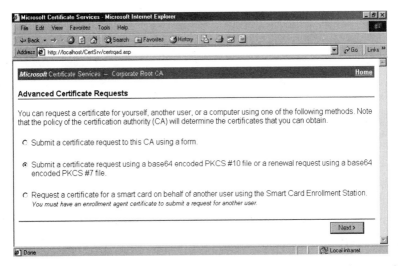

Figure 6-16. *Use the Advanced Certificate Requests page to choose the type of request you are submitting.*

to get more information on the error. You may need to re-create the certificate request or go back to ensure that you haven't accidentally inserted additional spacing or characters in the request submission.

8. If you are also the CA, you can use the Certification Authority snap-in to handle the request. See the "Approving and Declining Pending Certificate Requests" section of this chapter.

Once the request has been approved, use the Web-based interface to retrieve the signed certificate. To do this, complete the following steps:

1. Start your Web browser and type in the Certificate Services URL, such as *http://ca.microsoft.com/certsrv/.*

2. Under Select A Task, select Check On Pending Certificate, and then click Next.

3. You should see a list of pending requests. Requests are listed with a description and a date/time stamp. Select the request for the site you want to work with and then click Next.

Note If you cannot access the certificate file online, you can have the certificate administrator generate the certificate manually. See the "Generating Certificates Manually in the Certification Authority Snap-In" section of this chapter.

4. If a certificate has been issued for the request, you should see a page stating that the certificate you requested was issued to you. On this page, select Base 64 Encoded, and then click Download CA Certificate.

5. You should see a File Download dialog box. Select Save This File To Disk and then click OK.

6. Use the Save As dialog box to select a save location for the certificate file and then click Save. You should use .cer as the file extension. Then process and install the certificate as described in the "Processing Pending Requests and Installing Site Certificates" section of this chapter.

   Tip I recommend placing all certificate files and requests in a common folder on the Web server's local file system. You should safeguard this folder so that only administrators have access.

Processing Pending Requests and Installing Site Certificates

Once you receive the certificate back from the authority, you can install it by completing the following steps:

1. In the Internet Information Services snap-in, right-click the site for which you want to generate the certificate and select Properties.

2. From the Directory Security tab, select Server Certificate. This starts the Web Server Certificate Wizard. Click Next.

3. As shown in Figure 6-17, select Process The Pending Request And Install The Certificate, and then click Next.

4. Type the path and filename to the certificate file returned by the authority, or click Browse to search for the file. Click Next to continue.

Figure 6-17. *Process the pending request and install the certificate file.*

5. The next page provides summary information on the certificate. If this is the correct certificate, click Next, and then click Finish to complete the installation process. Otherwise, click Back to choose a different certificate file, and then repeat Steps 4 and 5.

6. Configure SSL and manage the certificate as described in the "Working with SSL" and "Managing Site Certificates in the Internet Information Services Snap-In" sections of this chapter.

Deleting Pending Certificate Requests

If you made a mistake in a certificate request that has already been generated, the only way to fix it is to delete the request and then create a new one. You can delete pending certificate requests by completing the following steps:

1. In the Internet Information Services snap-in, right-click the site for which you want to generate the certificate and select Properties.
2. From the Directory Security tab, select Server Certificate. This starts the Web Server Certificate Wizard. Click Next.
3. As shown in Figure 6-18, select Delete The Pending Request, and then click Next.

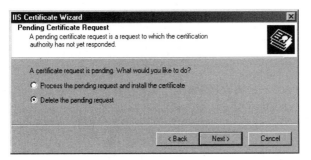

Figure 6-18. *If you or someone else instructs IIS to delete a pending request, you'll need to re-create the certificate request before you can try to install a certificate.*

4. Click Next and then click Finish. This deletes the request association in IIS but does not remove the actual request file. This file contains your site's public key and should be deleted.

Working with SSL

Installing a site certificate automatically enables SSL so that it can be used, but you may need to change the default settings. You'll need to configure and troubleshoot SSL as necessary.

Configuring SSL Ports

Once you install a certificate on a Web site, you can change the SSL port for the site. The SSL port is used for secure communications with client browsers. To view or change the SSL port, follow these steps:

1. In the Internet Information Services snap-in, right-click the site you want to work with, and then select Properties.
2. The SSL Port field on the Web Site tab shows the currently configured SSL port (if any).

3. As shown in Figure 6-19, change the SSL port by typing a new value in the SSL Port field. Multiple sites can use the same SSL port, provided that the sites are configured to use different IP addresses.

4. Click OK.

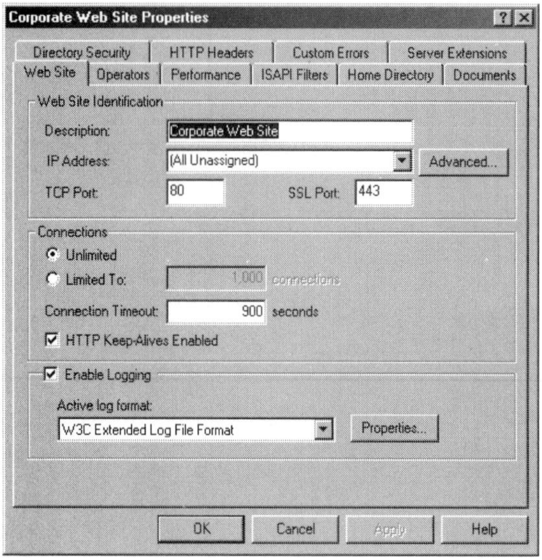

Figure 6-19. *Specify a port value for SSL.*

A site can also have multiple SSL identities (meaning the site can answer on different SSL ports). The SSL port configured on the Web Site tab is the one the site responds to by default. All other SSL ports must be specified in the browser request. For example, if you configure SSL for ports 443, 444, and 445, a request for *https://yoursite/* is handled by port 443 automatically, but you must specify the other ports to use them, such as *https://yoursite:445/*.

To configure multiple SSL identities for a site, complete these steps:

1. In the Internet Information Services snap-in, right-click the Web site you want to manage, and then select Properties.

2. On the Web Site tab, click Advanced. The Advanced Multiple Web Site Configuration dialog box is displayed.

3. As shown in Figure 6-20, use the Multiple SSL Identities For This Web Site panel to manage SSL port settings.

   • **Add**   Adds a new SSL identity. Click Add, select the IP address you want to use, and then type an SSL port value. Click OK when you are finished.

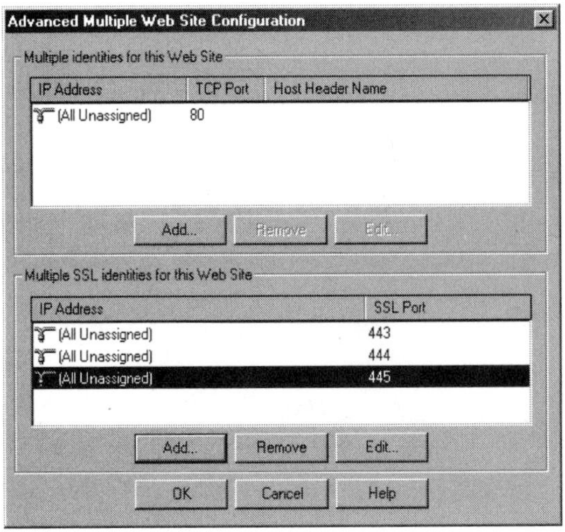

Figure 6-20. *Web sites can have multiple SSL identities. The port set on the Web Site tab is the primary identity. The others are alternatives that must be specified in a URL request.*

- **Remove** Allows you to remove the currently selected entry from the SSL Identities list box.
- **Edit** Allows you to edit the currently selected entry in the SSL Identities list box.

4. Click OK, and then click OK again to save your settings.

Adding the CA Certificate to the Client Browser's Root Store

Most root CA certificates issued by third-party CAs are configured as trusted CAs in Web browsers. However, if you are acting as your own CA, your root CA certificate won't be recognized and trusted by client browsers. To get browsers to trust the root CA certificate, the user must install the certificate in the browser's authorities store.

To install the root CA certificate, users need to complete the following steps:

1. Connect to your site using a secure URL that begins with *https://*.

2. As shown in Figure 6-21, the user's browser displays a security alert stating that there is a problem with the site's security certificate.

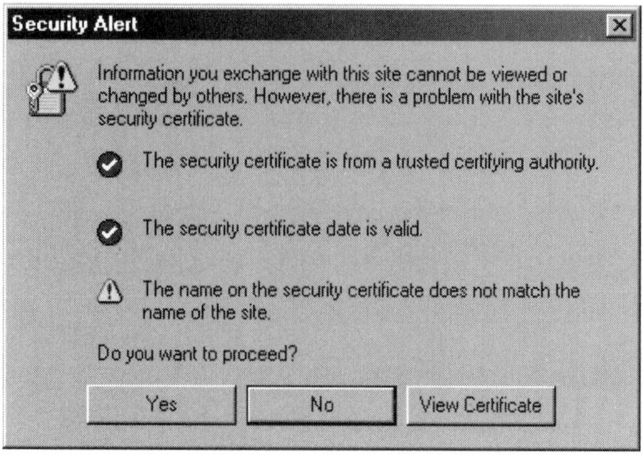

Figure 6-21. *A security alert warns that the browser doesn't trust your root CA.*

3. The alert is displayed because the user hasn't chosen to trust your root CA. At this point, the user can elect to proceed by clicking Yes, to cancel the request by clicking No, or to view the root CA certificate by clicking View Certificate.

4. Click View Certificate. This displays the Certificate dialog box.

5. The General tab information should state that the CA Root certificate is not trusted. To enable trust, click Install Certificate.

6. This starts the Certificate Import Wizard. Click Next.

7. Choose Automatically Select The Certificate Store Based On The Type Of Certificate, as shown in Figure 6-22, and then click Next.

8. Click Finish. The default options allow the browser to select the certificate store based on the type of certificate.

9. Click OK and then click Yes to proceed. The user shouldn't see the security alert again.

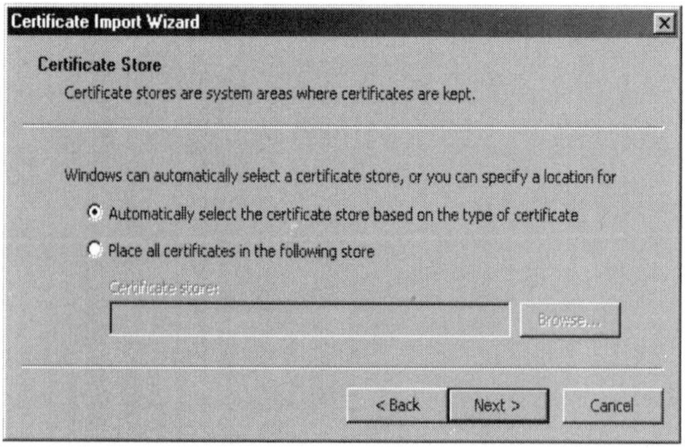

Figure 6-22. *Select Automatically to select the certificate store.*

Confirming that SSL Is Correctly Enabled

Secure connections can only be established when the browser connects to the server using a secure URL beginning with *https://*. Browsers display a warning if any embedded content (such as images) on a secure Web page are retrieved using an insecure (*http://*) connection. This warning tells users that some of the content on the page is insecure and asks them if they want to continue.

Once you've enabled SSL on your server, you should confirm that SSL is working and that the encryption level is set properly. To confirm that SSL is working in Internet Explorer, complete these steps:

1. Access your Web site using a secure URL beginning with *https://*. A padlock displayed in the bar at the bottom of the Internet Explorer window indicates that an SSL session has been established. If the padlock isn't displayed, the SSL session was not established.

2. Right-click anywhere on the Web page and then select Properties. This displays a Properties dialog box, which provides summary information on the Web page.

3. Click the Certificates button and then select the Details tab. Scroll down to display details concerning the certificate and the level of encryption used.

To confirm that SSL is working in Netscape Navigator, complete the following steps:

1. Access your Web site using a secure URL beginning with *https://*. The padlock in the lower right corner of the Navigator window should be closed instead of open. This indicates that an SSL session has been established. If the padlock is open, the SSL session was not established.

2. Click the padlock icon. This displays the Netscape Personal Security Manager, which also indicates the level of encryption currently being used.

Resolving SSL Problems

If SSL isn't working, ensure that you've installed the server certificate on the correct Web site and that you've enabled SSL on the site. These steps should resolve a server-based SSL problem.

If the encryption level isn't what you expected, you should check to make sure the browser supports the encryption level you are using. If a browser supports 128-bit encryption and the encryption level in use according to the browser's Properties dialog box is 40-bit, the problem is the server certificate. The server certificate must be upgraded to 128-bit encryption.

In Internet Explorer, check encryption support by completing the following steps:

1. From the Help menu, select About Internet Explorer.

2. The Cipher Strength field shows the level of encryption supported. You must have 128-bit support to establish a 128-bit session.

3. Click OK.

4. From the Tools menu, select Internet Options. From the Internet Options dialog box, select the Advanced tab.

5. Scroll down through the Advanced options until you see the Security heading. Ensure that Use SSL 2.0 and Use SSL 3.0 are selected.

6. Click OK.

In Netscape Navigator, check encryption support by completing these steps:

1. Click the padlock button on the Navigator's status bar. This displays the Netscape Personal Security Manager, which also indicates the level of encryption currently being used.

2. Click the Advanced tab, then select Options. There are three check boxes, all selected by default: Enable SSL Version 2, Enable SSL Version 3, and Enable TLS. Make sure both versions of SSL are selected at a minimum.

3. Click Close to save your settings.

Managing Site Certificates in the Internet Information Services Snap-In

Once you've installed a certificate on a Web site, you can use the Internet Information Services snap-in to manage it. Key management tasks are discussed in this section.

Viewing and Modifying Issued Certificates

Certificates contain the identity and geographic information specified in the original certificate request. They also have a number of properties set by the certification authority. These properties describe the certificate, set its authorized uses, and define the site for which the certificate is valid. If needed, you can modify the certificate to do the following:

- Update the friendly name assigned when the certificate was created
- Specify a detailed description of the certificate
- Enable or disable purposes for which the certificate can be used

You can view or modify a site's certificate by completing the following steps:

1. In the Internet Information Services snap-in, right-click the Web site you want to manage, and then select Properties.

2. On the Directory Security tab, click View Certificate. This displays the Certificate dialog box, shown in Figure 6-23.

Figure 6-23. *The Certificate dialog box provides summary information on the site certificate and can be used to modify properties and export the certificate to a file.*

3. To view properties set when the certificate was issued, click the Details tab. Fields on the Details tab include

   - **Version**   The X.509 version used in creating the certificate
   - **Serial Number**   The unique serial number for the certificate
   - **Signature Algorithm**   The encryption algorithm used to create the certificate's signature
   - **Issuer**   The issuer of the certificate
   - **Valid From**   The date from which the certificate is valid
   - **Valid To**   The date after which the certificate expires
   - **Subject**   Used to set the subject of the certificate, which typically includes the identification and geographic information
   - **Public Key**   The certificate's encrypted public key
   - **Thumbprint Algorithm**   The encryption algorithm used to create the certificate's thumbprint
   - **Thumbprint**   The encrypted thumbprint of the signature
   - **Friendly Name**   The descriptive name assigned to the certificate

4. To view or edit a list of purposes for which the certificate can be used, from the Details tab, click Edit Properties. You can then use the Certificate Properties dialog box, shown in Figure 6-24, to view or edit the certificate purposes.

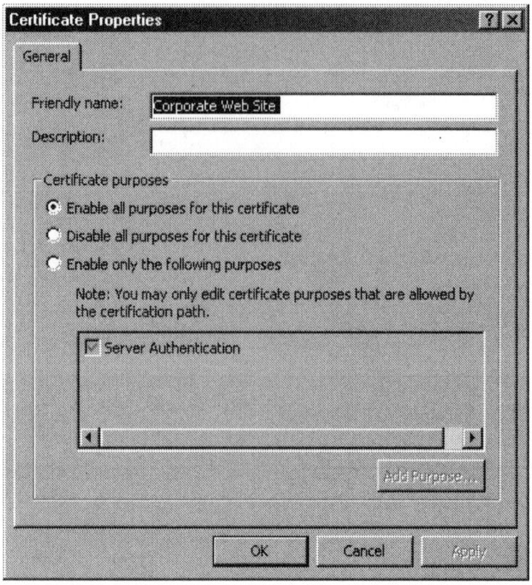

Figure 6-24. *Certificate purposes can be modified to meet the needs of your organization.*

Renewing, Removing, and Replacing Certificates

Normally, certificates are valid for one year from the date they were issued. This means certificates must be renewed on an annual basis. Certificates can also be removed or replaced as necessary. To renew, remove, or replace a certificate, follow these steps:

1. In the Internet Information Services snap-in, right-click the Web site you want to manage, and then select Properties.

2. Select the Directory Security tab and then click Server Certificate on the Secure Communications panel. This starts the Web Server Certificate Wizard. Click Next.

3. As shown in Figure 6-25, you can now elect to renew, remove, or replace the current certificate. Make your selection and then continue through the remaining wizard dialogs.

Figure 6-25. *You can renew, remove, or replace a certificate at any time using the Web Server Certificate Wizard.*

Exporting Site Certificates

You can export site certificates to a file, if necessary. To do this, complete the following steps:

1. In the Internet Information Services snap-in, right-click the Web site you want to manage, and then select Properties.

2. On the Directory Security tab, click View Certificate. This displays the Certificate dialog box, shown previously in Figure 6-23.

3. Select·the Details tab and then select Copy To File. This starts the Certificate Export Wizard. Click Next.

4. As shown in Figure 6-26, you can export the certificate file with or without the associated private key. If you want to export the private key, select the Yes option. Otherwise, select the No option. Click Next.

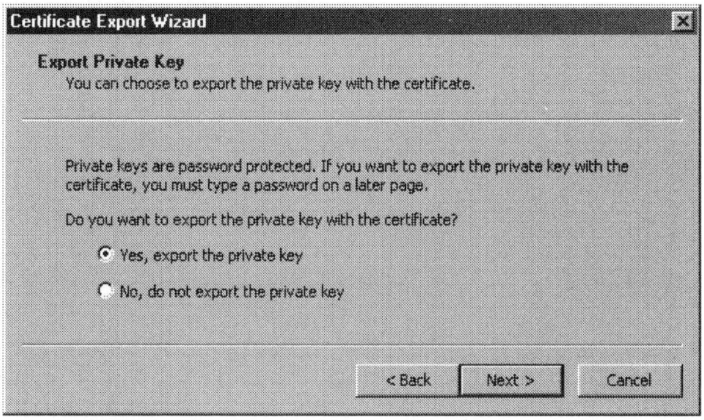

Figure 6-26. *You can export the certificate file with or without the private key. Select an option and then continue by clicking Next.*

5. The next page lets you choose the export file format. The default format should be adequate, so note the format that will be used, and then click Next.

6. If you elected to export the private key, you must now set a password for the certificate file. After you type and then confirm the password in the fields provided, click Next.

7. Specify the name of the file you want to export. Click Browse if you want to use the Save As dialog box to set the file location and name.

8. Click Next and then click Finish. Click OK to confirm a successful export. Click OK twice more to return to the Internet Information Services snap-in.

Ignoring, Accepting, and Requiring Client Certificates

Client certificates allow users to authenticate themselves through their Web browser. You may want to use client certificates if you have a secure external Web site, such as an extranet. If a Web site accepts or requires client certificates, you can configure client certificate mappings that permit access control to resources based on client certificates. A client certificate mapping can be mapped to a specific Windows account using a one-to-one mapping, or it can be mapped based on rules you specify.

By default, IIS doesn't accept or require client certificates. You can change this behavior. Keep in mind that accepting client certificates isn't the same as requiring client certificates. When a site requires client certificates, the site is secured for access using SSL only and cannot be accessed using standard HTTP. When a site accepts client certificates rather than requires them, the site can use either HTTP or HTTPS for communications.

To configure client certificate usage, follow these steps:

1. In the Internet Information Services snap-in, right-click the Web site you want to manage, and then select Properties.

2. Select the Directory Security tab and then click Edit on the Secure Communications panel. This displays the Secure Communications dialog box, shown in Figure 6-27.

3. If you want to require SSL (and preclude the use of insecure communications), select Require Secure Channel. Optionally, you can also select Require 128-Bit Encryption if your server has a 128-bit encryption installed and enabled.

4. On the Client Certificates panel, select the Ignore, Accept, or Require Client Certificates option as necessary.

Note   You can only require client certificates when secure SSL communications are required as well. Because of this, you must check Require Secure Channel when you want to require client certificates.

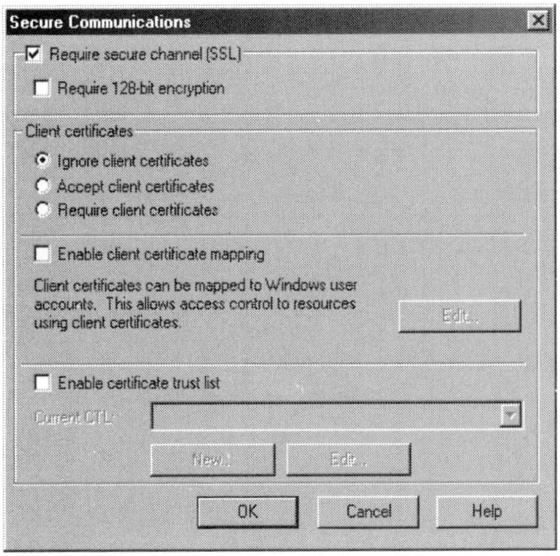

Figure 6-27. *Sites can ignore, accept, or require client certificates.*

5. If you want to map client certificates to Windows user accounts, select Enable Client Certificate Mapping, and then click Edit. Then use the Account Mappings dialog box to configure certificate mappings.

6. If you want to accept client certificates only from specific certification authorities, select Enable Certificate Trust List, and then click New. This starts the Certificate Trust List Wizard, which you can use to specify the root CA certificates that are trusted. Client certificates from trusted root CAs will be accepted. Client certificates from other root CAs will not be accepted.

7. Click OK twice.

Requiring SSL for All Communications

In some cases, you'll want to create sites that can only be accessed using secure communications. You can do this by requiring SSL and prohibiting the use of insecure communications. To require SSL for communications with a Web site, follow these steps:

1. In the Internet Information Services snap-in, right-click the Web site you want to manage, and then select Properties.

2. Select the Directory Security tab and then click Edit on the Secure Communications panel. This displays the Secure Communications dialog box, shown previously in Figure 6-27.

3. Select Require Secure Channel if you want to require SSL and preclude the use of insecure communications.

4. Optionally, select Require 128-Bit Encryption if your server has a 128-bit encryption installed and enabled.

5. Click OK twice.

Part III

Essential Services Administration

This part of the book focuses on the administration of essential services. By essential services, we mean those services you'll deploy time and again on your Web servers. Chapter 7 covers techniques for managing File Transfer Protocol (FTP). You'll find information on configuring FTP servers, controlling access to directories, managing user sessions, and maintaining FTP server security. Chapter 8 focuses on configuring and maintaining Simple Mail Transport Protocol (SMTP). You'll find detailed discussions on configuring SMTP servers, organizing messages for delivery, routing messages, message delivery options, and maintaining SMTP server security. The final chapter in this part, Chapter 9, examines indexing services. You'll learn to configure the Indexing Service, to create and manage catalogs, to optimize performance, and to test the indexing installation.

Chapter 7
Managing FTP Servers

File Transfer Protocol (FTP) is used to transfer files from one host to another. Managing FTP sites and servers is similar to managing World Wide Web sites and servers. You configure FTP sites for use on the Internet and on corporate intranets. Internet FTP sites typically use fully qualified domain names (FQDNs) and public Internet Protocol (IP) addresses. Intranet FTP sites typically use private IP addresses and computer names that resolve locally.

As with Web sites, FTP site properties identify a site, set its configuration values, and determine where and how documents are accessed. FTP site properties can be set at several levels:

- As global defaults
- As site defaults
- As directory defaults

Global defaults are set through the FTP Service Master Properties dialog box and apply to all new FTP sites created on the server. Individual defaults are set through the FTP Site Properties dialog box and apply only to the selected FTP site. Directory defaults are set through the directory Properties dialog box and apply only to the selected directory.

Understanding FTP

The sections that follow examine how FTP is used. You'll learn how FTP file transfers work, how FTP servers are accessed, and how FTP sessions are established.

FTP Essentials

FTP is a client/server protocol used for transferring files. Using FTP, you can log on to an FTP server, browse a directory structure to locate a file, and download the file. FTP also enables you to upload files to an FTP server. The difference between a file upload and a file download is important. When you upload a file, you transfer a file from a client to a server. When you download a file, you transfer a file from a server to a client.

With the increasing popularity of Hypertext Transfer Protocol (HTTP), the use of FTP is decreasing. While it is true that HTTP has taken over some of the functions of FTP, FTP continues to have a place when you need a dedicated resource for transferring files that is easy to use and to maintain. Like HTTP, FTP uses Transmission Control Protocol (TCP) as its transport protocol. Unlike HTTP, FTP is session-oriented. This means that FTP connections are persistent. When you connect to an FTP server, the connection remains open after you transfer files.

The maintenance of persistent connections requires system resources. A server with too many open connections quickly gets bogged down. Consequently, many FTP servers are configured to limit the number of open connections and to time out connections after a certain period of time. By default, Internet Information Services (IIS) FTP servers limit the number of connections to 100,000 and use a connection time-out of 900 seconds.

Because FTP is a client/server protocol, the successful transfer of files depends on several factors. A computer acting as a server must run FTP server software, such as IIS. A computer acting as a client must run FTP client software, such as Microsoft Internet Explorer 5.0 or the command-line FTP utility built into Microsoft Windows 2000.

File transfers can be either ASCII or binary. You can use ASCII file transfers when you are working with text documents and want to preserve the end-of-line designators. You must use binary file transfers when you are working with executables. You can use binary file transfers with other file types as well.

Controlling FTP Server Access

Most FTP clients and servers are configured to allow anonymous file transfers. In an anonymous file transfer, the server allows users to anonymously connect to the server and transfer files. As the name implies, anonymous file transfers are designed to allow anyone to connect to the server and transfer files. When you use Internet Explorer or another FTP client, anonymous transfers can be started automatically in most cases. For example, you could connect to the Microsoft FTP server by typing the following Uniform Resource Locator (URL) into your browser's Address field:

ftp://ftp.microsoft.com/public/

Here, ftp:// designates the protocol as FTP, ftp.microsoft.com identifies the server to which you want to connect, and public is the name of a directory on the server. Behind the scenes, the FTP client fills in the necessary username and password information. With an anonymous FTP connection, this means setting the username to anonymous and the password to your e-mail address or an empty string. If the client is unable to automatically fill in the necessary information, you'll be prompted for a username and password. Enter anonymous as the username and set the password to your e-mail address.

FTP servers can also be configured for restricted access. When you restrict access to a server, only authenticated users can gain access to the server. When users try to connect to the server, they are prompted to authenticate themselves by typing a username and password. The username and password must be for an account that exists on the local computer or in the domain the computer is a member of. Username and password information can also be specified in the URL used to access the server. To do this, use the following URL format:

ftp://username:password@hostname:port/path_to_resource

Here, ftp:// designates the protocol as FTP, username sets the account name, and password sets the account password. In the following example, the username is set to wrstanek and the password is set to mydingo123:

ftp://wrstanek:mydingo123@ftp.microsoft.com/public/

Being granted access to a server, either anonymously or through authentication, doesn't mean a user can upload or download files. The specific actions available to the user depend on the security settings. As discussed in Chapter 5, "Managing Web Server Security," security settings are set at two levels: Windows and IIS. Windows security settings are configured through user and group accounts, file and folder permissions, and group policy. IIS security settings are set through FTP server permissions, authentication, and Transmission Control Protocol/Internet Protocol (TCP/IP) access restrictions.

Working with FTP Sessions

Once a user is granted access to a server, either anonymously or through authentication, a TCP connection is established, and this connection remains open until the user session is terminated or the server issues a time-out. The FTP client and the server establish this connection using a three-way handshake. This handshake involves two dedicated TCP ports on the FTP server and two dynamically assigned TCP ports on the client that are mapped to the dedicated server ports.

Note TCP/IP connections are also established using a three-way handshake. TCP/IP connections are established at the Network Layer of the OSI model. FTP connections are established at the Application Layer.

The two ports used by FTP servers are ports 20 and 21, by default. Port 20 is used for sending and receiving FTP data and is only open when data is being transferred. Port 21 is used for sending and receiving FTP control information. Port 21 listens for clients that are trying to establish a connection. Once an FTP session is established with a client, the connection on port 21 remains open for the entire session.

The two ports used by FTP clients are dynamically assigned and range from 1024 to 5000 (see note). When an FTP session is started, the client opens a control port that connects to port 21 on the server. This connection is used to manage the FTP session. The client doesn't automatically connect to the data port on the server. This port connection is only established when data needs to be transferred between the client and server. When data needs to be transferred, the client opens a new data port and then connects to the server's data port (port 20 by default). Once the file transfer is complete, the client releases the data port. The next time data needs to be transferred the client opens a new data port, which typically isn't the same as the last port number used for data transfers.

> **Note** The dynamically assigned port numbers are outside the ranges that normally are reserved for other TCP and User Datagram Protocol (UDP) services. Thus, because ports 0 to 1023 are reserved for other TCP and UDP services, FTP uses ports ranging from 1024 to 5000 (limited by a Windows Registry setting with a theoretical limit of 65,535). You can find a complete list of current TCP and UDP ports used in \%SystemRoot%\System32\Drivers\Etc\Services.

Now that you know how FTP servers and clients use ports, let's look at how FTP sessions are established and then used in actual data transfers. The process of establishing and using an FTP session can be summarized as follows:

1. The FTP server listens for client requests on a dedicated control port. By default, the control port is 21.

2. When a user makes a request for resources on the FTP server, the client dynamically assigns a control port and then maps this control port to the server's control port. For example, the client may assign port 1025 and map this to server port 20.

3. Once a connection has been established with the server, the client and server can communicate over the control port.

4. Before the client initiates a data transfer, the client must dynamically assign a data port and map this to the server's data port. Each time a file is transferred, a new data port is opened by the client and then released. For example, port 1057 may be used for the first data transfer, port 1058 for the next data transfer, and so on.

5. The FTP session remains open until the session is terminated or the connection times out. The user or the server can terminate the session.

A useful tool for monitoring FTP sessions on clients and servers is Netstat. Netstat is a command-line utility that displays the status of network connections. When you call Netstat, you should specify that you want to see connections being used by TCP and that you want to redisplay the statistics at a specific interval. In this example, you tell Netstat to display connection statistics every 15 seconds:

```
netstat -p tcp 15
```

You can run Netstat on a client to monitor FTP activity. When the client establishes an FTP connection to the server, you'll see output similar to the following:

```
Active Connections

  Proto Local Address Foreign Address State
  TCP engsvr01:ftp engsvr01:1043 ESTABLISHED
  TCP engsvr01:1043 engsvr01:ftp ESTABLISHED
```

Here, the FTP connection is established on port 1043 and this port is mapped to the FTP control port. Whenever the client retrieves data from the server, a data port is mapped as well. After the data has been transferred, the data port will enter the TIME_WAIT state. The port remains in the TIME_WAIT state until it times out and is closed. The control port will continue to reflect the ESTABLISHED state as long as the connection is open. These port states are reflected in the following statements:

```
Active Connections

 Proto Local Address Foreign Address State
 TCP engsvr01:ftp-data engsvr01:1045 TIME_WAIT
 TCP engsvr01:ftp engsvr01:1043 ESTABLISHED
 TCP engsvr01:1043 engsvr01:ftp ESTABLISHED
```

When the client closes the connection to the FTP server, the only TCP entry that remains is the client to server control port mapping. As shown in this example, the client to server control port mapping enters the TIME_WAIT state and remains in this state until the session times out:

```
Active Connections

 Proto Local Address Foreign Address State
 TCP engsvr01:1043 engsvr01:ftp TIME_WAIT
```

Note Keep in mind that clients can establish multiple connections to a server. If this is the case for the client you are monitoring, you'll see multiple control and data ports in various states.

FTP Site Naming and Identification

Each FTP site deployed in your organization has a unique identity it uses to receive and respond to requests. The identity includes the following:

- A computer or Domain Name System (DNS) name
- A port number
- An IP address

The way these identifiers are combined to identify an FTP site depends on whether the host server is on a private or public network. On a private network, a computer called CorpFTP could have an IP address of 10.0.10.25. If so, the FTP site on the server could be accessed in these ways:

- Using the Uniform Naming Convention (UNC) path name: \\CorpFTP or \\10.0.10.25
- Using a URL: *ftp://CorpFTP/* or *ftp://10.0.10.25/*
- Using a URL and port number: *ftp://CorpFTP:21/* or *ftp://10.0.10.25:21/*

On a public network, a computer called MoonShot could be registered to use the DNS name ftp.microsoft.com and the IP address 207.46.230.210. If so, the FTP site on the server could be accessed in these ways:

- Using a URL: *ftp://ftp.microsoft.com/* or *ftp://207.46.230.210/*
- Using a URL and port number: *ftp://ftp.microsoft.com:21/* or *http://207.46.230.210:21/*

Using different combinations of IP addresses and port numbers, you can host multiple sites on a single computer. Hosting multiple sites on a single server has definite advantages. For example, rather than installing three different FTP servers, you could host ftp.microsoft.com, ftp.msn.com, and ftp.adatum.com on the same FTP server.

 Note Microsoft Windows 2000 Professional can host only one Web site and one FTP site. You must upgrade to Microsoft Windows 2000 Server to host multiple Web or FTP sites.

Managing Master FTP Service Properties

The master FTP service properties are used to set default property values for new FTP sites created on a server. Existing FTP sites on a server inherit changes you make to the master service properties. The only changes that are applied optionally are permission changes. If you set new access permissions, a prompt is displayed asking you to specify the sites and directories that should inherit the new access permissions.

To change the master FTP service properties for a server, follow these steps:

1. In the Internet Information Services snap-in, right-click the icon for the computer you want to work with and then select Properties. If the computer isn't shown, connect to it as discussed in the "Connecting To Other Servers" section of Chapter 2, "Core IIS Administration," and then perform these tasks.

2. From the Master Properties selection menu, select FTP Service, and then click the related Edit button. This opens the FTP Service Master Properties dialog box for the computer.

3. Use the tabs and fields of the FTP Service Master Properties dialog box to configure the default property values for new FTP sites. When you are finished making changes, click OK twice.

Creating FTP sites

When you install FTP Publishing Server for IIS, a default FTP site is created. Typically, the default FTP site is installed in Inetpub\Ftproot. By adding subdirectories to this location, you can create the directory structure of the FTP site. By adding files to this directory or to subdirectories, you provide content for users to download. Users can access the FTP site using the FTP server name or by typing an appropriate URL in their browsers.

You can create additional FTP sites by completing the following steps:

1. If you are installing the FTP site on a new server, ensure that the FTP Publishing Service has been installed on the server.

2. If you want the FTP site to use a new IP address, you must configure the IP address before installing the site. For details, refer to Chapter 15, "Managing TCP/IP Networking," in the *Microsoft Windows 2000 Administrator's Pocket Consultant*.

3. In the Internet Information Services snap-in, right-click the icon for the computer you want to work with, point to New, and then select FTP Site. If the computer isn't shown, connect to it as discussed in the "Connecting To Other Servers" section of Chapter 2, "Core IIS Administration," and then perform this task.

4. The FTP Site Creation Wizard is started. Click Next. In the Name field, type a descriptive name for the FTP site, such as Corporate FTP Server. Click Next.

5. As shown in Figure 7-1, use the IP Address selection list to select an available IP address. Select (All Unassigned) to allow FTP to respond on all unassigned IP addresses that are configured on the server. Multiple FTP sites can use the same IP address if the sites are configured to use different port numbers.

Note FTP has no equivalent of HTTP host headers. This means you cannot use host header names with FTP sites.

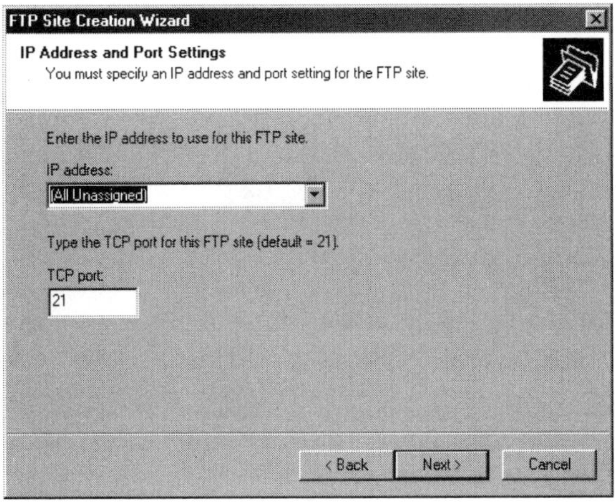

Figure 7-1. *Set the IP address and port values for the new FTP site.*

6. The TCP port for the FTP site is assigned automatically as port 21. If necessary, type a new port number in the TCP Port field. Multiple sites can use the same port if the sites are configured to use different IP addresses. Click Next.

7. The FTP Site Home Directory dialog box lets you set the home directory for the FTP site. Click Browse to search for a folder. This folder must be created before you can select it. If necessary, use Microsoft Windows Explorer to create the directory before you browse for a folder.

8. Next, as shown in Figure 7-2, you can set access permissions for the FTP site. Normally, you will want to set Read permissions only. The standard permissions are the following:

   • **Read** Allows users to download documents, meaning their clients can transfer documents from the server

   • **Write** Allows users to upload documents, meaning their clients can transfer documents to the server

9. Click Next and then click Finish. The FTP site is created automatically but not started. You should update the site's properties before you make it accessible to users.

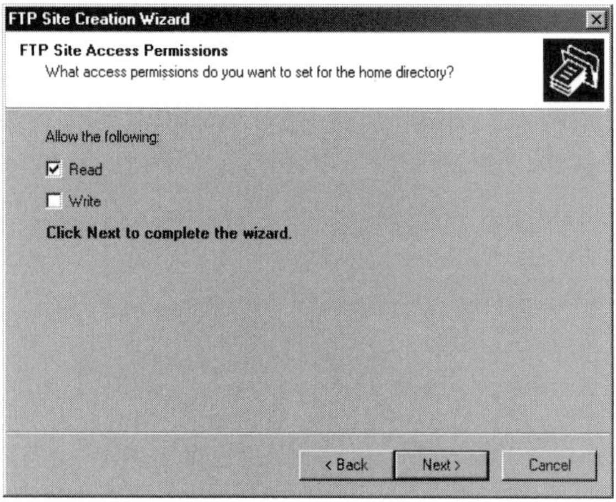

Figure 7-2. *Set access permissions for the FTP site.*

Managing FTP Sites

The sections that follow examine key tasks for managing FTP sites. Most FTP site properties are configured through the Internet Information Services snap-in.

Configuring an FTP Site's Home Directory

Each FTP site on a server has a home directory. The home directory is the base directory for all document transfers. The home directory is mapped to your site's domain name or to the server name. FTP clients connect to the server and access this directory by default.

You can view or change a site's home directory by completing the following steps:

1. Start the Internet Information Services snap-in and then, in the left pane (Console Root), click the plus sign (+) next to the computer you want to work with. If the computer isn't shown, connect to it as discussed in the "Connecting To Other Servers" section of Chapter 2, "Core IIS Administration."

2. Right-click the FTP site you want to manage and then select Properties.

3. Click the Home Directory tab, as shown in Figure 7-3.

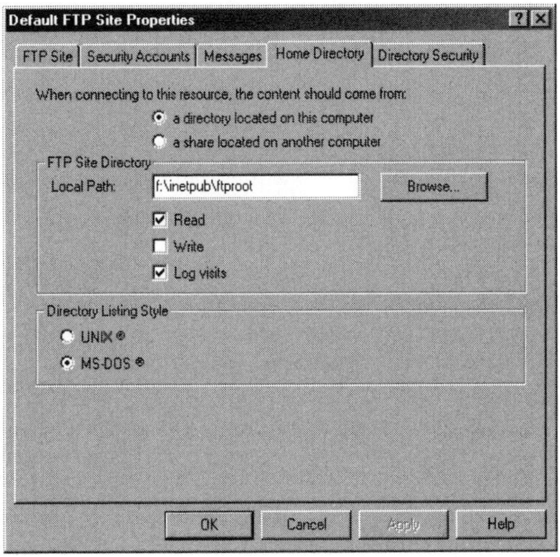

Figure 7-3. *You can change a site's home directory at any time.*

4. If the directory you want to use is on the local computer, select A Directory Located On This Computer, and then type the directory path in the Local Path field, such as C:\Inetpub\FTProot\. To browse for the folder, click Browse.

5. If the directory you want to use is on another computer and is accessible as a shared folder, select A Share Located On Another Computer, and then type the UNC path to the share in the Network Directory field. The path should be in the form \\ServerName\SharedFolder\, such as \\Gandolf\CorpFTP\. Afterward, click Connect As, and then enter the username and password that should be used to connect to the shared folder.

> **Note** If you do not specify a username and password, the user Everyone must have access to the shared folder. Otherwise, the network connection to the folder will fail.

6. Click OK.

Configuring Ports and IP Addresses Used by FTP Sites

Each FTP site has a unique identity. The identity consists of a TCP port and an IP address. The default TCP port is 21. The default IP address setting is to use any available IP address.

To change the identity of an FTP site, complete the following steps:

1. If you want the FTP site to use a new IP address, you must configure the IP address before updating the site. For details, refer to Chapter 15, "Managing TCP/IP Networking," in *Microsoft Windows 2000 Administrator's Pocket Consultant*.

2. Start the Internet Information Services snap-in and then, in the left pane (Console Root), click the plus sign (+) next to the computer you want to work with. If the computer isn't shown, connect to it as discussed in the "Connecting To Other Servers" section of Chapter 2, "Core IIS Administration."

3. Right-click the FTP site you want to manage and then select Properties. The dialog box shown in Figure 7-4 is displayed.

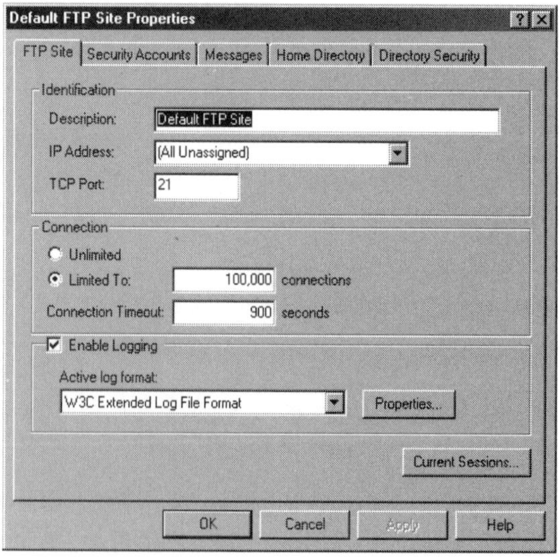

Figure 7-4. *You modify a site's identity through the FTP Site tab in the Properties dialog box.*

4. The Description field shows the descriptive name for the FTP site. The descriptive name is displayed in the Internet Information Services snap-in and isn't used for other purposes. You can change the current value by typing a new name in the Description field.

5. The IP address selection list shows the current IP address for the FTP site. If you want to change the current setting, use the selection list to select an available IP address, or select (All Unassigned) to allow FTP to respond on all unassigned IP addresses. Multiple FTP sites can use the same IP address if the sites are configured to use different port numbers.

6. The TCP port for the FTP site is assigned automatically to port 21. If necessary, type a new port number in the TCP Port field. Multiple FTP sites can use the same TCP port, if the sites are configured to use different IP addresses.

7. Click OK.

Restricting Incoming Connections and Setting Time-Out Values

Connection limits and time-out values are used to control the number of simultaneous FTP sessions that are allowed. Normally, FTP sites are limited to 100,000 connections and have a time-out of 900 seconds. If you have a server with limited resources, you may want to reduce the number of allowable connections. Keep in mind that once the limit is reached, no other clients are permitted to access the server. The clients must wait until the connection load on the server decreases.

The connection time-out value determines when idle user sessions are disconnected. With the default FTP site, sessions time out after they've been idle for 900 seconds (15 minutes). This is a good time-out for most FTP uses. If you find that users are complaining about getting disconnected from idle sessions, you may want to increase the time-out value.

You can modify connection limits and time-outs by completing the following steps:

1. Start the Internet Information Services snap-in and then, in the left pane (Console Root), click the plus sign (+) next to the computer you want to work with. Next, right-click the FTP site you want to manage, and then choose Properties.

2. The Connection panel has two option buttons: Unlimited and Limited To. The Unlimited option removes connection limits, which isn't a good idea for FTP servers. The Limited To option restricts the number of connections to a specific value. If you select the Limited To option, you must also specify the maximum number of connections that are permitted at any one time.

3. The Connection Timeout field controls the connection time-out. Type a new value to change the current time-out.

4. Click OK.

Note Each connection to an FTP server uses system resources. To reduce the drain on the server, you should set a specific connection limit. The default limit is to allow 100,000 simultaneous connections. On an average-sized server, this is a good value. If a server has limited resources or is used for other purposes, such as publishing your Web site, you may want to reduce this value. If a server is dedicated to FTP or is an enterprise class server, you may want to increase this value.

Creating Physical Directories for FTP Sites

FTP sites can be used for file uploads and downloads. Typically, directories used for uploading data are configured separately from directories used for retrieving data. Separate directory structures provide a clear separation between files that your organization has made available and files that users have uploaded. Here's a typical directory tree for an FTP site:

- **C:\Inetpub\FTProot**   Base directory for the site
- **C:\Inetpub\FTProot\Public**   Base directory for downloads
- **C:\Inetpub\FTProot\Upload**   Base directory for uploads

Once you establish the base directory structure, you can add directories to the tree. For example, a software company may have the following subdirectories under C:\Inetpub\FTProot\Public\:

- **Documentation**   Directory for product documentation
- **Patches**   Directory for patches to software
- **Service_Packs**   Directory for service packs

Tip To help visitors understand your site's directory structure, you should create a Welcome message that provides both an overview of how the site is meant to be used and a directory map. A directory map is a text file that describes, in detail, the available directories and what they are used for. Save the directory map as a .txt file in the base directory for the site.

You may want to configure separate FTP sites for uploads and downloads. On the upload site, you configure write-only access for upload directories. On the download site, you configure read-only access for download directories. In this way, visitors can only perform one very specific task at the site, and you have an easier job as an administrator.

Physical directories for FTP sites are created using Windows Explorer. You can create subdirectories within the home directory by completing the following steps:

1. Start Windows Explorer. Click Start, point to Programs, point to Accessories, and then select Windows Explorer.
2. In the Folders pane, select the home directory for the FTP site.

3. In the Contents pane, right-click and then select Folder from the New menu. A new folder is added to the Contents pane. The directory name is initialized to New Folder and selected for editing.

4. Edit the name of the directory and press ENTER. The best directory names are short but descriptive, such as Documentation, Service_Packs, or Patches.

5. The new folder inherits the default file permissions of the home directory and the default IIS permissions of the FTP site.

Tip The Internet Information Services snap-in doesn't automatically display new folders. You may need to click Refresh on the toolbar to display the folder.

Creating Virtual Directories for FTP Sites

Virtual directories are created in two stages. First, you create a physical directory. Then you create a virtual directory that maps to the physical directory. Virtual directories on FTP sites can be configured to allow file uploads, file downloads, or both. The way you control file transfers is simple. You set these configurations:

- Read access on directories that should allow downloads
- Write access on directories that should allow uploads
- Read and write access on directories that should allow uploads and downloads

Don't forget, however, that permissions at the file and folder level also control user permissions. With an anonymous connection, the Internet Guest account must have the appropriate directory permissions. With an authenticated connection, the user or a group in which the user is a member must have the appropriate directory permissions.

You can create a virtual directory by completing the following steps:

1. Start the Internet Information Services snap-in and then, in the left pane (Console Root), click the plus sign (+) next to the computer you want to work with.

2. Right-click the FTP site on which you want to create the virtual directory, point to New, and then select Virtual Directory. This starts the Virtual Directory Creation Wizard. Click Next.

3. In the Alias field, type the name you want to use to access the virtual directory. As with directory names, the best alias names are short but descriptive.

4. The next dialog box lets you set the path to the physical directory where your content is stored. Type the directory path or click Browse to search for a directory. The directory must be created before you can select it. If necessary, use Windows Explorer to create the directory before you browse for the directory.

5. Next, set access permissions for the virtual directory. Read permission allows users to download files. Write permission allows users to upload files.

6. Click Next and then click Finish. The virtual directory is created.

Redirecting Requests to a Network Share

If you use network-attached storage or have a dedicated server for file transfers, you can redirect a site's file requests to locations on a network share. To do this, complete the following steps:

1. In the Internet Information Services snap-in, right-click the FTP site you want to work with, and then select Properties.

2. Click the Home Directory tab and then select A Share Located On Another Computer.

3. Type the UNC path to the network share in the Network Directory field. The path should be in the form \\ServerName\SharedFolder\, such as \\Gandolf\CorpFTP\. Afterward, click Connect As and then enter the username and password that should be used to connect to the shared folder.

4. Click OK. Now all requests for files on the FTP site are mapped to files on the specified network share.

Setting the Directory Listing Style

When an FTP client accesses an FTP site, it automatically retrieves a directory listing from the server. The style of directory listing can be configured in one of two ways:

- **MS-DOS style**   Provides MS-DOS-style filenames, dates, and directory listings
- **UNIX style**   Provides UNIX-style filenames, dates, and directory listings

MS-DOS style listings are the preferred format as they are friendlier and easier to navigate. UNIX style listings are compatible with older browsers that may not understand the MS-DOS format. You set directory listing style at the site level. To do this, complete the following steps:

1. In the Internet Information Services snap-in, right-click the FTP site you want to work with, and then select Properties.

2. Click the Home Directory tab and then, under Directory Listing Style, select either UNIX or MS-DOS.

3. Click OK.

Setting Welcome, Exit, and Maximum Connection Messages

IIS FTP sites can display three different types of messages: Welcome, Exit, and Maximum Connection. These messages are called information messages and are set at the site level. Each FTP site configured on your server can have a different set of information messages. Each information message has a different use:

- **Welcome messages**   Welcome messages are displayed when users first connect to the FTP server. They can contain information about the purpose of the site, rules for using the site, locations of mirror sites, administrator contact, and more. The best Welcome messages are informative and contain 8 to 10 lines of text. To offset the message, you can start and end the message with a line of banner text, such as a line of asterisks.

- **Exit messages** Exit messages display final text to users when they leave your site. Exit messages are displayed when clients log off using the FTP command QUIT in an active session. Exit messages are not displayed when clients terminate an FTP session through a different technique, such as clicking Close in a browser window. Exit messages can be only one line in length and should be short and to the point.

- **Maximum Connection messages** Maximum Connection messages display when the server's connection threshold has been reached. These messages can only be one line in length and should be short and to the point. Keep in mind that you can change the number of simultaneous connections allowed. To do this, follow the procedure discussed in the "Restricting Incoming Connections and Setting Time-Out Values" section of this chapter.

You can configure information messages by completing the following steps:

1. In the Internet Information Services snap-in, right-click the FTP site you want to work with, and then select Properties.
2. Click the Messages tab.
3. In the Welcome text box, type your Welcome message.

Note Each line of text should end with a return (carriage return and line feed). If you don't end each line of text, Internet Explorer's FTP client might not display your message properly.

4. In the Exit text box, type your Exit message.
5. In the Maximum Connections text box, type your Maximum Connections message.
6. Click OK.

Managing FTP User Sessions

Each connection to an FTP site uses resources on the FTP server. To help you monitor resource usage, IIS allows you to view statistics on sessions. Each FTP site has separate session statistics.

Viewing FTP User Sessions

You can view session information for an FTP site by completing the following steps:

1. In the Internet Information Services snap-in, right-click the FTP site you want to work with, and then select Properties.

2. Click Current Sessions on the FTP Site tab. This displays the FTP User Sessions dialog box, shown in Figure 7-5. This dialog box displays the following information:

   • **Connected Users** The account name of authenticated users or the password value entered by anonymous users.

 Tip Keep in mind that anonymous users are asked to enter their e-mail address as the password value. You can distinguish between authenticated and anonymous users by the icon that is displayed. Icons for anonymous users have a red question mark. Icons for authenticated users have a standard user image.

   • **From** The IP address or DNS name of the computer from which the user is connecting.

   • **Time** The total elapsed time since the session started. The format is HH:MM:SS.

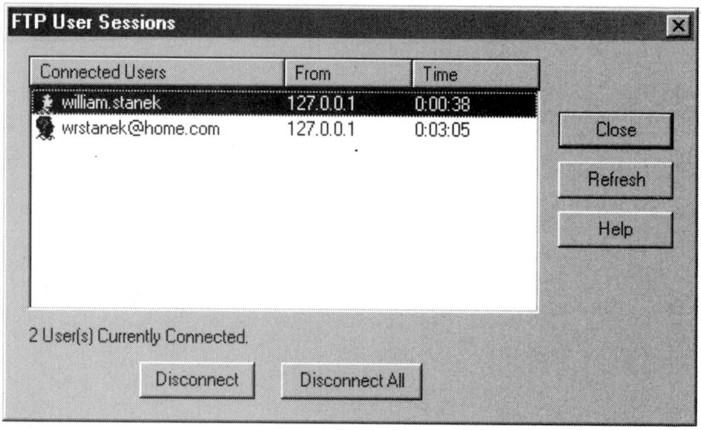

Connected Users	From	Time
william.stanek	127.0.0.1	0:00:38
wrstanek@home.com	127.0.0.1	0:03:05

FTP User Sessions

2 User(s) Currently Connected.

Close
Refresh
Help
Disconnect
Disconnect All

Figure 7-5. *Current FTP user sessions are displayed by username, IP address, and connection duration.*

3. Click Refresh to renew the session statistics, or click Close when you are finished monitoring user sessions.

Viewing the Total Number of Connected Users

IIS displays the total number of users that are connected to an FTP site in the lower left corner of the FTP User Sessions dialog box. You can access this dialog box and view the total number of connected users by completing the following steps:

1. In the Internet Information Services snap-in, right-click the FTP site you want to work with, and then select Properties.

2. Click Current Sessions on the FTP Site tab. This displays the FTP User Sessions dialog box.

3. The total number of connected users is displayed in the lower left corner of the dialog box. Click Refresh to get an updated count.

Terminating FTP User Sessions

You can terminate individual user sessions or all user sessions that are active on an FTP site. Typically, you want to do this when the session lasts too long or there are problems with resources on the server. If the user is uploading or downloading a file when you terminate the session, the file transfer will terminate immediately, and the user will get a message stating that the remote host has closed the connection.

To disconnect an individual session, follow these steps:

1. In the Internet Information Services snap-in, right-click the FTP site you want to work with, and then select Properties.

2. On the FTP Site tab, click Current Sessions.

3. Select the session you want to terminate and then click Disconnect.

4. When prompted to confirm the action, click Yes.

5. Click OK twice to return to the Internet Information Services snap-in.

To disconnect all user sessions on an FTP site, follow these steps:

1. In the Internet Information Services snap-in, right-click the FTP site you want to work with, and then select Properties.

2. Click Current Sessions on the FTP Site tab.

3. Click Disconnect All and then, when prompted to confirm the action, click Yes.

4. Click OK twice to return to the Internet Information Services snap-in.

Managing FTP Server Security

FTP server security is handled much like Web server security. You manage security at two levels: Windows and IIS. At the operating system level, you create user accounts, configure access permissions for files and directories, and set policies. At the IIS level, you set content permissions, authentication controls, and operator privileges.

Note Most FTP server security tasks are identical to those for Web server security. This section focuses only on what is different. For a complete discussion of IIS security, see Chapter 5, "Managing Web Server Security."

Managing Anonymous Connections

You manage anonymous access to FTP sites using a named account that has the appropriate permissions for the directories and files you make available for uploading and downloading files. By default, the anonymous access account is the Internet guest account (*IUSR_ComputerName*) discussed in Chapter 5, "Managing Web Server Security."

When anonymous access is enabled, users don't have to log on using a username and password. IIS automatically logs the user on using the anonymous account information provided for the resource. If anonymous access is not allowed, the site is configured for named account access only. Unlike Web sites, you can manage anonymous access only at the global or site level. You cannot manage anonymous access at the directory or file level.

Setting Anonymous Access Globally

You can manage anonymous access for all FTP sites on a server by completing the following steps:

1. In the Internet Information Services snap-in, right-click the icon for the computer you want to work with, and then select Properties. This displays a Properties dialog box.

2. Select FTP Service on the Master Properties selection list, and then click Edit. This opens the FTP Service Master Properties dialog box for the computer.

3. Select the Security Accounts tab in the Properties dialog box, as shown in Figure 7-6.

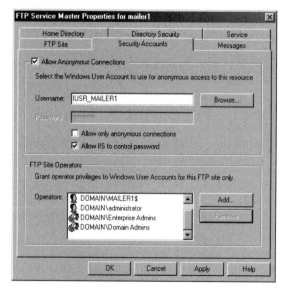

Figure 7-6. *Use the Security Accounts tab to configure anonymous access.*

4. To enable anonymous access, select Allow Anonymous Connections, and complete the remaining steps in this procedure.

5. To disable anonymous access, clear Allow Anonymous Connections, and skip the remaining steps in this procedure. With anonymous connections disabled, only authenticated users can access the server. You must configure local or domain accounts that can be used to access the sites on this server.

6. The Username field specifies the account used for anonymous access to the resource. If you desire, type the account name you want to use instead of the existing account, or click Browse to display the Find User dialog box.

7. Allow Only Anonymous Connections prevents users from logging on to the server with usernames and passwords. Select this option if you want only the anonymous user account to be available. If you want to allow users to log on to the server with named accounts, clear this option.

8. Allow IIS To Control Password determines whether IIS controls the password for the anonymous access account or you do. In most cases, you'll want IIS to control the account if it is defined on the local system. If this is the case, select this check box. Otherwise, clear this check box and type in the password for the anonymous access account.

9. Click OK, and then click OK again to save your settings. All FTP sites on the server inherit the changes automatically.

Setting Anonymous Access Locally

You can manage anonymous access for a specific FTP site by completing these steps:

1. In the Internet Information Services snap-in, right-click the FTP site you want to work with, and then select Properties.

2. Click the Security Accounts tab.

3. To enable anonymous access, select Allow Anonymous Connections, and complete the remaining steps in this procedure.

4. To disable anonymous access, clear Allow Anonymous Connections, and skip the remaining steps in this procedure. With anonymous connections disabled, only authenticated users can access the site. You must configure local or domain accounts that can be used to access the site.

5. The Username field specifies the account used for anonymous access to the resource. If you desire, type the account name you want to use instead of the existing account, or click Browse to display the Find User dialog box.

6. Allow Only Anonymous Connections prevents users from logging on to the site with usernames and passwords. Select this option if you want only the anonymous user account to be available. If you want to allow users to log on to the site with named accounts, clear this option.

7. Allow IIS To Control Password determines whether IIS controls the password for the anonymous access account or you do. In most cases, you'll want IIS to control the account if it is defined on the local system. If this is the case,

select this check box. Otherwise, clear this check box and type in the password for the anonymous access account.

8. Click OK.

Configuring Windows Permissions on FTP Servers

Every folder and file used by IIS can have different access permissions. These access permissions are set at the Windows security level. Anytime you work with file and folder permissions on an FTP server, you should keep the following in mind:

- Only administrators should have full control over folders and files. If users have full control, they'll be able to create, rename, and delete resources.

- Authenticated users should be assigned specific permissions based on the types of tasks they need to perform. Users who can download files should have Read permission on the appropriate folders and files. Users who can upload files should have Write permission on the appropriate folders (and Read permission if you want them to view folder contents).

- The special group Everyone and the Internet Guest account should have limited permissions. The Default FTP Site inherits its permissions from the InetPub directory, which means the group Everyone has Full Control permission over the directory. This is a security risk and should be changed immediately. Set Read permission on folders and files used with downloads. Set Write permission on folders used with uploads (and Read permission if you want users to view folder contents).

 Tip If you modify the properties of the base directory for the Default FTP Site, you'll need to clear the Allow Inheritable Permissions From Parent check box before you can set specific permissions on the directory.

Configuring FTP Server Permissions

FTP sites and directories have permissions in IIS in addition to the Windows security settings. These permissions are set the same for all users. This means you cannot set different permissions for different users at the IIS level. You can, however, create specific areas of your FTP that are designed for these specific functions:

- Download only
- Upload only
- Download and upload

You can set FTP permissions globally through the master properties or locally at the site or directory level. When you set FTP permissions in the master properties, you must also specify how these properties are inherited. If a site or directory has settings that conflict with permission changes you've made, you are given the opportunity to override the site or directory permissions with the global permissions. Similarly, if you make site-level permission changes that conflict with existing permissions on a subdirectory, you are given the opportunity to override the site or directory permissions with the local permissions. In both cases, the changes are applied when you choose to override the existing permissions.

Setting FTP Permissions Globally

To set FTP permissions globally, complete the following steps:

1. In the Internet Information Services snap-in, right-click the icon for the computer you want to work with, and then select Properties. This displays a Properties dialog box.

2. Select FTP Service on the Master Properties selection list and then click Edit. This opens the FTP Service Master Properties dialog box for the computer.

3. As shown in Figure 7-7, click the Home Directory tab, and then use the fields on the FTP Site Directory panel to set the permissions that you want sites and directories on this computer to inherit. The available options are the following:

   • **Read**   Allows users to read or download files stored in the directory

   • **Write**   Allows users to upload files to the directory

   • **Log Visits**   Used with server logging to log requests related for resource files

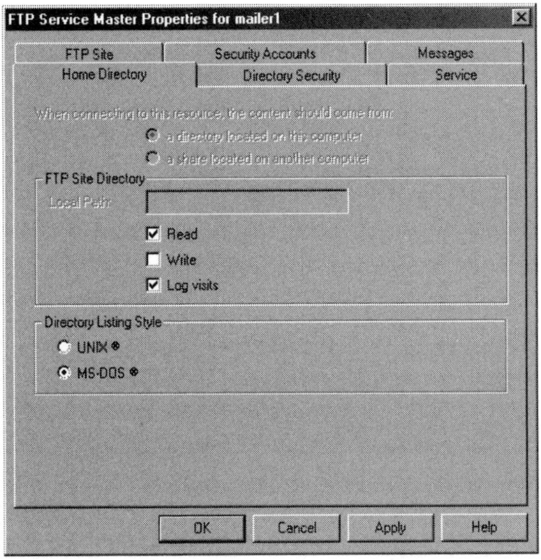

Figure 7-7. *Use the Properties dialog box to configure FTP permissions.*

4. Click Apply. Before applying permission changes, IIS checks the existing permissions in use for all FTP sites and directories within FTP sites. If a site or directory node uses a different value for a permission, an Inheritance Overrides dialog box is displayed. Use this dialog box to select the site and directory nodes, which should use the new permission value, and then click OK.

Setting FTP Permissions Locally

To set FTP permissions for a site or directory, complete the following steps:

1. In the Internet Information Services snap-in, right-click the site or directory.

2. Click the Home Directory, Directory, or Virtual Directory tab as appropriate. This displays the dialog box shown in Figure 7-8. Then use the following fields to set the permissions for the selected resource:

   - **Read** Allows users to read or download files stored in the directory

   - **Write** Allows users to upload files to the directory

   - **Log Visits** Used with server logging to log requests related for resource files

3. Click Apply. Before applying FTP permission changes, IIS checks the existing permissions in use for all subdirectories. If a subdirectory uses a different value for a permission, an Inheritance Overrides dialog box is displayed. Use this dialog box to select the site and directory nodes, which should use the new permission value, and then click OK.

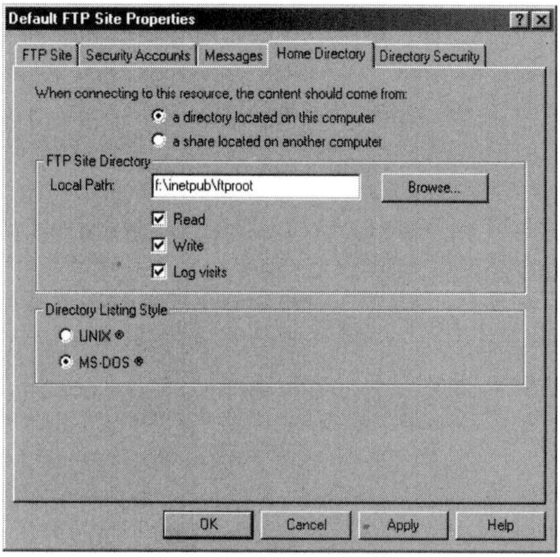

Figure 7-8. *Use the Properties dialog box to configure FTP permissions.*

Configuring IP Address and Domain Name Restrictions

By default, FTP resources are accessible to all IP addresses, computers, and domains, which presents a security risk that may allow your server to be misused. To control use of resources, you may want to grant or deny access by IP address, network identification, or domain. As with other FTP server settings, restrictions can be applied through the Master FTP server properties or through the properties for individual sites, directories, and files.

- Granting access allows a computer to make requests for resources but doesn't necessarily allow users to work with resources. If you require authentication, users still need to authenticate themselves.

- Denying access to resources prevents a computer from accessing those resources. Consequently, users of the computer can't access the resources—even if they could have authenticated themselves with a username and password.

You can establish or remove restrictions globally through the FTP Service Master Properties dialog box by completing the following steps:

1. In the Internet Information Services snap-in, right-click the icon for the computer you want to work with, and then select Properties. This displays a Properties dialog box.

2. Select FTP Service on the Master Properties selection list and then click Edit. This opens the FTP Service Master Properties dialog box for the computer.

3. Select the Directory Security tab, as shown in Figure 7-9.

Figure 7-9. *You can grant or deny access by IP address, network identification, and domain.*

4. Click Granted Access to grant access to specific computers and deny access to all others.

5. Click Denied Access to deny access to specific computers and grant access to all others.

6. Create the grant or deny list. Click Add, and then, in the Computer dialog box, specify Single Computer or Group Of Computers.

  * For a single computer, type the IP address for the computer, such as 192.168.5.50.

  * For groups of computers, type the Network ID, such as 192.168.0.0, and the subnet mask, such as 255.255.0.0.

7. If you want to remove an entry from the grant or deny list, select the related entry in the restrictions list, and then click Remove.

8. Click Apply. Before applying changes, IIS checks the existing restrictions for all FTP sites and directories within FTP sites. If a site or directory node uses a different value, an Inheritance Overrides dialog box is displayed. Use this dialog box to select the site and directory nodes that should use the new setting, and then click OK.

You can establish or remove restrictions at the site or directory level by completing these steps:

1. In the Internet Information Services snap-in, right-click the site or directory that you want to work with. This displays a Properties dialog box.

2. Select the Directory Security tab.

3. Click Granted Access to grant access to specific computers and deny access to all others.

4. Click Denied Access to deny access to specific computers and grant access to all others.

5. Create the grant or deny list. Click Add and then, in the Grant Access On or Deny Access On dialog box, specify Single Computer or Group Of Computers.

  * For a single computer, type the IP address for the computer, such as 192.168.5.50.

  * For groups of computers, type the subnet address, such as 192.168.0.0, and the subnet mask, such as 255.255.0.0.

6. If you want to remove an entry from the grant or deny list, select the related entry in the restrictions list, and then click Remove.

7. Click Apply. Before applying changes, IIS checks the existing restrictions for all child nodes of the selected resource (if any). If a child node uses a different value, an Inheritance Overrides dialog box is displayed. Use this dialog box to select the site and directory nodes that should use the new setting, and then click OK.

Configuring FTP Site Operators

You can designate FTP site operators for each FTP site on your server. FTP site operators constitute a special group of users who have limited administrative privileges. Operators cannot configure properties that affect IIS, the host computer, or the network.

To specify operator assignments for all FTP sites on a server, complete the following steps:

1. In the Internet Information Services snap-in, right-click the icon for the computer you want to work with, and then select Properties. This displays a Properties dialog box.

2. Select FTP Service on the Master Properties selection list and then click Edit. This opens the FTP Service Master Properties dialog box for the computer.

3. Select the Security Accounts tab. The Operators list box shows the currently configured operators. The global group Administrators is the only operator configured by default.

4. To add an operator, click Add. This displays the Select Users Or Groups dialog box, which you can use to select users and groups that should be configured as operators.

5. To remove an operator, select the operator in the Operators list box and then click Remove.

6. Click OK or Apply to complete the operator assignment.

To specify operator assignments for a specific FTP site, complete these steps:

1. In the Internet Information Services snap-in, right-click the site that you want to work with. This displays a Properties dialog box.

2. Select the Operators tab. The Operators list box shows the currently configured operators. The global group Administrators is the only operator configured by default.

3. To add an operator, click Add. This displays the Select Users Or Groups dialog box, which you can use to select users and groups that should be configured as operators.

4. To remove an operator, select the operator in the Operators list box, and then click Remove.

5. Click OK or Apply to complete the operator assignment.

Chapter 8

Configuring and Maintaining SMTP

Simple Mail Transfer Protocol (SMTP) is used to send and receive messages over the Internet. Most organizations use the SMTP features in Internet Information Services (IIS) to send e-mail rather than to allow World Wide Web servers to receive e-mail—and this is the purpose for which the SMTP service was designed. If you need a general purpose Internet mail server for corporate or Internet service provider (ISP) use, you should not use the SMTP service in IIS. Instead, you should use a full-featured messaging server, such as Microsoft Exchange 2000 Server.

When you install the SMTP service as part of an IIS installation, a default SMTP virtual server is created. The default virtual server is preconfigured so that locally generated messages can be handled and delivered. The configuration restricts the sending of messages that are generated by remote users, which does include the Internet Guest account and any other named user on the Web server. The configuration also restricts relaying of e-mail through the SMTP virtual server. With these settings, the default virtual server can be used in most environments without having to make further adjustments. That said, there are many times when you'll want to optimize configuration settings to meet the needs of your environment.

Managing SMTP is much different from any administration process you must perform in your normal duties as a Web administrator. Instead of managing content or file transfers, you are managing the way in which e-mail messages are handled and delivered. Before diving in to core administration tasks, let's look at SMTP fundamentals. A discussion of fundamentals will help build the essential background for successful SMTP administration.

Using SMTP

The SMTP service is designed to provide basic messaging services for one or more domains and can be configured in many different ways. You manage the configuration of SMTP through virtual servers. To understand how SMTP is used and managed, you need to understand the following concepts:

- How e-mail domains are used
- How the mail root is used
- How SMTP messages are processed

Understanding E-Mail Domain Usage

The SMTP service uses the e-mail address provided in a message's To, Cc, Bcc, and From fields to determine how the message should be handled. To, Cc, and Bcc fields are used to determine where the message should be delivered. The From field determines from where the message originated.

E-mail addresses, such as williams@tech.microsoft.com, have three components:

- An e-mail account, such as williams
- An at symbol (@), which separates the account name from the domain name
- An e-mail domain, such as tech.microsoft.com

The key component that determines how the SMTP server handles messages is the e-mail or service domain. Service domains can be either local or remote. A local service domain is a Domain Name System (DNS) domain that is serviced locally by the SMTP server. A remote service domain is a DNS domain that is serviced by another SMTP server or mail gateway.

Any message with a local domain name in a message's To, Cc, or Bcc fields is delivered locally. If a domain is local, you can designate it as the default domain or an alias domain. The default domain serves as the default for all messages transferred into or out of the domain. Messages addressed to the default domain are stored in the virtual server's Drop directory. Outgoing messages that do not have a domain set in the From field of the e-mail address use the default domain as their domain of origin. An SMTP virtual server can have only one default domain.

Any other local domains that you create on the server are specified as alias domains. Alias domains allow you to create secondary domains that point to the default domain and use its settings. When working with alias domains, keep in mind that any message sent to an alias domain is stamped with the default domain name. This means the alias domain uses the same configuration settings and the same Drop directory as the default domain. For example, an SMTP virtual server could specify tech.microsoft.com as the default domain and dev.microsoft.com as an alias domain. Any messages that specify either of these domains are handled locally by the SMTP virtual server on which they are configured and are stamped with the default domain name.

Any message with a nonlocal domain in a message's To, Cc, or Bcc fields is queued for delivery to a remote server. If you have unique delivery requirements for a specific remote domain, you can add a remote domain to the SMTP server and configure settings that allow you to handle its messages appropriately. For example, you could configure a remote domain with separate outbound security that requires message encryption. Or you could forward messages destined for a remote domain through a specific mail server designated as a smart host.

Understanding the Mailroot

When you install SMTP using the default settings, a default virtual server is installed as well. The default virtual server uses the Inetpub\Mailroot folder to manage message submission and delivery. You can install additional SMTP virtual servers. When you do this, each virtual server has a separate Mailroot that is located in the directory you specify during creation.

Each Mailroot has seven subfolders associated with it. These folders are used as follows:

- **Badmail**   Used to store messages that are undeliverable and cannot be returned to the sender. Each badmail message has an error message associated with it that can be used to help diagnose the problem. You should periodically monitor the Badmail folder to ensure messages are flowing through the system as expected.

- **Drop**   Drop box for all incoming messages addressed to recipients homed on the server, such as the virtual server's postmaster. If an incoming message is addressed to a local recipient, the SMTP service moves the message from the Queue folder to this folder. This folder becomes the final destination.

- **Mailbox**   Used to store mailboxes.

- **Pickup**   Used as a pickup point for messages that are to be delivered by the SMTP service. The SMTP service monitors this mailbox continuously for new messages. Any message placed in this folder is picked up by the SMTP service and transferred to the Queue folder for further processing and delivery.

- **Queue**   Holds messages that are ready for processing and delivery. Messages are transferred to the Queue folder from the Pickup folder and when they are received by SMTP. Messages that the SMTP service is unable to deliver due to bad connections or busy destination servers are stored in the Queue folder as well. These messages remain in the Queue folder until they can be delivered or until they are deemed undeliverable and transferred to the Badmail folder.

- **Route**   Used to store temporary data needed to route messages along specific paths. Typically used when you configure a route domain for an SMTP virtual server.

- **SortTemp**   Serves as a temporary sorting area for messages. Temporary files are created in this directory and are cleared out after messages are sorted and queued for delivery.

When you configure SMTP for use on a server, you should periodically monitor the Badmail and Queue folders. The Badmail folder provides the best indicator that you may have a problem with SMTP. Messages in this folder couldn't be delivered to the intended recipients, and they couldn't be returned to the sender. If the number of messages in this folder is growing, your mail server might have a problem accessing the network or delivering mail. Likewise, if the number of queued messages is growing and messages aren't clearing out of the Queue folder, your mail server might have a problem connecting to the network or delivering mail.

Understanding Mail Processing

The SMTP service is very systematic in the way it processes mail messages. Mail messages can originate from two sources:

- **Pickup folder**   Message files placed in the Pickup folder by an application, such as an Active Server Page (ASP), or by a user, such as an administrator
- **SMTP**   Message files received using the SMTP network protocol

When a message is copied to the Pickup folder or comes in through the SMTP network protocol, it is placed in the Queue folder for processing and delivery. What happens to a message next depends on the type of recipient. Mail recipients fall into two categories:

- **Local recipients**   A local recipient is a recipient with an e-mail domain serviced locally by the SMTP server. Locally serviced domains are the default domain and any alias domains configured on the server. Mail messages for local recipients are handled locally.
- **Remote recipients**   A remote recipient is a recipient with an e-mail domain serviced remotely by the SMTP server. Mail messages for remote recipients can be relayed directly, routed through DNS, or forwarded to a designated mail gateway.

Note   The e-mail domain is the portion of the e-mail address to the right of the at symbol (@). For example, the e-mail domain for the williams@tech.microsoft.com adress is tech.microsoft.com.

If a message is for local recipients, it is moved from the Queue folder to the Drop folder designated for the default domain. After the message is placed in the Drop folder, the SMTP service is done processing the message. By default, the Drop folder is located at Inetpub\Mailroot\Drop. However, the location of the Drop folder is configurable and can be changed using the Properties dialog box for the default domain.

If a message is for remote recipients, the recipients for the message are sorted by domain so the SMTP service can deliver the messages to these recipients as a group and thereby attempt to deliver multiple messages in a single mail session. After sorting, the message is queued for delivery.

Messages in the queue are handled in first in, first out order, meaning the first message into the queue is the first message SMTP attempts to deliver. When a message is at the front of the queue, the SMTP service attempts to connect to the destination mail server. If the SMTP service is able to establish a connection, the recipients are verified, the message is sent, and it is up to the destination server to confirm receipt. If the destination server fails to respond or is not ready to receive the message, the message remains in the queue and the SMTP service attempts to deliver the message according to the retry intervals you've specified. Processing will continue on lower-ranked messages while the SMTP service waits to retry delivery.

Messages that cannot be delivered within a specific expiration period are marked as nondeliverable, and the SMTP service generates a nondelivery report. The nondelivery report provides an error message that explains why delivery failed along with the original message. The SMTP service then attempts to deliver this report to the sender of the original message.

The message delivery process for the nondelivery report is the same as it is for any other message. The SMTP service places the message in the Queue folder and processes the message according to whether the sender is a local or remote recipient. However, if the nondelivery report cannot be delivered to the sender of the original message, the nondelivery report is moved to the Badmail folder, and the SMTP service is finished processing the message.

Core SMTP Administration

Core SMTP administration has to do with creating SMTP virtual servers, managing a server's port and Internet Protocol (IP) address configuration, checking server health, and monitoring user sessions. These tasks are examined in the sections that follow.

Creating SMTP Virtual Servers

When you install the SMTP service, a default SMTP virtual server is created. The default SMTP virtual server handles message delivery for the default domain and any other domains you've configured. In most cases, you won't need to create an additional SMTP virtual server. However, if you are hosting multiple domains and you want to have more than one default domain, you may want to create additional SMTP virtual servers to service these domains. You may also want to create additional virtual servers when you need to set separate messaging restrictions on each domain that you host.

You can create additional SMTP virtual servers by completing the following steps:

1. If you are installing the SMTP virtual server on a new server, ensure that the SMTP service has been installed on the server.

2. If you want the virtual server to use a new IP address, you must configure the IP address before installing the site. For details, refer to Chapter 15, "Managing TCP/IP Networking," in *Microsoft Windows 2000 Administrator's Pocket Consultant.*

3. In the Internet Information Services snap-in, right-click the icon for the computer you want to work with, point to New, and then select SMTP Virtual Server. If the computer isn't shown, connect to it as discussed in the "Connecting To Other Servers" section of Chapter 2, "Core IIS Administration," and then perform this task.

4. The New SMTP Virtual Server Wizard is started, as shown in Figure 8-1. In the Description field, type a descriptive name for the Web site, such as TechNet SMTP Server, and then click Next.

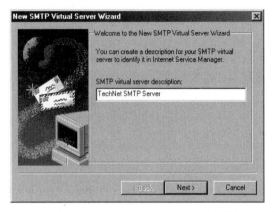

Figure 8-1. *Use the New SMTP Virtual Server Wizard to create the additional virtual server.*

5. Use the IP Address selection list to select an available IP address. Choose (All Unassigned) to allow SMTP to respond on all unassigned IP addresses that are configured on the server. The TCP port is assigned automatically to port 25. Click Next to continue.

 Note The IP address and TCP port combination must be unique on every virtual server. Multiple virtual servers can use the same port, provided that the servers are configured to use different IP addresses.

6. The next dialog box lets you set the home directory for the virtual server. Click Browse to search for a folder. This folder must be created before you can select it. If necessary, use Microsoft Windows Explorer to create the directory before you browse for a folder. Click Next to continue.

Tip For SMTP to function properly, the special group Everyone needs Full Control over the home directory and the associated subdirectories.

7. Next, you must specify the default domain for the virtual server. The default domain is a DNS domain that is serviced locally by the SMTP server. Typically, the default domain is the domain name specified in the DNS tab of the TCP/IP Properties dialog box for the server.

8. Click Finish to create the virtual server. If the default startup setting for the SMTP service is set to Automatic, the new SMTP virtual server should start

automatically as well. However, if you select an IP address and TCP port combination that is already in use, the virtual server will not start automatically, and you'll need to change the IP address or TCP port before you can start the virtual server.

9. Configure the virtual server as detailed in the sections of this chapter entitled "Handling Incoming Connections," "Handling Outgoing Connections," and "Managing Messaging Delivery."

Configuring Ports and IP Addresses Used by SMTP Servers

Each SMTP virtual server has a unique identity. The identity includes TCP port and IP address settings. The default TCP port is 25. The default IP address setting is to use any available IP address. To change the identity of an SMTP virtual server, complete the following steps:

1. If you want the SMTP virtual server to use a new IP address, you must configure the IP address before updating the site. For details, refer to Chapter 15, "Managing TCP/IP Networking," in *Microsoft Windows 2000 Administrator's Pocket Consultant*.

2. Start the Internet Information Services snap-in and then, in the left pane (Console Root), click the plus sign (+) next to the computer you want to work with. If the computer isn't shown, connect to it as discussed in the "Connecting To Other Servers" section of Chapter 2, "Core IIS Administration."

3. Right-click the SMTP virtual server you want to manage and then choose Properties. The dialog box shown in Figure 8-2 is displayed.

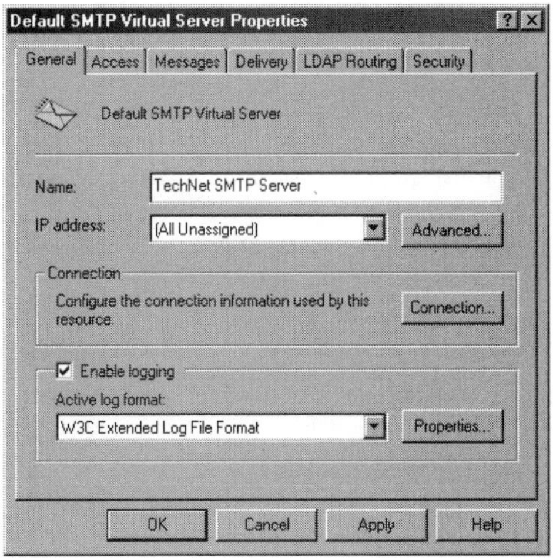

Figure 8-2. *You modify a site's identity through the General tab in the Properties dialog box.*

4. The Name field shows the descriptive name for the SMTP virtual server site. The descriptive name is displayed in the Internet Information Services snap-in and isn't used for other purposes. You can change the current value by typing a new value in the Name field.

5. The IP Address selection list shows the current IP address for the SMTP virtual server. If you want to change the current setting, use the selection list to select an available IP address or choose (All Unassigned) to allow SMTP to respond on all unassigned IP addresses. Multiple SMTP virtual servers can use the same IP address, provided that the servers are configured to use different port numbers.

6. The TCP port for the SMTP virtual server is assigned automatically to port 25. If you want to change the default value, display the Advanced dialog box by clicking Advanced. Next, select the IP address entry that you want to change and then click Edit. Type a new port number in the TCP Port field and click OK. Then click OK again to save your settings. Multiple File Transport Protocol (FTP) sites can use the same TCP port, provided that the sites are configured to use different IP addresses.

7. Click OK to close the Properties dialog box.

Configuring Multiple Identities for SMTP Virtual Servers

In some instances, you may want a single SMTP virtual server to have multiple identities. An SMTP virtual server is capable of handling incoming messages on multiple IP addresses and ports. For example, you could configure the server to receive mail on multiple TCP ports.

To assign multiple identities to an SMTP virtual server, complete the following steps:

1. In the Internet Information Services snap-in, right-click the SMTP virtual server you want to manage, and then choose Properties.

2. On the General tab, click Advanced, and then use the Advanced dialog box shown in Figure 8-3 to configure new IP address and TCP port settings. The key buttons on this dialog box are the following:

   - **Add** Adds a new identity. Click Add, select the IP address you want to use, and then type a TCP port. Click OK when you are finished.

   - **Edit** Allows you to edit the currently selected entry in the Address list box.

   - **Remove** Allows you to remove the currently selected entry from the Address list box.

3. Click OK, then click OK again to save your settings.

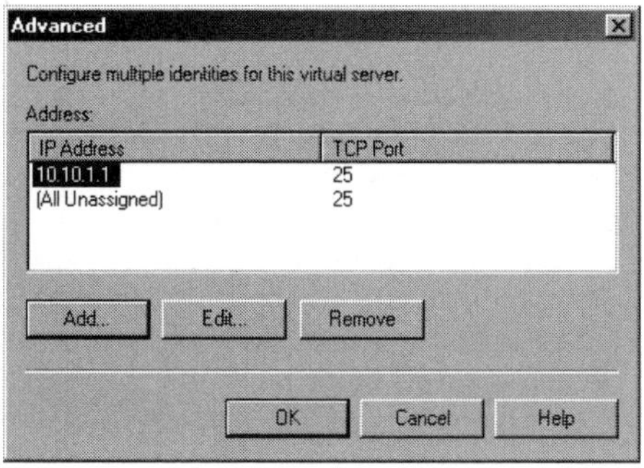

Figure 8-3. *SMTP virtual servers can respond on multiple IP addresses and ports. Configure additional identities using the Advanced dialog box.*

Monitoring SMTP Virtual Server Health

When you configure SMTP for use on a server, you should periodically monitor the folders under the Mailroot. These folders provide the best indicator as to the health of the SMTP installation. The key folders you'll want to monitor are the following:

- **Badmail** Messages in this folder couldn't be delivered to the intended recipients, and they couldn't be returned to the sender. If the number of messages in this folder is growing, your mail server may have a problem accessing the network or delivering mail. Try pinging the external network or the problem servers.

- **Drop** Messages in this folder have been processed by SMTP and are addressed to locally serviced domains. You may find messages addressed to postmaster@yourwebserver.com here. Read the messages and forward them as necessary to individuals in your organization.

- **Queue** Messages in this folder have been sorted and are queued for delivery to remote domains. If the number of queued messages is growing and messages aren't clearing out of this folder, your server may have a problem connecting to the network or delivering mail. Try pinging the external network or the problem servers.

- **Pickup** Messages should pass through this folder quickly. If messages remain in this folder, they may be unreadable, or there may be a problem with the SMTP service. You may, for example, have set permissions on the folder that don't allow the SMTP service to read its contents. Check the folder permissions and the status of the SMTP service.

Note Each SMTP virtual server has a separate Mailroot. The location of the Mailroot was set when the SMTP virtual server was installed. Note also that alternate Badmail folders can be configured on the Messages tab in the Properties dialog box for the virtual server.

Managing User Sessions

A user session is started each time a user connects to a virtual server. The session lasts for the duration of the user's connection. Each virtual server tracks user sessions separately. By viewing the current sessions, you can monitor server load and determine which users are logged on to a server as well as how long users have been connected. If an unauthorized user is accessing a virtual server, you can terminate the user session, which immediately disconnects the user. If you want to disconnect all users that are accessing a particular virtual server, you can do this as well.

To view or end user sessions, complete the following steps:

1. Start the Internet Information Services snap-in, and then double-click the entry for the virtual server you want to work with.

2. You should now see a node called Current Sessions. When you select this node in the left pane, current sessions are displayed in the right pane.

3. To disconnect a single user, right-click a user entry in the right pane, and then select Terminate.

4. To disconnect all users, right-click a user entry in the right pane, and then select Terminate All.

Configuring Service Domains

SMTP virtual servers are configured to support specific service domains. The only types of service domains you can create are alias and remote domains. The default domain is set automatically when you install the virtual server. If necessary, you can set an alias domain as the default.

Viewing Configured Service Domains

Before you create additional service domains on an SMTP virtual server, you should check the domains that are already being serviced by the SMTP virtual servers installed on the Web server. Each virtual server has separate service domains. You can view the configured service domains by completing the following steps:

1. Start the Internet Information Services snap-in and then double-click the entry for the virtual server you want to work with.

2. You should now see a node called Domains. When you select this node in the left pane, configured service domains are displayed in the right pane, as shown in Figure 8-4. The domain entries depict two characteristics:

   • **Domain Name**   The DNS name of the service domain, such as microsoft.com

   • **Type**   The type of the service domain as Local (Default), Local (Alias), or Remote

3. To view the properties of a service domain, right-click the domain entry, and then select Properties from the shortcut menu.

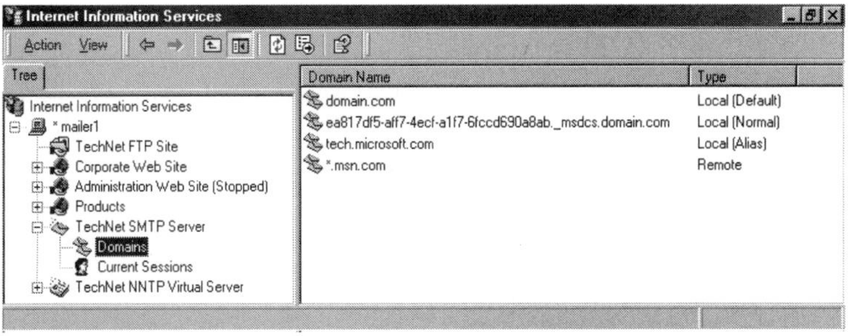

Figure 8-4. *SMTP virtual servers can have local alias, local default, and remote service domains.*

Working with Local Domains

Local service domains are domains that are serviced locally by SMTP. Two types of local domains are available: default and alias. The default domain serves as the default for incoming and outgoing messages. Alias domains allow you to create secondary domains that point to the default domain and use its settings. Messages addressed to the default domain and any associated alias domains are stored in the virtual server's Drop directory. Outgoing messages use the default domain as their domain of origin.

With local domains you have several administration options. You can

- Create alias domains
- Set an existing alias domain as the default
- Configure Drop direction location and quota settings

Creating Alias Domains

Alias domains allow you to create secondary domains that point to the default domain. Alias domains use the same configuration settings and the same Drop directory as the default domain.

You can create an alias domain by completing the following steps:

1. Start the Internet Information Services snap-in, and then double-click the entry for the virtual server you want to work with.
2. Right-click Domains, point to New, and then select Domain. This starts the New SMTP Domain Wizard.
3. Select Alias as the domain type and then click Next.
4. Type the DNS domain name of the alias in the Name field. You cannot use wildcards on the domain name. For example, you can use tech.microsoft.com, but you cannot use *.microsoft.com.
5. Click Finish to create the alias domain.

Setting the Default Domain

The default domain serves as the default for all messages transferred into or out of the domain. Messages addressed to the default domain are stored in the virtual server's Drop directory. Outgoing messages that do not have a domain set in the From field of the e-mail address use the default domain as their domain of origin. An SMTP virtual server can have only one default domain.

The default domain name is set automatically when you install the SMTP virtual server. If you need to set a new default service domain, you'll need to create an alias domain with the new settings you want to use, and then set the alias domain as the default service domain. To set an existing alias domain as the default service domain, follow these steps:

1. Start the Internet Information Services snap-in, and then double-click the entry for the virtual server you want to work with.

2. Select the Domains node in the left pane. You should see a list of service domains configured on the server.

3. Right-click the alias domain that you want to be the default, and then select Set As Default from the shortcut menu.

Changing the Drop Directory Settings for the Default Domain

The Drop directory is the final destination for all incoming messages addressed to local domains. This means messages addressed to the local domain and any alias domains are transferred from the Queue to the Drop directory. By default, the Drop directory is located at Inetpub\Mailroot\Drop. You can change the drop directory settings by completing the following steps:

1. Start the Internet Information Services snap-in, and then double-click the entry for the virtual server you want to work with.

2. Select the Domains node in the left pane. You should see a list of service domains configured on the server.

3. Right-click the default domain and then select Properties. The Properties dialog box shown in Figure 8-5 is displayed.

4. Type the new location of the Drop directory in the field provided, or click Browse to search for a folder. The folder you want to use must be created before you can select it, and it must be on a local drive. If necessary, use Windows Explorer to create the directory before you browse for a folder.

5. You can enforce a quota policy for the Drop directory by selecting Enable Drop Directory Quota. Otherwise, clear this option.

 Tip Quotas are useful to restrict the total size of the messages stored in the Drop directory. Quotas are enforced according to the quota policies configured for the directory owner. For more information about working with quotas, see the *Windows 2000 Server Administrator's Companion*.

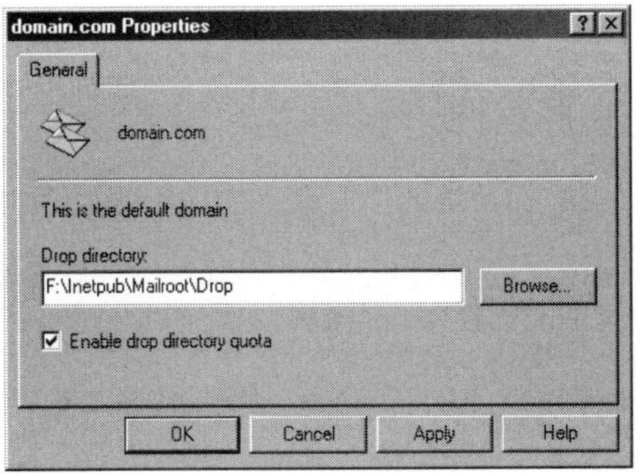

Figure 8-5. *The Drop directory is used by the default domain and all alias domains configured on the virtual server. You can change the directory location and quota configuration at any time.*

6. Click OK.

Working with Remote Domains

Any message with a nonlocal destination address is queued for delivery to a remote server. By default, the SMTP Service forwards messages directly to the destination SMTP servers, as listed in DNS. If you have unique delivery requirements for a specific remote server, you can add a remote domain to the SMTP virtual server and configure the necessary delivery requirements.

Once you create a remote domain, you have many different configuration options. The key options are the following:

- To set relay restrictions
- To configure support for Extension to SMTP (ESMTP) or standard SMTP
- To set outbound access and authentication security
- To queue messages for remote triggered delivery
- To configure route domains with smart hosts

Creating Remote Domains

Remote domains allow you to set delivery paths and routing for other SMTP servers and mail gateways. You typically configure remote domains for domains to which you commonly send messages. For each remote domain, you can set specific delivery options and require authentication before delivering mail to the domain.

You can create a remote domain by completing the following steps:

1. Start the Internet Information Services snap-in, and then double-click the entry for the virtual server you want to work with.

2. Right-click Domains, point to New, and then select Domain. This starts the New SMTP Domain Wizard.

3. Select Remote as the domain type and then click Next.

4. Specify the address space of the domain. Typically, this is the DNS domain name of the remote domain.

 Tip You can also use a wildcard character in the name so that all-inclusive domains use the same settings. Use an asterisk (*) as the first character, followed by a period (.), and then enter the remaining portion of the domain name, such as *.com for all .com domains or *.microsoft.com for all domains ending with microsoft.com.

5. Click Finish to create the remote domain. Select Domains in the left pane of the Internet Information Services snap-in. Right-click the remote domain entry in the right pane and then select Properties. You should now set properties for routing and securing message delivery to the remote domain. Click OK when your changes are completed.

Setting and Removing Relay Restrictions for Remote Domains

Mail relaying allows external users to use your mail system to relay messages bound for another organization. By default, the SMTP service is configured to prevent mail relaying, and you typically should maintain this setting to prevent the systems from being used to distribute spam. In this way, external users are unable to relay mail through your SMTP virtual server. Sometimes, however, you'll want users to be able to relay mail to designated mail gateways. The way you do this is to create a remote domain that specifies the target service domain and then authorizes mail relaying to this service domain.

You can set or remove relay restrictions by completing the following steps:

1. Start the Internet Information Services snap-in, and then double-click the entry for the virtual server you want to work with.

2. Select the Domains node in the left pane. You should see a list of service domains configured on the server.

3. Right-click the remote domain to which you want to relay mail and then select Properties. The Properties dialog box shown in Figure 8-6 is displayed.

4. To allow mail relaying to the remote domain, select Allow Incoming Mail To Be Relayed To This Domain.

5. To prevent mail relaying to the remote domain, clear Allow Incoming Mail To Be Relayed To This Domain.

6. Click OK.

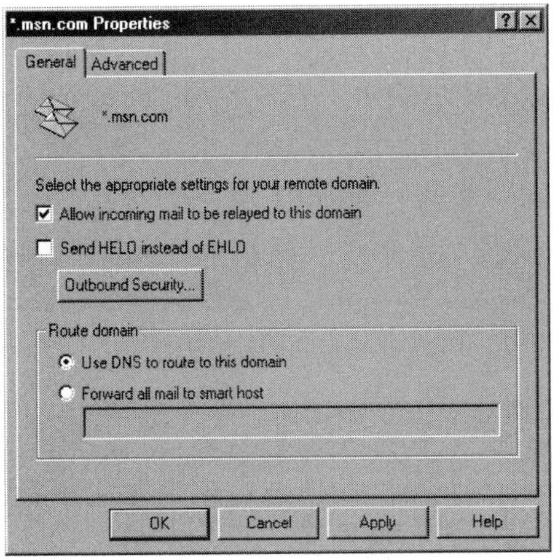

Figure 8-6. *You can configure remote domains to allow or prevent mail relaying. Mail relaying is prevented by default.*

Switching SMTP Modes Used with Remote Domains

The SMTP service supports standard SMTP and ESMTP. Although ESMTP is more efficient and secure than SMTP, you may want to configure a specific remote domain to use SMTP instead. The primary scenario under which you would do this is when the e-mail system in the remote domain doesn't support ESMTP and you are receiving error messages when initiating the ESMTP session.

By default, SMTP virtual servers always try to initiate ESMTP sessions using the EHLO session command, but you can change this to the more widely compatible SMTP HELO command. The SMTP service initiates SMTP sessions with other mail servers by issuing a HELO start command. The SMTP service initiates ESMTP sessions with other mail servers by issuing an EHLO start command.

You can change SMTP modes by completing the following steps:

1. Start the Internet Information Services snap-in, and then double-click the entry for the virtual server you want to work with.

2. Select the Domains node in the left pane. You should see a list of service domains configured on the server.

3. Right-click the remote domain you want to work with and then select Properties. The Properties dialog box shown previously in Figure 8-6 is displayed.

4. The Send HELO Instead Of EHLO check box controls the use of SMTP or ESMTP. To use SMTP, select this option. To use ESMTP (which is the default), clear this option.

5. Click OK.

Queuing Messages for Remote Triggered Delivery

The SMTP service can hold mail for mail clients or gateways that periodically connect to a virtual server and download mail. In this case, the client initiates delivery of the mail by issuing an ATRN command. The ATRN command tells the SMTP service to start sending messages to the remote domain. When you configure remote triggered delivery, you must specify the domain accounts in the enterprise that are authorized to use this feature. You do this by adding the domain accounts to an authorization list.

You can enable remote triggered delivery for named accounts in a remote domain by completing the following steps:

1. Start the Internet Information Services snap-in, and then double-click the entry for the virtual server you want to work with.

2. Select the Domains node in the left pane. You should see a list of service domains configured on the server.

3. Right-click the remote domain you want to work with and then select Properties.

4. Select the Advanced tab, as shown in Figure 8-7.

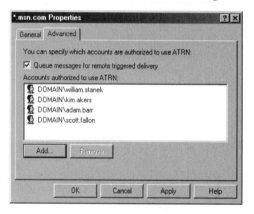

Figure 8-7. *You can queue messages addressed to specific users in a remote domain; then the user's mail client can trigger delivery of those messages.*

5. To enable remote triggered delivery, select Queue Messages For Remote Triggered Delivery.

6. To specify an authorized account, click Add. This displays the Select Users Or Groups dialog box, which you can use to select users or groups that are in the same Active Directory domain forest or tree.

7. To remove an authorized account, select the account in the Accounts Authorized list box and then click Remove.

8. Click OK.

Configuring Authentication for Remote Domains

By default, the SMTP service doesn't authenticate connections to remote domains. This means the connectors anonymously access remote domains to send messages. You can configure an SMTP virtual server to pass authentication credentials to remote domains, however. The key reasons to do this are when a specific level of authentication is required to access a remote domain or when you are sending messages to a specific address in the remote domain that requires authentication.

Several types of authentication can be used:

- **Basic**   Standard authentication with wide compatibility. With basic authentication, the username and password specified are passed as clear text to the remote domain.

- **Windows Security Package**   Secure authentication for Windows-compatible domains. With this authentication level, the username and password specified are passed securely to the remote domain using Windows security.

- **Transport Layer Security (TLS) Encryption**   Encrypted authentication for servers with smart cards or X.509 certificates. This type of authentication is combined with basic or Windows authentication.

To configure outbound security for a remote domain, follow these steps:

1. Start the Internet Information Services snap-in, and then double-click the entry for the virtual server you want to work with.

2. Select the Domains node in the left pane. You should see a list of service domains configured on the server.

3. Right-click the remote domain you want to work with and then select Properties.

4. Click Outbound Security on the General tab to display the dialog box shown in Figure 8-8.

5. To set standard authentication for wide compatibility, select Basic Authentication.

6. To set secure authentication for Windows-compatible domains, select Windows Security Package.

7. Each authentication mode has associated User Name and Password fields. Use these fields to set the authentication credentials. If the remote domain is in the same Active Directory domain forest or tree, click Browse to find an account in the remote domain using the Select User dialog box, and then type the account password.

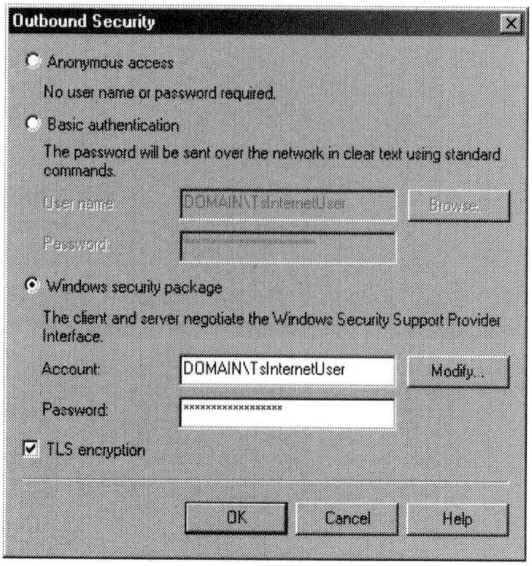

Figure 8-8. *Select the outbound security options and add TLS encryption if supported by the remote domain.*

8. If you want to encrypt message traffic and the destination servers in the remote domain support smart cards or X.509 certificates, select the TLS Encryption check box.

9. Click OK.

Caution When you select TLS encryption, the destination servers in the remote domain must support smart cards or X.509 certificates. If the servers do not, all messages sent to the remote domain will be returned with a nondelivery report.

Configuring Smart Hosts for Remote Domains

You can route all outgoing messages for a remote domain through a smart host instead of sending them directly to the destination domain. This allows you to route messages for the remote domain to a specific server. The goal is to route messages over a connection that may be more direct or less costly than the standard route.

You can add or remove a smart host for a remote domain by completing the following steps:

1. Start the Internet Information Services snap-in, and then double-click the entry for the virtual server you want to work with.

2. Select the Domains node in the left pane. You should see a list of service domains configured on the server.

3. Right-click the remote domain you want to work with and then select Properties.

4. To add a smart host, select Forward All Mail To Smart Host, and then type the IP address or the DNS name of the smart host in the field provided.

Tip   If you use an IP address to identify a smart host, enclose the IP address in brackets [] to prevent the SMTP service from attempting to perform a DNS lookup on the address. Note also that smart host settings for remote domains override smart host settings configured for the SMTP virtual server itself.

5. To remove a smart host, select Use DNS To Route To This Domain.

6. Click OK.

Renaming and Deleting Service Domains

You cannot rename a service domain. You can, however, create a new alias or remote domain using the new information, and then delete the existing service domain. For example, if you created a service domain called tec.microsoft.com that should have been tech.microsoft.com, you'll need to create a new service domain and then delete the old service domain. Keep in mind that you cannot delete the default domain. If you need to rename the default domain, you'll need to do the following:

1. Create an alias domain with the correct information.

2. Set the alias domain as the default.

3. Delete the old default domain.

You can delete a service domain by completing the following steps:

1. Start the Internet Information Services snap-in, and then double-click the entry for the virtual server you want to work with.

2. Select the Domains node in the left pane. You should see a list of service domains configured on the server.

3. Right-click the remote domain you want to delete, and then select Delete. When prompted to confirm the action, click Yes.

Handling Incoming Connections

Incoming connections to virtual servers can be controlled in several different ways. You can do the following:

- Grant or deny access using IP addresses or Internet domain names
- Require secure incoming connections
- Require authentication for incoming connections
- Restrict concurrent connections and set connection time-out values

Each of these tasks is discussed in the sections that follow.

 Note With SMTP, both incoming and outbound connection restrictions can be configured. To learn how to configure outbound connections, see the "Handling Outgoing Connections" section of this chapter.

Securing Access by IP Address, Subnet, or Domain

By default, virtual servers are accessible to all IP addresses, which presents a security risk that may allow your messaging system to be misused. To control use of a virtual server, you may want to grant or deny access by IP address, subnet, or domain.

- Granting access allows a computer to access the virtual server but doesn't necessarily allow users to submit or retrieve messages. Users still need to authenticate themselves if you require authentication.
- Denying access prevents a computer from accessing the virtual server. As a result, users of the computer cannot submit or retrieve messages from the virtual server—even if they could have authenticated themselves with a username and password.

To grant or deny access to a virtual server by IP address, subnet, or domain, follow these steps:

1. In the Internet Information Services snap-in, right-click the SMTP virtual server you want to manage, and then choose Properties.
2. Click Connection on the Access tab. As shown in Figure 8-9, the Computers list shows the computers that currently have connection controls.
3. To grant access to specific computers and deny access to all others, click Only The List Below.
4. To deny access to specific computers and grant all others access, click All Except The List Below.
5. Create the grant or deny list. Click Add and then, in the Computer dialog box, specify Single Computer, Group Of Computers, or Domain. When you have specified the computer or group, click OK.

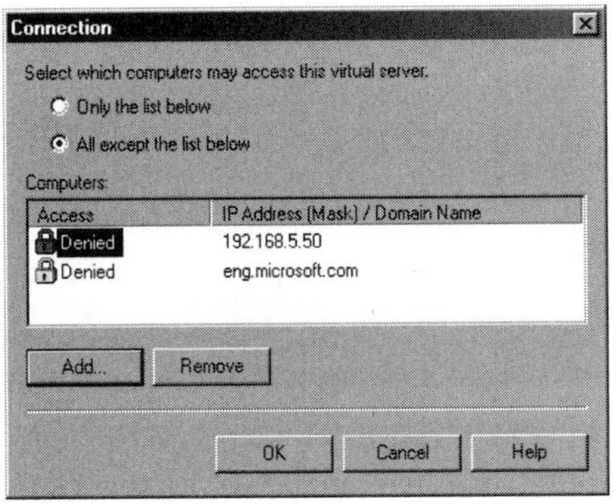

Figure 8-9. *Connections can be controlled by IP address, subnet, or domain.*

- With a single computer, enter the IP address for the computer, such as 192.168.5.50.

- With a group of computers, enter the subnet address, such as 192.168.5.0, and the subnet mask, such as 255.255.255.0.

- With a domain name, enter the fully qualified domain name (FQDN), such as eng.domain.com.

Caution   When you grant or deny by domain, the SMTP service must perform a reverse DNS lookup on each connection to determine if the connection comes from the domain. These reverse lookups can severely impact the performance of the SMTP service, and this performance impact increases as the number of concurrent users and connections increases.

6. If you want to remove an entry from the grant or deny list, select the related entry in the Computers list and then click Remove.

7. Click OK.

Controlling Secure Communications for Incoming Connections

By default, mail clients pass connection information and message data through an insecure connection. If corporate security is a high priority, however, your information security team may require that mail clients connect over secure communication channels. You configure secure communications as follows:

1. Create a certificate request for the SMTP virtual server for which you want to use secure communications. Each server that will be exchanging messages with other secure SMTP virtual servers must have a certificate.

2. Submit the certificate request to a certificate authority. The certificate authority will then issue you a certificate (usually for a fee).

3. Install the certificate on the SMTP virtual server. Repeat Steps 1 to 3 for each SMTP virtual server that needs to communicate over a secure channel.

4. Configure the server to require secure communications on a per-virtual server basis.

Following this procedure, you could create, install, and enable a certificate for use on a virtual server by completing the following steps:

1. In the Internet Information Services snap-in, right-click the SMTP virtual server on which you want to secure communications, and then select Properties.

2. On the Access tab, click Certificate. This starts the Web Certificate Wizard. Use the wizard to create a new certificate.

3. Send the certificate request to your certificate authority (CA). When you receive the certificate back from the CA, access the Web Certificate Wizard from the virtual server's Properties dialog box again. Now you'll be able to process the pending request and install the certificate.

4. When you are finished installing the certificate, don't close the Properties dialog box. Instead, click Communicate on the Access tab.

5. In the Security dialog box, click Require Secure Channel, and then, if you've also configured 128-bit security, select Require 128-Bit Encryption.

6. Click OK, then click OK again to save your settings.

Controlling Authentication for Incoming Connections

The SMTP service supports the following authentication modes:

- **Anonymous**   With anonymous authentication, users are able to anonymously connect to the server and submit messages for delivery. Most Web servers have SMTP virtual servers configured for anonymous connections. This allows applications and external users to submit mail for delivery to the domain without needing to be authenticated. The way you prevent users from abusing the system is to set restrictions that allow only authorized users to relay mail on the server.

- **Basic Authentication**   With basic authentication, users are prompted for logon information before they are allowed to connect to the SMTP virtual server. When the logon information is entered, the information is transmitted unencrypted across the network. If you've configured secure communications on the server as described under "Controlling Secure Communications for Incoming Connections," you can require that clients use Secure Sockets Layer (SSL). When you use SSL with basic authentication, the logon information is encrypted before transmission.

- **Windows Security Package**   With Windows authentication, the SMTP service uses standard Windows security to validate the user's identity. Instead of prompting for a username and password, clients relay the logon credentials users supply when they log on to Windows. These credentials are fully encrypted without the need for SSL and include the username and password needed to log on to the network.

All three authentication methods are enabled by default for SMTP virtual servers. As necessary, you can enable or disable support for these authentication methods. The steps you perform are as follows:

1. In the Internet Information Services snap-in, right-click the SMTP virtual server that you want to work with, and then select Properties.

2. On the Access tab, click Authentication. This displays the dialog box shown in Figure 8-10.

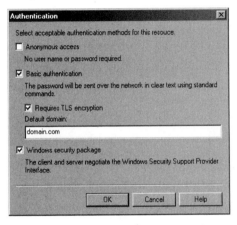

Figure 8-10. *Authentication methods can be enabled or disabled to meet the needs of your organization. With basic authentication, it is often helpful to set a default domain as well.*

3. You can now choose the acceptable authentication methods. Keep in mind that if you disable anonymous access, clients must authenticate themselves before they can submit messages for delivery, and you may need to reconfigure Web-based applications on your server so that they use authentication.

4. If you enable basic authentication, you can set a default domain that should be used when no domain information is supplied during the logon process. Setting the default domain is useful when you want to ensure that clients authenticate properly.

5. With basic authentication, you can also require TLS encryption. With TLS encryption, clients must have smart cards or certificates installed to establish a secure connection to the server.

6. Click OK, then click OK again to save your settings.

Restricting Incoming Connections and Setting Time-Out Values

You can control incoming connections to SMTP virtual servers in two key ways. You can set a limit on the number of simultaneous connections, and you can set a connection time-out value.

Normally, SMTP virtual servers accept an unlimited number of connections, and this is an optimal setting in most environments. However, when you are trying to prevent a virtual server from becoming overloaded, you may want to limit the number of simultaneous connections. Once the limit is reached, no other clients are permitted to access the server. The clients must wait until the connection load on the server decreases.

The connection time-out value determines when idle connections are disconnected. Normally, connections time out after they've been idle for 10 minutes. In most situations, a 10-minute time-out is ideal. Still, there are times when you'll want to increase the time-out value, and this primarily relates to clients that get disconnected when transferring large messages. If you discover that clients get disconnected during large message transfers, the time-out value is one area to look into.

You can modify connection limits and time-outs by completing the following steps:

1. In the Internet Information Services snap-in, right-click the SMTP virtual server that you want to work with, and then select Properties.

2. Click Connection on the General tab. This displays the Connections dialog box, shown in Figure 8-11.

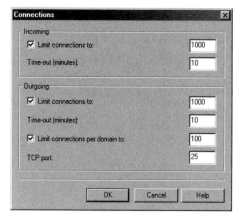

Figure 8-11. *Connection limits and time-outs can help reduce server load. They can also help in resolving connection problems.*

3. All the changes you'll make are to the fields on the Incoming panel. To set a connection limit, select Limit Connections To and then type the limit value. To remove connection limits, clear Limit Connections To.

4. The Time-Out field controls the connection time-out. Type the new time-out value in minutes. In most cases, you'll want to use a time-out value between 10 and 30 minutes.

5. Click OK, then click OK again to save your settings.

Handling Outgoing Connections

As with incoming connections, you can control outgoing connections to external SMTP virtual servers in several different ways. You can do the following:

- Require authentication for outgoing connections
- Restrict concurrent connections and set connection time-out values
- Configure message limits
- Handle nondelivery, bad mail, and unresolved recipients
- Set relay restrictions for message delivery

Each of these tasks is discussed in the sections that follow.

Configuring Outbound Security

By default, SMTP virtual servers deliver messages to other servers without authenticating themselves. This mode of authentication is referred to as anonymous. You can also configure SMTP virtual servers to use basic or Windows authentication. However, you rarely will use an authentication method other than anonymous with SMTP virtual servers.

One time that you'll use basic or Windows authentication with outgoing connections is when the SMTP virtual server must deliver all e-mail to a specific server or e-mail address in another domain. In other words, the server only delivers mail to one destination and doesn't deliver mail to other destinations. If you need to configure authentication for e-mail delivered to a particular server and need to deliver mail to other servers, you should configure a remote service domain to send mail to that specific server and use anonymous authentication for all other mail.

To view or change the outbound security settings for an SMTP virtual server, complete the following steps:

1. In the Internet Information Services snap-in, right-click the SMTP virtual server that you want to work with, and then select Properties.

2. On the Delivery tab, click Outbound Security. To use standard delivery for outgoing messages, select Anonymous Access.

3. To set basic authentication for outgoing messages, select Basic Authentication, and then, under User Name and Password, type the account name and password that are required to connect to the remote server.

4. To set Windows authentication for outgoing messages, select Windows Security Package, and then, under Account and Password, type the Windows account name and password that are required to connect to the remote server.

5. When you require authentication, you can also require encryption. To do this, select TLS Encryption.

> **Note** When you select TLS encryption, the destination servers must support smart cards or X.509 certificates. If the servers do not, all messages sent to noncompliant servers will be returned with a nondelivery report.

6. Click OK, then click OK again to save your settings.

Controlling Outgoing Connections

With SMTP virtual servers, you have much more control over outgoing connections than you do incoming connections. You can limit the number of simultaneous connections and the number of connections per domain. These limits set the maximum number of simultaneous outbound connections. By default, the total number of connections is limited to 1000, and the total number of connections per domain is limited to 100. To improve performance, you should optimize these values based on the capacity of your Web server.

You can set a connection time-out that determines when idle connections are disconnected. Normally, outbound connections time out after they've been idle for 10 minutes. Sometimes, you'll want to increase the time-out value, and this primarily relates to times when you are experiencing connectivity problems and messages aren't getting delivered.

You can also map outbound SMTP connections to a TCP port other than port 25. If you are connecting through a firewall or proxy, you may want to map outgoing connections to a different port and then let the firewall or proxy deliver the mail over the standard SMTP port (port 25).

You set outgoing connection controls by completing the following steps:

1. In the Internet Information Services snap-in, right-click the SMTP virtual server that you want to work with, and then select Properties.

2. Click Connection on the General tab. This displays the Connections dialog box shown previously in Figure 8-11.

3. All the changes you'll make are to the fields on the Outgoing panel. To remove outgoing connection limits, clear Limit Connections To. To set an outgoing connection limit, select Limit Connections To, and then type the limit value.

4. The Time-Out field controls the connection time-out. Type the new time-out value in minutes. In most cases, you'll want to use a time-out value between 10 minutes and 30 minutes.

5. To set an outgoing connection limit per domain, select Limit Connections Per Domain To and then type the limit value. You can remove the per-domain limit by clearing Limit Connections Per Domain To.

6. To map outgoing connections to a different port, type the outbound port that the firewall or proxy expects in the TCP Port field.

7. Click OK, then click OK again to save your settings.

Configuring Outgoing Message Limits for SMTP

Outgoing message limits can be used to control SMTP usage and to improve throughput for message delivery. You can set the maximum allowable message size for incoming messages. Clients attempting to send messages larger than this size get a nondelivery report that states the message exceeds this limit. The default limit is 2048 KB.

You can set the maximum size of all messages that can be sent in a single connection. The session limit should always be set so that it is several times larger than the message size limit. The default limit is 10,240 KB. Clients attempting to send multiple messages in sessions whose total size exceeds this limit receive a nondelivery report stating that the maximum session size has been exceeded.

You can control the number of messages that can be sent in a single connection. When the number of messages exceeds this value, the SMTP service starts a new connection and transfer continues until all messages are delivered. Optimizing this value for your environment can improve server performance, especially if users typically send large numbers of messages to the same external domains. The default is 20. So, if you had 50 messages queued for delivery to the same destination server, the SMTP service would open three connections and use these connections to deliver the mail. Because message delivery would take less time if you optimize the number of connections, you can considerably enhance the SMTP service's performance.

You can also control the number of recipients for a single message. When the number of recipients exceeds this value, the SMTP service opens a new connection and uses this connection to process the remaining recipients. The default is 100. Using the 100-recipient limit, a message queued for delivery to 300 recipients would be sent over three connections. Again, because message delivery would take less time if you optimize the number of connections, you can considerably enhance the SMTP service's performance.

You set outgoing connection controls by completing the following steps:

1. In the Internet Information Services snap-in, right-click the SMTP virtual server that you want to work with, and then select Properties.
2. Select the Messages tab, as shown in Figure 8-12.

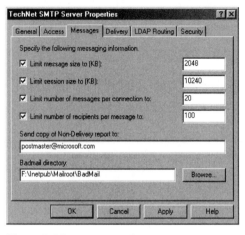

Figure 8-12. *Messaging limits can be used to control SMTP usage and to improve performance.*

3. Use the message size limit to strictly control the maximum message size. To disable this limit, clear Limit Message Size To. Otherwise, select the Limit Message Size To check box and use the related field to set a message size limit.

4. Use session limits to strictly control the maximum size of all messages that can be sent in a single session. To disable this limit, clear Limit Session Size To. Otherwise, select the Limit Session Size To check box and use the related field to set a session size limit.

5. Use the messages per connection limit to force the SMTP service to open new connections when multiple messages are queued for delivery to the same destination. To disable this limit, clear Limit Number Of Messages Per Connection To. Otherwise, select the Limit Number Of Messages Per Connection To check box and use the related field to set a limit.

6. Use recipient limits to force the SMTP service to open new connections when messages are addressed to lots of recipients. To disable this limit, clear Limit Number Of Recipients Per Message To. Otherwise, select the Limit Number Of Recipients Per Message To check box and use the related field to set a limit.

7. Click OK.

Handling Nondelivery, Bad Mail, and Unresolved Recipients

When a message is undeliverable or a fatal error occurs during delivery, the SMTP service generates a nondelivery report that it attempts to deliver to the sender. SMTP virtual server options provide several ways to handle nondelivery.

For tracking purposes, you can send a copy of all nondelivery reports to a specific e-mail address. The e-mail address specified is also placed in the Reply-To field of the nondelivery report. This allows users to respond to the error message and potentially reach someone who can help resolve the problem.

If a nondelivery report cannot be delivered to the sender, a copy of the original message is placed in the Badmail folder. Messages placed in the Badmail folder cannot be delivered or returned. You can use the Badmail folder to track potential abuse of your messaging system. By default, the Badmail folder is located at Inetpub\Mailroot\Badmail. You can change the location of the Badmail folder at any time as long as you use a local drive.

You can configure these nondelivery options by completing the following steps:

1. In the Internet Information Services snap-in, right-click the SMTP virtual server that you want to work with, and then select Properties.
2. Select the Messages tab, as shown previously in Figure 8-12.
3. In the Send Copy Of Non-Delivery Report To field, type the e-mail address of the organization's postmaster account or other account that should receive a copy of nondelivery reports.
4. In the Badmail Directory field, type the full path to the directory in which you want to store bad mail. If you don't know the full path, click Browse, and then use the Browse For Folder dialog box to find the folder you want to use.
5. Click OK.

Setting and Removing Relay Restrictions

Mail relaying can occur when users outside the organization use your mail system to send messages bound for another organization. The SMTP service normally prevents unauthorized users and computers from relaying mail through your organization—and you typically should use this setting. In this way, only users and computers that are able to authenticate themselves can use your mail system to relay messages.

If necessary, you can grant or deny relaying permissions to specific computers, networks, and domains, overriding the default configuration. To do this, follow these steps:

1. In the Internet Information Services snap-in, right-click the SMTP virtual server that you want to work with, and then select Properties.
2. Select the Access tab and then click Relay. You should now see the Relay Restrictions dialog box shown in Figure 8-13.

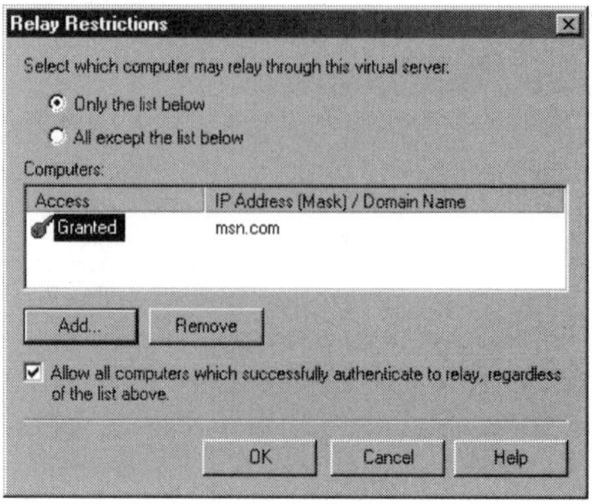

Relay Restrictions   ☒

Select which computer may relay through this virtual server:

⊙ Only the list below

○ All except the list below

Computers:

Access	IP Address [Mask] / Domain Name
✔ Granted	msn.com

[Add...]   [Remove]

☑ Allow all computers which successfully authenticate to relay, regardless of the list above.

[OK]   [Cancel]   [Help]

Figure 8-13. *If necessary, you can grant some computers the right to relay mail through your organization.*

3. To grant relay rights to specific computers and deny relay rights to all others, click Only The List Below.

4. To deny relaying for specific computers and grant all others the right to relay, click All Except The List Below.

• Create the grant or deny list. Click Add and then, in the Computer dialog box, specify Single Computer, Group Of Computers, or Domain. When you have specified the computer or group, click OK.

• With a single computer, enter the IP address for the computer, such as 192.168.5.50.

• With a group of computers, enter the subnet address, such as 192.168.5.0, and the subnet mask, such as 255.255.255.0.

• With a domain name, enter the FQDN, such as eng.domain.com.

 Caution When you grant or deny relaying by domain, the SMTP service must perform a reverse DNS lookup on each connection to determine if the connection comes from the domain. These reverse lookups can severely impact the performance of the SMTP service, and this performance impact increases as the number of concurrent users and connections increases.

5. If you want to remove an entry from the grant or deny list, select the entry in the Computers list, and then click Remove.

6. By default, any computer that can authenticate itself is permitted to relay messages through the SMTP virtual server. To change this behavior and strictly control relaying using the authorization list, clear Allow All Computers Which Successfully Authenticate To Relay.

7. Click OK.

Managing Message Delivery

SMTP delivery options determine how mail is delivered once a connection has been established and the receiving computer has acknowledged that it is ready to receive the data transfer. This section shows you how to use the configuration options that determine how message delivery and transfer occurs.

You can set the following options to control message delivery:

- Outbound retry intervals
- Outbound and local delay notification
- Outbound and local expiration time-out values
- Message hop count
- Domain name options
- Reverse DNS lookups
- External DNS server lists

Setting Outbound Retry Intervals, Delay Notification, and Expiration Time-Out

Once a connection has been established and the receiving computer has acknowledged that it is ready to receive the data transfer, the SMTP service attempts to deliver messages queued for delivery to the computer. If a message cannot be delivered on the first attempt, the SMTP service tries to send the message again after a specified time. The SMTP service keeps trying to send the message at the intervals you've specified until the expiration time-out is reached. When the time limit is reached, the message is returned to the sender with a nondelivery report. The default expiration time-out value is two days.

After each failed attempt to deliver a message, a delay notification is generated and queued for delivery to the user who sent the message. Notification doesn't occur immediately after failure. Instead, the delay notification message is sent only after the notification delay interval, and then only if the message hasn't been delivered already. The default notification delay value is 12 hours.

The SMTP service handles delay notification and expiration time-out values differently, depending on whether the message originated within the organization or outside the organization. Messages that originate within the organization are handled using the local delay notification and expiration time-out values. Messages that originate outside the organization are handled using the outbound delay notification and expiration time-out values.

You can view or change the retry interval, delay notification, and expiration time-out by completing the following steps:

1. In the Internet Information Services snap-in, right-click the SMTP virtual server that you want to work with, and then select Properties.

2. Click the Delivery tab as shown in Figure 8-14, then use the following options to set the retry values:

   * **First Retry Interval** Sets the amount of time to wait after the first delivery attempt. The default is 15 minutes.

   * **Second Retry Interval** Sets the amount of time to wait after the second delivery attempt. The default is 30 minutes after the first retry interval.

   * **Third Retry Interval** Sets the amount of time to wait after the third delivery attempt. The default is 60 minutes after the second retry interval.

   * **Subsequent Retry Interval** Sets the amount of time to wait after the fourth and subsequent delivery attempts. The default is 240 minutes.

3. Set the outbound delay notification and expiration time-out values using the Delay Notification and Expiration Timeout fields on the Outbound panel. These values can be set in minutes, hours, or days, and apply to messages addressed to remote domains and other external locations.

4. Set the local delay notification and expiration time-out values using the Delay Notification and Expiration Timeout fields on the Local panel. These values can be set in minutes, hours, or days, and they can apply to messages addressed to local and alias service domains.

5. Click OK.

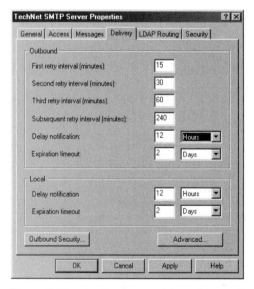

Figure 8-14. *Use the options of the Delivery tab to control message delivery in the organization.*

Setting Message Hop Count

Messages can be routed through many different servers before reaching their final destination. The number of servers a message passes through is called the hop count. As an administrator, you can control the maximum allowable hop count and you'll usually want to do this to prevent a message from being misrouted repeatedly.

The default maximum hop count is 15, which works well for most network configurations. However, if users frequently get nondelivery reports that state the maximum hop count was reached and the message wasn't delivered, you may want to consider increasing the maximum allowable hop count. The number of Received lines in the message header determines the total hops.

Caution Don't automatically increase the hop count without first examining the SMTP routing on your network. Nondelivery reports due to the hop count can also point to SMTP routing problems.

You can view or set the maximum hop count by completing the following steps:

1. In the Internet Information Services snap-in, right-click the SMTP virtual server that you want to work with, and then select Properties.
2. On the Delivery tab, click Advanced. This displays the Advanced Delivery dialog box.
3. If you want to change the hop count, type a new value in the Maximum Hop Count field. Valid values are between 10 and 256.
4. Click OK, then click OK again to save your settings.

Setting Domain Name Options

Domain names play an important role in determining how mail is delivered, and you have two options for configuring domain name usage. You can set a masquerade domain, and you can set a FQDN for the SMTP virtual server.

A masquerade domain replaces the local domain name in any Mail From lines in the message header. Mail From information is used to determine the address for sending nondelivery reports and does not replace the From lines in the message body that are displayed to mail clients. The name replacement occurs on the first hop only.

The FQDN of the virtual server is used in mail delivery. The server must have an FQDN, and this FQDN is associated with an e-mail domain through a DNS mail exchanger record. You have two options for specifying an FQDN:

• You can use the name specified on the Network Identification tab of the System utility.

• You can specify a unique FQDN for the SMTP virtual server you are configuring.

The name on the Network Identification tab is used automatically. If you change the name on this tab, the new name is used the next time the computer is rebooted. No action is required to update the FQDN for the virtual server. However, if you want to override the setting on the network identification tab, you can do so by specifying a unique FQDN for the SMTP virtual server.

You can set the masquerade domain name or override the default FQDN by completing the following steps:

1. In the Internet Information Services snap-in, right-click the SMTP virtual server that you want to work with, and then select Properties.

2. On the Delivery tab, click Advanced. This displays the Advanced Delivery dialog box shown in Figure 8-15.

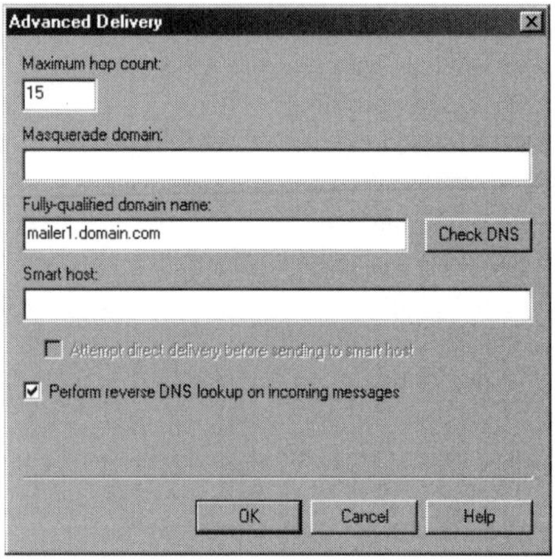

Figure 8-15. *Domain name options play an important role in determining how mail is delivered.*

3. In the Masquerade Domain field, type the domain name where you would like nondelivery reports to be sent. This will replace the default domain name in outgoing message headers.

4. If you want to override the default FQDN, type a new value in the Fully-Qualified Domain Name field. Click Check DNS to ensure you've entered the correct value and that DNS resolution is configured properly.

5. Click OK, then click OK again to save your settings.

Configuring Reverse DNS Lookups

With reverse lookups enabled, the SMTP service attempts to verify that the mail client's IP address matches the host and domain submitted by the client in the start session command. If the IP and DNS information match, the SMTP service passes the message through without modifying its contents. If the IP and DNS information cannot be verified, the SMTP service modifies the message header so that the key word "unverified" is inserted on the Received line of the message header.

As stated previously, reverse lookups can severely impact the performance of the SMTP service, and this performance impact increases as the number of concurrent users and connections increases. Because of this, you'll want to be very cautious of enabling reverse lookups.

To enable reverse DNS lookups, complete the following steps:

1. In the Internet Information Services snap-in, right-click the SMTP virtual server that you want to work with, and then select Properties.

2. On the Delivery tab, click Advanced. This displays the Advanced Delivery dialog box shown previously in Figure 8-15.

3. To enable reverse lookups, select Perform Reverse DNS Lookup On Incoming Messages. Clear this option to disable reverse lookups.

4. Click OK, and then click OK again to save your settings.

Routing Outgoing Messages to Smart Hosts

You can route all outgoing messages through a smart host instead of sending them directly to the destination domain. This allows you to route messages to a specific server that can relay or deliver the messages. The goal is to route messages over a connection that may be more direct or less costly than the standard route.

You can add or remove a smart host for a remote domain by completing the following steps:

1. In the Internet Information Services snap-in, right-click the SMTP virtual server that you want to work with, and then select Properties.

2. On the Delivery tab, click Advanced. This displays the Advanced Delivery dialog box shown previously in Figure 8-15.

3. To add a smart host, type the IP address or DNS name of the smart host in the Smart Host field. If you want the SMTP service to attempt direct delivery before using the smart host, select Attempt Direct Delivery Before Sending To Smart Host.

Tip If you use an IP address to identify a smart host, enclose the IP address in brackets [] to prevent the SMTP service from attempting to perform a DNS lookup on the address. Note also that smart host settings for remote domains override smart host settings configured for the SMTP virtual server itself.

4. To remove a smart host, delete the contents of the Smart Host field.

5. Click OK, then click OK again to save your settings.

Chapter 9

Administering the Indexing Service

The Indexing Service is used to build catalogs of documents that can be searched. When you add this capability to a World Wide Web site, it allows users to search for topics of interest using a standard Hypertext Markup Language (HTML) form. Like Internet Information Services (IIS), the Indexing Service is integrated into the Microsoft Windows operation system and can be used on intranets, extranets, and the Internet. As the Web administrator, you set up the catalogs the Indexing Service needs, configure content indexing, and manage indexing on a day-to-day basis.

Managing the Indexing Service is much different from managing IIS. Before you can use the Indexing Service, you must do the following tasks:

1. Install the Indexing Service on the site or virtual server you want to index. The Indexing Service is configured to start manually by default. You'll need to change this so that the Indexing Service starts automatically.

2. Create a catalog of documents to be searched. Each catalog should associate with a specific Web site and can be optionally associated with a Network News Transfer Protocol (NNTP) virtual server as well.

3. Specify the directories and files to be indexed. You specify content indexing options using the Internet Information Services snap-in.

4. Create a search page on the Web site. This page is used to access the catalog and retrieve information that matches the user's search parameters. The search page must specify the physical location of the catalog using the CiCatalog variable. Other variables are available to configure index searching as well.

Once you install and configure the Indexing Service, the service automatically creates and updates indexes. The service also attempts to manage its catalogs so that the data they contain are consistent and current. Data within catalogs occasionally gets out of sync, and when this happens, you may need to rebuild the catalog or force the Indexing Service to rescan directories for documents that should be indexed. These and other administration tasks are covered in this chapter.

Getting Started with the Indexing Service

The Indexing Service extracts information from designated documents and organizes the results into a catalog that can be searched quickly and easily. The extracted information includes the content (text) within documents as well as document properties, such as the document title and author. To understand how the Indexing Service works, let's look at the following subjects:

- How you can use and install the Indexing Service
- How the Indexing Service builds indexes and catalogs
- How you can search and manipulate indexes

Using the Indexing Service

The Indexing Service indexes the following types of documents:

- HTML (.htm or .html)
- ASCII text files (.txt)
- Microsoft Word documents (.doc)
- Microsoft Excel spreadsheets (.xls)
- Microsoft PowerPoint presentations (.ppt)
- Internet mail and news (when you index NNTP virtual servers)

Other documents for which a document filter is installed can be indexed as well. If the Indexing Service isn't installed on your Web server, you can install it using the Windows Components Wizard. To access and use this wizard, follow these steps:

1. Log on to the computer using an account with administrator privileges.
2. Click Start, point to Settings, and then click Control Panel.
3. Double-click Add/Remove Programs. This displays the Add/Remove Programs dialog box.
4. Start the Windows Components Wizard by clicking Add/Remove Windows Components.
5. Select Indexing Service and then click Next to continue. The wizard will then install the Indexing Service.

Once you've installed the Indexing Service, you manage the service using the Indexing Service snap-in for the Microsoft Management Console (MMC) or the Indexing Service node in Computer Management. Regardless of the option you choose, you can work with both local and remote servers using the same techniques. The only task that is different is connecting to remote servers.

With the snap-in, you set the server you want to work with when you add the snap-in to a management console. Here are the steps for adding the Indexing Service snap-in to a management console and selecting a server to work with:

1. Open the Run dialog box by clicking Start and then clicking Run.

2. Type **mmc** in the Open field and then click OK. This opens the Microsoft Management Console (MMC).

3. In MMC, click Console, and then click Add/Remove Snap-In. This opens the Add/Remove Snap-In dialog box.

4. On the Standalone tab, click Add.

5. In the Add Standalone Snap-In dialog box, click Indexing Service, and then click Add.

6. Select Local Computer to connect to the computer on which the console is running. Or select Another Computer and then type the name of a remote computer.

7. Click Finish. Afterward, click Close, and then click OK.

With Computer Management, you connect to the local server automatically when you start the utility. You can connect to a different computer by right-clicking the Computer Management node, selecting Connect To Another Computer, and then following the prompts. Figure 9-1 shows the Indexing Service node in Computer Management. As you can see, selecting the Index Service node displays an overview of the currently installed catalogs, which include the default System and Web catalogs. The catalog summary provides the following information:

- **Catalog**   The descriptive name set when the catalog was created

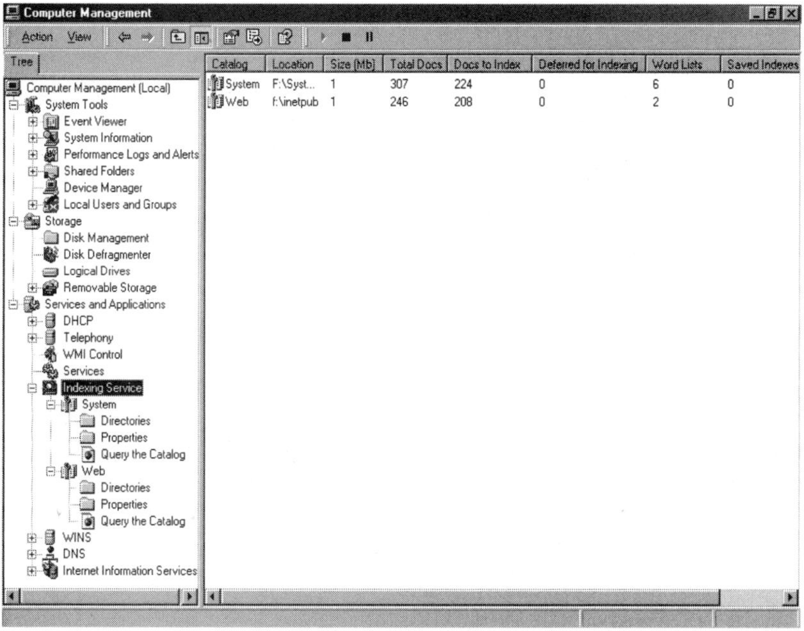

Figure 9-1. *Use the Indexing Service node in Computer Management to manage the Indexing Service.*

- **Location** The physical location of the catalog, such as D:\Catalogs\WWW\
- **Size (Mb)** The size of the catalog in megabytes

> **Note** The typical catalog is 25 percent to 40 percent of the total size of the documents indexed. This means that if you index 1 gigabyte (GB) of documents you'll need an additional 250 MB–400 MB of storage space for the associated catalog.

- **Total Docs** The total number of documents designated for indexing in this catalog
- **Docs to Index** The total number of documents that remain to be indexed
- **Deferred for Indexing** The total number of documents that need to be indexed but cannot be indexed because they are in use

> **Note** The Indexing Service defers indexing of documents being used and will attempt to index the documents when they are no longer in use.

- **Word Lists** The number of word lists associated with the catalog and stored in system memory
- **Saved Indexes** The number of saved indexes within the catalog
- **Status** The status of the indexing process

If you access the Indexing Service using Computer Management, you'll find that two default catalogs were created when you installed the service. These catalogs are the following:

- **System** The System catalog contains an index of all documents on all hard drives attached to the server.
- **Web** The Web catalog contains an index of the default Web site.

> **Tip** I recommend deleting the System catalog. This catalog typically isn't used on an IIS server, and maintaining the catalog uses system resources that could be better used elsewhere.

You can create additional catalogs at any time. When you create a catalog, you can associate the catalog with a Web site and an NNTP virtual server. The service then uses the indexing settings on the directories associated with the site or virtual server to determine which documents should be indexed. You configure indexing settings on directories using the Internet Information Services snap-in.

Indexing Service Essentials

The Indexing Service stores catalog information in Unicode format. This allows the service to index and query content in multiple languages. The Indexing Service performs three main functions to process document contents:

- **Indexing** Indexing is the process of extracting information from documents. The index contains contents from the main body of documents but doesn't include words on any exception word lists associated with the catalog. Indexes are compressed to save space.

- **Catalog building** Catalog building is the process of storing the index information in a named location. Catalogs contain extracted content in the form of indexes and stored properties for a set of documents.

- **Merging** Merging is the process of combining temporary indexes to create combined or master indexes. Merging indexes improves performance of the Indexing Service and reduces the amount of random access memory (RAM) used to store temporary indexes in memory.

Indexing and catalog building take place automatically in the background when the Indexing Service is running. When first started, the Indexing Service takes an inventory of the directories associated with each catalog to determine which documents should be indexed. This process is referred to as scanning. The Indexing Service can perform two types of scans:

- Full
- Incremental

Full scans take a complete look at all documents associated with a catalog. The Indexing Service performs a full scan under the following circumstances:

- When the service is run for the first time after installation
- When a folder is added to a catalog
- As part of recovery if a serious error occurs
- When you manually choose to do so

Incremental scans only look at documents modified since the last full or incremental scan. The Indexing Service performs incremental scans under the following circumstances:

- When you start or restart the Indexing Service
- When you change a local document
- When the Indexing Service loses change notifications
- Any time you manually start an incremental scan

> **Note** File system change notifications are important parts of the incremental scanning process. Change notifications are generated by the operating system and read by the Indexing Server whenever local documents are modified. In most cases, change notifications for documents on remote systems will not reach the local Indexing Service. To account for this, the Indexing Service periodically performs incremental scans on any remote directories associated with a catalog.

After completing a scan of documents to be indexed, the Indexing Service begins to build the necessary catalogs. It does this by reading each document using a document filter. Filters are software components that interpret the structure of a particular kind of document, such as an ASCII text file, a Word document, or HTML document. Using the appropriate filter, the Indexing Service extracts the document contents and property values, storing the property values and the path to the document in the index. Next, the Indexing Service uses the filter to determine the language the document is written in and breaks the document body (content) into individual words. Each supported language has an exception list that provides a list of words that the Indexing Service should ignore.

You'll find exception lists in the \%SystemRoot%\System32 directory. These files are stored as ASCII text files and are named Noise.*lang*, where *lang* is a three-letter extension that indicates the language of the exception list. You can add entries to or remove entries from the exception list using a standard text editor or word processor.

The Indexing Service also stores values of selected document properties in the property cache. The property cache is a storage place for values of properties that you may want to search on or display in the list of search results. Within the property cache, there are two storage levels: primary and secondary. The primary storage level is for values that are frequently accessed, and, as such, these values are stored in a way that makes them quick and easy to retrieve. The secondary storage level is for additional values that are used infrequently.

After discarding words on the exception list and updating the property cache, the Indexing Service stores the remaining document content in a word list. Each document can have one or more word lists associated with it. Word lists are combined to form temporary indexes called shadow indexes. Shadow indexes are stored on disk in a compressed file format. Multiple shadow indexes can be, and usually are, in the catalog at any given time. Over time, the number of shadow indexes can grow substantially. This occurs as documents are added to and modified within indexed directories.

The Indexing Service uses a process called shadow merge to combine word lists and temporary indexes, thereby reducing the number of temporary resources used and improving the overall responsiveness of the service. Shadow merges occur during scans and as part of the normal housekeeping process implemented by the Indexing Service. The key events that trigger a shadow merge are when there are too many word lists stored in memory (20 by default) or when the total size of all word lists exceeds a preset value (256 KB by default).

The end result of the indexing process is a master index. Each catalog has one, and only one, master index. The master index is created the first time you create a catalog and is kept up to date by periodically merging it with shadow indexes to create a new master index. This process of merging shadow indexes with the master index is called master merge. Once a master merge has occurred, there will be only one saved index associated with a catalog. This index is the master index.

Master merges are triggered automatically based on the size of the shadow indexes, the amount of free disk space on the catalog drive, and the number of document changes in indexed directories. Automatic master merges, regardless of condition, are scheduled to occur nightly at 12:00 midnight as well. If necessary, you can force a master merge. The key reason for forcing a master merge is to force the Indexing Service to update a catalog so that all changes are reflected in search results immediately. As you might imagine, the master merge process is resource-intensive, so you normally wouldn't force a master merge during peak usage hours.

Settings that control scanning, merging, and other Indexing Service processes are found in the Registry and are stored here:

```
HKEY_LOCAL_MACHINE
\SYSTEM
\CurrentControlSet
\Control
\ContentIndex
```

Registry settings that control scanning and merging include the following:

- **MasterMergeCheckpointInterval** Sets the interval for determining whether a master merge should be performed. The default value is 2048 seconds.

- **MasterMergeTime** Sets the default time for when a daily master merge should be performed. The default value is 0, meaning zero seconds after the start of a new day.

- **MaxFilesizeFiltered** Sets the maximum size of filtered content for a particular document. By default, this is set to 256 KB.

- **MaxFreshCount** Sets the maximum number of document updates and changes that triggers a master merge. By default, if more than 20,000 documents are changed, a master merge is triggered.

- **MaxIndexes** Sets the maximum number of indexes that should be associated with a catalog before shadow merging is forced. By default, if more than 25 indexes are associated with a catalog, the Indexing Service will perform a shadow merge.

- **MaxShadowIndexSize** Sets a maximum size value for shadow indexes in 128 KB increments. Used with MinDiskFreeForceMerge to force master merges when disk space is low and the size of the shadow index exceeds this value. The default is 15 (15 * 128 KB = 1920 KB).

- **MaxWordLists** Sets the maximum number of word lists that can exist in a catalog. When this number is exceeded, a shadow merge is triggered. By default, this value is set to 20.

- **MaxWordlistSize** Sets the maximum size of all word lists associated with a catalog. This value is set in increments of 128 KB and when exceeded, a shadow merge is triggered. By default, this value is set to 20 (20 * 128 KB = 2560 KB).

- **MinDiskFreeForceMerge** Sets a minimum free disk space value. If a drive containing catalogs has less disk space than this value, and the total size used by shadow indexes exceeds MaxShadowIndexSize, the Indexing Service performs a master merge. The default is 15 MB.

- **MinSizeMergeWordlists** Sets the minimum size threshold for merging word lists with a shadow index. If the word lists' size exceeds this value, a shadow merge is triggered. The default is 256 KB.

Searching Catalogs

Searching is the process of looking through the catalog to find information. Users can search the catalog in several different ways. The technique most used with Web servers is to build a query form that can be used to search the catalog. The Indexing Service includes a query form for each catalog that can be used to test the installation. You can also create query forms using Active Server Pages (ASPs) and Internet data query (IDQ) files.

With ASP, you create the query form and handle the results using a combination of server-side scripts that use ASP objects, HTML, and client-side scripts. The scripts you use can be written in any installed scripting language, and both Microsoft VBScript or Microsoft JScript are installed by default. Typically, you'll use the same page to implement the query form and display the results once the user has entered search parameters. For example, you could create a page called QUERY.ASP that implements the query form and has an embedded script that submits the search parameters and then formats the search results.

IDQ, on the other hand, is a special language designed for submitting queries to the Indexing Service. With IDQ, you create separate pages for handling each step in the query process. You use the following elements:

- An HTML page that ends with the .htm or .html extension to implement the query form

- An IDQ page that ends with the .idq extension to define the fixed query parameters for searches

- An HTML extension file that ends with the .htx extension to format the results of the query

An advantage of IDQ over ASP is that IDQ queries are much faster and more efficient in their use of Indexing Service resources. Regardless of whether you use ASP or IDQ to handle searches, you must set basic parameters that provide default values for the Indexing Service. The parameters you should set are summarized in Table 9-1.

Note Most organizations have Web developers whose job it is to create the Web pages needed for searching, handing, and displaying results. As the Web administrator, you assist the development team in setting parameters and publishing the Web pages when they are completed.

Table 9-1. Basic Parameters for the Indexing Service

Parameter	Description	Sample Value for IDQ
CiCatalog	Sets the file location of the catalog to be searched. If you don't set this parameter, the Indexing Service searches the Inetpub directory for a default catalog.	CiCatalog = D:\Catalogs\WWW
CiFlags	Sets the search flags for the query. The DEEP flag tells the Indexing Service to search all subdirectories within the current scope.	CiFlags = DEEP
CiMaxRecordsIn-ResultSet	Sets the maximum number of records to return in the result set.	CiMaxRecordsInResultSet = 100
CiMaxRecords-PerPage	Sets the maximum number of records to return in a single page.	CiMaxRecordsPerPage = 20
CiRestriction	Stores the search values entered by the user as passed from the query form.	CiRestriction = %CiRestriction%
CiScope	Sets the scope of the query within the catalog. If scope is set to /, the search begins at the top (or root) of the document tree.	CiScope = /Docs

Core Indexing Service Administration

Now that you know how the Indexing Service works, let's look at the core techniques for managing the Indexing Service. In this section, you learn how to specify the resources to index, create catalogs, tune performance, and more.

Setting Web Resources to Index

You configure Web resources for indexing using the Internet Information Services snap-in. Indexing settings can be applied globally or locally. Global settings affect all IIS Web sites that inherit the settings, which means that all indexable files on all sites and in all subdirectories use this setting. To configure global indexing settings, follow these steps:

1. In the Internet Information Services snap-in, right-click the computer node for the IIS server you want to work with, and then select Properties.

2. Click Edit on the Master Properties panel and then select the Home Directory tab.

3. Enable indexing for all Web sites on the server by selecting Index This Resource and then clicking OK. The indexing settings are inherited by all Web sites automatically. The changes also are automatically propagated to all directories within sites.

4. Disable indexing for all Web sites on the server by clearing Index This Resource and then clicking OK. Before applying these settings, IIS checks the existing settings in use for all Web sites. If a Web site uses a different value, an Inheritance Overrides dialog box is displayed. Use this dialog box to select the sites that should use the new setting, and then click OK.

Local settings can be applied to individual Web sites and directories. With sites, the root folder and all associated directories automatically inherit the site's indexing settings, meaning the indexable files within the root folder and associated directories use this setting. With directories, the selected directory and its subdirectories inherit the directory's indexing settings, meaning the indexable files within the selected directory and subdirectories use this setting.

To configure indexing settings for individual sites or directories, follow these steps:

1. In the Internet Information Services snap-in, right-click the Web site or directory you want to manage, and then select Properties.

2. Select the Home Directory, Directory, or Virtual Directory tab as appropriate.

3. Enable indexing for the currently selected resource and all its subdirectories by selecting Index This Resource and then clicking OK. The indexing settings are inherited automatically.

4. Disable indexing for the currently selected resource and all its subdirectories by clearing Index This Resource and then clicking OK. The indexing settings are inherited automatically.

Viewing and Creating Catalogs

Catalogs are created and managed at the site level. Each site that you want to index should have a catalog. A site can have multiple catalogs. For example, you could create a catalog for indexes of your product directories and another catalog for indexes of your services directories.

Each catalog you create should be created on a local file system and stored in a separate folder from other catalogs. To help manage multiple catalogs, you could create a top-level directory called Catalogs and then create subdirectories within this directory for each catalog you want to create. The catalog directory must be created before you create the catalog.

You create a catalog for a site by completing the following steps:

1. Start Computer Management, and then expand the Services And Applications node by clicking the plus sign (+) next to it.

Note When first accessed, Computer Management automatically con- nects to the local system. You can connect to a different computer by right-clicking the Computer Management node, selecting Connect To Another Computer, and then following the prompts. Keep in mind that you cannot add a catalog to a remote computer if the default administration shares on the remote computer have been removed.

2. Right-click the Indexing Service node, point to New, and then click Catalog. This displays the Add Catalog dialog box shown in Figure 9-2.

Figure 9-2. *Use the Add Catalog dialog box to create a new catalog on the server.*

3. In the Name field, type the name of the catalog.

4. In the Location field, type the complete file path to the catalog folder, or click Browse and then select the folder in which you want the catalog to be located.

5. Click OK. After you create a catalog, you must stop and then restart the In- dexing Service to populate the catalog with indexes.

Viewing Indexing Status

Indexing should be periodically monitored to make sure catalogs are being maintained. One of the values you can use to keep track of the Indexing Service is the indexing status. As Table 9-2 shows, the indexing status tells you the current state of the indexing engine. If users are experiencing problems retrieving search results, the Indexing Service may be paused or stopped, a merge may be in progress, or the service may be rescanning catalogs. Typically, you'll see an indexing state followed by the keyword Started. The Started keyword is a reference to the state of the Indexing Service itself. In this case, the service is active.

Table 9-2. Quick Reference for Indexing Service Status Conditions

Status	Description
(Blank)	Indexing Service is stopped and must be started to resume indexing.
Indexing Paused (High I/O)	Indexing is paused due to a high level of input/output (I/O) activity. You may want to close some applications to reduce the I/O activity.
Indexing Paused (Low Memory)	Indexing is paused because of low virtual memory. You may want to close some applications to make more memory available.
Indexing Paused (Power Management)	Indexing is paused to save battery power. Typically only seen on laptop systems.
Indexing Paused (User Active)	Indexing is paused to minimize interference with user activity. Users may be working with a large number of files that the indexer needs, or an administrator may be making changes to the Indexing Service configuration in Computer Management.
Master Merge (Paused)	Master merge is paused because of low resource availability. You may have a problem with the amount of memory, file space, or throughput of the system.
Merge	A merge is in progress. Merging is resource-intensive and may cause a temporary performance problem on the system.
Query Only	Indexing Service is started and is available only for querying.
Recovering	Indexing Service is recovering the catalog from an abrupt shutdown.
Scan Required	One or more documents have been added or modified within directories of this catalog. The indexer should perform a scan automatically. If it doesn't, check the Windows Event log.
Scanning	One or more directories are being scanned for newly added or modified documents.
Scanning (NTFS)	One or more NTFS volumes are being scanned for new or modified documents.
Started	Indexing Service for this catalog has started.
Starting	Indexing Service is in the process of starting.
Stopped	Indexing of the catalog has been stopped.

You can view Indexing Service status conditions by completing the following steps:

1. Start Computer Management, and then expand the Services And Applications node by clicking the plus sign (+) next to it.

2. Select the Indexing Service node in the left pane. The right pane displays the status conditions for each individual catalog. Keep in mind each catalog can have a different status condition.

Starting, Stopping, and Pausing the Indexing Service

The Indexing Service can be started, stopped, and paused like any other service. Users can perform queries and obtain results only when the Indexing Service is running. Users will not be able to obtain query results when the Indexing Service is stopped or paused.

You can manage the Indexing Service by completing the following steps:

1. Start Computer Management, and then expand the Services And Applications node by clicking the plus sign (+) next to it.

2. Select the Indexing Service node in the left pane. The right pane displays the status conditions for each individual catalog.

3. Right-click the Indexing Service node in the left pane. You can now do the following:

   - Select Start to start the Indexing Service.
   - Select Stop to stop the Indexing Service.
   - Select Pause to pause the Indexing Service. After you pause indexing, click Start to resume normal operations.

Note   Whenever you stop and then restart indexing, the Indexing Service performs an incremental scan of all the catalogs associated with all the sites on the server.

Setting Indexing Service Properties

The Indexing Service has several properties that can be configured to customize the way indexing works. These properties are summarized in Table 9-3. As with most other Indexing Service properties, you can set these values globally or locally. Global property settings are inherited by all catalogs unless you override the global settings.

Table 9-3. Configurable Properties for the Indexing Service

Property Tab	Property	Description
Generation	Index Files With Unknown Extensions	Specifies whether the Indexing Service indexes files with unregistered extensions. These files are indexed by default, which could slow down the indexing process if you have a large number of files with unregistered extensions.
	Generate Abstracts	Specifies whether the Indexing Service generates abstracts for files found in a search and returns them with the results. Abstracts contain key information gathered from documents that match the search parameters. Abstracts are generated by default.
	Maximum Size	Sets the maximum number of characters in the abstracts returned with a search. The default value is 320. The range of permitted values is from 10 to 10,000. Keep in mind this property is only available when you enable Generate Abstracts.
Tracking	Add Network Shares Automatically	Specifies whether the Indexing Service automatically uses network share names as aliases for shared network drives. If you don't select this option, you must manually configure aliases for each network share you want to index, as described in the "Adding Physical Directories to a Catalog" section of this chapter.

You configure global property settings by completing the following steps:

1. Start Computer Management, and then expand the Services And Applications node by clicking the plus sign (+) next to it.
2. Right-click the Indexing Service node and then select Properties.
3. On the Generation tab, you set properties that control the way indexing and search results are handled. Set or clear these properties as appropriate.
4. On the Tracking tab, you set properties for tracking network shares. Set or clear the related property as appropriate.
5. Click OK. If you want catalogs to inherit these values, check the properties of each catalog to ensure that Inherit Above Settings From Service is selected as appropriate on the Generation and Tracking tabs.

Individual catalogs can inherit or override the global settings. To perform these tasks, complete the following steps:

1. Start Computer Management. Expand the Services And Applications node by clicking the plus sign (+) next to it, and then expand the Indexing Service node.

2. You should see a list of catalogs configured on the server. Right-click the catalog you want to work with and then select Properties.

3. On the Generation tab, you set properties that control the way indexing and search results are handled. If you want the catalog to inherit the global settings, select Inherit Above Settings From Service. Otherwise, clear this check box and then change the properties as necessary.

4. On the Tracking tab, you set properties for tracking network shares. If you want the catalog to inherit the global settings, select Inherit Above Settings From Service. Otherwise, clear this check box and then change the properties as necessary.

5. Click OK.

Optimizing Indexing Service Performance

You can optimize the Indexing Service performance based on expected usage. You do this by controlling the way the Indexing Service manages the indexing and querying processes. Each process has different performance settings that can be set by using fixed or custom optimization values. For indexing, the performance options are the following:

- **Lazy**   The Indexing Service minimizes the amount of system resources reserved for indexing. Additionally, the Indexing Service doesn't immediately respond to change notification requests from the operating system, and consequently reduces the frequency of scanning. Best for environments in which documents are updated or modified infrequently.

- **Moderate**   The Indexing Service reserves the normal amount of system resources for indexes and attempts to handle change notification requests in a timely manner. This is the default setting. Best for the typical environment in which changes are made daily to documents configured for indexing.

- **Instant**   The Indexing Service reserves additional system resources for indexing and aggressively responds to change notification requests, which means higher than normal scanning for new and changed documents. As a result, document changes and additions appear quickly in catalogs. Best for environments in which documents are changing rapidly and in which you need to reflect the changes quickly.

The available optimization settings are

- **Low Load**   The Indexing Service reduces the amount of system resources reserved for querying. Therefore, the Indexing Service can handle only a limited number of simultaneous queries. Best for environments in which queries are infrequent. If the number of queries increases too much, the responsiveness of the service will be poor.

- **Moderate Load**   The Indexing Service reserves the normal amount of system resources for querying, and attempts to handle multiple simultaneous requests. This is the default setting. Best for the typical environment in which users are regularly performing queries, and you want to handle them appropriately.

- **Heavy Load**   The Indexing Service reserves additional system resources for querying and is able to handle a larger than usual number of simultaneous requests. Best when you need to handle a large number of queries and don't care if the Indexing Service uses more memory and central processing unit (CPU) time than usual.

You can optimize the Indexing Service performance by completing the following steps:

1. Start Computer Management, and then expand the Services And Applications node by clicking the plus sign (+) next to it.

2. Select the Indexing Service node in the left pane. The right pane displays the status conditions for each individual catalog.

3. Right-click the Indexing Service node in the left pane and then select Stop.

4. Right-click the Indexing Service node again, point to All Tasks, and then select Tune Performance. The Indexing Service Usage dialog box shown in Figure 9-3 is displayed.

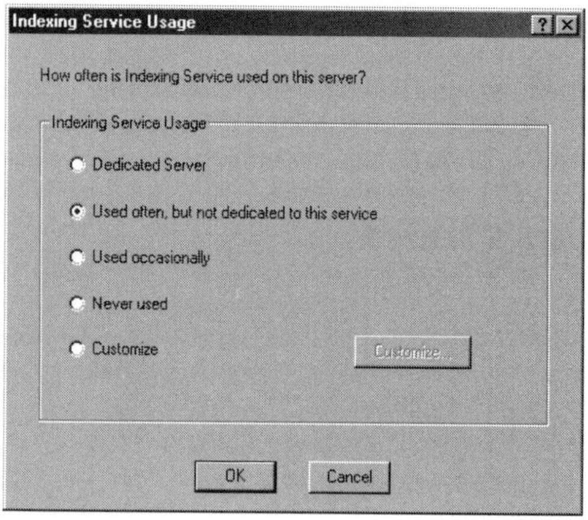

Figure 9-3. *Use the Indexing Service Usage dialog box to optimize indexing and querying.*

5. You can set a fixed or custom optimization value. To set fixed values, select one of the following options on the Indexing Service Usage dialog box:

   * **Dedicated Server**   Sets instant indexing and heavy load querying options.

   * **Used Often, But Not Dedicated To This Service**   Sets lazy indexing and moderate load querying options.

   * **Used Occasionally**   Sets lazy indexing and low load querying options.

   * **Never Used**   Disables the Indexing Service (as if you had disabled it from the Services node). Once selected, the Indexing Service stops permanently unless you re-enable it manually.

6. To set a custom optimization value, select the Customize option and then click the Customize button. As shown in Figure 9-4, you can do the following:

   * Use the Indexing slider to configure indexing as Lazy, Moderate, or Instant. The moderate value is the middle option, and it isn't labeled.

   * Use the Querying slider to configure querying handling as Low Load, Moderate Load, or Heavy Load. The moderate value is the middle option, and it isn't labeled.

7. Click OK. Click OK again to save your settings and return to the Computer Management snap-in.

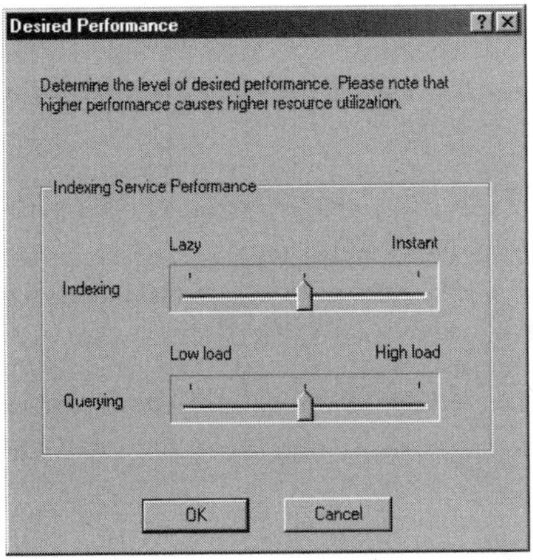

Figure 9-4. *You can customize the way indexing and querying are performed using the Desired Performance dialog box.*

Managing Catalogs

The Indexing Service stores all of the information you are indexing in catalogs. Catalogs contain the extracted contents from the main body of documents as well as metadata that describes the document and its properties. During the catalog creation process, you specify which Web site you want to associate the catalog with. Once you create a catalog for a Web site, users can search it using a Web-based query form.

Catalogs are maintained automatically by the Indexing Service and are updated through the scan and merge processes. You can manually control catalogs as well by starting, stopping, or pausing the update monitor for the catalog. You can also force the Indexing Service to merge separate indexes into the master to improve the overall performance and responsiveness of the Indexing Service.

Viewing Catalog Properties and Directories Being Indexed

Each catalog configured on the server has a separate set of properties that you can manage. These properties control the tracking of network shares, the generation of document abstracts, and the indexing configuration. You can configure catalogs to have unique property settings or to inherit global properties from the Indexing Service.

Catalogs can be associated with a Web site, an NNTP site, and one or more external directories. External directories can include local and remote resources. When you associate a catalog with a Web or NNTP site, you use the Internet Information Services snap-in to specify which resources are indexed. When you associate a catalog with a network share, you can elect to index the directory when you add it to the catalog.

To view the current property settings for a catalog as well as the directories that are currently being indexed, follow these steps:

1. Start Computer Management. Expand the Services And Applications node by clicking the plus sign (+) next to it, and then expand the Indexing Service node.

2. You should see a list of catalogs configured on the server. Expand a catalog node by clicking the plus sign (+) next to it. Select the Directories node in the left pane to display a list of external directories associated with a catalog in the right pane.

3. If you want to view the properties of a catalog, right-click the catalog you want to work with and then select Properties. This displays a Properties dialog box that you can use to view or set properties.

Adding Physical Directories to a Catalog

You can add external directories to a catalog that can be indexed along with the content of a Web or NNTP site. These external directories can be on the local file system or on a remote file system. If you don't select Add Network Share Alias Automatically, you must manually configure aliases for each network share you want to index.

To add an external directory to a catalog, follow these steps:

1. Start Computer Management. Expand the Services And Applications node by clicking the plus sign (+) next to it, and then expand the Indexing Service node.

2. You should see a list of catalogs configured on the server. Right-click the catalog you want to work with, point to New, and then select Directory. This displays the Add Directory dialog box shown in Figure 9-5.

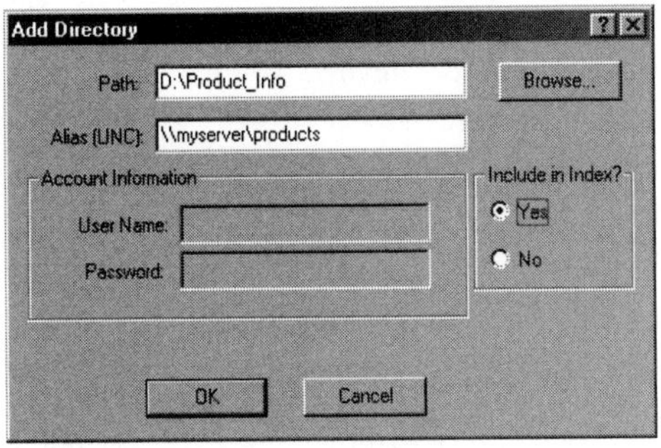

Add Directory	? X
Path: D:\Product_Info	Browse...
Alias (UNC): \\myserver\products	
Account Information	Include in Index?
User Name:	● Yes
Password:	○ No
OK	Cancel

Figure 9-5. *You can add physical directories to a catalog and map them to aliases using this dialog box.*

3. In the Path field, type the complete file path to the directory you want to index. If you do not know the directory path, click Browse to search for the directory.

4. If you are configuring indexing for a network share, type the network share alias that you want to use for this directory in the Alias (UNC) field. This alias should be in Uniform Naming Convention (UNC) format and is returned in the search results sent to clients. For example, you could set the Alias \\myserver\data to map to the actual network share path \\Galileo\reports\fy2001.

Tip When you work with remote systems, you must allow the Indexing Service to map administrative shares. If unable to map administrative shares, the Indexing Service will not be able to index content.

5. If you are configuring indexing for a network share, you can also set the User Name and Password that the Indexing Service can use to authenticate on the remote system.

6. Next, select Yes to specify whether the directory should be included in the catalog index. Select No to exclude the directory from the index.

7. Click OK.

Forcing Full and Incremental Directory Rescans

The Indexing Service watches for change notification requests from the operating system to determine if files have been added to or changed within directories set for indexing. When a request is received, the Indexing Service schedules the related directory for an incremental scan. At times, the Indexing Service may lose change notifications. This can happen during periods of high I/O or CPU processing; the Indexing Service may not be able to keep up with the change notifications. It can also happen when the Indexing Service is unable receive change notifications for directories on remote systems.

Typically, you can identify a problem with scanning by searching for documents that have been updated recently or added to an indexed directory. If the search results do not contain references to these documents, you may need to force a full or incremental rescan. You can do this only at the external directory level.

To force a directory rescan of an external directory, follow these steps:

1. Start Computer Management. Expand the Services And Applications node by clicking the plus sign (+) next to it, and then expand the Indexing Service node.

2. You should see a list of catalogs configured on the server. Double-click the catalog you want to work with, and then select the related Directories node.

3. In the right pane, you should see a list of external directories configured for the catalog. Right-click the directory you want to work with, point to All Tasks, and then select Rescan (Full) or Rescan (Incremental) as appropriate.

4. When prompted, confirm the action by clicking Yes. Keep in mind that rescans of directories with a large number of documents can be resource-intensive. This means you'll use additional CPU, memory, and file I/O resources during the rescan.

Starting, Stopping, and Pausing Individual Catalogs

When you need to perform a large number of updates to directories monitored by a catalog, it is a good idea to temporarily pause or stop the catalog. Pausing or stopping the catalog tells the Indexing Service that it shouldn't handle change notification requests for this catalog. The difference between pausing and stopping a catalog is important. When you stop a catalog, the Indexing Service stops both indexing and querying activities, meaning that the related directories are no longer indexed and that users cannot search the catalog. When you pause a catalog, Indexing Service stops indexing but still allows current queries to be completed.

To start, stop, or pause a catalog, complete the following steps:

1. Start Computer Management. Expand the Services And Applications node by clicking the plus sign (+) next to it, and then expand the Indexing Service node.

2. Right-click the catalog you want to work with, point to All Tasks, and then select Start, Pause, or Stop as appropriate.

Note   The Indexing Service automatically performs an incremental scan when you stop and then restart a catalog. This ensures that updated or new documents are indexed as appropriate.

Merging Catalogs

As the Indexing Service updates the catalog, it creates temporary indexes, called shadow indexes, which extend the master index. These shadow indexes reflect the changes within catalog directories. Over time, the number of shadow indexes can grow substantially, and this is reflected in the number of Saved Indexes associated with a catalog. Because shadow indexes contain additional pointers and information, they use more space than a fully merged master index. As the number of shadow indexes grows, the responsiveness of queries against the catalog can slow.

You can improve the responsiveness of the Indexing Service and reduce storage space usage by merging the temporary indexes with the master index. To perform this task, complete the following steps:

1. Start Computer Management. Expand the Services And Applications node by clicking the plus sign (+) next to it, and then expand the Indexing Service node.

2. Right-click the catalog you want to work with, point to All Tasks, and then select Merge.

3. When prompted to confirm the action, click Yes. As with rescanning, the merge process can be resource-intensive, and you may temporarily reduce the responsiveness of the Indexing Service. The net gain, however, is that once merging is completed, the Indexing Service should be more responsive to user queries.

Specifying Web or NNTP Sites to Include in Catalogs

Each catalog can be associated with one Web site and one NNTP site. After you associate a site with a catalog, you can use the Internet Information Services snap-in to specify the resources that should be indexed. You specify the site to include in a catalog by completing these steps:

1. Start Computer Management. Expand the Services And Applications node by clicking the plus sign (+) next to it, and then expand the Indexing Service node.

2. Right-click the catalog you want to work with, and then select Properties. Click the Tracking tab.

3. As shown in Figure 9-6, you can now take one of the following actions:

   * Use the WWW Server selection menu on the Tracking tab to specify the Web site that you want to associate with a catalog

   * Use the NNTP Server selection menu on the Tracking tab to specify an NNTP site that you want to associate with a catalog

4. Click OK.

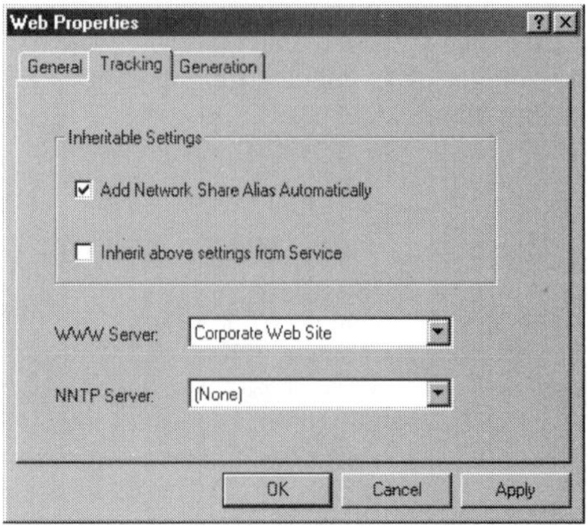

Figure 9-6. *Specify the site to index on the Tracking tab.*

Testing Catalogs with Queries

After you configure a catalog for indexing, you should query the catalog to ensure you get the expected results. The Indexing Service has a built-in query form to perform this task. To access this form and enter a query, follow these steps:

1. Start Computer Management. Expand the Services And Applications node by clicking the plus sign (+) next to it, and then expand the Indexing Service node.

2. You should see a list of catalogs configured on the server. Double-click the catalog you want to work with, and then select Query The Catalog in the left pane.

3. As shown in Figure 9-7, type the query you want to use in the field labeled Enter Your Free Text Query Below, and then click Search. If indexing is configured correctly, the Indexing Service should display search results. Then click on a document title or path entry to ensure that documents can be accessed from the results page. If you experience problems with either of these procedures, you should check the indexing configuration.

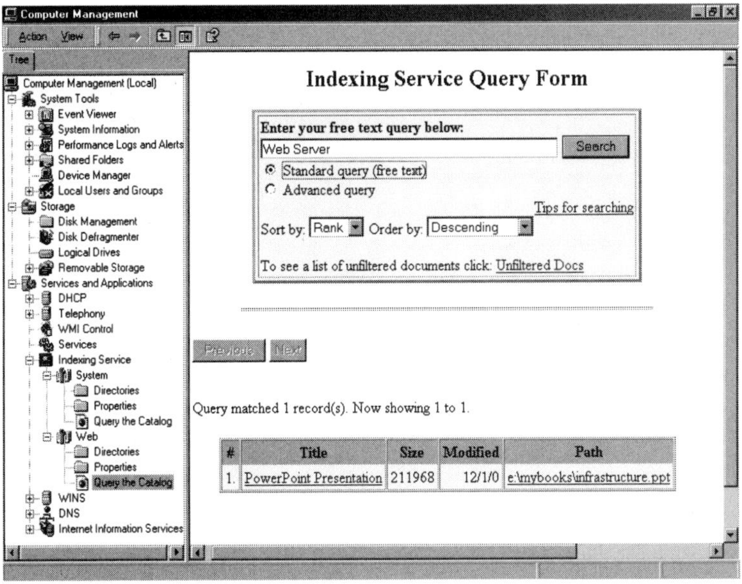

Figure 9-7. *After you configure indexing, check the configuration using the predefined query form.*

Part IV

Performance, Optimization, and Maintenance

Part IV covers administration tasks you'll use to enhance and maintain Internet Information Services (IIS). Chapter 10 provides the essentials for monitoring IIS and solving performance problems related to the operating system and hardware configuration. Chapter 11 provides an essential background on access logs and then details how to configure server logs. Chapter 12 explores IIS optimization. You'll learn how to update registry settings for IIS and how to work with the IIS metabase.

The subjects covered in this part of the book are extremely important to your success. Far too often, administrators forget that IIS is a collection of services that must be closely monitored, updated, and maintained. Through regular monitoring and maintenance, you can uncover problems that, when corrected, can improve the overall performance of the server. Servers also need to be optimized for current loads and resource allocations. Otherwise, users may experience decreased responsiveness, unstable service levels, and outages.

Chapter 10

Performance Tuning and Monitoring

Monitoring and performance tuning are essential parts of Web administration. You monitor servers to ensure they are running smoothly and troubleshoot problems as they occur. You tune the performance of servers to achieve optimal performance based on the current system resources and traffic load. Microsoft Windows 2000 includes several tools that you'll use to monitor Internet Information Services (IIS). The key tools are Performance Monitor, Windows event logs, and the IIS access logs. You'll often use the results of your monitoring to optimize IIS.

Performance tuning is as much an art as it is a science. You often tune performance based on trial and error. You adjust the server, monitor the server's performance over time, and then gauge the success of the updated settings. If things aren't working as expected, you adjust the settings again. In an ideal world, you'd have staging or development servers that are similar in configuration to your production servers to work with while tuning server performance. Then, once you've made adjustments that work in staging, you could configure these changes on the production servers.

Monitoring IIS Performance and Activity

Monitoring IIS isn't something you should do haphazardly. You need to have a clear plan—a set of goals that you hope to achieve. Let's look at some reasons you may want to monitor IIS and the tools you can use to do this.

Why Monitor IIS?

Troubleshooting performance problems is a key reason for monitoring. For example, users may be having problems connecting to the server, and you may want to monitor the server to troubleshoot these problems. Here, your goal would be to track down the problem using the available monitoring resources and then to solve it.

Another common reason for wanting to monitor IIS is to use the results to improve server performance. Improving server performance can reduce the need for costly additional servers or additional hardware components, such as central processing units (CPUs) and memory. This allows you to squeeze additional processing power out of the server and budget for when you really need to purchase new servers and components.

To achieve optimal performance, you need to identify performance bottlenecks, maximize throughput, and minimize the time it takes for World Wide Web applications to process user requests. You achieve this by doing the following:

- Monitoring memory and CPU usage and taking appropriate steps to reduce the load on the server, as necessary. Other processes running on the server may be using memory and CPU resources needed by IIS. Resolve this issue by stopping nonessential services and moving support applications to a different server.

- Resolving hardware issues that may be causing problems. If slow disk drives are delaying file reads, work on improving disk input/output (I/O). If the network cards are running at full capacity, install additional network cards for performing activities, such as backups.

- Optimizing Web pages and applications running on IIS. You should test Web pages and IIS applications to ensure the source code performs as expected. Eliminate unnecessary procedures and optimize inefficient processes.

Unfortunately, there are often tradeoffs to be made when it comes to resource usage. For example, as the number of users accessing IIS grows, you may not be able to reduce the network traffic load, but you may be able to improve server performance by optimizing Web pages and IIS applications.

Getting Ready to Monitor

Before you start monitoring IIS, you may want to establish baseline performance metrics for your server. To do this, you measure server performance at various times and under different load conditions. You can then compare the baseline performance with subsequent performance to determine how IIS is performing. Performance metrics that are well above the baseline measurements may indicate areas where the server needs to be optimized or reconfigured.

After you establish the baseline metrics, you should formulate a monitoring plan. A comprehensive monitoring plan involves the following steps:

1. Determine which server resources should be monitored to help you accomplish your goal.
2. Set filters to reduce the amount of information collected.
3. Configure performance counters to watch the resource usage.
4. Log the usage data so that it can be analyzed.
5. Analyze the usage data and replay the data as necessary to find a solution.

These procedures are examined later in the chapter under "Monitoring IIS Performance." While you should develop a monitoring plan in most cases, there are times when you may not want to go through all these steps to monitor IIS. In this case, use the steps that make sense for your situation.

Monitoring Tools and Resources

The primary tools you'll use to monitor IIS are

- **Performance Monitor** Configure counters to watch resource usage over time. Use the usage information to gauge the performance of IIS and determine areas that can be optimized.

- **Access logs** Use information in the access logs to find problems with pages, applications, and IIS. Entries logged with a status code beginning with a 4 or 5 indicate a potential problem.

- **Event logs** Use information in the event logs to troubleshoot system-wide problems, including IIS and Indexing Service problems.

Many other monitoring tools are available in the Microsoft Windows 2000 Resource Kit. The resource kit tools you'll want to use include

- **HTTP Monitoring Tool** Monitors Hypertext Transfer Protocol (HTTP) activity on the server and records the tracking information to a file or to the Windows Event logs. The information tracked can alert you to changes in HTTP activity. You can import the output file generated by the tool directly into Microsoft SQL Server as well.

- **Playback** Playback is a tool suite that includes two components: PLAYBACK.EXE and RECORDER.DLL. RECORDER.DLL records ongoing activity at a Web site so that it can be played back. PLAYBACK.EXE plays back the recorded activity on a Web site so that you can simulate real-world traffic on development or testing servers.

- **Web Application Stress Tool** Simulates Web activity so that you can evaluate server performance. Parameters you can set include the number of users, the frequency of requests, and the type of request. The tool produces a detailed report that tells you the number of requests, number of errors, elapsed time for processing requests, and more.

- **Web Capacity Analysis Tool (WCAT)** Tests different server and network configurations using workload simulations and content developed specifically for WCAT. When you change your hardware and software configuration and repeat the testing, you can identify how the new configuration affects server response.

Detecting and Resolving IIS Errors

IIS records errors in two locations: the IIS access logs and the Windows event logs. In the access logs, you'll find information related to missing resources, failed authentication, and internal server errors. In the event logs, you'll find IIS errors, IIS application errors, and errors related to other applications running on the server.

Examining the Access Logs

Access logs are created when you enable logging for Web, File Transfer Protocol (FTP), and Simple Mail Transfer Protocol (SMTP) sites. Every time someone requests a file from your Web site, an entry goes into the access log, making the access log a running history of resource requests. Because each entry has a status code, you can examine entries to determine the success or failure of a request. Failed requests have a status code beginning with a 4 or 5.

The most common error you'll see is a 404 error, which indicates that a resource was not found at the expected location. You can correct this problem by doing the following:

- Placing the file in the expected location
- Renaming the file if the current name is different than expected
- Modifying the linking file to reflect the correct name and location of the file

If you want to find the access log for a particular site, follow these steps:

1. Start the Internet Information Services snap-in and then, in the left pane (Console Root), click the plus sign (+) next to the computer you want to work with. If the computer isn't shown, connect to it as discussed in Chapter 2, "Core IIS Administration," in the section called "Connecting To Other Servers."

2. Right-click the Web, FTP, or SMTP site you want to manage, and then select Properties.

3. On the Enable Logging panel, you'll find a Properties button. Click this button to display a dialog box similar to the one shown in Figure 10-1.

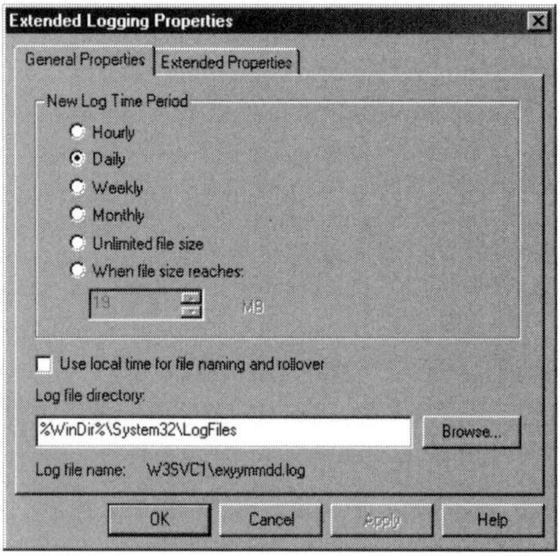

Figure 10-1. *The Logging Properties dialog box tells you where logs are being written.*

4. The Log File Directory field shows the top-level directory for this site's logs. The default top-level directory is \%WinDir%\System32\LogFiles.

5. The Log File Name field shows the subdirectory and log file naming format. For example, if the name shows \W3SVC1\EXYYMMDD.LOG, you'll find the site's logs in the W3SVC1 subdirectory. The current log is the file in this subdirectory with the most recent date and time stamp. All other logs are archive files that could be moved to a history directory.

Now that you know where the log files are located for the site, you can search for errors in the log file. Because logs are stored as ASCII text, one way to do this would be to open a log in Microsoft Notepad or another text editor and search for error codes, such as 404. Another way to search for errors would be to use the FIND command. At a command prompt, you could search for 404 errors in any log file within the current directory using the following command:

```
find "404" *
```

Once you identify missing files, you can use any of the previously recommended techniques to resolve the problem. You'll learn more about access logs and status codes in Chapter 11, "Tracking User Access and Logging."

Examining the Event Logs

Event logs provide historical information that can help you track down problems with services, processes, and applications. The events tracked are controlled by the event-logging service. When this service is started, user actions and system resource usage events can be tracked via the following event logs:

- **Application Log**   Records events logged by applications, such as IIS.
- **Directory Service**   Records events logged by Active Directory and its related services.
- **DNS Server**   Records Domain Name System (DNS) queries, responses, and other DNS activities.
- **File Replication Service**   Records file replication activities on the system.
- **Security Log**   Records events you've set for auditing with local or global group policies. Note that administrators must be granted access to the security log through user rights assignment.
- **System Log**   Records events logged by the operating system or its components, such as the failure of a service to start at bootup.

You access the event logs by completing the following steps:

1. Open the Start menu, select Programs, select Administrative Tools, and then select Event Viewer. This starts Event Viewer.

2. Event Viewer displays logs for the local computer by default. If you want to view logs on a remote computer, right-click the Event Viewer entry in the

console tree (left pane), and then select Connect To Another Computer. In the Select Computer dialog box, enter the name of the computer you want to access, and then click OK.

3. Select the log you want to view, as shown in Figure 10-2. Use the information in the Source column to determine which service or process logged a particular event.

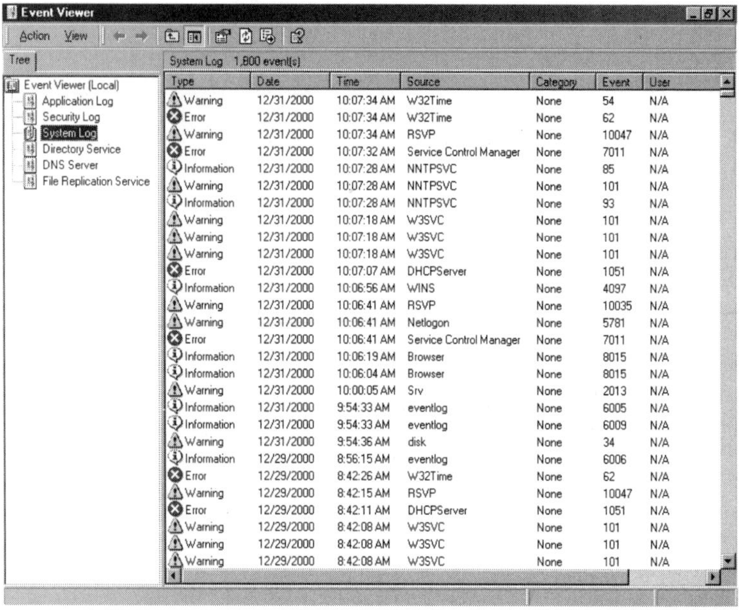

Figure 10-2. *Event Viewer displays events for the selected log.*

Entries in the main panel of Event Viewer provide a quick overview of when, where, and how an event occurred. To obtain detailed information on an event, double-click on its entry. The event type precedes the date and time of the event. Event types include:

- **Information**   An informational event, which is generally related to a successful action.

- **Success Audit**   An event related to the successful execution of an action.

- **Failure Audit**   An event related to the failed execution of an action.

- **Warning**   A warning. Details for warnings are often useful in preventing future system problems.

- **Error**   An error, such as the failure of a service to start.

Note   Warnings and errors are the two key types of events that you'll want to examine closely. Whenever these types of events occur and you are unsure of the cause, double-click on the entry to view the detailed event description.

In addition to type, date, and time, the summary and detailed event entries provide the following information:

- **Source**   The application, service, or component that logged the event
- **Category**   The category of the event, which is almost always set to None, but is sometimes used to further describe the related action
- **Event**   An identifier for the specific event
- **User**   The user account that was logged on when the event occurred, if applicable
- **Computer**   The name of the computer on which the event occurred
- **Description**   In the detailed entries, a text description of the event
- **Data**   In the detailed entries, any data or error code output by the event

The sources you'll want to look for include:

- **Active Server Pages (ASPs)**   Applications and ASP engines
- **CERTSVC**   Certificate services
- **Ci**   The Indexing Service
- **MSDTC**   Microsoft Distributed Transaction Coordinator
- **MSFTPSVC**   The FTP service
- **NNTPSVC**   The Network News Transfer Protocol (NNTP) service
- **SMTPSVC**   The SMTP service
- **W3SVC**   The World Wide Web service

If you want to see only warnings and errors, you can filter the log by completing the following steps:

1. From the View menu, select the Filter option. This opens the dialog box shown in Figure 10-3.
2. Clear the following check boxes: Information, Success Audit, and Failure Audit.
3. Select the Warning and Error check boxes.
4. Click OK. You should now see a list of warning and error messages only. Read these messages carefully and take steps to correct any problems that exist.

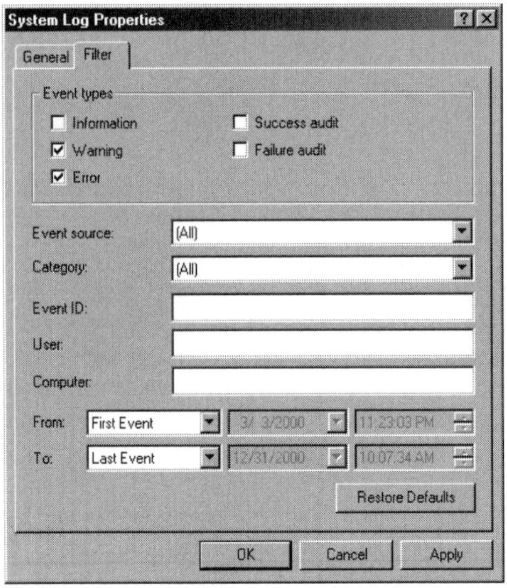

Figure 10-3. *You can filter events so that only warnings and errors are displayed.*

Monitoring IIS Performance

Performance Monitor is the tool of choice for monitoring IIS performance. Performance Monitor graphically displays statistics for the set of performance parameters you've selected for display. These performance parameters are referred to as counters. When you install IIS on a system, Performance Monitor is updated with a set of counters for tracking IIS performance. These counters can be updated when you install additional services and add-ons for IIS as well.

Performance Monitor creates a graph depicting the counters you're tracking. The update interval for this graph is configurable but, by default, is set to 1 second. As you'll see when you work with Performance Monitor, the tracking information is most valuable when you record performance information in a log file so that it can be played back. Also, Performance Monitor is helpful when you configure alerts to send messages when certain events occur, such as when an automatic IIS restart is triggered.

The sections that follow examine key techniques you'll use to work with Performance Monitor. You start Performance Monitor by selecting the Performance Monitor option from the Administrative Tools menu.

Choosing Counters to Monitor

The Performance Monitor only displays information for counters you're tracking. More than a hundred IIS counters are available, provided you've installed the related service. Counters are organized into object groupings. For example, all ASP-related counters are associated with the *Active Server Pages* object. You'll find counter objects for other services as well. A complete list of IIS-related counter objects follows:

- **Active Server Pages**   Counters for ASP scripts and applications running on the server
- **FTP Service**   Counters for the FTP service
- **HTTP Indexing Service**   Counters for the Indexing Service for Web sites, active queries, and caching results
- **Indexing Service**   Counters for Indexing Service that relate to indexing processes, word lists, and queries
- **Indexing Service Filter**   Counters provide additional performance information related to content filters and indexing speed related to filters
- **Internet Information Services Global**   Counters for all Internet services (WWW, FTP, SMTP, NNTP, and so on) running on the server
- **NNTP Commands**   Counters related to NNTP commands that users are executing on the server
- **NNTP Server**   Counters that track overall NNTP performance, such as the number of articles sent, received, and posted per second
- **SMTP NTFS Store Driver**   Counters for tracking the total number of messages and message streams
- **SMTP Server**   Counters that track overall SMTP performance, such as the number of messages sent and received per second
- **Web Service**   Counters for the World Wide Web Publishing Service

Counters for monitoring performance are summarized by issue and object in Table 10-1. The easiest way to learn about these counters is to read the explanations available in the Add Counters dialog box. Start Performance Monitor, click the Add button on the toolbar, and then select an object in the Performance Object field. Afterward, click the Explain button and then scroll through the list of counters for this object.

Table 10-1.   Key Counters Used to Monitor Server Performance

Issue	Counter	Object Available For
ASP sessions	Session Duration	Active Server Pages
	Sessions Current	Active Server Pages
	Sessions Timed Out	Active Server Pages
	Sessions Total	Active Server Pages
ASP transactions	Transactions Aborted	Active Server Pages
	Transactions Committed	Active Server Pages
	Transactions Pending	Active Server Pages

(continued)

Table 10-1. *(continued)*

Issue	Counter	Object Available For
	Transactions Total	Active Server Pages
	Transactions/Sec	Active Server Pages
Bandwidth usage	Current Blocked Async I/O Requests	Internet Information Services Global, Web Service, FTP Service
	Measured Async I/O Bandwidth usage	Internet Information Services Global, Web Service
	Total Allowed Async I/O Requests	Internet Information Services Global, Web Service
	Total Blocked Async I/O Requests	Internet Information Services Global, Web Service
	Total Rejected Async I/O Requests	Internet Information Services Global, Web Service
Caching and Memory	File Cache Flushes, URI Cache Flushes	Internet Information Services Global
	File Cache Flushes, URI Cache Flushes	Internet Information Services Global
	File Cache Hits, URI Cache Hits	Internet Information Services Global
	File Cache Hits %, URI Cache Hits %	Internet Information Services Global
	File Cache Misses, URI Cache Misses	Internet Information Services Global
	Maximum File Cache Memory Usage	Internet Information Services Global
	Script Engines Cached	Active Server Pages
	Template Cache Hit Rate	Active Server Pages
	Template Notifications	Active Server Pages
	Templates Cached	Active Server Pages
Connections	Connection Attempts/Sec	Web Service
	Current Anonymous Users	Web Service, FTP Service
	Current Connections	Web Service, FTP Service
	Current File Cache Memory Usage	Internet Information Services Global
	Maximum Connections	Web Service, FTP Service
	Current Files Cached	Internet Information Services Global

(continued)

Table 10-1. *(continued)*

Issue	Counter	Object Available For
	Current NonAnonymous Users	Web Service, FTP Service
	Maximum Anonymous Users	Web Service, FTP Service
	Maximum NonAnonymous Users	Web Service, FTP Service
	Total Anonymous Users	Web Service, FTP Service
	Total Connection Attempts	Web Service, FTP Service
	Total Logon Attempts	Web Service, FTP Service
	Total NonAnonymous Users	Web Service, FTP Service
Errors	Errors During Script Runtime	Active Server Pages
	Errors From ASP Preprocessor	Active Server Pages
	Errors From Script Compiler	Active Server Pages
	Errors/Sec	Active Server Pages
	Not Found Errors/Sec	Web Service
	Requests Not Authorized	Active Server Pages
	Requests Not Found	Active Server Pages
	Requests Rejected	Active Server Pages
	Requests Timed Out	Active Server Pages
	Service Uptime	Web Service, FTP Service
	Total Not Found Errors	Web Service
Indexing	Active Queries	HTTP Indexing Service
	Queries Per Minute	HTTP Indexing Service
	Total Queries	HTTP Indexing Service
	Total Indexing Speed	Indexing Service Filter
Requests	Get Requests/Sec	Web Service
	Head Requests/Sec	Web Service
	ISAPI Extension Requests/Sec	Web Service
	Post Requests/Sec	Web Service
	Put Requests/Sec	Web Service
	Request Bytes In Total	Active Server Pages
	Request Bytes Out Total	Active Server Pages
	Requests Executing	Active Server Pages
	Requests Queued	Active Server Pages
	Requests Rejected	Active Server Pages
	Requests Succeeded	Active Server Pages
	Requests Timed Out	Active Server Pages
	Requests Total	Active Server Pages
	Requests/Sec	Active Server Pages

(continued)

Table 10-1. *(continued)*

Issue	Counter	Object Available For
Throughput	Bytes Received/Sec	Web Service, FTP Service
	Bytes Sent/Sec	Web Service, FTP Service
	Bytes Total/Sec	Web Service, FTP Service
	Files Received/Sec	Web Service, FTP Service
	Files Sent/Sec	Web Service, FTP Service
	Files/Sec	Web Service, FTP Service
	Total Files Received	Web Service, FTP Service
	Total Files Sent	Web Service, FTP Service
	Total Files Transferred	Web Service, FTP Service

When Performance Monitor is monitoring a particular object, it can track all instances of all counters for that object. Instances are multiple occurrences of a particular counter. For example, when you track counters for the Web Service object, you often have a choice of tracking all Web site instances or specific Web site instances. Following this, if you configured CorpWeb, CorpProducts, and CorpServices sites, you could use Web Service counters to track a specific Web site instance or multiple Web site instances.

To select which counters you want to monitor, complete the following steps:

1. Start Performance Monitor by selecting the Performance Monitor option from the Administrative Tools menu.

2. Performance Monitor has several different views. Click View Chart on the toolbar to ensure you are in Chart view.

3. To add counters, click Add on the toolbar. This displays the Add Counters dialog box shown in Figure 10-4. The key fields are the following:

   - **Use Local Computer Counters**   Configure performance options for the local computer.

   - **Select Counters From Computer**   Enter the Uniform Naming Convention (UNC) name of the IIS you want to work with, such as \\ENGSVR01.

   - **Performance Object**   Select the type of object you want to work with, such as *Active Server Pages*.

   - **All Counters**   Select all counters for the current object.

   - **Select Counters From List**   Select one or more counters for the current object. For example, you could select Requests Not Found, Requests Queued, and Requests Total.

   - **All Instances**   Select all counter instances for monitoring.

   - **Select Instances From List**   Select one or more counter instances to monitor. For example, you could select instances of Anonymous Users/Sec for individual Web sites or for all Web sites.

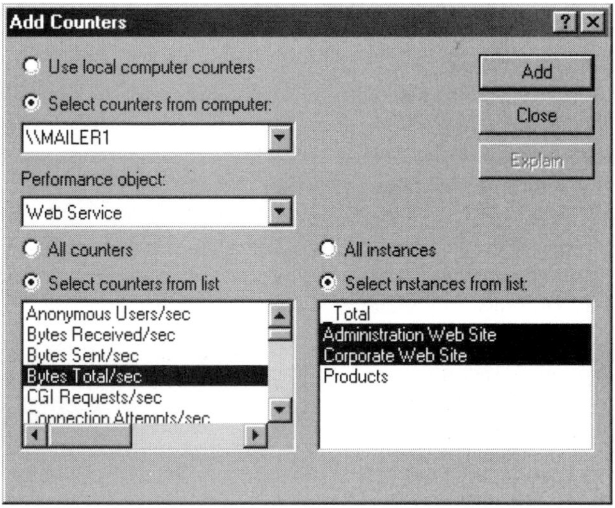

Figure 10-4. *Select the counter you want to monitor.*

Tip   Don't try to chart too many counters or counter instances at once. You'll make the display too difficult to read and you'll use system resources—namely, CPU time and memory—that may affect server responsiveness.

4. When you've selected all the necessary options, click Add to add the counters to the chart. Repeat this process as necessary to add other performance parameters.

5. Click Close when you're finished.

Creating and Managing Performance Monitor Logs

You can use performance logs to track the performance of IIS, and you can replay them later. As you set out to work with logs, keep in mind that the parameters you track in log files are recorded separately from the parameters you're charting in the Performance Monitor window. You can configure log files to update counter data automatically or manually. With automatic logging, a snapshot of key parameters is recorded at specific time intervals, such as every 15 seconds. With manual logging, you determine when snapshots are made. Two types of performance logs are available:

- **Counter logs**   These logs record performance data on the selected counters when a predetermined update interval has elapsed.

- **Trace logs**   These logs record performance data whenever their related events occur.

Creating and Managing Performance Logging

To create and manage performance logging, complete the following steps:

1. Access the Performance console by selecting the Performance option on the Administrative Tools menu.

2. Expand the Performance Logs And Alerts node by clicking the plus sign (+) next to it. If you want to configure a counter log, select Counter Logs. Otherwise, select Trace Logs.

3. As shown in Figure 10-5, you should see a list of current logs (if any) in the right pane. A green log symbol next to the log name indicates logging is active. A red log symbol indicates logging is stopped.

Figure 10-5. *Current performance logs are listed with summary information.*

4. You can create a new log by right-clicking in the right pane and selecting New Log Settings from the shortcut menu. A New Log Settings box appears asking you to give a name to the new log settings. Type a descriptive name here before continuing.

5. Click Add to add the counters you wish to log. Click OK to return to the Performance tool.

6. To manage an existing log, right-click its entry in the right pane and then select one of the following options:

   • **Start** Activates logging
   • **Stop** Halts logging
   • **Delete** Deletes the log
   • **Properties** Displays the Log Properties dialog box

Creating Counter Logs

Counter logs record performance data on the selected counters at a specific sample interval. For example, you could sample performance data for the Web service every 5 minutes. To create a counter log, complete the following steps:

1. Select Counter Logs in the left pane of the Performance console, and then right-click in the right pane to display the shortcut menu. Select New Log Settings.

2. In the New Log Settings dialog box, type a name for the log, such as HTTP Performance Monitor or Total Request Monitor, then click OK.

3. In the General tab, click Add to display the Select Counters dialog box. This dialog box is identical to the Add Counters dialog box shown previously in Figure 10-4.

4. Use the Select Counters dialog box to add counters for logging. Click Close when you're finished.

5. In the Sample Data Every field, type in a sample interval and select a time unit in seconds, minutes, hours, or days. The sample interval specifies when new data is collected. For example, if you select a sample interval of 15 minutes, the log is updated every 15 minutes.

6. As shown in Figure 10-6, click the Log Files tab and then specify how the log file should be created using the following fields:

   * **Location**   Sets the folder location for the log file.

   * **File Name**   Sets the name of the log file.

   * **End File Names With**   Sets an automatic suffix for each new file created when you run the counter log. Logs can have a numeric suffix or a suffix in a specific date format.

   * **Start Numbering At**   Sets the first serial number for a log that uses an automatic numeric suffix.

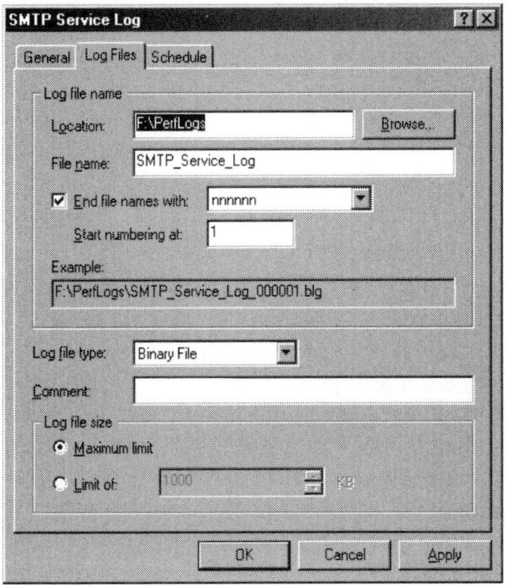

Figure 10-6. *Configure the log file format and usage.*

- **Log File Type** Sets the type of log file to create. Use Text File – CSV for a log file with comma-separated entries. Use Text File – TSV for a log file with tab-separated entries. Use Binary File to create a binary file that can be read by Performance Monitor. Use Binary Circular File to create a binary file that overwrites old data with new data when the file reaches a specified size limit.

 Tip If you plan to use Performance Monitor to analyze or view the log, use one of the binary file formats.

- **Comment** Sets an optional description of the log, which is displayed in the Comment column.
- **Maximum Limit** Sets no predefined limit on the size of the log file.
- **Limit Of** Sets a specific limit in kilobytes on the size of the log file.

7. As shown in Figure 10-7, click the Schedule tab and then specify when logging should start and stop.

8. You can configure the logging to start manually or automatically at a specific date. Select the appropriate option and then specify a start date if necessary.

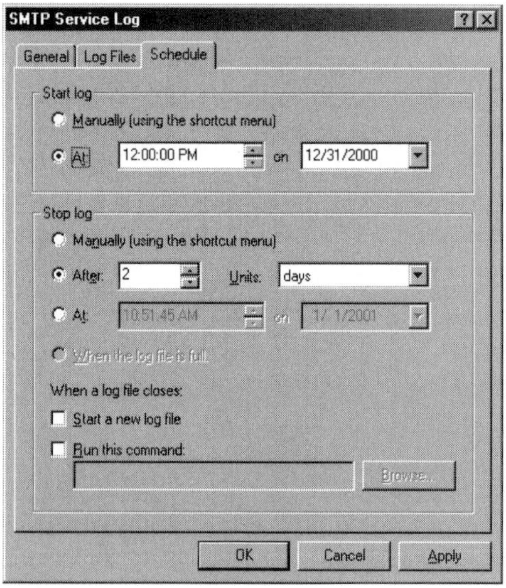

Figure 10-7. *Specify when logging starts and stops.*

Tip Log files can grow in size very quickly. If you plan to log data for an extended period, be sure to place the log file on a drive with lots of free space. Remember, the more frequently you update the log file, the higher the drive space and CPU resource usage on the system.

9. The log file can be configured to stop in the following ways:

   * Manually
   * After a specified period of time, such as 7 days
   * At a specific date and time
   * When the log file is full (if you've set a specific file size limit)

10. Click OK when you've finished setting the logging schedule. The log is then created and you can manage it as explained in the "Creating and Managing Performance Logging" section of this chapter.

Creating Trace Logs

Trace logs record performance data whenever events for their source providers occur. A source provider is an application or operating system service that has traceable events. On domain controllers, you'll find System, Local Security Authority, and Active Directory:NetLogon providers. On other servers, the System and Local Security Authority providers probably will be the only providers available.

To create a trace log, complete the following steps:

1. Select Trace Logs in the left pane of the Performance console, and then right-click in the right pane to display the shortcut menu. Select New Log Settings.

2. In the New Log Settings dialog box, type a name for the log, such as Disk I/O Trace or Network TCP/IP Trace, then click OK. This opens the dialog box shown in Figure 10-8.

3. If you want to trace operating system events, select the Events Logged By System Provider option button. As shown in Figure 10-8, you can now select system events to trace.

Caution Collecting page faults and file detail events puts a heavy load on the server and causes the log file to grow rapidly. Because of this, you should collect page faults and file details only for a limited amount of time.

4. If you want to trace another provider, select the Nonsystem Providers option button and then click Add. This displays the Add Nonsystem Providers dialog box, which you'll use to select the provider to trace.

5. When you're finished selecting providers and events to trace, click the Log Files tab. You can now configure the trace file as detailed in Step 6 of the

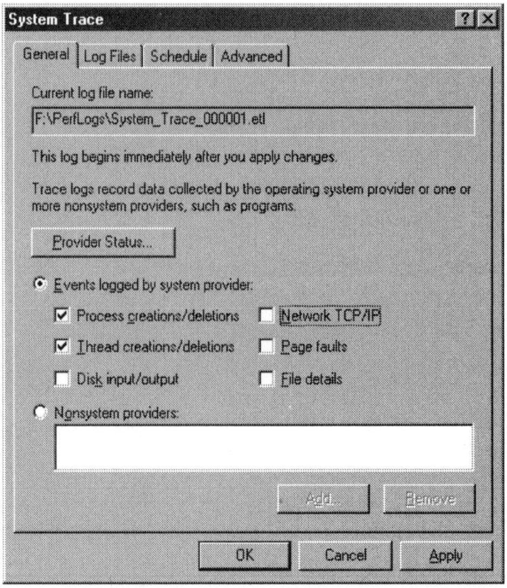

Figure 10-8. *Use the General tab to select the provider to use in the trace.*

"Creating Counter Logs" section of this chapter. The only change is that the log file types are different. With trace logs, you have two log types:

- **Sequential Trace File** Writes events to the trace log sequentially up to the maximum file size (if any)
- **Circular Trace File** Overwrites old data with new data when the file reaches a specified size limit

6. Select the Schedule tab and then specify when tracing starts and stops.

7. You can configure the logging to start manually or automatically at a specific date. Select the appropriate option and then specify a start date if necessary.

8. You can configure the log file to stop manually, after a specified period (such as 7 days), at a specific date and time, or when the log file is full (if you've set a specific file size limit).

9. When you finish setting the logging schedule, click OK. The log is then created and can be managed, as explained in the "Creating and Managing Performance Logging" section of this chapter.

Replaying Performance Logs

When you're troubleshooting problems, you'll often want to log performance data over an extended period and analyze the data later. To do this, complete the following steps:

1. Configure automatic logging as described in the "Creating Counter Logs" section of this chapter.

2. Load the log file in Performance Monitor when you're ready to analyze the data. To do this, click View Log File Data on the Performance Monitor toolbar. This displays the Select Log File dialog box.

3. Use the Look In selection list to access the log directory, and then select the log you want to view. Click Open.

4. Counters you've logged are available for charting. Click Add on the toolbar and then select the counters you want to display.

Configuring Alerts for Performance Counters

You can configure alerts to notify you when certain events occur or when certain performance thresholds are reached. You can send these alerts as network messages and as events that are logged in the application event log. You can also configure alerts to start applications and performance logs.

To add alerts in Performance Monitor, complete the following steps:

1. Select Alerts in the left pane of the Performance console, and then right-click in the right pane to display the shortcut menu. Select New Alert Settings.

2. In the New Alert Settings dialog box, type a name for the alert, such as ASP Error Alert or High User Connection Alert. Then click OK. This opens the dialog box shown in Figure 10-9.

3. In the General tab, type an optional description of the alert in the Comment field. Then click Add to display the Select Counters To Log dialog box. This

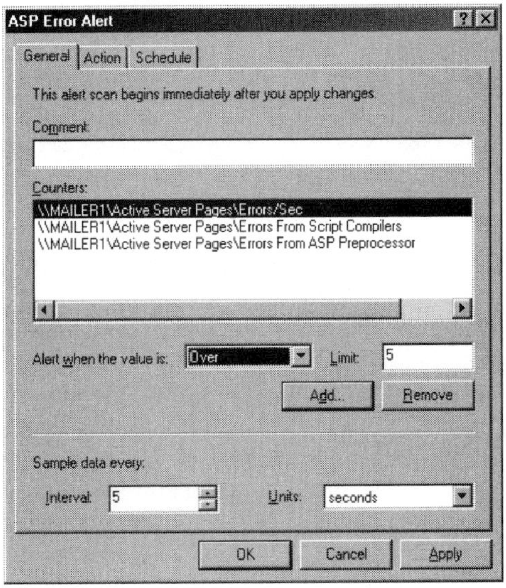

Figure 10-9. *Use the Alert dialog box to configure counters that trigger alerts.*

dialog box is identical to the Add Counters dialog box shown previously in Figure 10-4.

4. Use the Select Counters To Log dialog box to add counters that trigger the alert. Click Close when you're finished.

5. In the Counters panel, select the first counter and then use the Trigger Alert When Value Is field to set the occasion when an alert for this counter is triggered. Alerts can be triggered when the counter is over or under a specific value. Select Over or Under and then set the trigger value. The unit of measurement is whatever makes sense for the currently selected counters. For example, to alert if processor time is over 95 percent, you would select Over, and then type **95**. Repeat this process to configure other counters you've selected.

6. In the Sample Data Every field, type in a sample interval and select a time unit in seconds, minutes, hours, or days. The sample interval specifies when new data is collected. For example, if you set the sample interval to 5 minutes, the log is updated every 5 minutes.

 Caution Don't sample too frequently. You'll use system resources and may cause the server to seem unresponsive to user requests.

7. Select the Action tab, as shown in Figure 10-10. You can now specify any of the following actions to take place when an alert is triggered:

- **Log An Entry In The Application Event Log** Creates log entries for alerts
- **Send A Network Message To** Sends a network message to the computer specified
- **Start Performance Data Log** Sets a counter log to start when an alert occurs
- **Run This Program** Sets the complete file path of a program or script to run when the alert occurs

Tip You can run any type of executable file, including batch scripts with the .bat or .cmd extension and Windows scripts with the .vb, .js, .pl, or .wsc extension. To pass arguments to a script or application, use the options of the Command Line Arguments panel. Normally, arguments are passed as individual strings. However, if you select Single Argument String, the arguments are passed in a comma-separated list within a single string. The Sample Arguments List at the bottom of the panel shows how the arguments would be passed.

8. Select the Schedule tab and then specify when alerting starts and stops. For example, you could configure the alerts to start on a Friday evening and stop

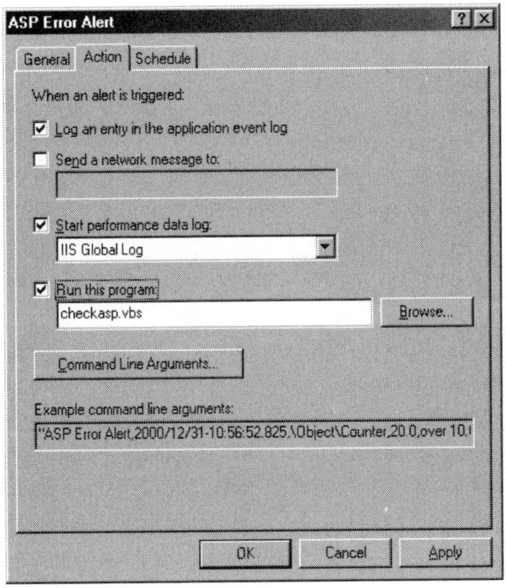

Figure 10-10. *Set actions that are executed when the alert occurs.*

on Monday morning. Then, each time an alert occurs during this period, the specified actions are executed.

 9. You can configure alerts to start manually or automatically at a specific date. Select the appropriate option and then specify a start date if necessary.

10. You can configure alerts to stop manually, after a specified period of time such as 7 days, or at a specific date and time.

11. When you've finished setting the alert schedule, click OK. The alert is then created and you can manage it in much the same way that you manage counter and trace logs.

Tuning Web Server Performance

Now that you know how to monitor your Web servers, let's look at how you can tune the operating system and hardware performance. The areas I'll examine are the following:

- Memory usage and caching
- Processor utilization
- Disk I/O
- Network bandwidth and connectivity

Monitoring and Tuning Memory Usage

Memory is often the source of performance problems, and you should always rule out memory problems before examining other areas of the system. One of the key reasons memory can be such a problem is that the IIS file cache is configured to use up to half of the available system memory by default. This means that on a system with 512 MB random access memory (RAM), the IIS file cache could use as much as 256 MB of memory. (Of course, the amount of memory used for caching depends on the number of files and the frequency of requests.)

Caching and virtual memory settings can also present a problem. Adding memory when there is a caching or virtual memory problem on the server won't solve performance problems. Because of this, you should always check for memory, caching, and virtual memory problems at the same time.

To rule out memory, caching, and virtual memory problems with the server, you should do the following:

- Configure application performance
- Configure data throughput

Once you've performed these tasks and rebooted the server, you can monitor the server's memory usage to check for problems.

Setting Application Performance

Application performance determines the responsiveness of foreground and background applications that may be running on the system. In most cases, you want a server to be equally responsive to foreground and background applications rather than give precedence to an application the Web administrator may be running on the computer. To ensure the server is responsive to background applications, follow these steps:

1. Click Start, point to Settings, and then select Control Panel. Double-click System. This starts the System utility.

2. Access the Advanced tab in the System utility and then display the Performance Options dialog box by clicking Performance Options.

3. Select Background Services and then click OK.

Setting Data Throughput

If you use the server primarily as a Web server, you should configure the server as an application server. This setting optimizes the server for networking performance, makes more memory available to Web applications, and enhances the multiprocessor capabilities of the server. To configure the server as an application server, complete the following steps:

1. Click Start, point to Settings, and then click Network And Dial-Up Connections.

2. Right-click Local Area Connection and then select Properties. This displays the Properties dialog box shown in Figure 10-11.

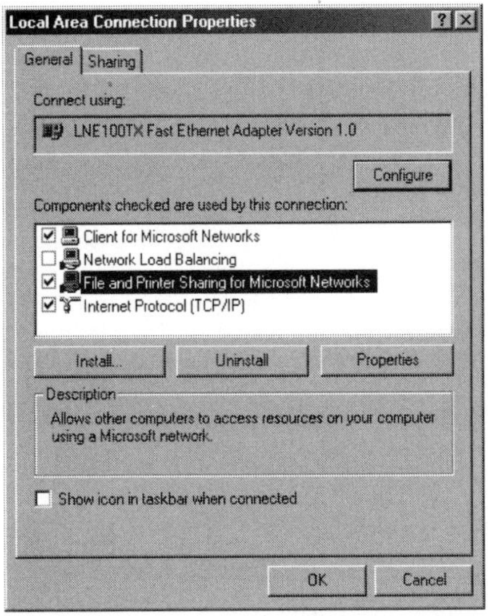

Figure 10-11. *Use the Local Area Connection Properties dialog box to configure file and printer sharing settings for the Web server.*

Note   Servers with multiple network interface cards will have multiple network connections shown in Network And Dial-Up Connections. You should optimize each of these connections appropriately.

3. Select File And Printer Sharing For Microsoft Networks and then click Properties.

4. On the Server Optimization tab, select Maximize Data Throughput For Network Applications. Click OK.

5. You will need to reboot the server for these changes to take effect.

Checking Memory, Caching, and Virtual Memory Usage

Now that you've optimized the system, you can determine how the system is using memory and check for problems. Table 10-2 provides an overview of counters that you'll want to track to uncover memory, caching, and virtual memory (paging) bottlenecks. The table is organized by issue category.

Table 10-2. Uncovering Memory-Related Bottlenecks

Issue	Counters to Track	Details
Physical and virtual memory usage	Memory\Available Kbytes Memory\ Committed Bytes	Memory\Available Kbytes is the amount of physical memory available to processes running on the server. Memory\Committed Bytes is the amount of committed virtual memory. If the server has very little available memory, you may need to add memory to the system. In general, you want the available memory to be no less than 5% of the total physical memory on the server. If the server has a high ratio of committed bytes to total physical memory on the system, you may need to add memory as well. In general, you want the committed bytes value to be no more than 75% of the total physical memory.
Memory caching	Memory\Cache Bytes Internet Information Services Global\ Current File Cache Memory Usage\ Internet Information Services Global\ File Cache Hits % Internet Information Services Global\ File Cache Flushes	Memory\Cache Bytes represents the total size of the file system cache. Internet Information Services Global\Current File Cache Memory Usage represents the current memory used by the IIS file cache. Internet Information Services Global\File Cache Hits % represents the ratio of cache hits to total cache requests, and reflects how well the settings for the IIS file cache are are working. A site with mostly static files should have a very high cache hit percentage (70%–85%). Internet Information Services Global\File Cache Flushes tells you how quickly IIS is flushing files out of cache. If flushes are occurring too quickly, you may need to increase the time-to-live value for cached objects (ObjectCacheTTL). If flushes are occurring too slowly, you may be wasting memory and may need to decrease the time-to-live value for cached objects.
Memory page faults	Memory\Page Faults/sec Memory\ Pages Input/ sec Memory\ Page Reads/sec	A page fault occurs when a process requests a page in memory and the system cannot find it at the requested location. If the requested page is elsewhere in memory, the fault is called a soft page fault. If the requested page must be retrieved from disk, the fault is called a hard page fault. Most processors can handle large numbers of soft faults. Hard faults, however,

(continued)

Table 10-2. *(continued)*

Issue	Counters to Track	Details
		can cause significant delays. Page Faults/sec is the overall rate at which the processor handles all types of page faults. Pages Input/sec is the total number of pages read from disk to resolve hard page faults. Page Reads/sec is the total disk reads needed to resolve hard page faults. Pages Input/sec will be greater than or equal to Page Reads/sec and can give you a good idea of your hard page fault rate. If there are a high number of hard page faults, you may need to increase the amount of memory or reduce the cache size on the server. Memory used by IIS is controlled by the MemCacheSize and MaxCachedFileSize settings.
Memory paging	Memory\Pool Paged Bytes, Memory\Pool Nonpaged Bytes	These counters track the number of bytes in the page and nonpaged pool. The paged pool is an area of system memory for objects that can be written to disk when they aren't used. The non-paged pool is an area of system memory for objects that cannot be written to disk. If the size of the page pool is large relative to the total amount of physical memory on the system, you may need to add memory to the system. If the size of the nonpaged pool is large relative to the total amount of virtual memory allocated to the server, you may want to increase the virtual memory size.

Monitoring and Tuning Processor Usage

The CPU does the actual processing of information on your server. As you examine the performance of a server, you should focus on the CPUs after memory bottlenecks have been eliminated. If the server's processors are the performance bottleneck, adding memory, drives, or network connections won't overcome the problem. Instead, you may need to upgrade the processors to faster clock speeds or add additional processors to increase the upper capacity of the server. You could also move processor-intensive applications, such as SQL Server, to another server.

Before you make a decision to upgrade CPUs or add additional CPUs, you should rule out problems with memory and caching. If signs still point to a processor problem, you should monitor the performance counters discussed in Table 10-3. Be sure to monitor these counters for each CPU installed on the server.

Table 10-3. Uncovering Processor-Related Bottlenecks

Issue	Counters to Track	Details
Thread queuing	System\Processor Queue Length	This counter displays the number of threads waiting to be executed. These threads are queued in an area shared by all processors on the system. If this counter has a sustained value of 2 or more threads, you'll need to upgrade or add processors.
CPU usage	Processor\ % Processor Time	This counter displays the percentage of time the selected CPU is executing a nonidle thread. You should track this counter separately for all processor instances on the server. If the % Processor Time values are high while the network interface and disk I/O throughput rates are relatively low, you'll need to upgrade or add processors.
ASP performance	Active Server Pages\Request Wait Time Active Server Pages\Requests Queued Active Server Pages\ Requests Rejected Active Server Pages\Requests/sec	These counters indicate the relative performance of IIS when working with ASPs. Active Server Pages\Request Wait Time is the number of milliseconds the most recent request was waiting in the queue. Active Server Pages\Requests Queued is the number of requests waiting to be processed. Active Server Pages\Requests Rejected is the total number of requests not executed because there weren't resources to process them. Active Server Pages\Requests/sec is the number of requests executed per second. In general, you don't want to see requests waiting in the queue and, if requests are queuing, the wait time should be very low. You also don't want to see requests rejected because resources aren't available. Keep these problems relative to the number of requests handled per second. You may notice some variance under peak loads. To resolve these issues you may need to upgrade or add processors.

Real World In many cases, a single server may not be sufficient to handle the network traffic load. In this case, you may need to scale your site across multiple servers. For example, you could replicate the site to additional servers and then distribute the traffic across these servers using a load balancer. If you already have a multiple-server Web farm, you could add additional Web servers.

Monitoring and Tuning Disk I/O

With today's high-speed disks, the disk throughput rate is rarely the cause of a bottleneck. That said, however, accessing memory is much faster than accessing disks. So, if the server has to do a lot of disk reads and writes, the overall performance of the server can be degraded. To reduce the amount of disk I/O, you want the server to manage memory very efficiently and page to disk only when necessary. You monitor and tune memory usage as discussed previously in the "Monitoring and Tuning Memory Usage" section of this chapter.

Beyond the memory tuning discussion, you can monitor some counters to gauge disk I/O activity. Specifically, you should monitor the counters discussed in Table 10-4.

Table 10-4. Uncovering Drive-Related Bottlenecks

Issue	Counters to Track	Details
Overall drive performance	PhysicalDisk\ % Disk Time in conjunction with Processor\% Processor Time and Network Interface Connection\Bytes Total/sec	If the % Disk Time value is high and the processor and network connection values are not high, the system's hard drives may be creating a bottleneck. Be sure to monitor % Disk Time for all hard drives on the server.
Disk I/O	PhysicalDisk\Disk Writes/sec, PhysicalDisk\ Disk Reads/sec, PhysicalDisk\Avg. Disk Write Queue Length, PhysicalDisk\Avg. Disk Read Queue Length Physical Disk\Current Disk Queue Length	The number of writes and reads per second tells you how much disk I/O activity there is. The write and read queue lengths tell you how many write or read requests are waiting to be processed. In general, you want there to be very few waiting requests. Keep in mind that the request delays are proportional to the length of the queues minus the number of drives in a RAID set.

Note Counters for physical and logical disks may need to be enabled before they are available. To enable these objects, type the following commands at a command prompt:

Diskperf –y for a hard drive

Diskperf –yv for a software RAID set

Monitoring and Tuning
Network Bandwidth and Connectivity

No other factor weighs more in a visitor's perceived performance of your server than the network that connects your server to the visitor's computer. The delay, or latency, between when a request is made and the time it is received can make all the difference. If there is a high degree of latency, it doesn't matter if you have the fastest server on the planet. The user experiences a delay and perceives that your servers are slow.

Generally speaking, the latency the user experiences is beyond your control. It is a function of the type of connection the user has and the route the request takes through the Internet to your server. The total capacity of your server to handle requests and the amount of bandwidth available to your servers are factors under your control, however. Network bandwidth availability is a function of your organization's connection to the Internet. Network capacity is a function of the network cards and interfaces configured on the servers.

A typical network card is equipped to handle a 100 Mbps Fast Ethernet connection with fair efficiency, which is much more traffic than the typical site experiences and much more traffic than the typical server can handle. Because of this, your organization's bandwidth availability is typically the limiting factor. If you have a shared T1 for all Internet activity, your servers are sharing the 1.4 Mbps connection with all other Internet traffic. If you have a dedicated T1 for your Web servers, your servers have 1.4 Mbps of bandwidth availability. If you have multiple T1s or a T3, the bandwidth available to your servers could range from 3 Mbps to 45 Mbps.

To put this in perspective, consider that the number of simultaneous connections your network can handle is relative to the speed of the connection, the average size of the data transferred per connection, and the permitted transfer time. For example, if you have a T1 and the typical data transfer per connection is 50 KB and transfer time allowable is 15 seconds, your connection could handle this capacity:

- 21 data transfers per second, or
- 294 simultaneous transfers

On the other hand, if you have a T1 and the typical data transfer per connection is 250 kilobytes and transfer time allowable is 15 seconds, your connection could handle this capacity:

- 15 data transfers per second, or
- 60 simultaneous transfers

The capacity of your network card can be a limiting factor in some instances. Most servers use 10/100 network cards, which can be configured in many different ways. Someone may have configured a card for 10 Mbps, or the card may be configured for half duplex instead of full duplex. If you suspect a capacity problem with a network card, you should always check the configuration.

Real World A T1 connection is a useful example for many commercial sites. Larger commercial sites are typically co-located at a hosting service, such as Genuity, and may have 100 Mbps or greater connections to the Internet. If this is the case for your site, keep in mind that some devices configured on your network may restrict the permitted bandwidth. For example, your company's firewall may be configured so that it only allows 5 Mbps for Web, 2 Mbps for FTP, and 1 Mbps for SMTP.

To determine the throughput and current activity on a server's network cards, you can check the following counters:

- Network\Bytes Received/sec
- Network\Bytes Sent/sec
- Network\Bytes Total/sec
- Network Current Bandwidth

If the total bytes-per-second value is more than 50% of the total capacity under average load conditions, your server may have problems under peak load conditions. You may want to ensure that operations that take a lot of network bandwidth, such as backups, are performed on a separate interface card. Keep in mind that you should compare these values in conjunction with PhysicalDisk\% Disk Time and Processor\% Processor Time. If the process time and disk time values are low but the network values are very high, there may be a capacity problem.

IIS provides several ways to restrict bandwidth usage and to improve bandwidth-related performance. These features are the following:

- Bandwidth throttling
- Connection limitations
- HTTP compression

Configuring Bandwidth Throttling and Connection Limits

You can restrict bandwidth usage by enabling bandwidth throttling and limiting the maximum number of allowable connections. Bandwidth throttling restricts the total bandwidth available to a service or individual sites. Connection limitations restrict the total number of allowable connections to a service. Because users may be denied service when these values are exceeded, you should only enable these features when you are sure that this setting is acceptable.

Before you restrict bandwidth, you should monitor the network object counters discussed earlier in the chapter. If these counters indicate a possible problem, restricting bandwidth is one answer. You can configure bandwidth throttling for all Web and FTP sites on a server by completing the following steps:

1. In the Internet Information Services snap-in, right-click the icon for the computer that you want to work with, and then select Properties.

2. On the Internet Information Services tab, select the Enable Bandwidth Throttling check box.

3. In the Maximum Network Use box, type the maximum number of kilobytes per second (Kbps) you want IIS to use. Remember, this value is for all Web and FTP sites.

4. Click OK.

While you cannot configure bandwidth throttling for individual FTP sites, you can configure throttling for individual Web sites. To do so, complete these steps:

1. In the Internet Information Services snap-in, right-click the Web site you want to work with, and then select Properties.

2. On the Performance property sheet, select Enable Bandwidth Throttling.

3. In the Maximum Network Use box, type the maximum number of kilobytes per second you want the site to use.

4. Click OK.

Setting connection limits for Web and FTP sites was covered previously in this book. To learn how to configure limits for Web sites, see the "Restricting Incoming Connections and Setting Time-Out Values" section of Chapter 3, "Configuring Web Sites and Servers." For FTP sites, see the similarly named section in Chapter 7, "Managing FTP Servers."

Configuring HTTP Compression

With HTTP compression enabled, the Web server compresses files before sending them to client browsers. File compression reduces the amount of information transferred between the server and the client, which in turn can reduce network bandwidth usage, network capacity, and transfer time. For HTTP compression to work, the client browser must support HTTP 1.1, and this feature must be enabled. Although most current browsers support HTTP 1.1 and have the feature enabled by default, older browsers may not support HTTP 1.1. Older browsers will still be able to retrieve files from your site, but they won't be taking advantage of HTTP compression.

Before you enable compression, you should monitor the current processor usage on the server. HTTP compression adds to the overhead on the server, meaning it will increase overall processor utilization. If your site uses dynamic content extensively and process utilization (% Processor Time) is already high, you may not want to upgrade or add processors before enabling HTTP compression.

Once you've completed your processor evaluation and have decided to use HTTP compression, you can enable this feature by completing the following steps:

1. In the Internet Information Services snap-in, right-click the icon for the computer that you want to work with, and then select Properties.

2. Under Master Properties, select WWW Service, and then click Edit.

3. Select the Service tab, as shown in Figure 10-12.

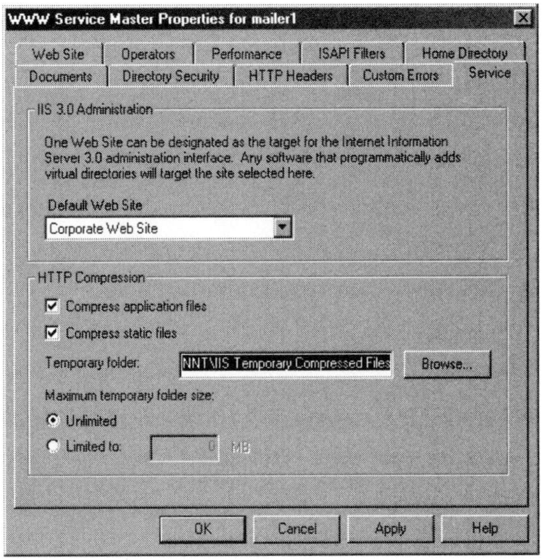

Figure 10-12. *Use the Service tab to configure HTTP compression.*

4. To compress dynamic content, such as ASPs, select Compress Application Files. Compressed dynamic files are stored in memory.

5. To compress static files, such as HTML pages, select Compress Static Files. Compressed static files are stored on disk in the directory specified by the Temporary Folder field.

6. The Temporary Folder field is used to specify where compressed static files are stored until the time-to-live period expires. When using compression for static files, type the name and path of the directory you want to use. Or click Browse to locate a directory where compressed files will be stored.

Note The directory must be on a local drive on a Windows NT file system partition. Additionally, the directory should not be shared and cannot be a compressed directory.

7. To limit the size of the static file cache, select Limited To, and then type a limit in megabytes for the directory.

8. Click OK twice.

Chapter 11

Tracking User Access and Logging

One of your primary responsibilities as a Web administrator may be to log access to your company's Internet servers. As you'll see in this chapter, enabling logging on Hypertext Transfer Protocol (HTTP), File Transfer Protocol (FTP), and Simple Mail Transfer Protocol (SMTP) servers isn't very difficult. What is difficult, however, is gathering the correct access information and recording this information in the proper format so that it can be read and analyzed. Software that you use to analyze access logs is called tracking software. You'll find many different types of tracking software. Most commercial tracking software produces detailed reports that include tables and graphs that summarize activity for specific periods. For example, you could compile tracking reports daily, weekly, or monthly.

You can configure logging for HTTP, FTP, and SMTP servers. The file format for access logs can be configured in several different ways. You can configure standard logging, open database connectivity (ODBC) logging, and extended logging. With standard logging, you choose a log file format and rely on the format to record the user access information you need. With ODBC logging, you record user access directly to an ODBC-compliant database, such as Microsoft SQL Server 2000. With extended logging, you can customize the logging process and record exactly the information you need to track user access.

Tracking Statistics: The Big Picture

Access logs are created when you enable logging for an HTTP, FTP, or SMTP server. Every time someone requests a file from your World Wide Web site, an entry goes into the access log, making the access log a running history of every successful and unsuccessful attempt to retrieve information from your site. Because each entry has its own line, entries in the access log can be easily extracted and compiled into reports. From these reports, you can learn many things about those who visit your site. You can do the following:

- Determine the busiest times of the day and week
- Determine which browsers and platforms are used by people who visit your site
- Discover popular and unpopular resources
- Discover sites that refer users to your site

- Learn more about the effectiveness of your advertising
- Learn more about the people who visit your site
- Obtain information about search engine usage and keywords
- Obtain information about the amount of time users spend at the site

Access logs can be configured in several different formats. The available formats are

- **National Center for Supercomputing Applications (NCSA) Common Log File Format (Web and SMTP Only)** Use the common log format when your reporting and tracking needs are basic. With this format, log entries are small, and this reduces the amount of storage space required for logging.

- **Microsoft Internet Information Services (IIS) Log File Format** Use the IIS format when you need a bit more information from the logs but don't need to tailor the entries to get detailed information. With this format, log entries are compact, and this reduces the amount of storage space required for logging.

- **World Wide Web Consortium (W3C) Extended Log File Format** Use the extended format when you need to customize the information tracked and obtain detailed information. With this format, log entries can become large, and this greatly increases the amount of storage space required. Recording lengthy entries can affect the performance of a busy server as well.

- **ODBC Logging** Use the ODBC format when you want to write access information directly to an ODBC-compliant database. With ODBC logging, you'll need tracking software capable of reading from a database. Entries are compact, however, and data can be read much more quickly than from a standard log file. Keep in mind that ODBC logging is more processor-intensive when you log directly to a local database instance.

> **Tip** Microsoft distributes a tool for converting a log file to NCSA common log file format. The tool is called CONVLOG, and it is located in the \%WinDir%\System32 directory. You can use CONVLOG to convert logs formatted using IIS and W3C extended log file formats to NCSA common log file format. The tool also performs reverse Domain Name System (DNS) lookups during the conversion process. This allows you to resolve some Internet Protocol (IP) addresses to domain names.

Because an understanding of what is written to log files is important to understanding logging itself, the sections that follow examine each of the available file formats. After this discussion, you'll be able to determine what each format has to offer and, hopefully, to better determine when to use each format.

Working with the NCSA Common Log File Format

NCSA common log file format is the most basic log format. The common log format is a fixed ASCII format in which each log entry represents a unique file request. You'll use the common log format when your tracking and reporting needs are basic. More specifically, the common log format is a good choice when you only need to track certain items, such as

- Hits (the number of unique file requests)
- Page views (the number of unique page requests)
- Visits (the number of user sessions in a specified period)
- Other basic access information

With this format, log entries are small, and this reduces the amount of storage space required for logging. Each entry in the common log format has only seven fields. These fields are

- Host
- Identification
- User Authentication
- Time Stamp
- HTTP Request Type
- Status Code
- Transfer Volume

As you'll see, the common log format is easy to understand, which makes it a good stepping-stone to more advanced log file formats. The following listing shows entries in a sample access log that are formatted using the NCSA common log file format. As you can see from the sample, log fields are separated by spaces.

```
192.168.11.15 - ENGSVR01\wrstanek [15/Jan/2001:18:44:57 -0800]
"GET / HTTP/1.1" 200 1970
192.168.11.15 - ENGSVR01\wrstanek [15/Jan/2001:18:45:06 -0800]
"GET /home.gif HTTP/1.1" 200 5032
192.168.11.15 - ENGSVR01\wrstanek [15/Jan/2001:18:45:28 -0800]
"GET /main.htm HTTP/1.1" 200 5432
192.168.11.15 - ENGSVR01\wrstanek [15/Jan/2001:18:45:31 -0800]
"GET /details.gif HTTP/1.1" 200 1211
192.168.11.15 - ENGSVR01\wrstanek [15/Jan/2001:18:45:31 -0800]
"GET /menu.gif HTTP/1.1" 200 6075
192.168.11.15 - ENGSVR01\wrstanek [15/Jan/2001:18:45:31 -0800]
"GET /sidebar.gif HTTP/1.1" 200 9023
192.168.11.15 - ENGSVR01\wrstanek [15/Jan/2001:18:45:31 -0800]
"GET /sun.gif HTTP/1.1" 200 4706
192.168.11.15 - ENGSVR01\wrstanek [15/Jan/2001:18:45:38 -0800]
"GET /moon.gif HTTP/1.1" 200 1984
192.168.11.15 - ENGSVR01\wrstanek [15/Jan/2001:18:45:41 -0800]
"GET /stars.gif HTTP/1.1" 200 2098
```

Most other log file formats build off the NCSA file format, so, it is useful to examine how these fields are used.

Host Field

Host is the first field in the common log format. This field identifies the host computer requesting a file from your Web server. The value in this field is either the IP address of the remote host, such as 192.168.11.15, or the fully qualified domain name of the remote host, such as net48.microsoft.com. The following example shows an HTTP query initiated by a host that was successfully resolved to a domain name:

```
net48.microsoft.com - ENGSVR01\wrstanek [15/Jan/2001:18:44:57 -
0800] "GET / HTTP/1.1" 200 1970
```

IP addresses are the numeric equivalent of fully qualified domain names. You can often use a reverse DNS lookup to determine the actual domain name from the IP address. When you have a domain name or resolve an IP address to an actual name, you can examine the name to learn more about the user accessing your server. Divisions within the domain name are separated by periods. The final division identifies the domain class, which can tell you where the user lives and works.

Domain classes are geographically and demographically organized. Geographically organized domain classes end in a two- or three-letter designator for the state or country in which the user lives. For example, the .ca domain class is for companies in Canada. Demographically organized domain classes tell you the type of company providing network access to the user. Table 11-1 summarizes these domain classes.

Table 11-1. Basic Domain Classes

Domain Name	Description
.com	Commercial; users from commercial organizations
.edu	Education; users from colleges and universities
.gov	U.S. government; users from U.S. government agencies, except military
.mil	U.S. military; users who work at military installations
.net	Network; users who work at network service providers, and other network-related organizations
.org	Nonprofit organizations; users who work for nonprofit organizations

Identification Field

The Identification field is the second field in the common log format. This field is meant to identify users by their username but in practice is rarely used. Because of this, you will generally see a hyphen (-) in this field, as in the following:

```
net48.microsoft.com - ENGSVR01\wrstanek [15/Jan/2001:18:44:57 -
0800] "GET / HTTP/1.1" 200 1970
```

If you do see a value in this field, keep in mind that the username is not validated. This means it could be made up and shouldn't be trusted.

User Authentication Field

The User Authentication field is the third field in the common log format. If you have a password-protected area at your Web site, users must authenticate themselves with a username and password that is registered for this area. After users validate themselves with their username and password, their username is entered in the User Authentication field. In unprotected areas of a site, you will usually see a hyphen (-) in this field. In protected areas of a site, you will see the account name of the authenticated user. The account name can be preceded by the name of the domain in which the user is authenticated, as shown in this example:

```
net48.microsoft.com - ENGSVR01\wrstanek [15/Jan/2001:18:44:57 -
0800] "GET / HTTP/1.1" 200 1970
```

Time Stamp Field

The Time Stamp field is the fourth field in the common log format. This field tells you exactly when someone accessed a file on the server. The format for the Time Stamp field is as follows:

```
DD/MMM/YYYY:HH:MM:SS OFFSET
```

such as:

```
15/Jan/2001:18:44:57 -0800
```

The only designator that probably doesn't make sense is the offset. The offset indicates the difference in the server's time from Greenwich Mean Time (GMT) standard time. In the following example, the offset is -8 hours, meaning that the server time is 8 hours behind GMT:

```
net48.microsoft.com - ENGSVR01\wrstanek [15/Jan/2001:18:44:57 -
0800] "GET / HTTP/1.1" 200 1970
```

HTTP Request Field

The HTTP Request field is the fifth field in the common log format. Use this field to determine the method that the remote client used to request the resource, the resource that the remote client requested, and the HTTP version that the client used to retrieve the resource. In the following example, the HTTP Request field information is bold:

```
192.168.11.15 - ENGSVR01\wrstanek [15/Jan/2001:18:45:06 -0800]
"GET /home.gif HTTP/1.1" 200 5032
```

Here, the transfer method is GET, the resource is /HOME.GIF, and the transfer method is HTTP 1.1. One thing you should note is that resources are specified using relative Uniform Resource Locators (URLs). The server interprets relative URLs. For example, if you request the file *http://www.microsoft.com/home/main.htm,* the server will use the relative URL /home/MAIN.HTM to log where the file is found. When you see an entry that ends in a slash, keep in mind that this refers to the default document for a directory, which is typically called INDEX.HTM or DEFAULT.ASP.

Status Code Field

The Status Code field is the sixth field in the common log format. Status codes indicate whether files were transferred correctly, were loaded from cache, were not found, and so on. Generally, status codes are three-digit numbers. As shown in Table 11-2, the first digit indicates the class or category of the status code.

Table 11-2. Status Code Classes

Code Class	Description
1XX	Continue/protocol change
2XX	Success
3XX	Redirection
4XX	Client error/failure
5XX	Server error

Because you'll rarely see a status code beginning with 1, you only need to remember the other four categories. A status code that begins with 2 indicates the associated file transferred successfully. A status code that begins with 3 indicates that the server performed a redirect. A status code that begins with 4 indicates some type of client error or failure. Last, a status code that begins with 5 tells you that a server error occurred.

Transfer Volume Field

The last field in the common log format is the Transfer Volume field. This field indicates the number of bytes transferred to the client because of the request. In the following example, 4096 bytes were transferred to the client:

```
net48.microsoft.com - ENGSVR01\wrstanek [15/Jan/2001:18:45:06 -
0800] "GET / HTTP/1.1" 200 4096
```

You'll only see a transfer volume when the status code class indicates success. If another status code class is used in field six, the Transfer Volume field will contain a hyphen (-) or a 0 to indicate that no data was transferred.

Working with the Microsoft IIS Log File Format

Like the common log format, the Microsoft IIS log file format is a fixed ASCII format. This means the fields in the log are of a fixed type and cannot be changed. It also means the log is formatted as standard ASCII text and can be read with any standard text editor or compliant application.

You'll use the IIS format when you need a bit more information than the common log format provides but don't need to tailor the entries to get detailed information. As the log entries are compact, the amount of storage space required for logging is much less than the expanded or ODBC logging formats.

The following listing shows entries from a sample log using the IIS log file format. The IIS log entries include common log fields such as the client IP address, authenticated username, request date and time, HTTP status code, and number of bytes received. IIS log entries also include detailed items such as the Web service name, the server IP address, and the elapsed time. Note that commas separate log fields, and entries are much longer than those in the common log file format.

```
192.14.16.2, -, 12/28/2000, 20:55:25, W3SVC1, ENGSVR01,
192.15.14.81, 0, 594, 3847, 401, 5, GET, /localstart.asp, -,
192.14.16.2, ENGSVR01\wrstanek, 12/28/2000, 20:55:25, W3SVC1,
ENGSVR01, 192.15.14.81, 10, 412, 3406, 404, 0, GET, /
localstart.asp, |-|0|404_Object_Not_Found,
192.14.16.2, -, 12/28/2000, 20:55:29, W3SVC1, ENGSVR01,
192.15.14.81, 0, 622, 3847, 401, 5, GET, /IISHelp/iis/misc/
default.asp, -,
192.14.16.2, ENGSVR01\wrstanek, 12/28/2000, 20:55:29, W3SVC1,
ENGSVR01, 192.15.14.81, 10, 426, 0, 200, 0, GET, /IISHelp/iis/
misc/default.asp, -,
192.14.16.2, ENGSVR01\wrstanek, 12/28/2000, 20:55:29, W3SVC1,
ENGSVR01, 192.15.14.81, 10, 368, 0, 200, 0, GET, /IISHelp/iis/
misc/contents.asp, -,
192.14.16.2, -, 12/28/2000, 20:55:29, W3SVC1, ENGSVR01,
192.15.14.81, 0, 732, 3847, 401, 5, GET, /IISHelp/iis/misc/
navbar.asp, -,
192.14.16.2, -, 12/28/2000, 20:55:29, W3SVC1, ENGSVR01,
192.15.14.81, 0, 742, 3847, 401, 5, GET, /IISHelp/iis/htm/core/
iiwltop.htm, -,
192.14.16.2, ENGSVR01\wrstanek, 12/28/2000, 20:55:29, W3SVC1,
ENGSVR01, 192.15.14.81, 20, 481, 0, 200, 0, GET, /IISHelp/iis/
misc/navbar.asp, -,
192.14.16.2, ENGSVR01\wrstanek, 12/28/2000, 20:55:29, W3SVC1,
ENGSVR01, 192.15.14.81, 91, 486, 6520, 200, 0, GET, /IISHelp/iis/
htm/core/iiwltop.htm, -,
```

The fields supported by IIS are summarized in Table 11-3. Note that the listed field order is the general order used by IIS to record fields.

Table 11-3. Fields for the IIS Log File Format

Field Name	Description	Example
Client IP	IP address of the client	192.14.16.2
Username	Authenticated name of the user	ENGSVR01\wrstanek
Date	Date at which the transaction was completed	12/28/2000
Time	Time at which the transaction was completed	20:55:29
Service	Name of the Web service logging the transaction	W3SVC1
Computer Name	Name of the computer that made the request	ENGSVR01

(continued)

Table 11-3. *(continued)*

Field Name	Description	Example
Server IP	IP address of the Web server	192.15.14.81
Elapsed Time	Time taken (in milliseconds) for the transaction to be completed	40
Bytes Received	Number of bytes received by the server in client request	486
Bytes Sent	Number of bytes sent to the client	6520
Status Code	HTTP status code	200
Windows Status Code	Error status code from Windows	0
Method Used	HTTP request method	GET
File URI	The requested file	/localstart.asp
Referer	The referer—the location the user came from	http://www.microsoft.com/

Working with the W3C Extended Log File Format

The W3C extended log file format is much different than either of the previously discussed log file formats. With this format, you can customize the information tracked and obtain detailed information. When you customize an extended log file, you select the fields you want the server to log, and the server handles the logging for you. Keep in mind that each additional field you track adds to the size of entries recorded in the access logs, and this can greatly increase the amount of storage space required.

The following listing shows sample entries from an extended log. Note that, as with the common log format, extended log fields are separated with spaces.

```
#Software: Microsoft Internet Information Services 5.0
#Version: 1.0
#Date: 2000-12-29 05:27:58
#Fields: date time c-ip cs-username s-ip s-port cs-method cs-uri-
stem cs-uri-query sc-status cs(User-Agent)
2000-12-29 05:27:58 192.14.16.2 ENGSVR01\wrstanek 192.14.15.81 80
GET /iishelp/iis/htm/core/iierrcst.htm - 304 Mozilla/
4.0+(compatible;+MSIE+5.01;+Windows+NT+5.0)
2000-12-29 05:28:00 192.14.16.2 ENGSVR01\wrstanek 192.14.15.81 80
GET /iishelp/iis/htm/core/iierrdtl.htm - 304 Mozilla/
4.0+(compatible;+MSIE+5.01;+Windows+NT+5.0)
2000-12-29 05:28:02 192.14.16.2 ENGSVR01\wrstanek 192.14.15.81 80
GET /iishelp/iis/htm/core/iierrabt.htm - 200 Mozilla/
4.0+(compatible;+MSIE+5.01;+Windows+NT+5.0)
2000-12-29 05:28:02 192.14.16.2 ENGSVR01\wrstanek 192.14.15.81 80
GET /iishelp/iis/htm/core/iierradd.htm - 200 Mozilla/
```

```
4.0+(compatible;+MSIE+5.01;+Windows+NT+5.0)
2000-12-29 05:28:05 192.14.16.2 ENGSVR01\wrstanek 192.14.15.81 80
GET /iishelp/iis/htm/core/iiprstop.htm - 200 Mozilla/
4.0+(compatible;+MSIE+5.01;+Windows+NT+5.0)
```

The first time you look at log entries that use the extended format, you might be a bit confused. The reason for this is that the extended logs are written with server directives as well as file requests. The good news is that server directives are always preceded by the hash symbol (#), easily allowing you to distinguish them from actual file requests. The key directives you'll see are the directives that identify the server software and the fields being recorded. These directives are summarized in Table 11-4.

Table 11-4. Directives Used with the Extended Log File Format

Directive	Name Description
Date	Identifies the date and time the entries were made in the log
End-Date	Identifies the date and time the log was finished and then archived
Fields	Specifies the fields and the field order used in the log file
Remark	Specifies comments
Software	Identifies the server software that created the log entries
Start-Date	Identifies the date and time the log was started
Version	Identifies the version of the extended log file format used

Most extended log fields have a prefix. The prefix tells you how a particular field is used or how the field was obtained. For example, the *cs* prefix tells you the field was obtained from a request sent by the client to the server. Field prefixes are summarized in Table 11-5.

Table 11-5. Prefixes Used with the Extended Log Fields

Prefix	Description
c	Identifies a client-related field
s	Identifies a server-related field
r	Identifies a remote server field
cs	Identifies information obtained from a request sent by the client to the server
sc	Identifies information obtained from a request sent by the IIS server to the client
sr	Identifies information obtained from a request sent by the Web server to a remote server (used by proxies)
rs	Identifies information obtained from a request sent by a remote server to the IIS server (used by proxies)
x	Application-specific prefix

All fields recorded in an extended log have a field identifier. This identifier details the type of information a particular field records. To create a named field, the IIS server can combine a field prefix with a field identifier, or it can simply use a field identifier. The most commonly used field names are summarized in Table 11-6. As you examine the table, keep in mind that most of these fields relate directly to the fields we've already discussed for the common and extended log file formats. Again, the key difference is that the extended format can give you information that is much more detailed.

Table 11-6. Field Identifiers Used with the Extended File Format

Field Type	Actual Field Name	Description
Bytes Received	cs-bytes	Number of bytes received by the server.
Bytes Sent	sc-bytes	Number of bytes sent by the server.
Client IP Address	c-ip	IP address of the client that accessed the server.
Cookie	cs(Cookie)	Content of the cookie sent or received (if any).
Date	date	Date on which the activity occurred.
Http Status	sc-status	HTTP status code.
Method Used	cs-method	HTTP request method.
Protocol Version	cs-protocol	Protocol version used by the client.
Referer	cs(Referer)	Previous site visited by the user. This site provided a link to the current site.
Server IP	s-ip	IP address of the IIS server.
Server Name	s-computername	Name of the IIS server.
Server Port	s-port	Port number to which client is connected.
Service Name and Instance Number	s-sitename	Internet service and instance number that was running on the server.
Time	time	Time the activity occurred.
Time Taken	time-taken	Time taken (in milliseconds) for the transaction to be completed.
URI Query	cs-uri-query	Query parameters passed in request (if any).
URI Stem	cs-uri-stem	Requested resource.
User Agent	cs(User-Agent)	Browser type and version used on the client.
User Name	c-username	Name of an authenticated user (if available).
Win32 Status	sc-win32-status	Error status code from Windows.

In addition to being able to log access requests, IIS can also log process accounting information related to HTTP requests. Process accounting information is helpful in determining the amount of central processing unit (CPU) resources a particular Web site is using, and service providers can use this information to determine resource usage on a per-site basis. However, keep in mind that process accounting only applies to resources used by out-of-process applications. Processing accounting does not cover resources used by pooled or in-process applications.

Table 11-7 provides an overview of fields used to log process accounting information. If you examine a log file with process accounting enabled and configured for logging, you'll find process accounting log entries interspersed with other logging information.

Table 11-7. Process Accounting Fields Used in Extended Logs

Field Type	Actual Field Name	Description
Active Processes	s-active-procs	Number of Common Gateway Interface (CGI) and out-of-process applications running when the log was recorded
Process Event	s-event	Event that was triggered
Process Type	s-proc-type	Type of process that triggered the event: CGI, out-of-process application, or all
Total Kernel Time	s-kernel-time	Total kernel mode processor time (in seconds) used during the current interval
Total Page Faults	s-page-faults	Number of memory references that resulted in memory page faults
Total Processes	s-total-procs	Number of CGI and out-of-process applications created during the current interval
Total Terminated Processes	s-stopped-procs	Number of CGI and out-of-process applications stopped due to process throttling
Total User Time	s-user-time	Total user mode processor time (in seconds) used during the current interval

Working with ODBC Logging

You can use the ODBC logging format when you want to write access information directly to an ODBC-compliant database, such as Microsoft Access or SQL Server 2000. The key advantage of ODBC logging is that access entries are written directly to a database in a format that can be quickly read and interpreted by compliant software. The major disadvantage of ODBC logging is that it requires basic database administration skills to configure and maintain.

With ODBC logging, you must configure a Data Source Name (DSN) that allows IIS to connect to your ODBC database. You must also create a database that can be used for logging. This database must have a table with the appropriate fields for the logging data.

Typically, you'll use the same database for logging information from multiple sites, with each site writing to a separate table in the database. For example, if you wanted to log HTTP, FTP, and SMTP access information in your database, and these services were running on separate sites, you would create three tables in your database:

- HTTPLog
- FTPLog
- SMTPLog

These tables would have the columns and data types for field values summarized in Table 11-8. The columns must be configured exactly as shown in the table. Don't worry; IIS includes a SQL script that you can use to create the necessary table structures. This script is located in the \%WinDir%\System32\Inetsrv directory and is named LOGTEMP.SQL.

 Note If you use the LOGTEMP.SQL script, be sure to edit the table name set in the CREATE TABLE statement. The default table name is inetlog. For more information about working with SQL scripts, see *Microsoft SQL Server 2000 Administrator's Pocket Consultant*.

Table 11-8. Table Fields for ODBC Logging

Field Name	Field Type	Description
ClientHost	varchar(255)	IP address of the client that accessed the server
Username	varchar(255)	Name of an authenticated user (if available)
LogTime	datetime	Date and time on which the activity occurred
Service	varchar(255)	Internet service and instance number that was running on the server
Machine	varchar(255)	Name of the computer that made the request
ServerIP	varchar(50)	IP address of the IIS server
ProcessingTime	int	Time taken (in milliseconds) for the transaction to be completed
BytesRecvd	int	Number of bytes received by the server
BytesSent	int	Number of bytes sent by the server
ServiceStatus	int	HTTP status code
Win32Status	int	Error status code from Windows
Operation	varchar(255)	HTTP request method
Target	varchar(255)	Requested resource
Parameters	varchar(255)	Query parameters passed in request (if any)

Understanding Logging

When IIS logging is enabled, new log entries are generated whenever users access the server. This causes a steady increase in log file size and, eventually, in the number of log files. On a busy server, log files can quickly grow to several gigabytes and, therefore, you might need to balance the need to gather information against the need to limit log files to a manageable size.

Tip Keep in mind that log files are ASCII text files, and, if you need to, you can split or combine log files as you would with any ASCII file. If your server runs out of disk space when IIS is attempting to add a log entry to a file, IIS logging shuts down and logs a logging error event in the Application log. When disk space is available again, IIS resumes logging file access and writes a start-logging event in the Application log.

When you configure logging, you specify how log files are created and saved. Logs can be created according to a time schedule, such as hourly, daily, weekly, and monthly. Logs can also be set to a fixed file size, such as 100 MB, or they can be allowed to grow to an unlimited file size. The name of a log file indicates its log file format as well as the time frame or sequence of the log. The various naming formats are summarized in Table 11-9.

Table 11-9. Conventions for Log File Names by Log Format

Format	Log Period	Filename
IIS Log Format	By file size	INETSV*NN*.LOG
	Unlimited	INETSV*NN*.LOG
	Hourly	INYYMMDDHH.LOG
	Daily	IN*YYMMDD*.LOG
	Weekly	INYYMMWW.LOG
	Monthly	IN*YYMM*.LOG
NCSA Common Log File Format	By file size	NCSA*NN*.LOG
	Unlimited	NCSA*NN*.LOG
	Hourly	NCYYMMDDHH.LOG
	Daily	NCYYMMDD.LOG
	Weekly	NCYYMMWW.LOG
	Monthly	NC*YYMM*.LOG
W3C Extended Log File Format	By file size	EXTEND*NN*.LOG
	Unlimited	EXTEND*NN*.LOG
	Hourly	EXYYMMDDHH.LOG
	Daily	EXYYMMDD.LOG
	Weekly	EX*YYMMWW*.LOG
	Monthly	EX*YYMM*.LOG

By default, log files are written to the \%WinDir%\System32\LogFiles directory. You can configure logging to a different directory, such as D:\LogFiles. Regardless of whether you use the default directory location or assign a new directory location for logs, you'll find separate subdirectories for each service that is enabled for logging under the primary directory.

Subdirectories for sites are named using the following syntax:

- MSFTPSVC*N*
- W3SVC*N*
- SMT*PSVC*N*

where *N* is the index number of the service. The first server created is number 1, the second is number 2, and so on. Following this, you could have site directories named W3SVC1, W3SVC2, and so on.

> **Note** Because sites are often added and deleted from a server, you'll find that the index numbers for sites might not be consecutive. When you delete a site, IIS might not reuse the previously assigned index number for the next site you create.

Configuring Logging for HTTP, SMTP, and FTP

Now that you know how log files are used and created, let's look at how you can enable and configure logging. The sections that follow examine each of the available logging formats.

Configuring NCSA Common Log File Format

The NCSA common log file format is used with HTTP and SMTP sites only. Use the common log format when your reporting and tracking needs are basic. With this format, log entries are small, and this reduces the amount of storage space required for logging.

You enable logging and configure the common log file format by completing the following steps:

1. Start the Internet Information Services snap-in and then, in the left pane (Console Root), click the plus sign (+) next to the computer you want to work with. If the computer isn't shown, connect to it as discussed in the "Connecting To Other Servers" section of Chapter 2, "Core IIS Administration."

2. Right-click the HTTP or SMTP site you want to manage, and then select Properties.

3. Select Enable Logging to start logging, and then set the Active Log Format to NCSA Common Log File Format.

4. Click the Properties button to display the NCSA Logging Properties dialog box shown in Figure 11-1.

5. On the New Log Time Period panel, select one of the following time period options:

   - **Hourly** IIS creates a new log each hour.

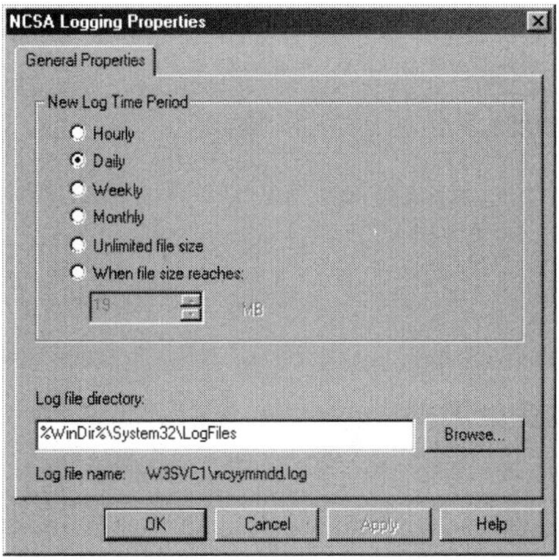

Figure 11-1. *Use the common log format when you have basic logging requirements.*

- **Daily**   IIS creates a new log daily at midnight.
- **Weekly**   IIS creates a new log file each Saturday at midnight.
- **Monthly**   IIS creates a new log file at midnight on the last day of the month.
- **Unlimited File Size**   IIS doesn't end the log file automatically. You must manage the log file.
- **When File Size Reaches**   If you select this option, you must set a maximum log file size in megabytes. When the log file reaches this size, a new log file is created.

6. By default, log files are located in a subdirectory under \%WinDir%\System32\Logfiles. If you want to change the default logging directory, type the directory path in the Log File Directory field, or click Browse to look for a directory that you want to use.

7. Click OK twice. The service directory and log file are created automatically, if necessary. If IIS doesn't have Read/Write permission on the logging directory, an error is generated.

Configuring Microsoft IIS Log File Format

The Microsoft IIS log file format can be used with HTTP, SMTP, and FTP sites. Use the IIS format when you need a bit more information from the logs but don't need to tailor the entries to get detailed information. With this format, log entries are compact, and this reduces the amount of storage space required for logging.

You enable logging and configure the IIS log file format by completing the following steps:

1. Start the Internet Information Services snap-in and then, in the left pane (Console Root), click the plus sign (+) next to the computer you want to work with. If the computer isn't shown, connect to it as discussed in the "Connecting To Other Servers" section of Chapter 2, "Core IIS Administration."

2. Right-click the HTTP, FTP, or SMTP site you want to manage, and then select Properties.

3. Select Enable Logging to start logging, and then set the Active Log Format to Microsoft IIS Log File Format.

4. Click the Properties button to display the Microsoft Logging Properties dialog box shown in Figure 11-2.

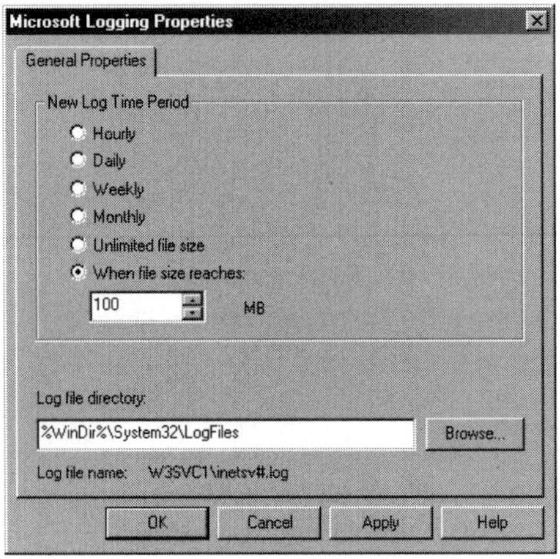

Figure 11-2. *Use the IIS log format when you have additional logging requirements but don't need to customize settings.*

5. On the New Log Time Period panel, select one of the following time period options:

   - **Hourly**   IIS creates a new log each hour.

   - **Daily**   IIS creates a new log daily at midnight.

   - **Weekly**   IIS creates a new log file each Saturday at midnight.

   - **Monthly**   IIS creates a new log file at midnight on the last day of the month.

   - **Unlimited File Size**   IIS doesn't end the log file automatically. You must manage the log file.

   - **When File Size Reaches**   If you select this option, you must set a maximum log file size in megabytes. When the log file reaches this size, a new log file is created.

6. By default, log files are located in a subdirectory under \%WinDir%\ System32\Logfiles. If you want to change the default logging directory, type

the directory path in the Log File Directory field, or click Browse to look for the directory that you want to use.

7. Click OK twice. The service directory and log file are created automatically, if necessary. If IIS doesn't have Read/Write permission on the logging directory, an error might be generated.

Configuring W3C Extended Log File Format

The W3C extended log file format can be used with HTTP, FTP, and SMTP sites. Use the extended format when you need to customize the information tracked and obtain detailed information. With this format, log entries can become large, and this greatly increases the amount of storage space required. Recording lengthy entries can impact the performance of a busy server as well.

You enable logging and configure the W3C extended log file format by completing the following steps:

1. Start the Internet Information Services snap-in and then, in the left pane (Console Root), click the plus sign (+) next to the computer you want to work with. If the computer isn't shown, connect to it as discussed in the "Connecting To Other Servers" section of Chapter 2, "Core IIS Administration."

2. Right-click the HTTP, FTP, or SMTP site you want to manage, and then select Properties.

3. Select Enable Logging to start logging, and then set the Active Log Format to W3C Extended Log File Format.

4. Click the Properties button to display the Extended Logging Properties dialog box shown in Figure 11-3.

5. On the New Log Time Period panel, select one of the following time period options:

   * **Hourly**   IIS creates a new log each hour.
   * **Daily**   IIS creates a new log daily at midnight.
   * **Weekly**   IIS creates a new log file each Saturday at midnight.
   * **Monthly**   IIS creates a new log file at midnight on the last day of the month.
   * **Unlimited File Size**   IIS doesn't end the log file automatically. You must manage the log file.
   * **When File Size Reaches**   If you select this option, you must set a maximum log file size in megabytes. When the log file reaches this size, a new log file is created.

6. By default, the extended format uses GMT to determine when to create new log files. This means daily, weekly, and monthly logs are generated at midnight GMT unless you specify otherwise. To use local time for determining when to create new logs, select Use Local Time For File Naming And Rollover.

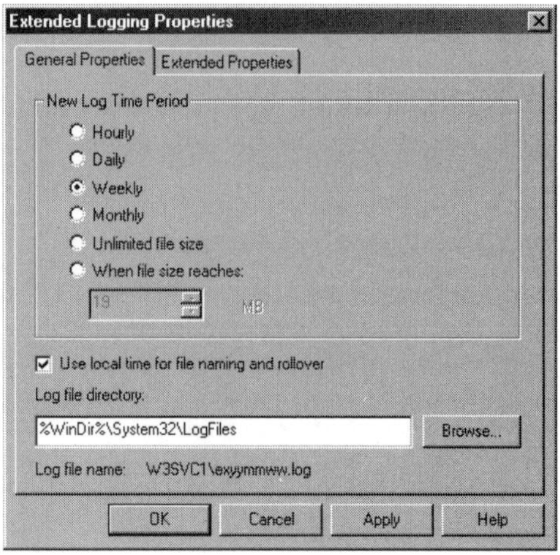

Figure 11-3. *Use the extended log format when you need to customize the logging process.*

7. By default, log files are located in a subdirectory under \%WinDir%\ System32\Logfiles. If you want to change the default logging directory, type the directory path in the Log File Directory field, or click Browse to look for a directory that you want to use.

8. Select the Extended Properties tab and then select the properties that you want to log. The fields you'll want to track in most cases are

- Date/Time
- Client IP Address/Server IP Address
- Method
- URI Stem/URI Query
- Protocol Status
- Bytes Sent/Bytes Received
- User Agent
- Cookie
- Referer

Note The more fields you track, the larger the log entries. Note also that process accounting fields are only available for HTTP sites.

9. Click OK twice. The service directory and log file are created automatically, if necessary. If IIS doesn't have Read/Write permission on the logging directory, an error might be generated.

Configuring ODBC Logging

You can configure ODBC Logging for HTTP, FTP, and SMTP sites. Use the ODBC format when you want to write access information directly to an ODBC-compliant database. With ODBC logging, you'll need tracking software capable of reading from a database. Entries are compact, however, and data can be read much more quickly than from a standard log file.

To use ODBC logging, you must perform the following tasks:

1. Create a database using ODBC-compliant database software. As long as IIS can connect to the database using an ODBC connection, the database doesn't have to reside on the IIS server. Microsoft Access can be used for small- to medium-sized sites with moderate traffic. For large or busy sites, use a more robust solution, such as SQL Server 2000.

2. Within the database, create a table for logging access entries. This table must have the field names and data types listed in Table 11-8. You can use the LOGTEMP.SQL script to create this table.

3. Next, create a DSN that IIS can use to connect to the database. You'll probably want to use a system DSN to establish the database connection. With SQL Server, you must specify the technique that should be used to verify the authenticity of the login identification (ID). If you use Microsoft Windows NT authentication, the account you specify when configuring IIS must have permission to write to the database. If you use SQL Server authentication, you can specify a SQL Server login ID and password to use.

4. Complete the process by enabling logging for the site and setting the active log format to ODBC logging. When you configure logging, you'll need to specify the DSN name, the table name, and the logon information.

The sections that follow describe how you can use SQL Server 2000 and IIS to configure ODBC logging. These sections assume a fair amount of knowledge of SQL Server 2000 and database administration. If you need more assistance, refer to the *Microsoft SQL Server 2000 Administrator's Pocket Consultant*.

Creating a Logging Database and Table in SQL Server 2000

You can use SQL Server 2000 as your logging server. To do this, you must create a database and configure a logging table. To create a database, complete the following steps:

1. Start Enterprise Manager and then, in the left pane (Console Root), click the plus sign (+) next to the server group you want to work with.

2. Click the plus sign (+) next to the server you want to work with again and then, if necessary, authenticate yourself, establish a connection, or both.

3. Right-click the Databases folder and then select New Database from the shortcut menu. This opens the Database Properties dialog box.

4. Select the General tab and type **LoggingDB** as the database name.

5. Click OK, and SQL Server creates the database.

Next, locate the LOGTEMP.SQL script. This script is located in the \%WinDir%\System32\Inetsrv directory on the IIS server. Edit the script so that it sets the table name you want to use for the site's log entries. For example, if you wanted to name the table HTTPLog, you would update the script as shown in the following listing:

```
use LoggingDB

create table HTTPLog (
ClientHost varchar(255),
username varchar(255),
LogTime datetime,
service varchar(255),
machine varchar(255),
serverip varchar(50),
processingtime int,
bytesrecvd int,
bytessent int,
servicestatus int,
win32status int,
operation varchar(255),
target varchar(255),
parameters varchar(255)
)
```

After you update the script, start Query Analyzer. In Query Analyzer, you can access scripts by clicking the Load SQL Script button on the toolbar and then entering the location of the script. Run the script by clicking Run. When the script completes, a new table should be created in the LoggingDB database. If necessary, make sure you connect to the SQL server using an account with database administrator privileges.

Creating a DSN for SQL Server 2000

Once you create the logging database and the input table, you can configure IIS to connect to the database. IIS connects to the database using a DSN. You must create the DSN on the IIS server.

To create a DSN, complete the following steps:

1. Start the Data Sources (ODBC) utility. Click Start, point to Settings, and then select Control Panel. On the Control Panel, double-click Administrative Tools, and then double-click Data Sources (ODBC).

2. On the System DSN tab, click Add. This displays the Create New Data Source dialog box.

3. Select SQL Server on the Driver selection list and then click Finish. As shown in Figure 11-4, you should now see the Create A New Data Source To SQL Server dialog box.

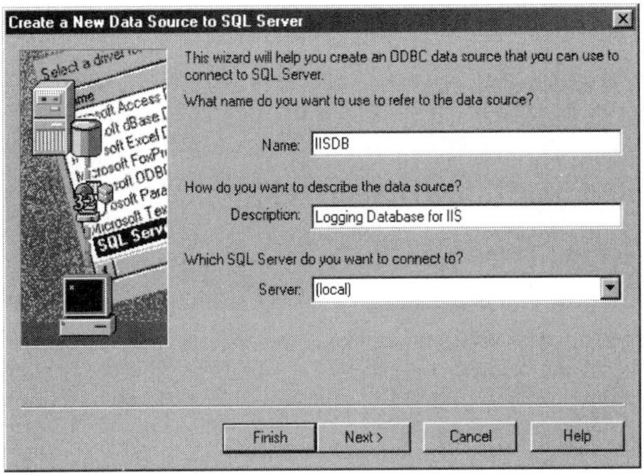

Create a New Data Source to SQL Server

This wizard will help you create an ODBC data source that you can use to connect to SQL Server.

What name do you want to use to refer to the data source?

Name: IISDB

How do you want to describe the data source?

Description: Logging Database for IIS

Which SQL Server do you want to connect to?

Server: (local)

[Finish] [Next >] [Cancel] [Help]

Figure 11-4. *Use the Create A New Data Source To SQL Server dialog box to configure the data source.*

4. In the Name field, type the name of the DSN, such as **IISDB**.

5. In the Server field, type the name of the SQL Server to which you want to connect, or select (Local) if SQL Server is running on the same hardware as IIS.

6. Next, as shown in Figure 11-5, specify the technique that should be used to verify the authenticity of the login ID. If you use Windows NT authentication, the account you specify when configuring IIS must have permission to write to the logging database. If you use SQL Server authentication, you can specify a SQL Server login ID and password to use.

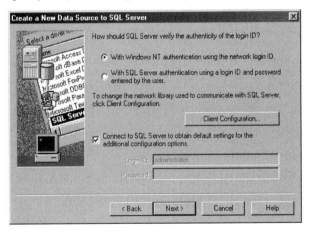

Create a New Data Source to SQL Server

How should SQL Server verify the authenticity of the login ID?

○ With Windows NT authentication using the network login ID.

○ With SQL Server authentication using a login ID and password entered by the user.

To change the network library used to communicate with SQL Server, click Client Configuration.

[Client Configuration...]

☑ Connect to SQL Server to obtain default settings for the additional configuration options.

Login ID: administrator

Password:

[< Back] [Next >] [Cancel] [Help]

Figure 11-5. *Set the authentication method for the DSN connection.*

7. Click Next and then click Finish to complete the process. If Windows is unable to establish a connection to the database, you might need to recheck the information you've entered to ensure that it is correct. You might also need to confirm that the account you are using has the appropriate permissions in the database.

Enabling and Configuring ODBC Logging in IIS

To complete the configuration process, you must enable and configure ODBC logging in IIS. Complete the following steps:

1. Start the Internet Information Services snap-in and then, in the left pane (Console Root), click the plus sign (+) next to the computer you want to work with. If the computer isn't shown, connect to it as discussed in the "Connecting To Other Servers" section of Chapter 2, "Core IIS Administration."

2. Right-click the HTTP, FTP, or SMTP site you want to manage, and then select Properties.

3. Select Enable Logging to start logging, and then set the Active Log Format to ODBC Logging.

4. Click Properties to display the ODBC Logging Properties dialog box shown in Figure 11-6.

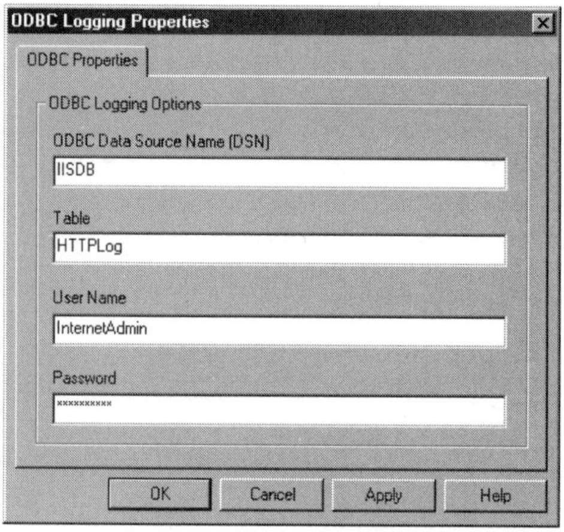

Figure 11-6. *Use ODBC logging when you need to write to a database.*

5. Type the name of the DSN in the ODBC Data Source Name (DSN) field. The DSN name must be exactly as you defined it.

6. Type the name of the logging table in the Table field.

7. If you are using Windows authentication, set the User Name and Password fields to the appropriate values for the account you want to use to log on to the database.

8. Click OK, and then click OK again to save your settings.

Disabling Logging

If you don't plan to generate reports from access logs for a particular site, you might not want to log user access to the site. In this case, you can disable logging for the site by completing the following steps:

1. Start the Internet Information Services snap-in and then, in the left pane (Console Root), click the plus sign (+) next to the computer you want to work with. If the computer isn't shown, connect to it as discussed in the "Connecting To Other Servers" section of Chapter 2, "Core IIS Administration."

2. Right-click the HTTP, FTP, or SMTP site you want to manage, and then select Properties.

3. Clear Enable Logging and then click OK.

Chapter 12

IIS Optimization and the Metabase

Previous chapters in this part of the book focused on techniques you can use to monitor Internet Information Services (IIS) and to optimize server hardware. In this chapter, you'll learn how to optimize IIS and its related services. You'll learn techniques for improving IIS performance, configuring automatic restarts of IIS, and getting the most from IIS applications. You'll also learn advanced techniques for managing IIS through the Microsoft Windows Registry and the IIS metabase.

The Windows Registry contains configuration settings for the operating system, the server hardware, and all applications installed on the server, including IIS. The metabase contains configuration settings that are specific to the sites you've implemented on a particular World Wide Web server. While most configuration settings can be managed through the IIS properties dialog boxes, some properties can be changed only through direct editing of the registry or the metabase. These settings typically are advanced values that should be changed only when you have unique needs.

Strategies for Improving IIS Performance

In this section, I examine strategies you can use to improve the performance of IIS. The focus of this section is on improving the overall responsiveness of IIS, and not the underlying server hardware.

Removing Unnecessary Applications and Services

One of the most obvious ways to improve IIS performance is to remove resource drains on the server. Start by removing applications that might be affecting the performance of IIS, including

- Microsoft SQL Server
- Microsoft Exchange Server
- File and print services
- UNIX services

If necessary, move these applications to a separate server. This will give IIS more resources to work with. For applications that you can't move, see if there is a way to run the applications only during periods of relatively low activity. For example, if you are running server backups daily, see if you can schedule backups to run late at night when user activity is low.

System services are another area you can examine to see if there are unnecessary resource drains. Every service running on the server uses resources that can be used in other ways. Services that aren't necessary should be stopped and then set to start manually. Before you stop any service, you should check for dependencies to ensure that your server isn't adversely affected.

If you have a dedicated IIS server, the following services are not required in most instances:

- Alerter
- ClipBook
- Computer Browser
- DHCP Client
- DHCP Server
- Fax Service
- File Replication
- Infrared Monitor
- Internet Connection Sharing
- Messenger
- NetMeeting Remote Desktop Sharing
- Network DDE
- Network DDE DSDM
- NWLink NetBIOS
- NWLink IPX/SPX
- Print Spooler
- TCP/IP NetBIOS Helper Service
- Telephony
- Telnet
- Uninterruptible Power Supply

Optimizing Content Usage

The responsiveness of your server is tied directly to the content you are publishing. You can often realize substantial performance benefits by optimizing the way content is used. IIS can handle both static and dynamic content. While static content is passed directly to the requesting client, dynamic content must be processed before it can be passed to the client. This places a resource burden on the server that can be reduced by using static content.

Note I'm not advocating replacing all dynamic content with static content. Dynamically generated content is a powerful tool for building highly customized and full-featured sites. However, if there are places that you are using dynamic content for no specific reason, you may want to rethink this strategy.

When you use static content, keep in mind that you should set expire headers whenever possible. Expire headers allow the related files to be stored in the client's cache, and this can greatly improve performance on repeat visits when the original content hasn't changed. For details on setting expire headers, see the "Customizing Web Site Content and HTTP Headers" section of Chapter 4, "Customizing Internet Information Services."

With dynamic content, you should limit your use of Common Gateway Interface (CGI) applications. CGI applications require more processor and memory resources than their Internet Server Application Programming Interface (ISAPI) and Active Server Page (ASP) counterparts. Because of this, you should replace or convert CGI applications to ISAPI or ASP. When you have a choice of using ISAPI or ASP, you should use ISAPI. ISAPI applications run faster than ASP applications, although they often require more development time.

Additionally, whenever you work with ISAPI or ASP applications, try to push as much of the processing load onto the client as possible. This reduces the server resource requirements and greatly improves application responsiveness. One example of pushing processing to the client is to use client-side scripting to evaluate form submissions before data is sent to the server. This technique reduces the number of times information is sent between the client and the server; therefore, it can greatly improve the overall performance of the application.

To improve content-related performance, you might also want to

- **Analyze the way content is organized on your hard drives** In most cases, you should keep related content files on the same logical partitions of a disk. Keeping related files together improves IIS file caching.

- **Defragment your drives periodically** Over time, drives can become fragmented, and this decreases read/write performance. To correct this, periodically defragment your server's drives. Many defragmentation tools allow you to automate this process so that you can configure a scheduled job to automatically defragment drives without needing administrator intervention.

- **Reduce the size of content files** The larger the file size, the more time it takes to send the file to a client. If you can optimize your source Hypertext Markup Language (HTML) or ASP code and reduce the file size, you can increase the performance and responsiveness of your Web server. Some of the biggest bandwidth users are multimedia files. Compress image, video, or audio files using an appropriate compression format whenever possible.

- **Store log files on separate disks from content files** Logging activity can reduce the responsiveness of a busy server. One way to correct this is to store access logs on a different physical drive from the one storing your site's content files. In this way, disk writes for logging are separate from the disk reads or writes for working with content files, which can greatly improve the overall server responsiveness.

- **Log only essential information**   Trying to log too much information can also slow down a busy server. With the World Wide Web Consortium (W3C) extended logging format, you can reduce logging overhead by logging only the information that you need to generate reports and removing logging for nonessential information. With any type of logging, you can reduce logging overhead by organizing different types of content appropriately and then disabling logging on directories containing content whose access doesn't need to be logged. For example, you could place all of your image files in a directory called Images, and then disable logging on this directory.

Optimizing ISAPI and ASP Applications

Improperly configured and poorly optimized applications can be major resource drains on an IIS server. To get the most from the server, you need to optimize the way applications are configured. To optimize applications:

- **Enable ISAPI application caching**   IIS can cache ISAPI applications in memory. This allows frequently used applications to be accessed quickly. You can control caching with the metabase property CacheISAPI.

- **Manage application buffering and flushes appropriately**   Application buffering allows all output from an application to be collected in the buffer before being sent to the client. This cuts down on network traffic and response times. However, users don't receive data until the page is finished executing, which can give the perception that a site isn't very responsive. You can control application buffering with the metabase property AspBufferingOn.

- **Disable application debugging**   Application debugging slows IIS performance considerably. You should only use debugging for troubleshooting. Otherwise, debugging should be disabled. You can control debugging with the metabase property AppAllowDebugging.

- **Run isolated applications only when necessary**   Pooled and out-of-process applications use additional system resources and have slightly lower performance than in-process applications. For more information, see the "Using and Running Applications" section of Chapter 4, "Customizing Internet Information Services."

- **Manage session configuration appropriately**   As the usage of your server changes, so should the session management configuration. By default, session management is enabled for all applications. If your applications don't use sessions, however, you are wasting system resources. Instead of enabling sessions by default, you should disable sessions by default and then enable sessions for individual applications. You can control sessions with the metabase properties AspAllowSessionState, AspSessionMax, and AspSessionTimeout.

- **Set a meaningful session time-out**   The session time-out value is extremely important in determining the amount of resources used in session management. Set this value accurately. Sessions should time out after an appropriate period. Configure session time-out with the metabase property AspSessionTimeout.

- **Set appropriate script and connection time-out values** ASP scripts and user connections should time out at an appropriate interval. By default, ASP scripts time out after 90 seconds and user connections time out after 15 minutes. Zombie scripts and open connections use resources and can reduce the responsiveness of the server. To reduce this drain, set appropriate time-outs. These time-outs should be set based on the way your site is used. You can control script and connection time-outs with the metabase properties AspScriptTimeout and ConnectionTimeout, respectively.

Optimizing IIS Caching and Queuing

IIS uses many different memory-resident caches and queues to manage resources. If you make extensive use of dynamic content or have a heavily trafficked site, you should optimize the way these caches and queues work for your environment. You might want to

- **Lengthen connection queues used with HTTP keep-alives** When you use HTTP keep-alives, IIS maintains connections for a user's HTTP session in the connection queue. By default, this queue can hold a maximum of 15 connections at any one time. If this value does not meet your needs, you can modify it using the metabase property ServerListenBackLog. In most cases, you'll want to set this value to the maximum number of connection requests you want the server to maintain.

- **Consider enabling thread gating** Thread gating dynamically controls the number of concurrently executing threads with a goal of ensuring that requests are serviced in a timely manner. When enabled, thread gating occurs when processor utilization drops below 50 percent or rises above 80 percent. When processor utilization drops below 50 percent, which could indicate that threads are blocked or that the load is light, IIS increases the number of active threads so that other requests can be serviced. When processor utilization exceeds 80 percent, indicating a heavy load, IIS deactivates threads to reduce the amount of context switching. To control thread gating, you'll use the metabase properties AspThreadGateEnabled, AspThreadGateLoadLow, and AspThreadGateLoadHigh.

- **Consider changing the IIS File Cache settings** By default, IIS uses up to 50 percent of the server's physical memory. This value ensures that IIS works well with other applications that might be running on the server. If the server is dedicated to IIS or has additional memory available, you might want to increase this setting to allow IIS to use more memory. To control IIS file caching, you'll create and then set the Windows Registry value MemCacheSize.

- **Consider changing the maximum cached file size** By default, IIS only caches files that are 256 KB or less in size. If you have large data or multimedia files that are accessed frequently, you might want to increase this value to allow IIS to cache larger files. Keep in mind that with file sizes over 256 KB you'll reach a point at which caching won't significantly improve performance. The reason for this is that with small files, the overhead of reading from disk rather than the file cache is significant, but with large files, the disk read might not be the key factor in determining overall performance. To control the maximum cached file size, you'll create and then set the Windows Registry value MaxCachedFileSize.

- **Consider adjusting the time-to-live value for cached resources**   By default, IIS purges from cache any resources that haven't been requested within the last 30 seconds. If you have additional memory on the server, you might want to increase this value so that files aren't removed from cache as quickly. To control the time-to-live value for cached resources, you'll create and then set the Windows Registry value ObjectCacheTTL.

- **Consider modifying the ASP template cache**   The ASP template cache controls the number of ASP pages that are cached in memory. By default, IIS will cache up to 250 files. This might not be enough on a site with lots of ASP content. Template cache entries can reference one or more entries in the ASP Script Engine Cache. To control template caching, you'll set the metabase property AspScriptFileCacheSize.

- **Consider modifying the script engine cache**   The ASP Script Engine Cache is an area of memory directly accessible to the scripting engines used by IIS. As such, the preferred area for IIS to retrieve information from is the script engine cache. By default, the script engine cache can hold up to 125 entries. To control script engine caching, you'll set the metabase property AspScriptEngineCacheMax.

Configuring Automatic Restarts of IIS

Chapter 2, "Core IIS Administration," focused on core administration tasks for IIS. In that chapter, you learned how to manage services and how to use the IIS Reset utility. To get the best performance from IIS, configure the IIS Admin Service to automatically run the IIS Reset utility if a problem occurs with the service. This allows IIS to automatically recover from most situations that otherwise would have stopped IIS from handling user requests altogether.

You can configure automatic restart of IIS by completing the following steps:

1. In the Computer Management console, connect to the computer whose services you want to manage.

2. Expand the Services And Applications node by clicking the plus sign (+) next to it, and then select Services.

3. Right-click on IIS Admin Service, and then select Properties.

4. Select the Recovery tab. Set the First Failure, Second Failure, and Subsequent Failure fields to Run A File, as shown in Figure 12-1.

5. In the Run File panel, set the File field to **\%SystemRoot%\System32\ IISRESET.EXE**.

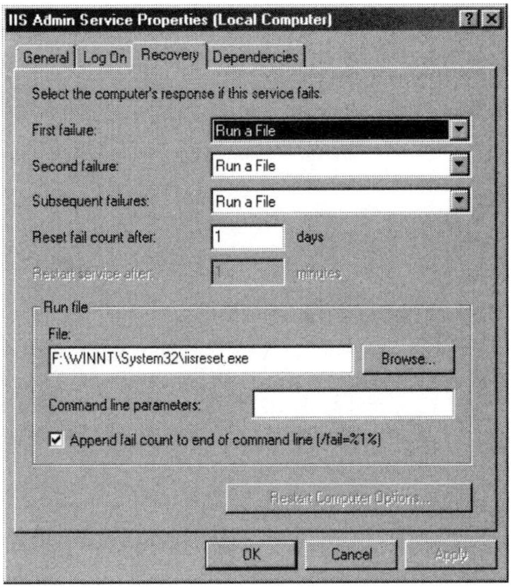

Figure 12-1. *Configure the IIS Admin Service to run the IIS Reset utility.*

6. Click OK.

Managing IIS Registry Settings

The Windows Registry stores configuration settings for the operating system, the server hardware, and all installed applications. The Registry is essential to the proper operation of the operating system. You should make changes to the registry only when you know how these changes will affect the system.

Working with the Registry

Registry settings are stored as keys and values. These keys and values are placed under a specific root key. The root key controls when and how other keys and values are used. The root keys are

- **HKEY_CLASSES_ROOT** Configuration settings for applications and files. Ensures the correct application is opened when a file is started through Microsoft Windows Explorer or object linking and embedding (OLE).

- **HKEY_CURRENT_CONFIG** Contains information about the hardware profile being used.

- **HKEY_CURRENT_USER** Controls configuration settings for the current user.

- **HKEY_LOCAL_MACHINE** Controls system-level configuration settings.

- **HKEY_USERS** Stores default user and other user settings by profile.

Under the root keys, you'll find the main keys that control various facets of the system, user, and application environments. These keys are organized into a tree structure in which folders represent keys. Settings that control the IIS Admin Service are stored under the following Registry path:

```
HKEY_LOCAL_MACHINE
 \SYSTEM
 \CurrentControlSet
 \Services
 \InetInfo
 \Parameters
```

Here, the key is Parameters. The values associated with this or any other key have three components: a value name, a value type, and an actual value. Numeric values are often expressed in hexadecimal format. Hexadecimal values use the prefix 0x, such as 0x19 for the decimal value 25. In the following example, the ListenBackLog value has a type of REG_DWORD and a value of 0x19:

```
ListenBackLog : REG_DWORD : 0x19
```

REG_DWORD is one of many possible value types. The complete list of value types follows:

- **REG_BINARY**   Sets a binary value. Binary values must be entered using base-2 (0 or 1).
- **REG_DWORD**   Sets a DWORD value, which is composed of hexadecimal data with a maximum length of 4 bytes.
- **REG_SZ**   Sets a string value containing a sequence of characters.
- **REG_EXPAND_SZ**   Sets an expandable string value, which is usually used with directory paths.
- **REG_MULTI_SZ**   Sets a multiple string value.

The main tool that you'll use to work with the Windows Registry is the Registry Editor (REGEDT32.EXE). You can start the Registry Editor by clicking Start and then selecting Run. Then, type **REGEDT32** in the Open field, and then click OK. If you are an experienced administrator, you might want to use a Windows script to manage the Registry. With scripts you can create, update, and delete Registry settings. A Microsoft Visual Basic, Scripting Edition (VBScript) script example that updates the ListenBackLog value follows:

```
'Initialize variables and objects
Dim Path
Path =
HKLM\SYSTEM\CurrentControlSet\Services\Inetinfo\Parameters\"
Set ws = WScript.CreateObject("WScript.Shell")

'Read and display key value
val = ws.RegRead(Path & "ListenBackLog")
WScript.Echo "Orginal ListenBackLog value: " & val

'Write new key value and then display new value
retVal = ws.RegWrite(Path & "ListenBackLog", 50, "REG_DWORD")
```

```
val = ws.RegRead(Path & "ListenBackLog")
WScript.Echo "Updated ListenBackLog value: " & val
```

Note A detailed discussion of scripting is beyond the scope of this book. A good resource for learning more about Windows scripting is the *Windows 2000 Scripting Bible.* See William R. Stanek, *Windows 2000 Scripting Bible* (IDG Books, June 2000).

Controlling IIS Through the Registry

Settings that control IIS are stored in the Registry under

```
HKEY_LOCAL_MACHINE\SYSTEM
  \CurrentControlSet
  \Services
  \Inetinfo
  \Parameters
```

After you've started the Registry Editor and accessed this location, the key values you might want to work with are

- **CacheSecurityDescriptor** Indicates whether security descriptors are cached for file objects. A value of 1 enables this feature. A value of 0 disables this feature. When enabled (the default setting), security descriptors for files are saved when caching a file object. As long as the file is cached, IIS will not need to re-access the file to determine access rights for new users. This value is most useful for sites that authenticate users and not useful for sites that allow anonymous access.

- **CheckCertRevocation** Indicates whether IIS checks to see if a client certificate is revoked. If you issue your own certificates and make local certificate checks, you might want to enable this feature. Otherwise, the feature should be disabled, which is the default. A value of 1 enables this feature.

- **DisableMemoryCache** Indicates whether IIS memory caching is enabled or disabled. By default, memory caching is enabled (meaning this value is set to 0). Disable memory caching only for testing or development purposes.

- **ListenBackLog** Specifies the maximum number of active connections that IIS maintains in the connection queue. The default value is 15 and the range of acceptable values is from 1 to 250.

- **MaxCachedFileSize** Determines the maximum size of a file that can be placed in the file cache. IIS will not cache files that are larger than this value. The default value is 262,144 bytes (256 KB).

- **MaxConcurrency** Specifies how many threads per processor should be allowed to run simultaneously if there is a pending input/output (I/O) operation. The default value (0) allows IIS to control the number of threads per processor. You can also set a specific value.

- **MaxPoolThreads** Sets the number of pool threads to create per processor. Each pool thread watches for a network request for a CGI application and processes it. This value does not control threads that are used by ISAPI applications. By default, the value is set to 4. On a single processor system, this means that only four CGI applications could run simultaneously.

- **MemCacheSize** Sets the maximum amount of memory that IIS will use for its file cache. If IIS does not need this much memory, it will be left for other applications to use. By default, IIS uses 50 percent of the available memory. The valid range is from 0 megabytes to the total amount of physical memory available in megabytes.

- **ObjectCacheTTL** Sets the length of time (in milliseconds) that objects are held in memory. If the object hasn't been used in this interval, it is removed from memory. The default value is 30 seconds (300,000 milliseconds).

- **PoolThreadLimit** Sets the maximum number of pool threads that can be created on the server. This limit is for all IIS threads. The default value is twice the size of physical memory in megabytes.

Controlling Indexing Service Through the Registry

Settings that control the Indexing Service are stored in the Registry under

```
HKEY_LOCAL_MACHINE
  \SYSTEM
  \CurrentControlSet
  \Control
  \ContentIndex
```

You'll find a detailed discussion of related settings and keys in the "Indexing Service Essentials" section of Chapter 9, "Administering the Indexing Service."

Settings for the World Wide Web Publishing, File Transfer Protocol (FTP), and Simple Mail Transfer Protocol (SMTP) Services are stored in separate registry keys. The path to these keys is

```
HKEY_LOCAL_MACHINE
  \SYSTEM
  \CurrentControlSet
  \Services
  \ServiceName
  \Parameters
```

ServiceName is the name of the service you want to work with. Services you might work with are

- MSFTPSVC for the FTP Service
- W3SVC for the World Wide Web Publishing Service
- SMTPSVC for the SMTP Service

Although most of the keys under this path are used only by IIS, you might want to set the AllowGuestAccess key value. This key value determines whether Guest logons are allowed for Internet services. By default, Guest logons are permitted, but you can disable this feature by setting the key value to 0.

For the World Wide Web Publishing Service, you might also want to work with the following key values:

- **SSIEnableCmdDirective** Determines whether Web pages can issue server-side include statements that execute shell commands. By default, the ability to execute shell commands is disabled (set to 0), and this is the value you should use in most cases. If you allow the direct execution of shell commands from Web pages, you might inadvertently open up the server to attack from malicious coders.

- **TryExceptDisable** Determines whether exception caching is enabled for debugging. The value is disabled by default (set to 0). If enabled (set to 1), the server stops when any exception is thrown and allows a developer to debug the application that threw the exception.

- **UploadReadAhead** When a client posts data to the server, this value determines the amount of data the server will read before passing control to the application responsible for handling the data. The default value is 48 KB.

- **UsePoolThreadForCGI** Determines whether CGI requests can use pooled threads. By default, this value is enabled (set to 1). If disabled, CGI requests don't use pooling and the Inetinfo value MaxPoolThreads doesn't apply.

Controlling Secure Sockets Layer Through the Registry

Settings that control Secure Sockets Layer (SSL) are stored in the Registry under

```
HKEY_LOCAL_MACHINE
  \SYSTEM \CurrentControlSet \Control \SecurityProviders \SCHANNEL
```

After you've started the Registry Editor and accessed this location, the key values you might want to work with are

- **EventLogging** Determines whether SSL connections are logged for Web sites configured on the server. By default, this value is enabled (set to 1). To disable this feature, set the value to 0.

- **ServerCacheTime** Determines the amount of time (in milliseconds) that an SSL session lasts. Establishing an SSL session is a time- and resource-intensive process. If you expect SSL sessions to last, on average, longer than the default value, you might want to modify this value. By default, an SSL session lasts 5 minutes (300,000 milliseconds). When the session expires, a new SSL session must be established.

Managing IIS Metabase Settings

The metabase is one of the most important components in an IIS installation. The metabase is where IIS stores configuration settings for sites and virtual servers. The metabase also contains default settings for sites and virtual servers, such as the Master WWW properties.

Examining and Editing the Metabase

The IIS metabase is stored in a structured file that is located in the \Inetsrv directory and is named METABASE.BIN. Although you should never access the file directly, there are many ways to view and modify the contents of this file. In the "Configuring IIS Backup and Recovery" section of Chapter 2, "Core IIS Administration," you learned how to create backup copies of the metabase and how to use these backup copies to recover the metabase to a specific point and time. Discussions in previous chapters showed you how to use standard administration tools, such as the Internet Information Services snap-in, to modify the configuration settings of IIS. Any configuration changes you make in the administration tools are in turn reflected in the IIS metabase.

Metabase contents can also be viewed and managed in a specially configured editor. The Windows 2000 Resource Kit includes Metabase Editor (METAEDIT.EXE). If you have the resource kit CD-ROM, you can install the Metabase Editor by double-clicking SETUP.EXE in the \Apps\Metaedit directory and following the prompts. After you install and run Metabase Editor, you'll find that working with the metabase is much like working with the Windows Registry Editor (REGEDT32.EXE).

As Figure 12-2 shows, configuration properties are organized into a hierarchy that follows a standard naming convention where each value has a key name and path. The key name is a location in the metabase. The path is a sequence of keys separated by a forward slash (/) that uniquely identifies the location of a key. The hierarchy follows this convention:

/LM/Service/Website/Root

where LM is a key that represents the local machine; *Service* is a placeholder that represents an Internet service, such as W3SVC or MSFTPSVC; *Website* is a placeholder that represents the site or virtual server instance; and *Root* is the virtual directory root.

To see how metabase paths are used, consider the following example. The metabase path /LM/W3SVC/1/Root represents the root of the first Web site instance installed on the local machine. Thus, if this value is associated with the path C:\Inetpub\Wwwroot, then the Uniform Resource Locator (URL) *http://www.domain.com/index.htm* could be mapped to the physical file path C:\Inetpub\Wwwroot\INDEX.HTM.

When you work with metabase properties, the inheritance rules discussed in previous chapters still apply. Properties that you set at the global level can apply to

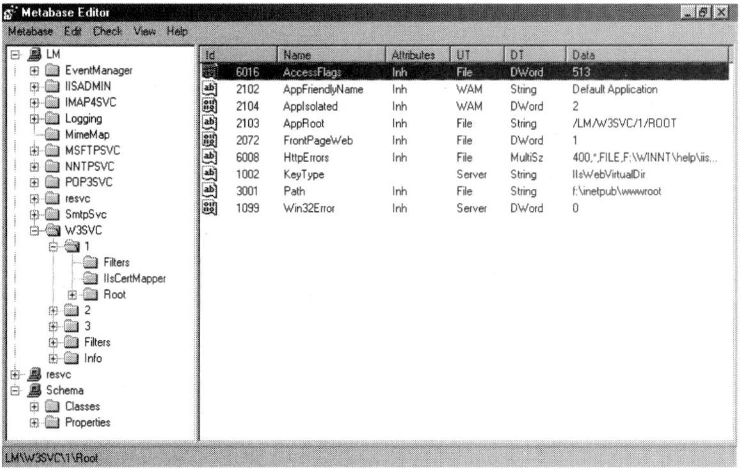

Figure 12-2. *Use the Metabase Editor to view and edit metabase properties.*

sites, directories within a site, and subdirectories within a directory. Properties
that you set at the local level can inherit properties you set at the global level.
Similarly, child nodes could inherit properties that you set for a site or a directory. Inheritance is automatic. You can, however, override inheritance. One way
to do this in the Metabase Editor is to remove the Inherit attribute from the property before you change its value. Another way to do this is to set a specific property value at the site level. For example, if you want to turn buffering on for an
individual site and not for all sites, you could set the AspBufferingOn property
for the specific site.

Modifying Metabase Properties

You can use the Metabase Editor or a Windows VBScript to modify metabase
properties. With the Metabase Editor, you can modify properties using techniques
similar to those for the Registry Editor. You can

- Browse the directorylike structure of the metabase until you find the property that you want to edit.

- Double-click the property and then edit the value using a dialog box similar
  to the one shown in Figure 12-3.

- Use the Data field to view or set the property value. When you are finished
  editing the property, click OK.

Note   As you work with metabase properties, keep in mind that new settings might not take effect until you restart the related service. For example, if you modify a Web site setting, you might need to stop and then
start the Web site for the changes to take effect.

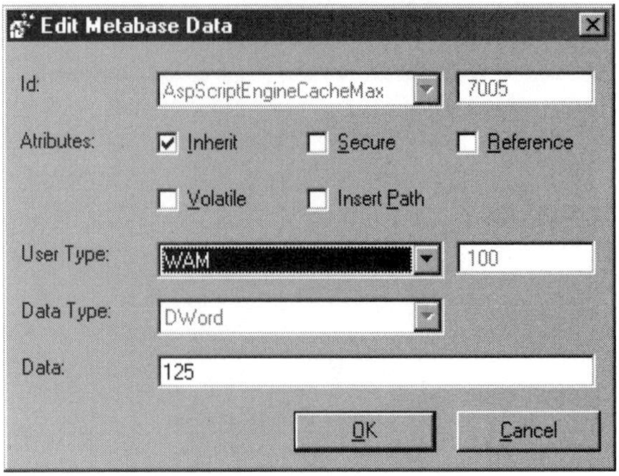

Figure 12-3. *After you locate a property, use the dialog box shown to edit its settings.*

You can also use the Metabase Editor to search for a property that you want to edit. To do this, follow these steps:

1. Press Ctrl+F or select Find from the View menu.

2. In the Find dialog box, type the property name in the field provided, and then click OK.

3. If the editor can find the property, the editor locates the property in the metabase tree and highlights it. Double-click the property and then edit the value using the dialog box provided. Click OK when you are finished.

4. If the editor cannot find the property, you'll see an error message. Make sure you've typed the property name correctly and try searching again.

As you can probably imagine, you can set hundreds of metabase properties. The ones you'll work with the most relate to global settings for Web servers. You'll find these properties in the metabase location \LM\W3SVC. The properties you'll want to work with include

- **AppAllowDebugging** Specifies whether ASP debugging is enabled on the server. When you enable this property, only one thread of execution is allowed for each IIS application you've configured on the server. This allows you to debug applications individually. By default, this value is set to FALSE. Set this value to TRUE only for debugging purposes.

- **AspAllowSessionState** Specifies whether sessions are enabled for applications. When you enable this property, IIS tracks information for user sessions. By default, this value is set to TRUE (enabling sessions). If sessions aren't used, however, you can achieve better performance by setting this value to FALSE and then enabling sessions in individual applications as needed using <% @ENABLESESSIONSTATE=TRUE %>.

- **AspBufferingOn**   Specifies whether ASP buffering is enabled. With buffering, output is collected in a buffer before it is sent to the client. By default, this value is set to TRUE (enabling buffering). If you set this property to FALSE, output from ASP scripts is sent to the client browser as it becomes available.

- **AspQueueConnectionTestTime**   Sets the interval used to determine if a client is still connected to the server. If a request has been in the queue longer than the test time, the server checks to see if the client is still connected before beginning execution. The default value is 3 seconds. This feature is designed to handle the problem of impatient users filling the request queue with numerous requests for the same page. ASP pages can also use the Response.IsClientConnected method to see if the client is still connected.

- **AspRequestQueueMax**   Specifies the default limit for ASP requests in the connection queue. The default value is 3000. The way you set this value depends on your applications. If the average request has a very short execution time and the time in the queue is short, you might want to increase this limit (particularly if you have a very busy server).

- **AspScriptEngineCacheMax**   Specifies the maximum number of scripts to cache in memory. A hit in the script engine cache means that you can avoid recompiling a template into byte code. The default value is 125.

- **AspScriptFileCacheSize**   Specifies the number of precompiled script files to store in the ASP Template Cache. The default value is 250. If you set this property to –1, all script files requested are cached. If you set this property to 0, no script files are cached.

- **AspSessionMax**   Sets the maximum number of concurrent user sessions for ASP applications. By default, sessions are limited by time and not the total number of connections.

- **AspSessionTimeout**   Determines when ASP sessions time out and have to be refreshed. By default, sessions time out after 20 minutes.

- **AspThreadGateEnabled**   Specifies whether thread gating is enabled. Thread gating is used to dynamically control threads of execution. By default, this value is set to FALSE. You can enable thread gating by setting this property to TRUE.

- **AspThreadGateLoadHigh**   Sets the high value for thread gating. IIS deactivates threads to reduce the amount of context switching when processor utilization rises above this value. This is a precautionary measure to improve performance under heavy loads.

- **AspThreadGateLoadLow**   Sets the low value for thread gating. IIS increases the number of active threads when processor utilization drops below this value. This is a precautionary measure in case there are blocking threads.

- **CacheISAPI**   Specifies whether ISAPI DLLs are cached in memory after use. By default, this property is set to TRUE and ISAPI DLLs remain in the cache until the server is stopped. If the property is FALSE, DLLs are unloaded from memory after use.

- **ConnectionTimeout** Specifies the time in seconds that the server will wait before disconnecting an inactive connection. The default value is 900 seconds (15 minutes).
- **DisableMemoryCache** Indicates whether IIS memory caching is enabled or disabled. By default, memory caching is enabled (meaning this value is set to 0). You should disable memory caching only for testing or development purposes.
- **ServerListenBackLog** Sets the request queue size. The default value is based on the AcceptEx operating system parameter and on the value of the ServerSize metabase property. If ServerSize is set to 1, the default for this property is 40. If ServerSize is set to 2, the default is 100. Valid values for this property range from 5 to 1000.
- **ServerSize** Specifies the general size of the server in terms of the number of client requests processed per day. A value of 0 indicates fewer than 10,000 requests per day, a value of 1 indicates between 10,000 and 100,000 requests per day, and a value of 2 indicates more than 100,000 requests per day.

Scripting the Metabase

Windows scripts provide another technique you can use to work with the metabase. To access metabase properties in a Windows script, you use the Active Directory Services Interface (ADSI) provider for IIS. This provider allows you to manipulate the IIS administrative objects. Key administrative objects that you'll work with include IIsComputer, IIsWebServer, and IIsFtpServer.

You can use the IIsComputer object to set global IIS properties and to manage metabase backups. Keep in mind that all child nodes (sites, directories, and others) can inherit global properties. The IIsComputer object is an ADSI container object that has this AdsPath:

```
IIS://MachineName
```

where *MachineName* can be any computer name or LocalHost, such as

```
IIS://engsvr01
```

In VBScript, you could get the IIsComputer object for ENGSVR01 using the following code:

```
'Initialize variables
Dim compObject, serverName
serverName = "engsvr01"
'Get IISWebServer object
Set compObject = GetObject("IIS://" & serverName)
```

Note A detailed discussion of scripting the metabase is beyond the scope of this book. If you want to learn Windows scripting, a good resource is the Microsoft *Windows 2000 Scripting Bible*. Once you know how to program Windows scripts, use the IIS online help documentation to get a better understanding of what objects are available and how those objects can be used.

You can then work with any of the IIsComputer object's methods and properties, such as these:

```
'Initialize variables
Dim compObject, serverName
serverName = "engsvr01"

'Get IISWebServer object
Set compObject = GetObject("IIS://" & serverName)

'Restore metabase configuration from last backup
compObject.Restore
```

You use the IIsWebServer object to set metabase properties that apply to a specific Web site and to set inheritable properties for directories and files. Methods are also available to control server operation. For example, you can use the Stop method to stop a site and then use the Start method to start the site.

Web sites are identified according to their index number in the metabase. The first Web site instance created on the server has an index number of 1, the second has an index of 2, and so on. The IIsWebServer object is an ADSI container object that has this AdsPath:

```
IIS://MachineName/W3SVC/N
```

MachineName can be any computer name or LocalHost, W3SVC identifies the Web service, and *N* is the index number of the site. In the following example, the AdsPath string specifies the first Web site instance on the server named ENGSVR01:

```
IIS://engsvr01/W3SVC/1
```

In VBScript, you can get the IIsWebServer object for the first Web site instance using the following code:

```
'Initialize variables
Dim webObject, serverName, webN
serverName = "engsvr01"
webN = "1"

'Get IISWebServer object
Set webObject = GetObject("IIS://" & serverName & "/W3SVC/" & webN)
```

You can then work with any of the IIsWebServer object's methods and properties, such as these:

```
'Initialize variables
Dim webObject, serverName, webN
serverName = "engsvr01"
webN = "1"

'Get IISWebServer object
Set webObject = GetObject("IIS://" & serverName & "/W3SVC/"& webN)

'Stop Web site
webObject.Stop

'Turn on ASP Buffering
webObject.AspBufferingOn = True

'Save the changed value to the metabase
webObject.SetInfo

'Start the Web server
webObject.Start
```

You can use the IIsFtpServer object to set metabase properties that apply to a specific FTP server and to set inheritable metabase properties for directories. As with the IIsWebServer object, methods are also available to control server operation. You can, for example, call the Pause method to pause the FTP server and then call the Continue method to resume operation.

FTP servers are identified according to their index number in the metabase. The first server has an index number of 1, the second has an index of 2, and so on. The IIsFTPServer object is an ADSI container object that has this AdsPath:

IIS://*MachineName*/MSFTPSVC/*N*

MachineName can be any computer name or LocalHost, MSFTPSVC identifies the FTP Service, and *N* is the index number of the server. In the following example, the AdsPath string specifies the first FTP server on ENGSVR01:

IIS://engsvr01/MSFTPSVC/1

In VBScript, you can get the IIsFtpServer object for the first FTP server instance using the following code:

```
'Initialize variables
Dim ftpObj, serverName, ftpM
serverName = "engsvr01"
ftpN = "1"

'Get IIsFtpServer object
Set ftpObj = GetObject("IIS://" & serverName & "/MSFTPSVC/ & tpN)
```

You can then work with any of the IIsFtpServer object's methods and properties, such as in the following:

```
'Initialize variables
Dim ftpObj, serverName, ftpN
serverName = "engsvr01"
ftpN = "1"

'Get IIsFtpServer object
Set ftpObj = GetObject("IIS://" & serverName & "/MSFTPSVC/"& ftpN)

'Stop FTP Server
ftpObj.Stop

'Enable anonymous access
ftpObj.AllowAnonymous = True

'Save the changed value to the metabase
ftpObj.SetInfo

'Start FTP Server
ftpObj.Start
```

Index

A

access logs
  error detection/resolution, 280–281
  formats of, 310
  Microsoft IIS log file format, 314–316, 323–325
  NCSA common log file format, 310–314, 322–323
  ODBC log file format, 319–320, 327–330
  overview of, 279
  W3C extended log file format, 316–319, 325–326
access permissions. *See* file and folder permissions
Access tab, Internet Information Services snap-in, 234–235
account lockout policies, guidelines for, 123
Active Directory Services Interface (ADSI)
  managing IIS with, 13
  manipulating IIS administrative objects, 348
Active Server Pages (ASPs). *See* Microsoft Active Server Pages (ASPs)
Add Counters dialog box, 288–289
administration techniques, 11–15
  using IIS administration objects, 13
  using IIS administration scripts, 13–14
  using IIS snap-in, 11
  using Internet Services Manager, 12
administrative tools
  Administrative Tools menu, 9–10
  installing, 10–11
  quick reference for, 10
  resource management with, 9–10
Administrative Tools menu, 9–10, 290
Administrator account, renaming for added security, 142
ADSI. *See* Active Directory Services Interface (ADSI)
Alert dialog box, 295–296
alerts, configuring, 295–297
alias domains, SMTP
  creating, 225
  renaming/deleting service domains, 233

Anonymous Access, log on process and, 114
anonymous authentication
  authentication modes and, 134
  SMTP, 236, 239
anonymous connections, FTP, 190, 206–208
application mappings, 82–85
  adding, 83–85
  components of, 78
  editing, 85
  removing, 85, 147
Application Protection
  ASP applications and, 3–4
  settings for, 82
applications
  advanced settings for, 76
  basic settings for, 76
  creating, 76–77
  creating pooled and nonpooled applications, 80–82
  deleting, 90
  enabling/disabling debugging, 88–89
  isolated, 89–90
  managing buffering for, 87
  managing session state for, 86
  overhead of, 79
  protection settings for, 77–78
  removing unnecessary, 333–334
  uploading, 89–90
  using and running, 77–80
applications, custom. *See* Microsoft Internet Information Services (IIS), custom applications
architecture, IIS, 17–18
ASCII
  log file formats and, 310, 314
  splitting and combining log files and, 321
auditing policies
  guidelines for, 123
  setting, 125–126
Audit Policy node, 126
authentication
  application components and, 78
  digest authentication and, 4
  enabling/disabling, 135–137
  FTP, 190–191
  modes of, 134
  process of, 134–135
  SMTP, 231–232, 236–237, 239
  understanding enhancements for, 8
Authentication Methods dialog box, 136
automatic restarts, IIS, 338–339

B

backup and recovery, 33–37
    certificate authorities (CAs) and,
        160–162
    configuring, 32–33
    creating backup configurations, 35
    deleting backup configurations, 37
    rebuilding corrupted IIS installation,
        36–37
    recovery options, 34
    restoring from backup config-
        urations, 36
    storing IIS Server configuration, 33–35
    using backup configurations, 34
Badmail folder, SMTP, 217, 223, 243
bandwidth
    configuring throttling, 305–306
    counters for, 286
    tuning and monitoring for Web
        servers, 304–307
baselines, for performance
    monitoring, 278
basic authentication, 134, 236, 239–240
bottlenecks. *See* performance bottlenecks
browser redirection, 63–69
    customizing, 67–69
    FTP sites and, 202
    IIS redirect variables, 68
    redirecting all requests, 65
    redirecting requests to other
        applications, 66–67
    redirecting requests to other
        directories or Web sites, 64
    retrieving files from a network share,
        65–66
browsers
    accessing Microsoft Certificate
        Services, 158–159
    browsing Web site files, 62
    disabling directory browsing, 143
    File Not Found error and, 61
    preventing caching, 94
    support for host headers, 45–46
buffering, managing, 87

C

caching
    counters for, 286
    Indexing Service property cache, 256
    managing in IIS, 82–85
    optimizing in IIS, 337–338
    preventing browser caching, 94
    tracking for Web servers, 299–300

CAs. *See* certificate authorities (CAs)
catalogs, 253–254, 268–273
    adding physical directories to, 268–269
    building, 255, 256
    default catalogs, 254
    full/incremental directories
        rescans, 270
    merging, 271
    searching, 258–259
    specifying Web/NNTP sites to include
        in, 271–272
    starting, stopping, and pausing,
        270–271
    testing with queries, 272–273
    viewing and creating, 261
    viewing properties and directories, 268
central processing units (CPUs), 5
CertControl, 158
CertEnroll, 158
certificate authorities (CAs), 159–160
    adding to client browser root store,
        177–178
    backing up, 160–161
    defined, 151–152
    installing, 156–157
    restoring, 162
    reviewing/renewing root CA
        certificate, 165–166
    SMTP incoming connections and,
        235–236
    third-party, 152–153
    types of, 154
Certificate dialog box, 165, 181–182
Certificate Export Wizard, 163, 183
certificate requests
    approving/declining, 163
    creating, 167–170
    deleting pending requests, 175
    processing pending requests, 174
    submitting to Certificate Services,
        172–174
    submitting to third-party authorities,
        170–171
certificates, 151–153. *See also* Microsoft
        Certificate Services
    client vs. server certificates, 151
    defined, 151
    exporting site certificates, 183–184
    generating manually, 163
    ignoring, accepting, and requiring,
        184–185
    renewing, removing, and replacing,
        182–183
    revoking, 164

certificates, *continued*
  using with virtual servers, 236
  viewing and modifying, 180–182
Certificate Services. *See* Microsoft
    Certificate Services
Certification Authority snap-in
  controlling certificates with, 154
  Issued Certificates node of, 163
  nodes of, 154–155
  Pending Requests node of, 163
  Revoked Certificates node of, 164
  starting/stopping Certificate Services
    with, 159–160
CertSrv, 158
CGI. *See* Common Gateway Interface
    (CGI)
change notifications, rescans and, 270
common files, IIS components, 6
Common Gateway Interface (CGI)
  application mappings and, 147
  dynamic content and, 335
common log format. *See* National Center
    for Supercomputing Applications
    (NCSA) common log file format
components, installing, 6–8
Component Services snap-in
  managing authentication, 78
  managing COM components, 75
  managing Web application accounts,
    115–116
compression, HTTP compression, 3,
    306–307
Computer Management console
  accessing IIS snap-in from, 22–23
  catalogs, adding directories to, 269
  catalogs, creating, 261
  catalogs, managing, 270–271
  catalogs, merging, 271
  catalogs, specifying Web/NNTP sites to
    include in, 271–272
  catalogs, testing with queries, 272–273
  configuring IIS automatic restarts,
    338–339
  configuring service startup, 31–32
  forcing full and incremental directory
    rescans, 270
  Indexing Service, managing, 263
  Indexing Service, node for, 253–254
  Indexing Service, optimizing, 266
  Indexing Service, setting properties,
    264–265
  Indexing Service, viewing status
    conditions, 263
  Services node of, 29

computer names, checking, 46–48
configuration backups
  creating, 35
  deleting, 37
  restoring from, 36
  uses of, 34
connection limits
  configuring, 305–306
  setting for FTP, 199–200
  setting for SMTP, 238–239
connections
  controlling incoming, 56–57
  counters for, 286–287
  IIS summary, 23
  tuning and monitoring for Web
    servers, 304–307
connections, SMTP incoming
  controlling authentication of, 236–237
  securing access to, 234–235
  security of, 235–236
  setting connection restrictions and
    time-outs, 238–239
connections, SMTP outgoing
  configuring message limits, 241–242
  configuring security, 239–240
  controlling, 240–241
  relay restrictions, 243–244
  troubleshooting, 243
Connections dialog box, 238–239
content
  analyzing hard drive organization of,
    335
  enabling/disabling expiration limits,
    94–95
  optimizing usage in IIS, 334–336
  static vs. dynamic, 334–335
  using ratings for, 96–97
CONVLOG tool, 310
core services, IIS, 30
counter logs
  creating, 290–293
  overview of, 289
counters
  for IIS, 285
  monitoring server performance, 285–
    288
  in Performance Monitor, 284–289
CSCRIPT.EXE, 15

D

data protection, using RAID for, 5
Data Source Names (DSNs)
  configuring for ODBC logging, 319

Data Source Names, *continued*
  creating for SQL Server 2000, 328–330
data throughput. *See* throughput
dead ends, preventing, 109
debugging, enabling/disabling, 88
delay notification, SMTP, 245–246
delivery. *See* message delivery, SMTP
Delivery tab, SMTP options, 246
Desired Performance dialog box, 267
digest authentication
  IIS authentication methods, 4
  overview of, 134
directories
  creating top level, 51
  disabling browsing, 143
  forcing full and incremental
    rescans, 270
  Microsoft Windows 2000 file and
    directory structure, 17
  setting defaults for, 41
  setting listing style for FTP sites, 202
  viewing with Indexing Services, 268
directories, Web sites
  configuring system directories, 60–61
  creating physical directories, 59
  creating virtual directories, 59–60
  deleting, 62
  modifying properties, 61
  physical and virtual directory
    structures, 58–59
  renaming, 61
Directory Properties dialog box, 41
disk drives
  optimizing, 335
  requirements for Internet servers, 5
disk I/O, tuning and monitoring for Web
    servers, 303
disk mirroring (RAID 1), 5
disk striping without parity (RAID 0), 5
disk striping with parity (RAID 5), 5
distributed authoring and versioning. *See*
    Web Distributed Authoring and
    Versioning (WebDAV)
DLLHOST.EXE, 89
DLLs. *See* dynamic-link libraries (DLLs)
DNS (Domain Name System), 42
documentation
  IIS component installation, 6
  IISHelp, 60–61
documents
  accessing and publishing with
    WebDAV, 133
  configuring default documents, 92–93
  configuring footers for, 93–94

documents, *continued*
  types indexed, 252
domain names. *See also* fully qualified
    domain names (FQDNs)
  FTP security and, 213
  IIS security and, 137–139
  InterNIC and, 42
  setting options, 247–248
Domain Name System (DNS), 42
domains. *See also* service domains, SMTP
  changing domain information, 47
  default domains, SMTP, 226
  securing virtual server access by,
    234–235
  specifying with URLs, 19–20
Drop directory, SMTP, 226–227
Drop folder, SMTP, 223
DSNs. *See* Data Source Names (DSNs)
dynamic-link libraries (DLLs)
  hosts, 18–19
  ISAPI extensions, 73
  ISAPI filters, 72–73

E

e-mail domains, 216. *See also* service
    domains
encryption, 149–151
  defined, 149
  strength of, 153
  TLS encryption, 232
enterprise root CA, 154, 156
enterprise subordinate CA, 154, 156
Error Mapping Properties dialog box, 102
error messages, 98–102
  configuring, 89
  editing custom settings, 102
  error handling options, 100
  handling 404 errors and preventing
    dead ends, 109
  standard HTTP error codes, 99
  status codes and, 98
  viewing custom settings, 101
errors
  404 errors, 109, 280
  counters for, 287
  detection/resolution, 279–284
  detection/resolution, access logs,
    280–281
  detection/resolution, events logs,
    281–284
  File Not Found error, 61
  filters for, 283–284
escape codes, URLs, 22

event logs, 279, 281–284
Event Viewer, 281–284
  event types and, 282
  filtering for warnings and errors, 283–284
  summary event information, 283
exit messages, FTP, 203
expiration time-out, SMTP, 245–246
extended logging, 309. *See also* World Wide Web Consortium (W3C) log file format
extensions, ISAPI, 73

F
fields
  Microsoft IIS log file format, 315–316
  NCSA common log file format, 312–314
  ODBC log file format, 320
  W3C extended log file format, 318–319
file and folder permissions
  guidelines based on content type, 118
  list of, 117
  overview, 117–118
  setting, 119–121
  viewing, 119
File Not Found error, 61
files, Web sites
  deleting, 63
  modifying properties, 62–63
  opening and browsing, 62
  renaming, 63
File Transfer Protocol (FTP)
  bundled with IIS, 3
  controlling server access, 190–191
  enabling logging, 309
  functions of, 189
  installing FTP service, 6
  overview, 189–190
  publishing service, 8–9
  sites, creating, 194–196
  sites, installing default, 7
  sites, using Microsoft IIS log file format, 323–325
  sites, using ODBC log file format, 327
  sites, using W3C log file format, 325–326
  sites, naming and identifying, 193–194
  working with FTP sessions, 191–193
File Transfer Protocol (FTP), security management, 205–213. *See also* security, Web servers
  configuring IP address and domain name restrictions, 210–212

File Transfer Protocol, security, *continued*
  configuring Server permissions, globally, 209
  configuring Server permissions, locally, 210
  configuring site operators, 213
  configuring Windows permissions, 208
  managing anonymous connections, 206–208
File Transfer Protocol (FTP), session management, 203–205
  terminating users sessions, 204–205
  viewing number of connected users, 204–205
  viewing users sessions, 203–204
File Transfer Protocol (FTP), site management, 196–203
  configuring home directory, 197–198
  configuring ports and IP addresses, 198–199
  creating physical directories, 200–201
  creating virtual directories, 201
  redirecting requests, 202
  setting connection limits/time-out values, 199–200
  setting directory listing style, 202
  welcome, exit, and maximum connection messages, 202–203
File Types dialog box, 105–106
filters
  filtering event logs for warnings and errors, 283–284
  indexing process and, 256
  ISAPI filters, 72–73
  ISAPI filters, global, 90–91
  ISAPI filters, local, 91–92
FIND command, searching for errors, 281
firewalls, 142
folders. *See* file and folder permissions
footers, configuring for documents, 93–94
forms, checking for malicious input, 146
FQDNs. *See* fully qualified domain names (FQDNs)
FrontPage 2000 Server, 6
FTP. *See* File Transfer Protocol (FTP)
FTP Restart, 3
FTP Service Master Properties dialog box, 189
FTP Site Creation Wizard, 196
fully qualified domain names (FQDNs). *See also* domain names
  FTP sites, 189
  SMTP virtual servers, 247

G

group accounts. *See* user and group accounts
group permissions. *See* permissions
group policies
  configuring with Group Policy snap-in, 121–122
  guidelines for, 123
  managing local policies, 122–123
  order of application, 121
  setting auditing policies, 125–126
  setting for IIS servers, 123–125
Group Policy snap-in, 121–122

H

handshake, FTP, 191
hard drives. *See* disk drives
hardware
  guidelines for Internet servers, 4–6
  troubleshooting, 278
headers, HTTP, 92, 95–96. *See also* host headers
hisecws, security templates, 144
HKEY_CLASSES_ROOT, 339
HKEY_CURRENT_CONFIG, 339
HKEY_CURRENT_USER, 339
HKEY_LOCAL_MACHINE, 339
HKEY_USERS, 339
home directory
  configuring for FTP sites, 197–198
  configuring for Web sites, 52–53
hop count, 247
Host field, NCSA common log file format, 312
host headers
  drawbacks of, 45–46
  FTP sites and, 195
  hosting multiple Web sites with, 3
hosting
  on FTP sites, 194
  multiple sites on a single server, 43–46
host names, configuring for Web sites, 53–55
hot fixes, Web server security and, 144–146
HTML (Hypertext Markup Language), 3, 251
HTTP. *See* Hypertext Transfer Protocol (HTTP)
HTTP Keep-Alives
  configuring, 57–58
  optimizing IIS and, 337
HTTP Monitoring tool, 279

HTTP Request field, NCSA common log file format, 313
Hypertext Markup Language (HTML), 3, 251
Hypertext Transfer Protocol (HTTP)
  compression, 306–307
  enabling logging, 309
  error codes, 99
  vs. FTP, 189–190
  headers, 92, 95–96
  HTTP Monitoring tool, 279
  IIS support for, 3
  Keep-Alives, 57–58
  request types used with ISAPI extensions, 73
  sites, using Microsoft IIS log file format, 323–325
  sites, using NCSA log file format, 322–323
  sites, using ODBC log file format, 327
  sites, using W3C log file format, 325–326
  WebDAV and, 132

I

Identification field, NCSA common log file format, 312
IDQ (Internet data query) files, 258–259
IIS. *See* Microsoft Internet Information Services (IIS)
IISAdmin
  default Web site directories, 49
  remote administration and, 143
  site control with, 60–61
IISADMPWD virtual directory, 146
IIS Certificate Wizard
  creating certificate requests, 167–168
  deleting pending certificate requests, 175
  processing pending certificate requests, 174
IISHelp
  default Web site directories, 49
  help documentation with, 60–61
IISRESET utility
  rebooting local and remote computers with, 28
  starting, stopping, and re-starting Internet services, 26
  switches of, 26–27
IISSamples, 49
incremental backups. *See* backup and recovery

indexing
  counters for, 287
  defined, 255
Indexing Service, 251–273
  catalogs, building, 256
  catalogs, installed, 253–254
  catalogs, searching, 258–259
  controlling through Registry, 314–343
  document types indexed by, 252
  installing, 252
  logging on with local system
    account, 112
  management options for, 252–253
  overview of, 9, 251
  processing documents, 255
  Registry settings for scanning and
    merging, 257–258
  shadow merges and master merges,
    256–257
  storing document values in property
    cache, 256
  types of scans performed by, 255–256
  using with IIS, 3
Indexing Service, catalog management,
    268–273
  adding physical directories to catalogs,
    268–269
  forcing full and incremental directories
    rescans, 270
  merging catalogs, 271
  specifying Web or NNTP sites to
    include in catalogs, 271–272
  starting, stopping, and pausing
    individual catalogs, 270–271
  testing catalogs with queries, 272–273
  viewing catalog properties and
    directories, 268
Indexing Service, core administration,
    260–267
  configuring Web resources for
    indexing, 260
  optimizing performance, 265–267
  setting properties, 263–265
  starting, stopping, and pausing
    indexing, 263
  viewing and creating catalogs, 261
  viewing indexing status, 261–263
Indexing Service Usage dialog box, 266
INETINFO.EXE, 18, 25
inherited permissions, overriding, 120
Internet data query (IDQ) files, 258–259
Internet Guest account, managing,
    113–115
Internet Information Services (IIS). See
    Microsoft Internet Information
    Services
Internet Information Services snap-in, 202
  accessing, 22–23
  Access tab, 234–235
  administrative tools and, 11
  associating catalogs with Web sites/
    NNTP sites, 268
  configuring FTP sites, connection
    limits and time-outs, 199–200
  configuring FTP sites, home directory,
    197–198
  configuring FTP sites, IP addresses and
    ports, 198–199
  configuring FTP sites, physical
    directories, 200–201
  configuring FTP sites, request
    redirection, 202
  configuring FTP sites, setting welcome,
    exit and maximum connection
    messages, 202–203
  configuring FTP sites, virtual
    directories, 201
  connecting to other servers, 24
  creating certificate requests, 167
  defining custom applications, 75–77
  deleting files, 63
  managing Internet services, 25–27
  managing resources, 27–28
  rebooting IIS servers, 28
  rebooting local/remote computers, 28
  renaming files, 63
  starting and using, 22–24
Internet Information Services snap-in,
    managing certificates, 180–185
  exporting site certificates, 183–184
  ignoring, accepting, and requiring
    client certificates, 184–185
  renewing, removing, and replacing
    certificates, 182–183
  requiring SSL for all communi-
    cations, 185
  viewing and modifying issued
    certificates, 180–182
Internet Network Information Center
    (InterNIC), 42
Internet Protocol (TCP/IP) Properties
    dialog box, 47
Internet Server Application Programming
    Interface (ISAPI)
  choosing over ASP or CGI, 335
  custom applications and, 71
  customizing IIS and, 71–73

Internet Server Application Programming
Interface, *continued*
ISAPI extensions, 73, 147
ISAPI filters, 72–73, 90–92
optimizing in IIS, 336–337
role in IIS architecture, 18–19
Internet servers, hardware for, 4–6
Internet services. *See also* Microsoft
Internet Information Services (IIS)
configuring backup and recovery for,
32–33
configuring startup, 31–32
installing, 8–9
starting, stopping, and restarting,
25–27
Internet Services Manager
administration techniques using, 12
IIS component installation and, 6
InterNIC (Internet Network Information
Center), 42
intranets, name resolution and, 42
IP addresses
checking, 46–48
configuring for FTP, 198–199
configuring for SMTP, 221–222
configuring for Web sites, 53–55
FTP security and, 210–212
IIS security and, 137–139
setting with Web Site Creation
Wizard, 50
viewing, 47
virtual server access by, 234–235
Web servers and, 46–48
Web sites and, 41–43
ISAPI. *See* Internet Server Application
Programming Interface (ISAPI)
Issued Certificates node, Certification
Authority snap-in, 163
IUSR_*ComputerName*, 112
IWAN_*ComputerName*, 112

J

Java Servlet Pages, 71
JScript, IIS installation and, 88
jump pages, advertising with, 108–109

K

keys
encryption and, 149–150
IIS metabase and, 13
Windows Registry, 339–340

L

legal notices, creating, 143–144
local group policies, 122–123
local permissions. *See* permissions
local recipients, SMTP, 218
local service domains, SMTP
changing Drop directory for default
domain, 226
creating alias domains, 225
setting default domains, 226
local system account, 112
logging, user access, 309–331
access log formats, 310
disabling, 331
log file naming conventions, 321
Microsoft IIS log file format,
configuring, 323–325
Microsoft IIS log file format, fields of,
315–316
Microsoft IIS log file format, overview
of, 314–315
NCSA common log file format,
configuring, 322–323
NCSA common log file format, Host
field, 312
NCSA common log file format, HTTP
Request field, 313
NCSA common log file format,
Identification field, 312
NCSA common log file format, Status
Code field, 314
NCSA common log file format, Time
Stamp field, 313
NCSA common log file format,
Transfer Volume field, 314
NCSA common log file format, User
Authentication field, 313
ODBC log file format, configuring,
327–330
ODBC log file format, overview of,
319–320
ODBC log file format, table fields
for, 320
types of logging, 309
understanding, 320–322
W3C extended log file format,
configuring, 325–326
W3C extended log file format,
directives used with, 317
W3C extended log file format, field
identifiers used with, 318
W3C extended log file format,
overview of, 316

logging, user access, *continued*
    W3C extended log file format, prefixes
        used with, 317–318
    W3C extended log file format, process
        accounting fields of, 319
Logging Properties dialog box, 280
logon accounts, 112–113
logs
    access logs, 280–281
    counter logs, 290–293
    events logs, 281–284
    finding location of, 280–281
    performance logs, logging over
        extended period, 294–295
    performance logs, creating and
        managing, 290
    reducing overhead of, 336
    trace logs, 293–294
LOGTEMP.SQL script, 320

M

mail processing, SMTP, 218–219
mail recipients, SMTP, 218
mail relaying. *See* relay restrictions
Mailroot folders, 217–218
    subfolders of, 217
    using separate folders for each virtual
        server, 223
marshalling, applications, 78
masquerade domains, 247
master FTP service properties, 194
master merges, Indexing Service, 256–257
Master Properties dialog box, 127–130
master Web service properties, 48
maximum connection messages, FTP
    sites, 203
memory
    counters for, 286
    requirements for Internet servers, 5
    Web servers, bottlenecks, 300–301
    Web servers, checking use of, 299
    Web servers, setting application
        performance, 298
    Web servers, setting data throughput,
        298–299
memory paging, 300–301
merges, Indexing Service
    master merges, 256–257
    merging catalogs, 271
    overview of, 255
    Registry settings for, 257–258
    shadow merges, 256–257

message delivery, SMTP
    configuring reverse DNS lookups,
        248–249
    routing outgoing messages to smart
        host, 249
    setting domain name options, 247–248
    setting message hop count, 247
    setting retry intervals, delay
        notification and expiration time-
        out, 245–246
message limits, SMTP, 241–242
metabase, 343
    examining and editing, 344–345
    modifying properties, 345–348
    scripting, 348–351
    Metabase Editor (METAEDIT.EXE),
        344–345
metrics, 278
Microsoft Active Server Pages (ASPs)
    built-in ASP objects, 74
    creating queries with, 258–259
    custom applications and, 71
    IIS support for, 3
    vs. ISAPI, 335
    modifying script engine cache, 338
    optimizing ASP applications, 336–337
    pre-built components for ASP
        applications, 75
    session counters, 285
    transaction counters, 285–286
    understanding, 74–75
Microsoft Certificate Services
    accessing in a browser, 158–159
    approving/declining certificate
        requests, 163
    backing up and restoring the CA,
        160–162
    creating certificate requests, 167–170
    deleting pending certificate
        requests, 175
    generating certificates manually, 163
    installing, 155–157
    overview of, 154–155
    processing pending certificate
        requests, 174
    reviewing/renewing root CA
        certificate, 165–166
    revoking certificates, 164
    stopping and starting, 159–160
    submitting certificate requests to,
        172–174
    submitting certificate requests to third-
        party authorities, 170–171

Microsoft Exchange 2000 Server, 215
Microsoft Internet Information Services
    (IIS)
  architecture, 17–18
  authentication, 8
  configuring ODBC logging, 330
  default user accounts, 9
  error detection, access logs, 280–281
  error detection, events logs, 281–283
  hardware guidelines for Internet
      servers, 4–6
  installing administration tools, 10–11
  installing components and default
      sites, 6–8
  installing Internet services, 8–9
  key features of, 3–4
  logging on with local system
      account, 112
  managing, configuring service
      recovery, 32–33
  managing, configuring service start up,
      31–32
  managing, core services, 30
  managing, starting stopping and
      pausing, 30–31
  managing, using Services node, 29–30
  performance tuning, configuring
      automatic restarts, 338–339
  performance tuning, optimizing
      content usage, 334–336
  performance tuning, optimizing IIS
      caching and queuing, 337–338
  performance tuning, optimizing ISAPI
      and ASP applications, 336–337
  performance tuning, removing
      unnecessary applications and
      services, 333–334
  reasons for monitoring, 277–278
  Registry and, 341–342
  resource management, 9–10
  servers, rebooting, 28
  servers, setting group policies, 123–125
  servers, storing configuration, 33–35
  Web administration techniques, 11–15
Microsoft Internet Information Services
    (IIS), backing up and recovering,
    33–37
  creating configuration backups, 35
  deleting backup configurations, 37
  rebuilding corrupted IIS installation,
      36–37
  restoring from backup configura-
      tions, 36
  storing IIS Server configuration, 33–35

Microsoft Internet Information Services
    (IIS), custom applications, 71–109
  ASP applications, 74–75
  configuring default documents, 92–93
  configuring document footers, 93–94
  ISAPI applications, 71–73
  ISAPI filters, global, 90–91
  ISAPI filters, local, 91–92
  managing, buffering, 87
  managing, deleting applications, 89–90
  managing, enabling/disabling
      debugging, 88–89
  managing, error messages
      configuration, 89
  managing, mapping and caching,
      82–85
  managing, parent paths, default ASP
      language, and ASP script
      time-out, 88
  managing, pooled and nonpooled
      applications, 80–82
  managing, session state, 85–87
  managing, uploading isolated
      applications, 89–90
  MIME types, basic, 103
  MIME types, common, 104
  MIME types, viewing and configuring,
      105–106
  tips, handling 404 errors and
      preventing dead ends, 109
  tips, updating sites to manage outages,
      107–108
  tips, using jump pages for advertising,
      108–109
  using content expiration, 94–95
  using content ratings, 96–97
  using custom HTTP headers, 95–96
  Web Server error messages,
      customizing, 100–102
  Web Server error messages, standard
      HTTP error codes, 99
  Web Server error messages, status
      codes and, 98
Microsoft Internet Information Services
    (IIS), log file format
  configuring, 323–325
  fields, 315–316
  overview, 314–315
  overview of, 310
Microsoft Internet Information Services
    (IIS), security, 127–141
  authentication modes, enabling/
      disabling, 135–137

Microsoft Internet Information Services,
  security, *continued*
  authentication modes, overview,
    134–135
  configuring IP address and domain
    name restrictions, 137–139
  WebDAV, accessing and publishing
    documents, 133
  WebDAV, permitting distributed
    authoring and versioning, 132–133
  Web server permissions, global,
    128–130
  Web server permissions, local, 130–132
  Web server permissions, overview,
    127–128
  Web site operators, assigning, 141
  Web site operators, overview, 140
  Web site operators, permitting
    operator administration, 141
Microsoft Management Console (MMC)
  snap-ins, 22, 252–253. *See also* by
  individual type
Microsoft Script Debugger, 88–89
Microsoft Visual Basic Scripting Edition
  (VBScript)
  checking for malicious users with, 146
  IIS installation and, 88
  managing Registry with, 340–341
  modifying metabase properties
    with, 345
Microsoft Windows 2000
  file and directory structure of, 17
  IIS directory based on file structure
    of, 58
  integration with IIS, 17–18
  naming conventions used by, 42
  permissions of, 18
Microsoft Windows 2000 Advanced
  Server, 6
Microsoft Windows 2000 Datacenter
  Server, 6
Microsoft Windows 2000 Professional
  limitations of, 44, 194
  using with IIS, 6
Microsoft Windows 2000 Resource
  Kit, 279
Microsoft Windows 2000 Server
  hosting multiple FTP sites, 194
  hosting multiple Web sites, 44
  using with IIS, 6
Microsoft Windows security
  file and folder permissions, guidelines
    based on content type, 118
  file and folder permissions, list of, 117

Microsoft Windows security, *continued*
  file and folder permissions, overview,
    117–118
  file and folder permissions, setting,
    119–121
  file and folder permissions,
    viewing, 119
  FTP site permissions, 208
  group policies, overview, 121–123
  group policies, setting auditing
    policies, 125–126
  group policies, setting for IIS servers,
    123–125
  SMTP authentication and, 236–237, 239
  user and group accounts, Internet
    Guest account, 113–115
  user and group accounts, logon
    accounts, 112–113
  user and group accounts,
    overview, 112
  user and group accounts, Web
    application account, 115–116
MIME. *See* Multipurpose Internet Mail
  Extension (MIME) types
MMC. *See* Microsoft Management Console
  (MMC) snap-ins
monitoring. *See* performance, tuning and
  monitoring
multiple identities, SMTP, 222–223
Multipurpose Internet Mail Extension
  (MIME) types
  basic, 103
  common, 104
  custom applications and, 71
  viewing and configuring, 105–106

N

name resolution, Web sites, 41–43
names
  checking computer names, 46–48
  domain names, FTP security and, 213
  domain names, IIS security and,
    137–139
  domain names, InterNIC and, 42
  domain names, setting options,
    247–248
  FTP sites, 193–194
  fully qualified domain names
    (FQDNs), FTP sites, 189
  fully qualified domain names
    (FQDNs), SMTP virtual
    servers, 247
  URL formats, 19–21

names, *continued*
  usernames, anonymous access and, 8
  usernames, URLs and, 20
  Web sites, hosting multiple sites on a
    single server, 43–46
  Web sites, host names, 53–55
  Web sites, IP addresses and name
    resolution and, 41–43
  Web sites, understanding identifiers, 43
naming conventions
  log files and, 321–322
  Uniform Naming Convention
    (UNC), 43
National Center for Supercomputing
    Applications (NCSA) common log
    file format, 310–314
  configuring, 322–323
  Host field, 312
  HTTP Request field, 313
  Identification field, 312
  overview of, 310–311
  Status Code field, 314
  Time Stamp field, 313
  Transfer Volume field, 314
  User Authentication field, 313
NetBIOS naming convention, 42
Network Identification tab, 248
Network News Transfer Protocol (NNTP)
  associating catalogs with, 268
  bundled with IIS, 3
  installing default sites, 7–8
  installing service, 6
  overview of, 9
  specifying sites to include in catalogs,
    271–272
networks, bandwidth and connectivity,
    304–307
  configuring HTTP compression,
    306–307
  configuring throttling and connection
    limits, 305–306
network shares
  redirecting requests to, 202
  retrieving files from, 65–66
New SMTP Virtual Server Wizard, 220
NNTP. *See* Network News Transfer
    Protocol (NNTP)
nondelivery reports, SMTP, 219, 243
nonpooled applications, 80–82

O

open database connectivity (ODBC) log
    file format
  configuring, creating DSN for SQL
    Server 2000, 328–330
  configuring, for IIS, 330
  configuring, creating logging database
    and table in SQL Server 2000,
    327–328
  overview, 309–310, 319–320
  table fields, 320
operators, FTP sites, 213
operators, Web sites
  administrative privileges of, 140
  assigning, 141
  overview, 140
  permitting operator administration, 141
outages
  avoiding, 107–108
  uninterruptible power supply (UPS)
    and, 6

P

passwords
  anonymous access and, 8
  guidelines for, 123
  URLs and, 20
paths
  IIS metabase and, 13
  managing parent paths, 88
Pending Certificate Request
  deleting, 175
  processing, 174
Pending Requests node, Certification
    Authority snap-in, 163
performance, IIS, 333–351
  configuring automatic restarts, 338–339
  optimizing content usage, 334–336
  optimizing IIS caching and queuing,
    337–338
  optimizing ISAPI and ASP applications,
    336–337
  removing unnecessary applications
    and services, 333–334
performance, Indexing Service, 265–267
performance, SMTP
  configuring outgoing message limits,
    241–242
  reverse lookups and, 244
performance bottlenecks
  drive-related, 303
  identifying, 278

performance bottlenecks, *continued*
    memory and virtual memory and,
        300–301
    processor-related, 302
performance logs
    creating and managing, 290
    logging over extended period, 294–295
    types of, 289
Performance Logs and Alerts node, 290
Performance Monitor
    choosing counters, 284–289
    configuring alerts, 295–297
    creating and managing performance
        logs, 290
    creating counter logs, 290–293
    creating trace logs, 293–294
    logging over extended period, 294–295
    overview of, 279
performance, tuning and monitoring,
        272–273
    creating plan for, 278
    error detection/resolution, access logs,
        280–281
    error detection/resolution, events logs,
        281–284
    establishing baselines for, 278
    Performance Monitor, choosing
        counters, 284–289
    Performance Monitor, configuring
        alerts, 295–297
    Performance Monitor, creating counter
        logs, 290–293
    Performance Monitor, creating trace
        logs, 293–294
    Performance Monitor, logging over
        extended period, 294–295
    Performance Monitor, creating and
        managing performance logs, 290
    tools and resources for, 279
    tuning and monitoring, 301–302
    Web servers, 297–307
    Web servers, disk I/O, 303
    Web servers, memory usage, 298–301
    Web servers, processor usage, 301–302
    Web servers, bandwidth and
        connectivity, 304–307
    why monitor IIS, 277–278
permissions. *See also* file and folder
        permissions
    access permissions, for virtual
        directories, 60
    access permissions, for Web sites, 51
    configuring Windows permissions, 208
    FTP servers, global permissions, 209

permissions, *continued*
    FTP servers, local permissions, 210
    modifying Web file setting, 62
    overriding inherited permissions, 120
    use of Microsoft Windows 2000
        permissions, 18
    Web servers, global permissions,
        128–130
    Web servers, local permissions,
        130–132
physical directories
    adding to catalogs, 268–269
    creating, 59
    creating for FTP sites, 200–201
    overview of, 58–59
Pickup folder, SMTP, 223
PICS (Platform for Internet Content
        Selection), 96–97
pipe character (|), malicious users
        and, 146
Platform for Internet Content Selection
        (PICS), 96–97
Playback tool, 279
pooled applications, managing, 80–82
ports
    configuring for FTP, 198–199
    configuring for SMTP, 221–222
    configuring for SSL, 175–177
    configuring for Web sites, 53–55
    firewalls and, 142
    specification by Web Site Creation
        Wizard, 50
    specification in URLs, 20
power outages
    avoiding, 107–108
    uninterruptible power supply (UPS)
        and, 6
private keys, encryption and, 149–150
private network addresses, 42
Process Accounting, 4
processors, 5
Process Throttling, 4
properties, Web sites
    configuring home directory for, 52–53
    configuring HTTP Keep-Alives, 57–58
    configuring multiple identities for,
        55–56
    configuring ports, IP addresses, and
        host names, 53–55
    controlling incoming connections,
        56–57
    managing master Web service
        properties, 48
    setting time-out values, 56–57

Properties dialog box
configuring custom applications, 81
configuring Web server
permissions, 130
modifying site identity with, 221
property cache, Indexing Service, 256
protection settings, for applications, 77–78
public keys, encryption and, 149–150

Q

queries
checking for malicious input in query
strings, 146
creating, 258
testing catalogs with, 272–273
Queue folder, SMTP, 217–218, 223
queuing messages
optimizing in IIS, 337–338
SMTP remote service domains and,
230–231

R

RAID, 5
recipients
local and remote, 218
unresolved, 243
recovery. *See* backup and recovery
Recreational Software Advisory Council
(RSAC), 96–97
redirection. *See* browser redirection
Registry
controlling IIS with, 341–342
controlling Indexing Service with,
314–343
controlling SSL with, 343
settings for scanning and merging,
257–258
working with, 339–341
Registry Editor (REGEDT32.EXE), 340
relay restrictions, 228–229, 243–244
remote administration, 143
remote connections, 24
remote recipients, SMTP, 218
remote service domains, SMTP
configuring authentication, 231–232
creating, 227–228
queuing messaging for remote
triggered delivery, 230–231
setting and removing relay restrictions,
228–229
switching SMTP modes, 229
requests, counters for, 287. *See also*
certificate requests

resources
administrative tools for management
of, 9–10
configuring Web resources for
indexing, 260
managing with IIS snap-in, 9–10
Microsoft Windows 2000 Resource
Kit, 279
starting, stopping, and pausing, 27–28
summary of IIS resources, 23–24
restoring. *See* backup and recovery
retry interval, SMTP, 246
reverse lookups
configuring, 248–249
DNS and, 139
SMTP performance and, 235
Revoked Certificates node, Certification
Authority snap-in, 164
routing
hop count and, 247
routing outgoing messages to smart
hosts, 249
RSAC (Recreational Software Advisory
Council), 96–97

S

scans
forcing full and incremental directories
rescans, 270
Indexing Service and, 255–256
registry settings for, 257–258
scripts, 13–15
administration techniques using, 13–14
CSCRIPT.EXE, 15
IIS scripting engine and, 88
managing Registry with, 340–341
metabase and, 348–351
quick reference for IIS Administration
scripts, 14
searches. *See also* Indexing Service
catalogs and, 258
using FIND command, 281
secure communications, SSL, 185,
235–236
Secure Sockets Layer (SSL)
adding CA certificates to client
browser root store, 177–178
configuring SSL ports, 175–177
confirming operation of, 179
controlling through Registry, 343
host headers and, 46
overview of, 4
requiring for all communications, 185

Secure Sockets Layer, *continued*
  resolving problems with, 179–180
  understanding encryption strength, 153
  using certificates, 151–153
  using encryption, 149–151
securews, security templates, 144
security
  managing logon and security, 8
  SMTP incoming connections, 235–236
security, FTP servers, 205–213
  configuring global permissions, 209
  configuring IP address and domain
    name restrictions, 210–212
  configuring local permissions, 210
  configuring site operators, 213
  configuring Windows permissions, 208
  managing anonymous connections,
    206–208
security, Web servers, 111–147
  enhancements, checking for malicious
    input, 146
  enhancements, creating legal notices,
    143–144
  enhancements, disabling default Web
    site, 142
  enhancements, disabling directory
    browsing, 143
  enhancements, disabling remote
    administration, 143
  enhancements, removing IISADMPWD
    virtual directory, 146
  enhancements, removing unused
    application mappings, 147
  enhancements, renaming Administrator
    account, 142
  enhancements, service packs, hot
    fixes, and templates, 144–146
  enhancements, using firewalls, 142
  IIS security, configuring IP address/
    domain name restrictions, 137–139
  IIS security, configuring WebDAV,
    132–133
  IIS security, configuring Web site
    operators, 140–141
  IIS security, setting authentication
    modes, 133–137
  IIS security, setting permissions,
    127–132
  levels of security for, 111
  Windows security, file and folder
    permissions, 116–121
  Windows security, group policies,
    121–126

security, Web servers, *continued*
  Windows security, user and group
    accounts, 112–116
Security Accounts tab, 206
Security tab, 119
Security Templates snap-in, 145
service domains, SMTP
  local, changing Drop directory, 226
  local, creating alias domains, 225
  local, setting default domains, 226
  local vs. remote, 216
  remote, configuring authentication,
    231–232
  remote, configuring smart hosts for,
    232–233
  remote, creating, 227–228
  remote, queuing messaging for remote
    triggered delivery, 230–231
  remote, setting and removing relay
    restrictions, 228–229
  remote, switching SMTP modes, 229
  renaming and deleting, 233
  types of, 225
  viewing configured domains, 224–225
service packs, Web server security and,
  144–146
services. *See* Internet services; Microsoft
  Internet Information Services (IIS)
Services node, 29–30
session state, 85–87
shadow merges, Indexing Service, 256–257
shared secret keys, encryption and,
  149–150
Simple Mail Transfer Protocol (SMTP),
  215–249
  administration, configuring ports/IP
    addresses, 221–222
  administration, configuring multiple
    identities, 222–223
  administration, creating virtual servers,
    219–221
  administration, managing users
    sessions, 224
  administration, monitoring virtual
    servers, 223
  bundled with IIS, 3
  concepts, e-mail domains, 216
  concepts, mail processing, 218–219
  concepts, mailroot folder, 217–218
  enabling logging on, 309
  incoming connections, access control,
    234–235
  incoming connections, authentication,
    236–237

Simple Mail Transfer Protocol, *continued*
  incoming connections, restrictions/
    time-outs, 238–239
  incoming connections, security,
    235–236
  installing default site, 7
  installing SMTP service, 6
  log formats, Microsoft IIS log file
    format, 323–325
  log formats, NCSA log file format,
    322–323
  log formats, ODBC log file format, 327
  log formats, W3C log file format,
    325–326
  message delivery, domain name
    options, 247–248
  message delivery, message hop
    count, 247
  message delivery, reverse DNS
    lookups, 248–249
  message delivery, routing messages to
    smart host, 249
  message delivery, time-outs, retry
    intervals, and delay notification,
    245–246
  outgoing connections, controlling,
    240–241
  outgoing connections, message limits,
    241–242
  outgoing connections, relay
    restrictions, 243–244
  outgoing connections, security, 239–240
  outgoing connections, trouble-
    shooting, 243
  overview of, 9
  service domains, configuring smart
    hosts, 232–233
  service domains, local, 225–227
  service domains, remote, 227–232
  service domains, renaming and
    deleting, 233
  service domains, viewing configured
    domains, 224–225
site certificates. *See* certificates
site operators, FTP security and, 213
sites. *See* Web sites
smart hosts
  configuring, 232–233
  routing outgoing messages to, 249
SMPs. *See* symmetric multiprocessors
    (SMPs)
SMTP. *See* Simple Mail Transfer Protocol
    (SMTP)
special characters, using in URLs, 21

SQL Server 2000
  creating DSN for, 328–330
  creating logging database and table in,
    327–328
stand-alone CA, 154, 156
stand-alone subordinate CA, 154, 156
standard logging, 309
start up, configuring, 31–32
statistics, FTP sessions, 203–204
Status Code field, NCSA common log file
    format, 314
status codes
  classes of, 98
  definition of, 98
subnets, 234–235
symmetric multiprocessors (SMPs), 5
system directories, configuring, 60–61

T
TCP (Transmission Control Protocol), 190
TCP/IP. *See* Transmission Control
    Protocol/Internet Protocol (TCP/IP)
templates
  configuring, 145–146
  options, 144
  Web server security and, 144–146
third-party authority
  root CAs issued by, 177
  submitting certificate requests to,
    170–171
thread gating, 337
throttling
  configuring bandwidth throttling,
    305–306
  Process Throttling, 4
throughput
  counters for, 288
  high speed disks and, 303
  setting for Web servers, 298–299
time-out values
  expiration time-out, 245–246
  for FTP, 199–200
  setting, 56–57
  for SMTP, 238–239
Time Stamp field, NCSA common log file
    format, 313
time-to-live values, 338
TLS. *See* transport layer security (TLS)
trace logs
  creating, 293–294
  overview of, 289
tracking software, 309

tracking user access. *See* logging, user access
Transfer Volume field, NCSA common log file format, 314
Transmission Control Protocol (TCP), 190
Transmission Control Protocol/Internet Protocol (TCP/IP)
name resolution and, 42
viewing and configuring, 47
transport layer security (TLS) encryption, 232
overview of, 4
troubleshooting. *See also* error messages
hardware, 278
SMTP outgoing connections, 243
SSL, 179–180
tuning. *See* performance, tuning and monitoring

U

Uniform Naming Convention (UNC), 43
Uniform Resource Locators (URLs), 19–22
escape codes, 22
format and specifications in, 19–21
function of, 19
special characters in, 21
uninterruptible power supply (UPS), 6
unique identifiers, FTP sites, 198
update sites, 107
UPS (uninterruptible power supply), 6
URLs. *See* Uniform Resource Locators (URLs)
user access, logging. *See* logging, user access
user and group accounts
IIS and Indexing Services and, 9
Internet Guest account, 113–115
logon accounts, 112–113
overview, 112
Web application account, 115–116
User Authentication field, NCSA common log file format, 313
usernames
anonymous access and, 8
URLs and, 20
users sessions, FTP
terminating, 204–205
viewing, 203–204
viewing number of connected users, 204–205
users sessions, SMTP, 224

V

value types, Windows Registry, 340
IIS key values, 341–342
SSL key values, 343
World Wide Web Publishing Service key values, 343
virtual directories
creating, 59–60
creating for FTP sites, 201
understanding, 58–59
virtual directories, certificates and, 158–159
virtual memory, bottlenecks, 299–300
virtual servers, IIS, 17
virtual servers, SMTP
creating, 219–221
monitoring health of, 223
using certificates with, 236
using multiple IP addresses and ports with, 223
Visual InterDev RAD remote deployment support, 7

W

WCAT (Web Capacity Analysis Tool), 279
Web administration techniques. *See* administration techniques
Web application account, 115–116
Web Application Stress tool, 279
Web browsers. *See* browser redirection; browsers
Web Capacity Analysis Tool (WCAT), 279
Web Distributed Authoring and Versioning (WebDAV)
accessing and publishing documents, 133
functions of, 132
overview of, 4
permitting distributed authoring and versioning, 132–133
Web pages, testing, 278
Web resources, configuring for indexing, 260
Web Server error messages. *See* error messages
Web servers, permissions. *See also* security, Web servers
overview, 127–128
setting globally, 128–130
setting locally, 130–132
Web servers, checking computer name and IP address of, 46–48

Web servers, tuning and monitoring,
    297–307
  bandwidth and connectivity, 304–307
  disk I/O, 303
  memory usage, 298–301
  processor usage, 301–302
Web services. *See* Microsoft Internet
    Information Services (IIS)
Web Site Creation Wizard
  setting access permissions for Web
    sites, 51
  setting IP addresses and ports with, 50
Web Site Properties dialog box, 41
Web sites
  associating catalogs with, 268
  configuring for IIS, 17
  creating, 48–52
  creating new MIME types for, 105
  disabling default, 142
  installing default sites, 7
  master Web service properties, 48
  specifying sites to include in catalogs,
    271–272
  SSL identities of, 177
Web sites, browser redirection, 63–69
  customizing, 67–69
  redirecting all requests, 65
  redirecting to applications, 66–67
  redirecting to other directories or Web
    sites, 64
  retrieving files from a network share,
    65–66
Web sites, managing content
  deleting files, 63
  modifying file properties, 62–63
  opening in browsing files, 62
  renaming files, 63
Web sites, managing directories
  configuring system directories, 60–61
  creating physical directories, 59
  creating virtual directories, 59–60
  deleting directories, 62
  modifying directory properties, 61
  physical and virtual directory
    structures, 58–59
  renaming directories, 61
Web sites, managing properties
  configuring home directory for, 52–53
  configuring HTTP Keep-Alives, 57–58
  configuring multiple identities for, 55–56
  configuring ports, IP addresses, and
    host names, 53–55
  controlling incoming connections, 56–57
  setting time-out values, 56–57

Web sites, naming and identifying
  hosting multiple sites on a single
    server, 43–46
  IP addresses and name resolution and,
    41–43
  understanding identifiers, 43
welcome messages, FTP sites, 202–203
wildcards, redirect, 68–69
Windows. *See* Microsoft Windows
Windows authentication, 134
Windows Components Wizard
  installing components with, 6
  installing Indexing Service, 252
Windows domain security, 8
Windows Explorer, 62
Windows Registry. *See* Registry
Windows Scripting Host
  managing IIS with, 13
  scripting the metabase, 348–351
Windows Security Package. *See* Microsoft
    Windows security
World Wide Web (WWW). *See* Web sites
World Wide Web Consortium (W3C) log
    file format
  configuring, 325–326
  directives used, 317
  field identifiers used, 318
  overview, 310, 316
  prefixes used, 317–318
  process accounting fields, 319
World Wide Web Publishing Service
  overview of, 9
  Registry key values for, 343

X

X.509 standard, 151. *See also* certificates

About the Author

William R. Stanek (win2000-consulting@tvpress.com) has over 15 years of hands-on experience with advanced programming and development. He is a leading network technology expert and an award-winning author. Over the years, his practical advice has helped programmers, developers, and network engineers all over the world. He is also a regular contributor to leading publications like *PC Magazine*, where you'll often find his work in the "Solutions" section. He has written, co-authored, or contributed to over 20 computer books. Current or forthcoming books include *Microsoft Windows 2000 Administrator's Pocket Consultant, Microsoft Exchange 2000 Server Administrator's Pocket Consultant, Microsoft SQL Server 2000 Administrator's Pocket Consultant,* and *Windows 2000 Scripting Bible.*

Mr. Stanek has been involved in the commercial Internet community since 1991. His core business and technology experience comes from over 11 years of military service. He has experience in developing server technology, encryption, Internet development, and a strong understanding of e-commerce technology and its deployment. During 1998 and 1999, he worked as a senior member of the technical staff at Intel Corporation's IDS business division at iCat (now part of Intel's Internet Online Services division). In 1999 and 2000 he worked for GeoTrust, an Application Services provider based in Portland, Oregon. There, he helped develop the ground-floor business strategies and long-range technology plans that have taken the company from a paper concept to a multimillion-dollar business.

Mr. Stanek has an M.S. degree with distinction in information systems and a B.S. degree, *magna cum laude,* in computer science. He is proud to have served in the Persian Gulf War as a combat crewmember on an electronic warfare aircraft. He flew on numerous combat missions into Iraq and was awarded nine medals for his wartime service, including one of the United States of America's highest flying honors, the Air Force Distinguished Flying Cross. He lives in the Pacific Northwest with his wife and children.

The author prepared and submitted the manuscript for this book in electronic form using Microsoft Word 2000 for Windows. Pages were composed by nSight, Inc., in Cambridge, MA, using Adobe PageMaker 6.5 for Windows, with text in Garamond Light and display type in ITC Franklin Gothic. Composed pages were delivered to the printer as electronic prepress files.

Cover Designer
Landor Associates

Cover Illustrator
Landor Associates

Layout Artist
Patty Fagan

Project Manager
Sarah Kimnach Hains

Tech Editor
Tony Northrup

Copy Editor
Amy Olener

Proofreader
Shimona Katz

Indexer
Jack Lewis

Editorial Assistant
Kathleen Pickett

Ready solutions *for the* IT administrator

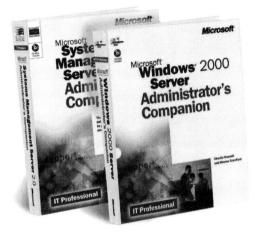

Powerhouse resources to minimize costs while maximizing performance

Deploy and support your enterprise business systems using the expertise and tools of those who know the technology best—the Microsoft product groups. Each RESOURCE KIT packs precise technical reference, installation and rollout tactics, planning guides, upgrade strategies, and essential utilities on CD-ROM. They're everything you need to help maximize system performance as you reduce ownership and support costs!

Microsoft Press® products are available worldwide wherever quality computer books are sold. For more information, contact your book or computer retailer, software reseller, or local Microsoft Sales Office, or visit our Web site at mspress.microsoft.com. To locate your nearest source for Microsoft Press products, or to order directly, call 1-800-MSPRESS in the U.S. (in Canada, call 1-800-268-2222).

Prices and availability dates are subject to change.

Microsoft® Windows® 2000 Server Resource Kit
ISBN   1-57231-805-8
U.S.A. $299.99
U.K.   £189.99 [V.A.T. included]
Canada $460.99

Microsoft Windows 2000 Professional Resource Kit
ISBN   1-57231-808-2
U.S.A. $69.99
U.K.   £45.99 [V.A.T. included]
Canada $107.99

Microsoft BackOffice® 4.5 Resource Kit
ISBN   0-7356-0583-1
U.S.A. $249.99
U.K.   £161.99 [V.A.T. included]
Canada $374.99

Microsoft Internet Explorer 5 Resource Kit
ISBN   0-7356-0587-4
U.S.A. $59.99
U.K.   £38.99 [V.A.T. included]
Canada $89.99

Microsoft Office 2000 Resource Kit
ISBN   0-7356-0555-6
U.S.A. $59.99
U.K.   £38.99 [V.A.T. included]
Canada $89.99

Microsoft Windows NT® Server 4.0 Resource Kit
ISBN   1-57231-344-7
U.S.A. $149.95
U.K.   £96.99 [V.A.T. included]
Canada $199.95

Microsoft Windows NT Workstation 4.0 Resource Kit
ISBN   1-57231-343-9
U.S.A. $69.95
U.K.   £45.99 [V.A.T. included]
Canada $94.95

mspress.microsoft.com

In-depth. Focused.
And
ready for work.

Get the technical drilldown you need to deploy and support Microsoft products more effectively with the MICROSOFT TECHNICAL REFERENCE series. Each guide focuses on a specific aspect of the technology—weaving in-depth detail with on-the-job scenarios and practical how-to information for the IT professional. Get focused—and take technology to its limits—with MICROSOFT TECHNICAL REFERENCES.

Data Warehousing with Microsoft® SQL Server™ 7.0 Technical Reference
ISBN 0-7356-0859-8

Microsoft SQL Server 7.0 Performance Tuning Technical Reference
ISBN 0-7356-0909-8

Building Applications with Microsoft Outlook® 2000 Technical Reference
ISBN 0-7356-0581-5

Microsoft Windows NT® Server 4.0 Terminal Server Edition Technical Reference
ISBN 0-7356-0645-5

Microsoft Windows® 2000 TCP/IP Protocols and Services Technical Reference
ISBN 0-7356-0556-4

Active Directory™ Services for Microsoft Windows 2000 Technical Reference
ISBN 0-7356-0624-2

Microsoft Windows 2000 Security Technical Reference
ISBN 0-7356-0858-X

Microsoft Windows 2000 Performance Tuning Technical Reference
ISBN 0-7356-0633-1

mspress.microsoft.com